The Black Box of Governance

In the world of corporate governance, the board of directors is often viewed as the "black box" of companies: only the board members who are seated at the meeting table understand how this "decision-making machine" works. In this book, a board member with over 25 years' experience pulls off the lid and shows both how boards have worked and how they could work.

This book is grounded in extensive research in three different surveys: one with more than 100 Brazilian directors, another with 340 board members from 40 countries, and a final one with 103 Brazilian directors serving on 238 boards. It also includes interviews with Ira Millstein, Sir Adrian Cadbury, Robert Monks and Mervyn King. The inner-workings of the board of directors are revealed:

- What keeps directors awake at night
- Obstacles to efficient decision-making
- Behavioral dynamics, both within the board and in relation to the management
- Pitfalls that arise from individual and group biases

Based on these insights and the author's own consulting and board experience, the book presents a guide to behavioral tools enabling directors and executives to confidently navigate the boardroom, improving interactivity and the efficiency of the decision-making process. Intended for directors and executives who are directly involved in the board's activities, as well as for leaders responsible for strategy implementation, this book provides a behavioral compass for all those interacting with the "black box."

Sandra Guerra has more than 25 years of experience in the board of directors and corporate governance. She was co-founder and chair of the Brazilian Institute for Corporate Governance (IBGC) and board governor of the International Corporate Governance Network (ICGN). She holds a Master of Science degree in business.

"*The Black Box of Governance* is an important read for both corporate directors and management, as well as for anyone who expects 'good governance' in the boardroom. It provides an international context – the issue is not restricted to one country, it's global."

Ira Millstein, corporate lawyer and senior partner
at Weil, Gotshal & Manges

"A very positive attribute of *The Black Box of Governance* is that, although based on research among the most renowned theorists, the author presents us with an eminently practical book."

Sergio Rial, Banco Santander's CEO in Brazil and
member of Delta Airlines' BoD

"... that's what makes this such a compelling read. It artfully weaves together a panoramic review of all the leading academic research on board governance with real-life stories told by real-life people, who speak candidly about the best and the worst of human nature in the high-stakes, sometimes inglorious world that is the boardroom. Each and every one of these stories rings true."

Karina Litvack, non-executive board director at
Eni S.p.A and director at BSR (Business for Social
Responsibility) and the CFA Institute

The Black Box of Governance

Boards of Directors Revealed by Those Who Inhabit Them

Sandra Guerra

Routledge
Taylor & Francis Group

NEW YORK AND LONDON

First published 2022
by Routledge
605 Third Avenue, New York, NY 10158

and by Routledge
2 Park Square, Milton Park, Abingdon, Oxon, OX14 4RN

Routledge is an imprint of the Taylor & Francis Group, an informa business

© 2022 Sandra Guerra

The right of Sandra Guerra to be identified as author of this work has been asserted by her in accordance with sections 77 and 78 of the Copyright, Designs and Patents Act 1988.

Library of Congress Cataloging-in-Publication Data
Names: Guerra, Sandra, author.
Title: The black box of governance : boards of directors revealed by those who inhabit them / Sandra Guerra.
Description: New York, NY : Routledge, 2022. | Includes bibliographical references and index.
Subjects: LCSH: Boards of directors. | Boards of directors—Brazil. | Corporate governance. | Corporate governance—Brazil. | Organizational behavior. | Organizational behavior—Brazil.
Classification: LCC HD2745 .G77 2022 (print) | LCC HD2745 (ebook) | DDC 658.4/22—dc23
LC record available at https://lccn.loc.gov/2021007726
LC ebook record available at https://lccn.loc.gov/2021007727

ISBN: 978-1-032-05223-6 (hbk)
ISBN: 978-1-032-05224-3 (pbk)
ISBN: 978-1-003-19664-8 (ebk)

Typeset in Sabon
by codeMantra

For Bengt Hallqvist, who opened the doors of corporate governance to me and, as a result, changed my life.

Contents

Foreword

Ira Millstein

The Black Box of Governance is an important read for both corporate directors and management, as well as for anyone who expects "good governance" in the boardroom. It provides an international context – the issue is not restricted to one country, it's global.

Sandra Guerra is uniquely qualified to author a comprehensive work detailing what truly goes on in the boardroom as well as how to improve board effectiveness. She has studied board behavior for more than two decades – both as a director and as an advisor to boards. Ms. Guerra was one of the founders and later Chair of the Brazilian Institute of Corporate Governance. As the principal of Better Governance, she has served as a valued advisor to boards of both public and private companies. In addition to surveying more than a hundred directors during the preparation of The Black Box, she conducted numerous in-depth interviews. For this English edition, she incorporated the results of additional research covering 340 directors serving on boards in 40 different countries. A well-known and deeply respected global expert on the topic, Ms. Guerra has access to top thinkers and practitioners.

Most importantly, Ms. Guerra is an experienced board director herself. She has not just observed from the sidelines how boards function (and misfunction) and directors behave (and misbehave). Her experience in The "Black Box" itself, and her extensive interactions with other directors, board chairs and management, inform her extensive research and provide a practitioner's reality check.

The author's suggestions for how to tackle challenges faced by directors are insightful and invaluable. But what makes The Black Box of particular practical value, and unique in the field, are the behavioral tools that Ms. Guerra provides to help boards navigate around the pitfalls caused by cognitive limitations and individual and group biases. The "caselet" approach, around which many of the challenges facing modern boards are introduced, is a particularly effective means to illustrate how such tools can significantly improve board and company performance. Setting the stage through caselets also allows all perspectives and motivations to be deconstructed, including those of directors, management and others who influence boardroom dynamics.

The publication of The Black Box in English makes Ms. Guerra's research and insights available to a global audience. Corporate governance practitioners will be talking about it for years.

Ira Millstein

Ira Millstein, a corporate lawyer and a senior partner at Weil, Gotshal and Manges, is one of the most highly regarded corporate governance experts in the United States and headed up the committee that drafted the OECD's – Organisation for Economic Co-operation and Development's – Corporate Governance Principles.

Foreword

Sérgio Rial

No matter how technical and analytical the board members may be, every single board of directors' effectiveness is affected – positively or negatively – by the behavioral aspects of each individual and/or of the group's own dynamics. In my experience as a director, and now again as a CEO, I have seen this influence on the decisions taken at the board meetings and on the interactions with the executives. It is precisely this observation that leads me to the belief nowadays that we are first and foremost psychological rather than logical beings. And, therefore, the limits of rationality and the emotional complexity of human beings can no longer simply be overlooked by the management and governance practices implemented in organizations. It is also essential to bear in mind that, along with the complexity that is inherent to group dynamics and the management of business as usual in any time or place, there is also the fact that boards have been trained to avoid surprises – and we are living in an era of "surprises."

This new century has proven to be much more challenging than we had anticipated. The word transformation has become a mantra, and at the heart of this process is the new role of senior leadership at every company, including the board itself. Since 2001, when we saw the magnitude of the attack on the Twin Towers in New York, we have witnessed successive financial crises, as well the split-up of the European Union with Brexit and the election of some present governments that tend to govern only for those who elected them rather than for society as a whole. A more polarized society emerges and democracies are being tested. The pandemic of COVID-19 has not made it any easier and has given rise to a number of new trends: low interest rates are here to stay for a longer period, remote everything is possible, structural unemployment is a sad new reality, human interaction is on the rise for the perception of value, the importance of after-sales services is increasing, a technological elite is emerging in the world, and from a governance point of view, tail risks are no longer remote possibilities.

At the same time, forecasting the unknown at the board level may not be a very good use of management's time. So, what to do? My recommendation is to stick to clear global trends and try to understand them. Boards need to stimulate the right level of common sense and equilibrium in order to analyze risks which in the past were for the most part immaterial, but no longer are. In view of their experience, directors should be capable of helping management to synthetize critical insights into these new fast-moving changes on the macro scene and at the consumer level. More and more, brands need to stand for their values, for their stories and more important, how they will embrace this new future.

Especially in light of this so unprecedented disruptive scenario and in line with the most recent studies in the area, I regard the behavioral approach as being one of the most innovative and relevant contributions to the area of business administration. And it is based on this perspective that we will be able to minimize what I call "dramatization of management," helping to develop two skills – more essential than ever – among executives and directors: the willingness to listen and the ability to ask. In the most complex decision-making processes, in general, the most important thing lies in our ability to listen. Willingness to really listen can overcome the natural obstacles to good communication when it goes beyond the sense of hearing and puts the focus of observation on the behaviors expressed as well. It is by listening to more than just the words themselves that we are able to articulate new perspectives and ask what may be of most importance.

In my opinion, management's biggest leverage factor is the questions it asks. When they listen more than usual and ask questions that go beyond the obvious, the board members have the chance to establish a relationship of trust with the executives, in which open, frank and transparent dialogue can construct the best answers, serving all stakeholders rather than just the shareholders. For this reason, it is my belief that among boards' most valuable tasks is that of providing the executives with quality technical support, asking constructive questions so that they can arrive at a short list of priorities and as a result of this come up with the best answers for each proposition. It is such a symbiotic relationship that I often say, "Show me your CEO and I will tell you who your board is." Therefore, I see the board as an integral and vital part of the success or failure of each and every one of the company's projects.

However, it is necessary to avoid this purpose from being idealized and separated from real practices and processes. This perception tends to emerge from the tendency to assume that good relations are characterized by unanimity between the parties and no tension whatsoever in the interactions. That would be a mistake since it is unlikely that there will be unanimity when people who are intelligent, independent and engaged are sitting around the table. Therefore, a certain amount of tension is a fundamental element of the relationship so that executives and directors can maintain their independent and diverse positions while seeking alignment and consensus regarding the strategic values and objectives of the business. It is this constructive tension that characterizes the functioning of the healthiest boards of directors, those that make their best contribution to the sustainable strategy of businesses, acting as a big nose, but never as a big finger.* These boards exist and are the majority.

We all know, of course, that harmful behavioral aspects also exist in boards of directors, but nobody likes to talk about it, although this discussion is crucial when it comes to identifying the paths to improving corporate governance practices. It is precisely for this reason that I regard this book by Sandra Guerra as an act of courage: her text is daring enough to bring up issues that we would prefer to keep hidden in the day-to-day management of companies. Not for the sole purpose of problematizing, but with the explicit aim of contributing to the search for possible solutions. Far from proposing far-fetched ready-made methods, the book deals with issues that actually occur on a daily basis in board rooms, triggering reflections so as to build TRUST – which is a key factor in the relationship between directors and executives.

Another very positive attribute of *The Black Box of Governance* is that, although based on research among the most renowned theorists, the author presents us with an eminently practical book. Put together from her own professional experience as an executive and as a board member, on the carrying out of three surveys with hundreds of directors in total and on a series of interviews with specialists in the field, Sandra has organized and offers us a consistent guide for applying the behavioral approach in the diagnosis and mitigation of the main dysfunctionalities of boards of directors and of the interaction between directors and executives. I was honored and pleased to take part in Sandra's venture, both as an interviewee and as the writer of one of the book's prefaces, as I am convinced that reading this book will be of great value to all those whose aim is to contribute to improving corporate governance practices – in particular when the construction of a constant introspective and truthful dialogue at the board level with management is the best antidote for what is to come. Improving the ability to listen and ask questions is what we most need in order to plan for a more unstructured time given that the world has become a lot more unpredictable.

Sérgio Rial

Sérgio Lires Rial, who is currently Banco Santander's CEO in Brazil and a member of Delta Airlines' BoD, was the bank's chairman when he gave this interview. He has substantial experience on other boards both in Brazil as well as abroad.

---

* "Nose in, fingers out" is a corporate governance mantra that makes it clear that the board should govern the organization, but not interfere in management's role of running it.

Foreword

Karina Litvack

This is no ordinary book on corporate governance. It is as close as one gets to settling down in Sandra's kitchen with a strong cup of coffee, or better yet, a stiff G&T, to listen to 25 years' worth of war stories. It is as close as one can get to learning from practical experience by learning from a book.

And that's what makes this such a compelling read. It artfully weaves together a panoramic review of all the leading academic research on board governance with real-life stories told by real-life people, who speak candidly about the best and the worst of human nature in the high-stakes, sometimes inglorious world that is the boardroom. Each and every one of these stories rings true. Each one provokes an "Ah yes, I've been there!", or an "Oh dear! And here I thought we had it bad," or indeed a "Hah, this is nothing!"

Because each of these lessons is universal. Each tells the tale of how groups of human beings interact when having to make decisions under pressure, only with one significant twist: these particular groups of human beings by and large comprise very accomplished professionals whose track record of competence and success has been rewarded with a position of great privilege and responsibility. They are people who are used to being at the top and expect to be listened to, yet now have to work collegially, in a setting where tension and dissent are good and necessary, but not so much that it tips into factionalism and dysfunction. Where the duty to offer frank and constructive challenge, even criticism, must be couched in the language of support, assistance and oversight. Where a balanced mix of competencies, unimpeachable integrity and loyalty to the company are a must, yet are far from sufficient, because high-functioning group dynamics are every bit as essential as technical prowess. Where independence is pivotal, yet largely impossible to gauge from a CV, because as experience has shown all too often, every box can be ticked, yet a person's character only becomes visible when put to the test. Where strong and wise leadership in the figure of the board chairman is crucial to bring out the best in every director, yet where the occupant of that chair must be an enabler, often a coach, always a primus inter pares who is answerable for the collective performance of the whole, rather than the undisputed autocrat who decides for the group.

That is quite a challenging brew. There is no degree or certificate that can teach these skills: they are learned and earned through experience, and no doubt the making of many mistakes. As someone who has committed my fair share of rookie mistakes in my boards, and no doubt will continue to do, I can attest to how delicate and perpetually challenging this job is. As Sandra articulates so eloquently, our job as directors is not just to read the papers, however diligently; not just to listen, however actively; nor just to pose incisive questions, and vote with our heads and our values. It is to be genuinely ambitious, to add value through outside perspectives that complement the inside knowledge that management brings to the table; to achieve the right balance of both cohesion and fresh thinking to reach better decisions than any one of us, executive or non-executive, could have done alone. And most challengingly of all in these extraordinary times of global health and climate crisis, it is to steer our companies through managing historic disruption, when neither the human brain, much less conventional corporate governance codes, are designed to model disruption.

In the mistakes and "lessons learned" that I myself collected along the way, I am reminded of a seemingly obvious lesson that Sandra captures so well in her discussion about the seemingly banal question of board minutes: one of my companies was the subject of a criminal enforcement action involving an incident that had occurred before any of my fellow directors or I had joined the Board. Still, how the Board conducted the requisite independent investigation of this affair nonetheless came under the Prosecutor's microscope, and I was subpoenaed to answer questions about how the Board had navigated these sensitive questions – in the full glare of the media spotlight. In the course of being cross-examined, I was aggressively challenged by Defence Counsel on why the strong concerns I was known to have voiced had not translated into abstentions or votes against in any of the minutes. The incident underlined the crucial importance – as Sandra wisely reminds us – of ensuring that the nuances of board debate and dissent are accurately and thoroughly recorded. As I learned that day, better to be the director who annoys the company secretary with seemingly trivial amendments to the minutes than to have to take the stand to explain away the discrepancy between what one said and what the record shows. Not only is it an insurance policy for the dissenting director, but most importantly it serves as robust evidence that the board did in fact do its job of debating difficult points, acted in good faith to balance all the arguments, and reached the best decision it could under the circumstances.

Like most of the directors Sandra has studied, I've had many a sleepless night agonizing over whether in the pecking order of battles to fight, I had picked the right ones, or had had the courage and wisdom to change my mind at the right time. Only time – and for the rare few, a court subpoena – will tell.

Karina Litvack

Karina Litvack is a non-executive Board Director at Eni S.p.A and a Director at Viridor, a KKR company, BSR (Business for Social Responsibility), and the CFA Institute. Karina provides a truly global and multi-stakeholder perspective of the governance scene. She was born in Canada, lives in the UK and serves on the boards of an Italian, a UK and two US companies. Additionally she is a corporate governance and sustainable investment expert who had a 25-year career in finance and sustainable business practice, prior to becoming a corporate board director.

Acknowledgments

This book exists only because César Souza is a determined and convincing person. If you don't yet know, by reading this book you will learn that César is a director, consultant and renowned author. We first sat together on a board of directors in 2011, and from that point on, I never had any peace. Every time the word "book" came up, César would nag me about the fact that I still hadn't written mine. He knew that I had co-authored books with multilateral organizations, but that was not what he was talking about. It was "my" book that he was complaining about. I always had a reason to put the project off for a little bit longer. Finally, César used an argument that decided it for me: "You don't have the right to keep this knowledge just for yourself." Before the end of that year, I was already conducting the first interview. I would like to express my thanks to César for mentoring me throughout the entire process of writing this book.

But difficulties remained for the book project. My intense work schedule was a real and tangible impediment. I needed help with the writing. Having been a journalist for the first ten years of my professional life, I know how to use the written word to express myself, but time – which is the greatest luxury of all nowadays – simply did not allow me to get into a rhythm that a project like this demands. And the search for assistance was no small matter either: I was not looking for the aid of a typical ghost-writer, because I knew exactly what I wanted to write and how I wanted to write it. I needed someone who could work from the content that I myself had actually developed and, in particular, someone who was confident enough of their own writing that they would not be upset by a potentially devastating revision in order for it to be the "way" I wanted it. Cristina Sant'Anna, who has been my friend since the time when we were both journalists, was the obvious choice. But it was a choice we avoided making for months on end, for fear that the project might ruin our friendship. She said: "Don't underestimate the clashes we may well have." We didn't underestimate them. We took great care with the project, but even more with our friendship that had lasted for decades. I am deeply grateful that Cristina agreed to take on the risk and gave herself body and soul to this project, with the quality that is her trademark.

For the current international edition, I also received valuable support from Mike Lubrano, who has been very rigorous and meticulous in helping adapt the form and content of the Portuguese version and its revisions into English. My permanent go-to conversation partner on governance issues since 1999, Mike has become a friend and I am sure that my career in this field would not be the same if I had not always been able to count on him being there for me.

This book also benefited from the generosity of 31 professionals of the very highest caliber from all over the world, who put aside their reservations and shared with me what really goes on in boardrooms. Some of them – governance experts such as Sir Adrian Cadbury,* Bengt Hallqvist,** Ira Millstein, Mats Isaksson, Mervyn King, Mike Lubrano, Robert Monks and Stephen Davis are quoted in the book. The candid observations shared "on the record" by board directors I interviewed, including Alexandre Gonçalves Silva, Betania Tanure, César Souza, Fernando Carneiro, Herman Bulls, Linda Parker Hudson, Luiz Carlos Cabrera, Paula Rosput Reynolds, Pedro Parente and Sérgio Rial are a central component of this work. At their request, the names of others have not been disclosed so that all the book's readers could take advantage of the cases they described. I am very grateful to all these experts, executives and board directors for the opportunity to learn more from them about the "black box" and share it with my readers.

This book also made use of three surveys that were answered anonymously: one by 102 Brazilian directors, another by 340 board members from 40 countries and the third by 103 Brazilian directors. I wish to thank everyone involved in the surveys for their attention and time spent on these exercises. My partner in the first survey was Rafael Liza Santos. We have worked together for many years, but with each new initiative, our partnership grows stronger and deeper. I am grateful for the enormous effort that Rafael put into everything from the design of the survey questionnaire to the completion of the study. In the second survey, Rafael and I were able to count on the leadership of Professor Lucas Barros, coordinator of the Post-Graduate Program in Controllership and Accounting (PPGCC) at FEA/USP. And the three of us express our thanks for the support of Alessandra Polastrini and Aline Moraes, who took meticulous care with the research graphs.

* The author interviewed Sir Adrian Cadbury (1929–2015) on December 4, 2013.
** The author interviewed Bengt Hallqvist (1930–2019) on October 5, 2016.

To top off all this effort, I had the privilege of having Ira Millstein, Karina Litvack and Sérgio Rial all accept my invitation to write a preface for this book. There is no way I can properly thank these three highly renowned and experienced professionals for their generosity.

Even with the support of all those I have just thanked, we still wouldn't have this revised and updated international edition of my book without the dedication of my overseas agent Daniela Manole, who promptly found the right publisher for the project. Special thanks also go to Meredith Norwich, senior editor at Routledge/Taylor & Francis, whose support has been invaluable throughout the entire editing process. And last but not least, I would like to thank the book's translator Mark Edward Murray for his careful work.

Introduction

One of my most treasured professional beliefs, confirmed over the 25 years I have been working as an advisor on corporate governance (CG) and as a board member, is today a deeply held conviction that CG "in appearance," adopted merely to comply with rules or even in an opportunistic way, is incapable of generating sustainable value. In fact, adopting CG practices principally for a show can destroy value. And in a big way.

This conclusion slowly took shape over all the years in which I have witnessed the adoption by companies of good CG practices – either out of enthusiasm for the potential results or out of fear of the consequences of not adopting them. In many cases, the path to improving governance is motivated by some perceived short- or medium-term gains, such as a reduction in the cost of capital via an Initial Public Offering (IPO) or even a decrease in the interest rates on loans. Up to this point, there is nothing to question: it is the short- and medium-term goals that lead to the long ones. The problem arises when the adoption of these positive CG practices is focused exclusively on complying with a set of rules and nothing else.

I have held this conviction for a long time. Back in 2007, I raised concerns, in an article for a magazine aimed at the capital market,[1] about possible inconsistencies around the adoption of good governance practices. In particular, I warned of the risks that some companies, motivated by the wrong reasons, could run and, worse, impose on stakeholders and the business environment as a whole. In the flood of public offerings, including IPOs, driven in large part by the excess liquidity that was observed on the international market at that time, I suspected that many companies pursued governance changes mostly for the sake of appearances and to meet the formal requirements to be a publicly held company, without actually carrying out a well-thought-out improvement process. In 2013, I further explored the consequences of this appearance of good governance in another article, this time in another publication.[2]

This superficial and somewhat opportunistic approach is generally guided by ready-made models, which have not been properly thought out and discussed internally. As a consequence, they do not produce a governance model that responds to the company's challenges at any given time, since they merely perform the role of 'seeming to be'. When this happens, a dichotomy is created between what actually occurs in the company and what its reports and documents disclose. This almost schizophrenia between the internal and external destroys value, undermining the environment of trust, reducing the ability to attract and retain managers and exposing the company to risks, at the very least, to its reputation.

This quest to "improve" CG to comply with the rules and satisfy market expectations, however, is not always ill-intentioned. I have observed that there is an honest belief that good governance is simply that: merely adopting and formalizing some rules. My argument was – and still is – that, to the contrary, true good governance "in reality" is adopted for its intrinsic value, which also ends up resulting in perceived value outside the company. To be sure, it is CG as practiced in everyday life that reveals its internal value in the management of conflicts of interest; in the more robust and effective decision-making processes; in the increased confidence that results from ethical and equitable practices; in attracting talent and so on. All of this is reflected in the organization's reputation, boosting external and internal confidence. It is the establishment of this culture that protects decision-making, leading to a more sustainable business. In the long term, this cycle creates tangible and intangible value and protects the company from destruction.

One need not be an expert to note that it was not governance "in reality" that prevailed in innumerable tragic episodes of corporate history. Although CG policies and standards of good practice have continuously evolved since the mid-1990s, when the CG movement got a major boost at the global level,* these failed to prevent the outbreak of successive scandals and corporate crises, with harmful consequences both from an economic point of view as well as from a social and environmental one.

Spectacular corporate failures, such as those at Enron, WorldCom and Tyco, at the start of the millennium, illustrated the marked destruction of value that can stem from poor governance. However, if not even that wave of failures could convince the most skeptical regarding the importance of good CG, real-life produced another unquestionable example: the disaster that was caused by the use of high-risk derivatives related to

---

* A summary of the history of the evolution of corporate governance can be found in Chapter 1.

subprime mortgages, which resulted in the international financial crisis of 2008, the consequences of which were hard felt throughout the world. In light of the magnitude of this example, not is hardly necessary to mention later cases such as MFGlobal (2011), Toshiba (2015), Volkswagen's dieselgate (2015) or that of Nissan (2018), along with so many others that continue to occur. There is no denying it: governance continues to fail, with devastating consequences, despite all of the attempts at institutional improvement made at various levels.

It is no exaggeration to state that governance "**in appearance**" prevailed in all of these cases. But for someone like me approaching three decades in CG, this finding is, at the very least, disturbing. Why do failures in CG practices continue to take place notwithstanding all the scrutiny of the last few years? For a long time, episodes of this type were explained by the belief that this is human nature: given the opportunity, a large number of us human beings behave improperly, cheating, speculating with other people's money, and are only motivated by personal gain. But there have already been studies that indicate that these beliefs can be challenged.[3] After all, even those who question the consistency of these studies can give themselves the benefit of another doubt: given that the number of people involved in the aforementioned episodes is very large, it does not seem reasonable to assume that they were all acting in bad faith, without the proper responsibility or merely focused on their own interests. So why did all these executives and directors fail to prevent actions that caused irreversible damage like the ones that we have witnessed?

Before I answer this question, I present another concept that I regard as indispensable and which refers to my own view on governance: the best CG is always that which tries to establish balanced relationships among all of the parties involved – executives, directors, owners, auditors and stakeholders. This balance should be strived for, even when the parties in question are separated by antagonistic views. The aim is to align them so that solutions that can provide a sustainable balance between these different governance agents prevail. Nevertheless, I am also fully aware that the apparent simplicity of this idea does not reduce the complexity entailed in applying it. It is precisely for this reason that good CG has been systematically denied by practice.

My view regarding the relevance of the virtuous integration of all these professionals with essential roles in governance originated during the initial phase of the **Brazilian Institute of Corporate Governance (IBGC)**. The IBGC's group of founders, of which I was a part, decided to expand the institute's scope of action. When it was first set up in 1995, the entity was called the IBCA – the Brazilian Institute of Directors. We started off with a focus on boards of directors, acknowledging their central role in the context of CG. But in 1999, which was the same year in which we were drafting the first edition of the Code of Best Practices, we decided to transform what was then called the IBCA into an organization involving all of the players in the governance scene. After all, we had never considered establishing a professional organization, as our intention had always been to improve the CG of organizations in the country as a whole. So, as a result of this decision, the Institute changed its name to the **IBGC**.

This theme was a recurring one in the long conversations I had with **Bengt Hallqvist,**[*] the determined Swede who brought the co-founders of the IBGC together in 1995 around the idea that it was essential to do governance very differently from how it had been practiced up until then by Brazil's companies. And it was the same again in October 2016, when I was with him in Stenungsund, a lovely seaside town surrounded by fjords where he then lived. On that day, **Bengt** again commented that, in all likelihood, when we widened the scope of the institute none of us was fully aware of the importance that this decision would have for the development of CG in Brazil. With his vast entrepreneurial experience developed in a number of companies and countries, as both an executive and a board director, **Bengt** was of the opinion that there had been a lot of progress in governance in Brazil over the course of these decades and that this success should be attributed to the expansion of IBGC's activity:

> What we did in Brazil had a huge impact on corporate governance and the basis of our success was the fact that we transformed the institute which initially was just focused on directors into what the IBGC is today, involving all the governance players: owners, managers and auditors as well as directors.

At the international level, the evolution of governance over the last few decades is also highlighted by **Stephen Davis,**[**] senior fellow and associate director for Harvard Law School's Program on Corporate Governance. Celebrating the 20th anniversary of the Global Conference on Corporate Governance, which was held in collaboration with the

---

[*] Bengt Hallqvist (1930–2019), who had a degree in Administration from Harvard Business School, developed his knowledge of governance based on his experience on 50 boards of directors, 12 of them as the chair, in 20 countries since 1979. Prior to this, he was the CEO of Volvo Latin America and of AEG Telefunken in Brazil, along with various other executive positions that he held around the world. He was awarded the *ICGN Awards* prize, in 2005, for Excellence in Governance. The author interviewed Bengt Hallqvist in Stenungsund, Sweden, on October 5, 2016.

[**] Stephen Davis, Ph.D. is one of the architects of today's global corporate governance framework and president of Davis Global Advisors. The author interviewed Stephen Davis in a virtual internet room, on August 8, 2020.

World Bank and chaired by him in July 2000 in the city of New Haven (United States), Davis believes that CG concepts and practices have spread significantly, having reached other stakeholders, such as institutional investors, who now understand that shareholders' long-term success also depends on the attention given to **ESG (Environmental, Social and Corporate Governance)** issues. **Mike Lubrano**[*] is another key player in the global corporate governance scene: starting off from an investor's perspective, he has played a key role in developing the CG guidelines that are used today by emerging markets investors, both in his capacity as manager of the corporate governance team at the IFC (International Financial Corporation) and then later as managing director, Corporate Governance and Sustainability for the Cartica Management, LLC. **Lubrano,** who, like me, was also one of those who took part in the 2000 Global Conference, is of the opinion that a network of experts and advocates began to emerge there, which gives CG a global boost:

> This network (which emerged from the 2000 conference) has been critical and is remarkable in that it has provided specialists who have established institutions, which you can count on for solving problems that arise or to take advantage of opportunities. Investors have benefitted from this network over the course of these two decades. These initial champions have been effective from the outset in raising the profile of issues such as the role of directors and to whom they should be accountable.

In his retrospective analysis of CG's progress, **Stephen Davis** also emphasized the evolution of the very definition of which factors are most relevant for the best performance of Boards of Directors (BoDs):

> Right from the early days, independence was seen as a key factor. But then it turned out to be an insufficient and even naïve concept. The directors don't just need to be independent: as well as a proper relationship between them, they also need to have in-depth knowledge of the business and know how to communicate not just with management and key shareholders, but also with the capital markets as a whole. They are not just the demographic representatives of the principal shareholders, and for this reason the board needs to be a diverse body, which brings different perspectives to the debate in order to address the company's future challenges rather than being

---

[*] Mike Lubrano is principal at Lubrano Advisory Services and Senior Advisor at Nestor Advisors. He is a regularly-cited expert on corporate governance issues and was co-founder of the Latin American Corporate Governance Roundtable. The author interviewed Mike Lubrano in a virtual internet room, on August 5, 2020.

focused on those of the past. Those are some of the insights that we have developed over the last 20 years, and for sure we have not yet been able to put them all into practice. We are still on this journey.

The BoD's leading role within the corporate governance scenario is unquestionable. This needs to be borne in mind whenever analyzing a board of directors: everything in governance is the result of a precise and specific context. Therefore, we are back to the question that I left unanswered. What could have occurred on the boards, which are the driving force of governance, that left them unable to prevent the enormous losses and failures that were observed?

The decision-making machine that is the BoD has been dissected by theoretical and practical studies regarding their roles, responsibilities, structure and functioning. Nevertheless, they continue to be viewed as a "black box."[*] After all, only board members actually know what goes on in there between the four walls of the boardroom. And what happens there? Which factors have the greatest potential to deflect the process from the best decisions or even make the group of directors' performance really dysfunctional – or, as some authors prefer to call it, pathological? This was how, instead of carrying out an autopsy on corporate scandals looking for the disease that had led to the collapse of the governance bodies, I discovered that the behavioral approach offered the best tool to observe relevant causes of the limitations and maladies of BoDs. Additionally, it offers opportunities to transform them into collective decision-making bodies that lead and inspire the creation of sustainable value for organizations.

Only based on a view of its interior, understanding the insides of the board – which is a living and dynamic being – is it feasible to understand that there are many other factors apart from the alleged rationality of the board's performance and of its decisions. Looking inside the black box paves the way to acknowledging that even those BoDs made up of the most competent, diligent and committed directors can fail disastrously.

The behavioral approach also enables us to demonstrate that boards and directors may be hijacked by cognitive biases to which all human beings are vulnerable. Moreover, these individual biases are added to those which are common to group dynamics, making the BoD dysfunctional and deflecting it from rationality. This approach once and for all challenges the view of those who continue to believe that human behavior is absolutely and exclusively guided by rationality. Even more so when

---

[*] Because of the practical difficulties of gaining close enough access to boards to study their inner workings, researchers of governance and board of directors have frequently referred to the body as a "black box."

this behavior occurs in such august environments as the boardrooms occupied by directors who are focused and capable. The chamber may indeed be august and the directors focused and capable, but that does not guarantee rational effectiveness, as this book aims to show.

It was based on this conviction, therefore, that I felt the need to thoroughly mull over these issues, and to muster the willingness, time and focus to write this book. I conducted 31 interviews with professionals of nine different nationalities in eight cities around the world: from Tokyo to Leipzig, from New Port to Dorridge, with the most recent interviews carried out in virtual meeting rooms during these COVID-19 times. In addition to reviewing the latest Brazilian and international literature on the behavioral approach and interviewing global governance experts, such as **Sir Adrian Cadbury,**[*] **Bengt Hallqvist,**[**] **Ira Millstein, Mats Isaksson, Mervyn King, Mike Lubrano, Robert Monks** and **Stephen Davis,** I dedicated myself to gaining a deeper understanding of CG practices in companies, based on the undertaking of three surveys: the first was a survey of 102 board members from the most significant organizations and from the widest possible range of Brazilian economic sectors, which was conducted between May 2015 and January 2016. Then, between June and October 2018, Professor Lucas Barros, Rafael Liza Santos and I conducted an international survey to which 340 directors from 40 countries responded. This time around, we peeped into the "black box" of boardrooms to investigate some of the main challenges faced by boards of directors in their quest for effective decision-making. We explored the unique perspective of board members themselves about the prevalence of group biases and other factors with the potential to harm or improve board performance. And last but not least, between October 2019 and January 2020, **Better Governance**[***] collected and analyzed the answers of 103 Brazilian directors serving on 238 boards to examine how their time is spent – both inside and outside the boardrooms.

Meanwhile, in order to further analyze the intricacies of CG and the functioning of BoDs and give this book valuable empirical perspective, I personally collected the opinions of some of the most experienced professionals who have already held – or still hold – the positions of Chief Executive Officer (CEO) and/or board member. Among those interviewed were **Alexandre Gonçalves Silva, Betania Tanure, César Souza, Fernando Carneiro, Herman Bulls, Linda Parker Hudson, Luiz Carlos Cabrera, Paula Rosput Reynolds, Pedro Parente** and **Sérgio Rial.**

---

[*] The author interviewed Sir Adrian Cadbury (1929–2015) on December 4, 2013.
[**] The author interviewed Bengt Hallqvist (1930–2019) on October 5, 2016.
[***] A consulting firm specialized in corporate governance that provides support for the improvement of the CG model and adoption of the best CG practices. The author is a founding partner of Better Governance.

A number of other directors and executives from around the world were interviewed, but their names are omitted in order to preserve confidentiality in the cases reported. The book is filled with short reports from these professionals and each chapter opens with a case that anticipates the issues covered in that chapter, with the episodes concluded at the climax of the chapter, when the ideas presented are understood and can be applied to the case. The situations reported derive from real events. But please do not even try to identify them: I have scrambled the circumstances, characters and characteristics of the cases that occurred in my interviewees' different countries in such a way that even I have a hard time remembering the precise outlines of their original stories. In this way, the real situations were transformed into the very purest fiction.

My main objective in writing this book is to share experiences and lessons learned about CG – both mine as well as of all the interviewees – with all those who, directly or indirectly, are involved with boards of directors or affected by their decisions and often wonder how they are taken. I hope that reading this book will be of use to directors and CEOs as well as to executives or managers who do not yet circulate in board meetings on a frequent basis. The same applies to consultants, auditors, lawyers, governance secretaries and chief governance officers, who serve boards, as well as students, researchers and experts on CG and boards of directors. My invitation is that, instead of standing outside, trying to understand "the decisions that emanate from that black box," you use the behavioral compass provided by this book to make your interaction with the board a more productive and effective one, involving each and every player in governance practices.

The first part of the book – **The black box** – consists of five chapters:

- **Chapter 1**, along with a brief history of CG, the interviewees help me to discuss the performance of boards.
- **Chapter 2** describes BoDs, presenting their main characteristics in terms of composition and discussing the effects of limited diversity. The chapter also presents the most detrimental individual behaviors of directors as reported in our first survey with 102 board members concluded in 2017.
- **Chapter 3** deals with the decision-making process subjected to intra- and extra-board tensions, highlighting the delicate relationship between the CEO and the other executives with the directors.
- **Chapter 4** deals with the solitary and so misunderstood role of the chair of the board: in the midst of so many tensions and individual dysfunctional behaviors, it is his/her responsibility to ensure that the board remains in good working order.
- **Chapter 5** points out the issues and disputes that most keep board members awake at night. The result of the research carried out with

these professionals reveals their concerns, headaches and regrets and also covers the behavioral factors involved.

The second part – **Thinking outside the box** – is divided into two chapters. After discussing the limits of rationality based mainly on the theoretical concepts of **Herbert Simon** and **Daniel Kahneman** (two winners of the Nobel Prize for Economics):

- **Chapter 6** applies the behavioral approach – from the individual point of view and the group view – to identify the cognitive biases that have the greatest influence on the decision-making process. And finally,
- **Chapter 7** provides a behavioral compass: a guide with instruments to minimize the effects of the biases on the performance of directors, either individually or in a group. The chapter goes on to explain how to apply these instruments, so that all professionals – whether board members, CEOs or executives in the different positions – can navigate more easily and confidently among the behavioral traps, improving the interactive process and increasing the efficiency of the board's decision-making and other duties. In providing these instruments, the chapter relies on literature that explores the architecture of choices. It is the concept of "nudge" "any aspect that alters people's behavior in a predictable way without forbidding any options or significantly changing their economic incentives."[4]

I hope this book will help you to be guided by **"governance in reality,"** leading you to contemplate the opportunity it presents to create value. Understanding good governance based on its principles – transparency, equity, accountability and corporate responsibility – and recognizing the considerable impact that people and their limited rationality have on the way that organizations are governed, will bring us closer to achieving that value.

The exploration of the behavioral world that is inherent to the dynamics of boards can be an enjoyable and thought-provoking experience. As you turn the pages, you will encounter routes, maps and equipment to guide you on your journey through this brave new world. Have a great trip!

Notes

1 Guerra, Sandra. Melhor não descuidar. As conquistas alcançadas em governança não eliminam os riscos de retrocesso. *Capital Aberto*, November 2007.
2 Guerra, Sandra. Governança Corporativa e Criação de Valor. *Criação de Valor da Associação Brasileira de Companhias Abertas* (ABRASCA), October 2013.

3 Da Silveira, Alexandre Di Miceli. Corporate scandals of the 21st century: Limitations of mainstream corporate governance literature and the need for a new behavioral approach. *Science Research Network*, November 2015. Available at https://papers.ssrn.com/sol3/papers.cfm?abstract_id=2181705. Accessed on August 11, 2020.
4 Thaler, Richard H.; Sunstein, Cass R. *Nudge: Improving decisions about health, wealth, and happiness*. New York: Penguin, 2009. Location 171 of 5708.

Part I

The Black Box

Chapter 1

The Decision-Making Machine

Chapter Summary

- A brief historical evolutionary background of corporate governance in the world from the 17th century to the regulatory advances and improvements in policies and practices that have been adopted since the financial crisis that got underway in 2007/2008.
- Interviewees such as **Adrian Cadbury, Ira Millstein, Mats Isaksson, Robert Monks** and **Mervyn King** discuss the workings of boards of directors (BoDs), identify obstacles, acknowledge the existence of failures and point out possible causes.
- The operation of BoDs, the highest corporate governance body, is scrutinized from the point of view of its roles, responsibilities, structure, dynamics and processes. A structural X-ray of the so-called black box.
- Right at the outset in this first chapter, a small box alerts you to the tensions in the relationship between board members and executives, giving a preview of the detailed breakdown of this topic that can be found in Chapter 3.
- Even though they are in accordance with the latest regulatory requirements and best Corporate Governance practices, BoDs fail: why? The answer for this will be sought over the course of the next few chapters.
- A caselet describing the dilemma of an independent board experiencing a dysfunctional situation opens and concludes the chapter, covering the chapter conceptual discussions.

> *"Good boards are pretty uncomfortable places and that's where they should be,"* was a statement made by Sir Christopher Hogg,[1] the former chairman of the Financial Reporting Council, the United Kingdom's regulatory body, in an article that I read a few years ago. And I can guarantee that I experienced this for three long months, while I argued about the viability of the Blue Bird Project with SanMartín's

BoD. There were nine directors in total, and I was the only independent one.

In February 2016, the executives began a series of meetings to present us with one of the most ambitious projects that was in progress in the group, which also promised to be one of the most profitable ones. At the end of the first meeting, my eight fellow board members already seemed to be convinced by the potentially extraordinary figures in terms of profitability, whereas I was uneasy. The risk potential seemed high to me. The executives had already assured us that the risk management model was being complied with; all the permits for the construction work had been issued; and the project had positive technical reports from environmentalists and lawyers who specialized in the environmental area. Nevertheless, I was still not totally convinced.

At the meetings that followed, I remained uncomfortable. The more the executives gave reassurances regarding the reliability of the numbers and the unlikelihood of a major environmental disaster, the more I clung to my suspicions. I questioned each aspect so thoroughly that I ended up by creating an almost hostile environment in relation to my role as an independent board member. I reached the point where I could feel that the atmosphere was very tense.

Fearing that the decision would be postponed, the chairman, who also held the position of Chief Executive Officer (CEO), silenced my solitary voice: "Relax, you are new to this sector. Just wait and see the leap that the shares will take at the end of the quarter, when the Blue Bird Project is announced." There was no need to wait until the end of March. Fifteen days after the announcement, the market had already established the price of the company's shares, which had risen by 25%. Despite this apparent momentary happy ending for SanMartín, the future would show that I was right...[*]

Since the 17th century, when the first commercial entities appeared in which ownership and management were separated, there has not been a single period in the corporate history in which the relevance and effectiveness of the performance of those running the company have not been questioned – to a greater or lesser degree. In the Dutch East India Company, a small group of managers, who were appointed for life, were regularly accused by the other shareholders of prioritizing matters related to war and politics rather than the enterprise's strictly commercial interests. It was therefore characterized as "one of the very first demonstrations of 'shareholder activism,'" which, since then, has presented three basic demands – which are still very much present centuries

---

[*] The story's conclusion will be presented at the end of this chapter.

later: (1) the provision of clear information, (2) the right to appoint managers and (3) changes to directors' remuneration.[2]

Although it was a successful enterprise for almost two centuries, neither the increasing pressure from shareholders outside of management nor the continued creation of new disciplinary mechanisms were able to prevent the Dutch East India Company from going bankrupt in 1799, buckling under competition from products from the New World and inundated with charges of fraud and corruption. Likewise, in the following centuries, the corporate history has shown that governance instruments, while continuously evolving, have not been able to prevent the worst business failures, always with disastrous direct and indirect social impacts. Indeed, this is still happening nowadays and what is observed is a cyclical trend: the advance of best policies and practices is successively fueled by crises and business scandals – always failing, however, in its aim of preventing them.

Institutional investors assumed greater political and economic power in the 1980s and 1990s, following the wave of hostile takeovers in the United States and Europe when defense mechanisms were created. Investors then began to exercise their fiduciary role of owners.[3] At the turn of the 21st century, the process of globalization of the real economy and the financial markets increased the complexity of the environment with the universalization of the risks and turbulence resulting, for example, from the crises in Asia, Russia and Brazil, while business scandals, such as Enron, WorldCom and Tyco highlighted the distrust and conflict between managers and shareholders.

In retrospect, there is no question that the unfolding of these scandals was the result of a combination of defective processes based on information asymmetry, divergence of interests and misguided purposes coupled with conspicuous doses of greed, and an absence of the basic principles of ethical conduct. "There is little doubt that the Enron collapse, the biggest bankruptcy in the history of the United States to date, was caused by corporate governance problems,"[4] experts afterward pointed out.

As yet another direct response to malpractice on the part of boards and senior management, 2002 saw the establishment of the Sarbanes-Oxley Act (SOX) in the United States. At that time, it seemed essential to impose heavy penalties on those who failed to adhere to the new governance standards, in addition to trying to restore confidence in companies' financial reports and the credibility of consulting firms and external auditors. In the corporate universe, this period was characterized by the adoption of a rigid model of compulsory adherence to a long list of control, monitoring and inspection mechanisms.

However, not even this imposed severity was able to prevent, deter or mitigate the systemic breakdown that would follow, which had its origins in the unbridled granting of subprime mortgage loans in the United

States. Erupting in 2007/2008, the mortgage default crisis had a domino effect and contaminated the global banking and financial systems, with consequences up to the present. The resulting monetary losses were no greater than the catastrophic impact the crisis had on the credibility of the relationship between shareholders and managers. "What did the administrators of these institutions do, including those who were handsomely remunerated?", small investors want to know. The question "where were the directors who failed to see the misconduct of the executives they were supposed to be guiding, supervising and controlling?", is still being asked by some of the leading experts in corporate governance (CG) who remain outraged.

There Is Only One Certainty: Boards Fail

These and other issues are still worrying experts of the caliber of Sir Adrian Cadbury,[*] who was one of the forerunners of the movement to improve corporate governance in the 1990s. Therefore, although he was one of the main promoters of the continuous evolution of CG mechanisms, he never failed to recognize that BoDs have often failed to prevent business scandals. In an interview granted, Sir Adrian commented on the main causes of dysfunctions in BoDs:

> If we start off with the scandals it seems to me that boards were not doing their job, they were not asking the right questions and they were not carrying out properly the functions of a board. The key thing that a board does is to appoint and monitor the chief executive, giving him/her as much support as they can, ensuring that he/she continues down the path that the board has set, because it is the board that decides the company's strategy, what its goals are, what its purpose is, and most important of all – what its values are. In the period when these companies went astray, boards were not carrying out their functions, they were quite prepared to let the executives do what they wanted and there were further problems such as incentive arrangements which encouraged risk taking and greed. I cannot explain what happened during that period: we saw the disaster building up, we observed an extraordinary disparity between the earnings of a few executives at the top and the rest of the workforce. This is something that a board should be concerned about because the company needs to be able to rely on a stable workforce, with there being the feeling throughout the entire company that the pay

[*] Sir Adrian Cadbury (1929--2015) was the author of the Cadbury Report, which, in 1992, established corporate governance standards for the United Kingdom. He was also the chairman of the board of Cadbury Schweppes. The author interviewed Sir Adrian Cadbury in Dorridge, England, on December 4, 2013.

structure is fair, so that everyone feels as if they part of the company, that they have all contributed to its results. When there is a huge gap between those at the top and the rest of the workforce there are marked social implications, the people in the workforce do not feel that they are valued, and the top executives become detached, they don't feel as if they're part of the company. There is a deterioration in the relationships and it is the board's job to be aware of this. After all, some companies got into trouble, not because of their structure as a whole, but because the people in charge did not tackle the problems that had been identified.

> Basically, in both cases, what we are talking about here is the result of greedy behavior on the part of the board and the executives, isn't it?

Yes, we are talking about greed, and sadly, about the ability of a few individuals who benefited from acting in a mercenary way. And that is what is wrong, it should not be possible for the executives who are at the top to be able to manipulate the compensation system by means of bonuses and options, however they may benefit in terms of the compensation paid by companies, which, at the end of the day, means that it is the customers and the community who are paying for the greed of a few. This is wrong, but it is the boards of these companies who are responsible.

> As a distant observer, what would be the signs of a dysfunctional board?

The most obvious sign is when the board is dominated by a single individual, whether it be the chairman of the board, the CEO or, occasionally, one of the external directors. So dominance – the silence of the external directors or the excessive power of a single person – is a clear sign that the board is not working properly. The key point here is that dominance prevents the board from operating properly: if someone merely listens, if there is no contribution from everyone, this indicates a dysfunctional board. On a good board of directors, all of the directors express their ideas and contribute to decisions and strategies. A dysfunctional board is one where there are no ideas expressed collectively and where one or another board member tries to exercise an undue influence.

The successive cycles between the outbreak of governance crises and the establishment of new rules and practices were analyzed by **Ira Millstein,**[*]

---

[*] Ira Millstein, corporate lawyer and a senior partner at Weil, Gotshal and Manges, is one of the most highly regarded corporate governance experts in the United States and headed up the committee that drafted the OECD's – Organisation for Economic

whose role in corporate governance in the United States can be compared to that of **Sir Adrian Cadbury** on the other side of the Atlantic. In an interview with the author, **Ira** pointed to the excess of regulatory mechanisms and, in particular, the pressure from the financial market for short-term results as being among the main obstacles to the sustainable management of companies:

> One of the current problems is that boards are overwhelmed with too many rules and regulations – they are spending too much time on compliance instead of on strategy and tactics. So, this is the starting point for my analysis: a lot of the things that I originally suggested were, and still are, necessary, but that wasn't the end of the story. Some of these rules have either been taken too far or become the central focus, at the expense of setting board strategy, in the boardroom. For example, do shareholders now have too much power, in the sense that activists want to change things even when not in the best interests of the company? Do all the rules, taken together, weaken boards? All of these rules were created to make boards better, not to help activists with different agendas. So I'm wondering more what makes a good board. Is it just the rules? Do we need more rules and regulations? No. Boards are already overwhelmed by them, spending too much time on compliance and not enough time on risk oversight. What is really being done on analyzing the business strategy and the compensation system in order to see whether compensation is good for the company or just good for the boards and for the executives? Despite all the rules, we are continuing to see matters that shouldn't be happening: in some cases, too much risk; and in other cases, compensation still not under control. In addition, the capital markets have changed, they have become short term oriented. Boards are worried about ending the quarter with a good result, because their compensation comes primarily from their stock packages; they want to see the stock going up. Unfortunately, we also have naked options[*] which can cash out right away. Even if we lengthen the time frame, the compensation system is still too closely tied to the stock market, which encourages a quarterly outlook, rather than the long term.

> **What should we focus our attention on in order to make boards of directors better?**

Co-operation and Development's – Corporate Governance Principles. The author interviewed Ira Millstein in New York, United States, on March 31, 2014.

[*] When the investor assumes the right to trade (buy and/or sell) a lot of shares in a company within a predetermined period, without, in fact, previously having owned the securities.

Boards of directors are made up of people and, therefore, when you are looking for a good board member, you should evaluate that person's personal attributes. Is he or she someone who has the courage and willingness to do the "right thing?" A professor, David W. Miller, had a definition for ethics that I regard as being the main attribute of a good board member: "Ethics is the art and discipline of discerning the right, the good and the fitting action to take, and having the creativity and courage to do it." Based on my own experiences counseling boards of directors for more than fifty years, I believe that directors, for the most part, want to do the right thing. Then the real question is whether they in fact have the courage to act?

(In Chapter 5, Ira Millstein provides his perspectives on three cases in which board members demonstrated this boldness in relation to deciding and taking action.)

With regard to the aspects related to the duties and performance of BoDs – before, during and after periods of governance crisis, **Mats Isaksson**[*] offers an unsettling perspective. Until March 2021, he was the Head of Corporate Governance and Corporate Finance at the Organization for Economic Cooperation and Development (OECD), which was responsible for formulating the G20/OECD Principles of Corporate Governance,[**] which have guided all the codes around the world on this subject since 1999:

> As an external observer I have always been fascinated by the work and the workings of the board of directors in large companies. Why do we have them? How to they fulfill their duties and what motivates its members? Boards consist of a relatively small group of highly qualified persons, not very well paid and still in charge of issues of strategic importance to large and complex organizations that on a daily basis are run by an army of experts and executives that understand and control every aspect of the business. And still, every time there is some sort of governance crisis or corporate scandals there is a call to put more and more responsibilities on the board of directors. There are suggestions to add yet one more independent director, create another board committee, additional compliance

[*] Mats Isaksson is an economist who in his former role as head of the OECD Corporate Governance and Corporate Finance Division led the development of the G20/OECD Principles of Corporate Governance. The author interviewed Mats Isaksson in Leipzig, Germany, on September 24, 2015.

[**] First issued in 1999, the Principles have become the international benchmark in corporate governance. They were adopted as one of the Financial Stability Board's Key Standards for Sound Financial Systems and endorsed by the G20 in 2015.

requirements, extended duties and so on. I am not saying that this is always the wrong avenue. But before we embark on it, we must have a good understanding of what a board reasonably can achieve compared to other company organs, such as the shareholder meeting and the executive. And on a more practical level, what differentiates a board that creates value for its shareholders from one that merely fulfills a formal function of discharging its formal responsibilities through box ticking. If it is overcharged and not allow to function well, the board may itself be part of the problem and the more responsibilities we load on it, the further away from a solution we may get. The correct distribution of authority and accountability between the different company organs, such as the shareholder meeting, the board and the executive should obviously the product of their different incentives and the need for checks and balances. But once this is formally established, it becomes an issue of skills, judgment and human capacity. And what is so fascinating with the quality of the board is that it is the product of both individual and collective skills. How do individual board members perceive their role? How often should the directors meet in order to interact effectively as a group? How long should the meetings last? Should we have fully professional boards, or part time boards that meet up six or eight times a year?

Without boards of directors, what would we have in their place?

The worst of all worlds is probably one in which we trust a corporate body with important responsibilities without knowing if it actually has the skills and means to carry them out. So, we need to set it up in a way where there is proportionality between board responsibilities and their ability to realistically and in a diligent way discharge these responsibilities. And the tendency at every scandal to vest the board with additional responsibilities or routines makes it more important than ever to understand and improve the functioning of the board. A task that I believe should be a priority not only for the shareholders that appoint the board but also for the directors themselves that are taking on an increasingly demanding job in large corporations. This inquiry will not only make for better run companies but it will also make us better prepared to discuss the role of the board in a rational way when the next corporate scandal triggers new calls for reform.

Robert Monks[*] takes an even more provocative approach than **Isaksson**. Monks, who is one of the pioneers of shareholder activism in the

---

[*] Robert Monks is a co-founder of Institutional Shareholders Services and the author of books such as *Corpocracy and Watching the Watchers*. The author interviewed Robert Monks in Pelican Hill, Newport Coast, California, United States, on September 13, 2013.

United States and is recognized for his fighting spirit, regards it as being almost beyond belief that BoDs continue to exist, especially in publicly traded companies. According to him, BoDs are a myth, "almost like Santa Claus":

> Basically, what I can conclude is that the boards of directors of public companies are a fiction. They are almost like Santa Claus, something that was invented because they perform a useful role in the public imagination. Nobody really wants boards to do what the public imagination believes they do. This is particularly true in the United States. The way that boards are structured, there is a permanent resistance against separating the roles of chairman of the BoD and CEO of the company. This means that the board, whose main responsibility is to monitor the CEO and choose a new one, when it is necessary, actually has its agenda predetermined, given that its meetings are chaired by the CEO. Simply by adopting this model is enough for serious people to know that there are no real boards of directors. The English are a little more sophisticated, but they have also lost the meaning of the board in the midst of their class system. They have boards that have clubbable people, so if you're a "clubbable" person you go on the boards and if you're not, you can't get on the board. The result of this is that it suits everyone to pretend that boards do what people say they ought to do. But, in my view, boards are a myth.

For his part, **Mervyn King,**[*] the most significant figure in corporate governance in South Africa who enjoys international recognition, compares companies to "incapacitated people," given that they do not think or act for themselves. He brings to the discussion once again a point that has already been emphasized by Ira Millstein, namely, that BoDs are made up of human beings – but he goes further. As far as King is concerned, board members are subject to the temptations and sins of the "corporate devil."

> I have always said that there is a corporate devil and that is why we have to be aware of its sins, including greed and self-centered concerns. You cannot be a board member and be afraid of taking some degree of risk, because it is your duty to take risks in order to achieve the rewards. You will be acting out of self-interest when you think, "I'd better protect myself. If something goes wrong, I could be sued".

---

[*] Mervyn King is chairman emeritus of the GRI (Global Reporting Initiative). King, who is a South African with a distinguished career as a supreme court judge in that country, chaired the King Committee on Corporate Governance, which produced South Africa's governance code. The code, the King Report on Corporate Governance is an international reference already in its 4th edition. The author interviewed Mervyn King in New York, United States, on April 1, 2014.

In that case, you will not be using your abilities in the company's best interest, in other words, on behalf of maximizing value. By itself, self-centered concern is a failure to fulfill the director's duty. Another corporate sin is arrogance. For example, a long-term strategy has been decided and afterwards, when it's compared to the other one, you think something like: "I have no idea what they are doing. They're out of their minds. Why are they moving out of Brazil? Why go to Peru? What's in Peru? Are they going crazy?" And there is still pride. You made a decision on the BoD that is being implemented. From your point of view, you think it is wrong, but instead of initiating a debate within the board, you give a TV interview criticizing it. You avoid discussing it because deep down you don't want egg on your face. These are the corporate devils that are constantly tempting us. Therefore, intellectual honesty is a critical issue. You have to honestly realize that you are acting on behalf of an inanimate and incapacitated person, that is, a company. The company has no heart, mind or soul, it has nothing; it is worse than a person who's a vegetable on account of a major car accident: he cannot think for himself; he is immobile and he's being kept alive by machines. The director becomes the heart, mind and soul of the company. He/she is the one who creates the company's reputation and steers the company in a direction. Based on the view of the company as an inanimate person, let's define the director's duties as being the heart, mind and soul of an incapacitated person, and doing so with good faith and diligence.

What the Black Box Is and How It Works?

In addition to the scandals and crises that have fueled the evolutionary cycle of corporate governance, there is another factor – antagonistic with the first – which has contributed to stimulate the creation and adoption of new rules and mechanisms aimed at ensuring the best practices and optimizing the results of the business. Ever since the start of the 21st century, research has reiterated the value of good governance, which can be defined nowadays as follows:

Corporate governance refers to the making of decisions, controlling their implementation and distributing the results fairly to the different parties involved. It is aimed at creating value over the long term and preserving the balance between the interests of the aforesaid parties.

In 2000, the consulting firm **McKinsey & Company**[5] carried out a study with international investors from 22 countries and identified that the group was willing to pay a premium of between 18% and 28% for shares of companies with superior governance practices. Since then, over the years, a number of studies have been conducted that associated good governance practices with perceived value. While in 2015, a group of researchers from four countries[6] once again found evidence that good corporate governance practices raise the value of companies in the four emerging markets that were studied (Brazil, India, Korea and Turkey). Among the aspects that are associated with value generation are financial transparency (disclosure) and the board's independence.

What is even more widely accepted is the fact that best CG practices increase access to financing, reduce the cost of capital and optimize operational performance, given that, along with other benefits, they provide a better allocation of resources and facilitate the relationship with related parties.[7] However, the positive effect of implementing CG standards also goes beyond the individual performance of companies: the governance structure is capable of influencing sectors of activity and even countries themselves. In this case, uncertainties in relation to corporate governance translate into an increased cost of capital and can even affect the functioning of a country's capital market, whether it extends to a group of companies or to a sector. In the **OECD's – Organization for Economic Cooperation and Development**'s – Corporate Governance Factbook 2019, the chair **Masato Kanda** reiterates the importance of CG for companies and countries:

> "Good corporate governance is an essential means to create an environment of market confidence and business integrity that supports capital market development and corporate access to equity capital for long-term productive investments. As a matter of fact, the quality of a country's corporate governance framework is of decisive importance for the dynamics and the competitiveness of a country's business sector."[8]

Over the course of the past decades, among the CG mechanisms, studies and research have devoted special attention to the BoD. The board's practices and processes are among the first elements analyzed in order to determine a company's level of governance and, notwithstanding the different perspectives and critical questions, there is a lot of agreement among experts regarding the importance of its existence and performance. According to some of the leading scholars in the field, the BoD can be defined as follows:

- The mainstay of corporate governance and the critical nexus in which the company's fate is decided;[9]

- It is the body that is ultimately responsible for ensuring the organization's integrity in all matters;[10]
- It occupies a critical position in the modern free enterprise system, with the responsibility and the opportunity to make a significant difference by presenting a competitive need, which can be used as a competitive differential;[11]
- It provides a governance safeguard for capital and managers and is an important internal control tool;[12]
- It is the corporation's key decision-making body on behalf of shareholders and the repository of the company's maximum power;[13]
- It is the heart of the governance system and a focal point for shareholders and the market system[14] due to the fact that it is among the most revered corporate governance instruments.[15]

However, there is a flagrant contradiction: despite the relevance of the BoD in companies' CG structure and the focus dedicated to this instrument in hundreds of studies, the BoD is also regarded as a black box, precisely because of the difficulty to obtain direct access to its internal operating rituals[16] – unless you are one of the board members sitting at the table. Even so, the never-ending quest for a more in-depth understanding of its workings has given rise to theoretical and practical studies, methodically dissecting the BoD from a number of angles: on the basis of its roles and responsibilities, its structure and operation, or its processes. A brief description of these various aspects will be presented below so that, in the following chapters, it will be possible to proceed from these descriptions in order to analyze the dynamics of the individual and group interactions, in addition to other factors with intangible characteristics which are also present in the workings of BoDs.

Roles and responsibilities – The BoD's duties relate to various corporate spheres:
  Strategy:

- To define the strategic direction in an integrated way with the executive board, supporting its implementation. When defining the strategy, the board should make sure that the choices are sustainable and that the externalities generated are taken into account, as well as its social responsibility;
- To regularly monitor the implementation of the strategy defined;
- To make decisions regarding relevant investment projects, within its approval authority level, including mergers and acquisitions;
- To keep the board focused on the organization's future, continually reassessing opportunities and threats, as well as the need to add or reformulate organizational competencies, allowing the organization to anticipate external changes.

Identity, values and governance:

- To act as guardian of the organization's principles and values, encouraging their discussion and definition;
- To ensure ethical conduct;
- To preserve the company's identity and ensure respect for the organization's culture. To assess when changes in culture are needed and support their implementation;
- To ensure that the organization listens to interested parties in order to take into account their point of view regarding the organization's performance. Special attention should be paid to investors, establishing a strategic dialogue channel in line with that administered by the investor relations area at the executive level;
- To act as guardian of the company's governance, heading up regular reviews of its practices.

Performance, risks, controls and audit:

- To oversee the economic, financial and operational performance;
- To ensure that there is a model of the set of risks to which the activity is exposed, a process for monitoring and mitigating the aforesaid risks, along with mechanisms so that the board oversees risk management on a regular basis;
- To ensure the existence of an internal control system that works with the proper independence and which reports directly to the board;
- To approve the financial statements and ensure that they faithfully and clearly express the organization's economic, financial and asset situation;
- To select the independent auditor, as well as to approve its annual work program, making an assessment of it at the end of the period.

People, organization and innovation:

- To hire and fire the CEO and to endorse the choice and dismissal of the executives who report to him/her;
- To carry out an assessment of the chief executive on an annual basis and to ensure that he/she does the same with his/her subordinates;
- To ratify that the board maintains a structured plan which is kept up to date for the emergency replacement of the main executive, as well as for his/her scheduled succession;
- To oversee the succession plans made out by the CEO for his/her subordinates;
- To carry out a structured assessment of the board on an annual basis which, at least every three years, should be aided by an external,

independent agent. The assessment should result in an improvement plan and also be used to fuel a skills, characteristics and styles matrix in order to plan the board's composition and renewal;

- To maintain a structured plan which is kept up to date in relation to the succession of directors;
- To define a compensation policy for the senior executives, guaranteeing a long-term view;
- To establish the CEO's goals, as well as to endorse the goals of his/her subordinates;
- To ensure that the organization remains competitive, innovative and up to date in terms of its technology;
- To ensure that the organization adopts policies and mechanisms for attracting, developing and retaining professionals, in advance of strategic demands.

This is a concise description of the board members' responsibilities, but with the spotlight intensely focused on boards with each new successive scandal or crisis, the duties of BoDs have continued to grow, as was previously pointed out by the OECD's Head of Corporate Governance and Corporate Finance, **Mats Isaksson**. Board members are overburdened, particularly regarding legal requirements and their consequent risks. There is even a new discussion in relation to this topic: how long will there be professionals who are willing to face this burden and take on these risks?

Structure – Based on the description already presented of its roles and duties, the BoD can be regarded as a "decision-making machine" and, therefore, its make-up has a very significant impact, given that the interaction between the board members is one of the determining factors for increasing or reducing its effectiveness. It is vital that the environment is one which is open to contradictory opinions, particularly in relation to decision-making, since those decisions that are questioned and scrutinized the most, tend to be the most robust ones. Therefore, in order to have a debate that is capable of clarifying all the proposals presented, it is necessary that the board's make-up includes the appropriate degree of diversity, with the concept here being extended to all of its aspects: education, knowledge, experience, gender, age, origin or geographical experience and cultural perspectives, as well as behavior and leadership styles. It is this willingness to accept contradictory opinions and the set of different worldviews that will allow the same object to be evaluated from a variety of perspectives – and that will enable the final decision to be the best one.

There is consistent research in the field of social psychology that proves the relevance of diversity in the interaction of groups.[17] There are situations, for example, in which not everybody agrees with a point of view, but where on account of the fact that they are in the minority, the person leaves out their opinion, failing to present it in a discussion. Therefore, a lack of diversity reduces the social influence of individuals and can even blind the board members, negatively affecting the quality of the decision-making process by creating an internal circle of dominant power[18] within the group. Other studies also indicate that groups with greater diversity perform better than those that are more homogeneous – not just because there is a more dynamic flow of new ideas, but also because diversity leads to more careful processing of information, which is not the case in more homogeneous groups.[19] In Chapter 2, when the profile of board members and some aspects of the dynamics of their interactions are covered, the current picture and the implications of gender diversity in BoDs will be analyzed.

Still looking at the structural aspect, the BoD performs its duties with the support of committees – collective bodies that are also made up of board members, but which have an accessory role, in other words they do not take any decision in isolation or act as a supervisory body.

Dynamics and processes – A crucial point for the BoD's best performance is for this body to have its own work plan in order not to be at the mercy of the agenda of topics brought up by the executives. This implies the prior definition by the board members of a working dynamic along with the establishment of priorities among the board's duties. For example, amount of time does not necessarily denote quality. However, a BoD that meets four times a year, essentially to approve the company's financial statements, is totally different from one that has monthly meetings – both in terms of the priority responsibilities as well as in relation to the dynamics and processes that should be implemented.

The Strained Interaction between Board Members and Executives

The relationship between the board and the senior management is an extremely complex one and, in some more extreme cases, can even become turbulent. The main reason for this lies in the fact that there is an apparent paradox: at the same time, the directors should both advise as well as supervise the managers, which often leads to a strained relationship. These two simultaneous responsibilities (supervising and advising) mean that the board members tend to adopt a more skeptical approach in order to maintain objectivity and assertiveness. However, in doing so, they tend to exacerbate the critical side, leaving the more constructive observations in the background.

The result is that this behavior puts executives on the defensive: they only offer the information that keeps them out of the hot-seat, opening up as little as possible at board meetings. In the case of boards that are very harsh and that adopt an inquisition-like approach, a love-hate relationship may be established. This dysfunction can even go as far as to result in something akin to Stockholm syndrome, when someone, after being subjected to intimidation for a long time, ends up becoming sympathetic and even feeling affection or friendship for their own aggressor. It is rare, but it does happen.

However, since the BoD is considered the "decision-making machine," how could the process possibly be efficient and effective in an environment that is not conducive to confidence and an unreserved exchange of information? According to **Pound**,[20] the fundamental problem in CG does not come from the imbalance of power, but rather from subtle failures resulting from the interaction between managers and board members in decision-making and in monitoring the business' progress. Therefore, the construction of a positive relationship that allows the flow and exchange of information, in addition to the maturity to accept contradictory opinions – appreciated by both groups: directors and executives – is an essential tool for making better decisions and will be discussed at length throughout this book, with the focus being on behavioral approach aspects.

It is also necessary to mention that BoDs have other internal conflicts, regarding the dynamics of the interactions between the group of directors themselves. One of them, for example, results from another apparent contradiction: it is recommended that the board's diversified make-up encourages and paves the way for contradictory opinions, but, at the same time that in the end, the directors can reach a cohesive position. This is an even more challenging task, bearing in mind that the decision-making process within the board takes place against a backdrop that is already affected by the strained relations with the executives. All of these aspects of group dynamics are so significant that Chapter 3 will be dedicated exclusively to this topic.

Another factor that is fundamental in order for the board to perform properly is the leadership role of the chairperson. This point is a complex one, as there are not yet many professionals who are capable of understanding the exact nature of this leadership, with it usually being confused with the pure and simple role of command and power. The board chair's operating profile should be that of a discussion enabler, obtaining the best from the board members and skillfully conducting the decision or supervision process, duly tested by contradictory opinions. There is a significant amount of room for progress here: as long as boards are headed up by leaders who do not understand and do not fulfill their real role, much of the body's capacity to generate value will continue to be wasted. In order to support their work, chairs have a board secretary, who in some countries is referred to as the governance secretary, and who is responsible for all the processes – agenda, minutes, documentation, board portal – and who reports directly to the board chair. The chairperson's role will be covered in detail in Chapter 4.

Even When Everything Is Being Complied with...

The effectiveness of BoDs has historically been related to their structure and functioning. As shown earlier on, a great deal of attention has already been paid to their composition, committees, as well as to the number and length of meetings, in addition to the quality of the pre-meeting reading material provided for information and the advance notice with which everything reaches the board members. The importance of all these elements is not disputed: there is no way to deny that a good BoD has to take into account all these basic and structural aspects. However, it is essential to distinguish that the board – first and foremost – is a group of highly qualified people, which is required to make decisions, define strategies, advise managers and oversee the execution of everything in an attentive way; and all of this has to be done as a group. Everything else stems from this vision of communication between people.

Essentially the board's performance depends on how its members interact with each other and how this collective decision-making body gets along with the senior executives. The researchers **Katharina Pick** and **Kenneth Merchant**[21] point out trends in groups that can overshadow the talents of intelligent and well-intentioned people, causing what they call blind spots, biases and inefficiencies, which can make boards ineffective. These factors can lead highly qualified BoDs to fail to identify risks and problems. In addition, according to these researchers, the groups make joint decisions that none of the individuals would take by themselves. Although the amount of time that the meetings have is always extremely limited, the trend is for the group to get bogged down on details that are not important to the quality of the decision to be taken.

Rules, practices and mechanisms are essential to the functioning of a good BoD, but none of this will result in better governance if the behavior and attitude of the individuals are not more conducive to efficiency within the governance apparatus. Almost 30 years after the corporate governance movement first got underway in the world, it is already possible to shift the focus to more subtle and sophisticated aspects of BoDs, which have not yet received the due attention. This is the case of the behavioral approach, which permeates the entire dynamics of boards as well as their interaction with the other corporate governance bodies.

It is possible to speculate that if we were to analyze these behavioral aspects more closely, we would find clearer evidence as to why companies that had a governance that was considered to be a model – at least when seen from the outside and from a distance – experienced notorious corporate scandals and/or ended up becoming landmark cases of business failure. Theoretically, it seems simple; however, in practice, it is the source of one of the biggest challenges for companies: when it comes to the BoD, everything can go wrong. By its very nature as a black box, if instead of creating value, the BoD is destroying it, this can go unnoticed, and this is extremely serious. In this case, the loss is substantial and irreversible, with a high financial cost and, generally, also significant reputational damage.

In the account given at the start of this chapter, the board member experienced a dysfunctional situation in San Martín's BoD, which made him helpless in light of the facts. The sequence of events ensured that he was proved right, but did not give him the satisfaction of having fulfilled his role as an independent director.

About two years after that fateful meeting at SanMartín's board of directors, I was having a cup of coffee early in the morning, while reading the news on my favorite business portal: suddenly, my hand stopped in mid-air, my mouth was half-open and my eyes froze. Yes, I was seeing it right. A serious ecological disaster on an unprecedented scale in the south of the country had caused unspecified environmental damage, resulting in many victims. The information at that point was imprecise. There was no confirmation of the total number of dead, but it was estimated to be more than fifty, in addition to hundreds of missing persons. At the epicenter of the tragedy, the successful company SanMartín, which up until that moment had not issued a statement about the accident. I had no doubt whatsoever: the description was clearly of the Blue Bird Project, which had both worried me and made me question its wisdom. I immediately felt a mixture of relief and sadness. Nine months after that meeting, I had made the difficult decision to resign from the position of independent director at SanMartín. At the time, it might not have been so obvious, but now the evidence that I was right leapt out at me from my notebook screen. At every subsequent meeting, I saw clear signs that the all-powerful controller, chairman, and CEO did not, in fact, appreciate my independent contribution. As far as he was concerned, the BoD was just another audience for his endless speeches. Questions were not appreciated and my peers did nothing but sing the praises of "our president's" initiatives. I could not in all good conscience continue to accept this spectacle, although the remuneration as a board member at SanMartín was very important at that point – not least because my wife had just lost her job. Once again, I breathed a sigh of relief. It was important to have insisted and succeeded in getting the minutes of the meetings to register my votes against the Blue Bird Project, in addition to all my considerations regarding the risks involved. Fortunately, I took the advice of a very experienced friend and sent a letter, stating the reasons for my resignation: the role of the board was wrong and I did not feel that I could exercise my duty as an independent director, in accordance with my conscience. However, none of this did anything to ease my sadness in relation to what had just occurred. I felt powerless: what can an independent board member do within a group of nine? How could I have predicted that, in reality, this board of directors only existed on paper?

Does the scenario look familiar? In the next chapters, the intricacies and the outlines of dysfunctional situations of BoDs will be addressed more clearly, and in addition tools and a compass will be offered so that directors and executives can navigate more easily through turbulent situations, improving their interaction and, in particular, the governance model in order to guarantee maximization of the company's value.

Notes

1 Wong, Simon C. Y. Boards: When best practice isn't enough. *McKinsey Quarterly*, 1–7, June, 2011. Available at http://ssrn.com/abstract=1872324. Accessed on May 28, 2016. Accessed on May 28, 2016.
2 Frentrop, Paul. *A history of corporate governance, 1602–2002.* Amsterdam: Deminor, 2003, 480p.
3 Brancato, Carolyn K. *Institutional investors and corporate governance: best practices for increasing corporate value.* Chicago: Irwin Professional Pub, 1996, p. xi–xxii.
4 Becht, Marco; Bolton, Patrick; Röell, Ailsa. Corporate governance and control. *ECGI – Finance Working Paper* nº 2, 2002. p. 1–128, 2002. Available at http://papers.ssrn.com/sol3/papers.cfm?abstract_id=343461. Accessed on December 2, 2015.
5 Mckinsey & Company. Investor opinion survey on corporate governance, p. 1–18, June 2000. Available https://www.oecd.org/daf/ca/corporate governanceprinciples/1922101.pdf Accessed on October 4, 2016.
6 Black, Bernard S.; De Carvalho, Antônio Gledson; Khanna, Vikramaditya;Kim, Woochan and Yurtoglu, Burcin. Which aspects of corporate governance do and do not matter in emerging markets. *Northwestern Law & Economics Research Paper* nº 14–22, 2019; ECGI – Finance Working Paper

n° 566/2018, University of Michigan Law & Econ Research Paper, p. 1–50, May, 2015. Available at http://ssrn.com/abstract=2601107. Accessed on January 1, 2016.

7 IFC; OCDE; Global Corporate Governance Forum. *Practical guide to corporate governance*. Experiences from the Latin American Companies Circle, Washington, DC: IFC, p.1–276, 2009.

8 OECD (2019), OECD Corporate Governance Factbook 2019. p.1–184. Available at http://www.oecd.org/corporate/corporate-governance-factbook.htm. Accessed on June 9, 2020.

9 Clarke, Thomas. *International corporate governance: A comparative approach*.1st ed. Nova York: Routledge, 2017.

10 Fuller, Joseph B.; Michael C. Jensen. What's a Director to Do? In *Best practice: Ideas and insights from the world's foremost business thinkers*, edited by Tom Brown and Robert Heller, p. 243–250. New York: Basic Books, 2003.

11 Charan, Ram. Introduction: Advancing the Practice of Corporate Governance. In: *Boards that deliver: Advancing corporate governance from compliance to competitive advantage*. 1st. ed. São Francisco: Jossey-Bass, p.ix-xiii, 2005.

12 Baysinger, Barry; Hoskisson, Robert E. The Composition of Boards of Directors and Strategic Control: Effects on Corporate Strategy. *The Academy of Management Review*, v. 15, n.1, p. 72–87, 1990.

13 Millstein, Ira M. A perspective on corporate governance: Rules, principles or both. In: *ICGN yearbook*. Washington, 2006. Available at http://www.icgn.org/conferences/2006/documents/mill stein.pdf. Accessed on October 10, 2006.

14 Cadbury, Adrian; Millstein, Ira. The new agenda for ICGN. *International Corporate Governance Network*, Discussion Paper n°1 for the ICGN 10th Anniversary Conference. London, July 2005. Available at http://www.icgn.org/conferences/2005/documents/cad bury_millstein.pdf. Accessed on October 10, 2006.

15 Zahra, Shaker A.; Pearce, John A. Boards of directors and corporate financial performance: A review and integrative model. *Journal of Management*, v. 15, n. 2, p. 291–334, 1989.

16 Leighton, David S. R; Thain, Donald H. How to pay directors. *Business Quarterly*, v. 58, n. 2, p. 30–44, 1993 apud Leblanc, Michel; Schwartz, Mark S. The black box of board process: Gaining access to a difficult subject. *The Authors*, v. 15, n. 5, p.843–851, 2007.

17 Sherif, Muzafer. *The psychology of social norms*. Nova York: Harper, 1936. Also in Asch, Solomon E., *Effects of group pressure upon the modification and distortion of judgments*. In H. Guetzkow (Ed.), Groups, leadership and men. Pittsburg: Carnegie Press, , p. 177–190, 1951.

18 Merchant, Kenneth A.; Pick, Katharina. *Blind spots, biases and other pathologies in the boardroom*. New York: Business Expert Press, 2010.

19 Phillips, Katherine W.; Liljenquist, Katie A.; Neale, Margaret A. Is the pain worth the gain? The advantages and liabilities of agreeing with socially distinct newcomers. *Personality and Social Psychology Bulletin*, v. 35, n.3, p. 336–350, 2009.

20 Pound, John. The promise of the governed corporation. *Harvard Business Review*, v. 73, n. 2, p. 89–98, 1995.

21 Merchant, Kenneth A.; Pick, Katharina. *Blind spots, biases and other pathologies in the boardroom*. New York: Business Expert Press, 2010.

Chapter 2

Alone, But Always Accompanied

Chapter Summary

- Although they sit around the same table with the willingness to make collective decisions, a number of factors can lead to dysfunctionalities, including among others: the structure and composition of the board of directors (BoD) and the quality of the interactions between the directors.
- Surveys all over the world as well as in Brazil describe the typical profile of a board director: male, aged between 50 and 60, and in general, a former executive.
- Other studies indicate that women are still a long way off from achieving a balanced presence in boardrooms or even as executives, although female participation in management is associated with better business performance (there is still some controversy regarding this last point).
- The similarity in terms of the profile of directors may produce positive results such as an affinity of interests and group cohesion. But there may also be negative results such as the absence of any opposition in the decision-making process.
- In the opinion of the 102 Brazilian board members interviewed by **Guerra and Santos**, technical skills are not enough, and there is also a need to have quality interactions. However, these dynamics are susceptible to harmful individual behaviors, such as the inability to listen, micromanagement, excessive vanity, lack of preparation for board meetings, and even bullying.
- Interviews with Brazilian and international directors and executives who share their experiences regarding how to reduce harmful behavior in boardrooms. Some of them are kept anonymous due to the fact that they reveal situations of dysfunctionalities experienced in BoDs.
- The caselet in this chapter explores the feeling of isolation of a board director and the quest for understanding the actual reasons for it is,

leading to interesting insights on the importance of the dynamics on a boardroom.

The initial sense of alienation was total. I felt absolutely isolated on that BoD, which, apart from myself, included seven other directors. After obtaining a degree in production engineering, I began a very successful career, firstly as a technician and then later as an executive, until I became the Chief Executive Officer (CEO) at an automated machinery company. While I was acting as CEO, I was invited to take up my first position as a board member. For the previous 27 years, I had been immersed in highly competitive corporate environments, both internal as well as external. Therefore, I assumed that my career and my last six years as CEO had provided me with the credentials for the position: I already knew everything I needed about business management; including regarding human relations in all their organizational aspects. Over the course of my career, I had learned to handle feedback that my approach, as would be expected of any good engineer, tended to be extremely logical and did not always take into account the human factors involved in companies and businesses. Therefore, I was sure that my marked sense of isolation was not due to any limitations that I might have on the human relations front: I had undergone lengthy coaching processes, leadership courses and training to develop relationship skills.

However, shortly after my first board meetings, I felt as if I had been parachuted into an unknown city, being the only person in the world who did not speak that country's language. Feeling confused, I could only attribute that unease to the fact that I did not have specific, in-depth knowledge of finance. At least, not of the level required by that complex and sophisticated business: I had become a board member at a privately owned and shared-control bank, La Rochelle, and the controlling group was made up of three different shareholders. Each of these "factions" had very different expectations as to the direction of the business – as did the directors elected by them. Everyone seemed to have other commitments; and everybody played their cards close to their chest. It was only possible to find out each person's position at the time of the vote. It was like being at a poker table rather than on the board of a major financial institution.

Even having identified this situation, I felt that the lack of integration was largely due to the fact that my financial knowledge was not on a par with that of my peers. Since this was my fault, I made an effort to make up for it. The attitude of the other board members suggested that none of them seemed to be inclined to help me in my *learning endeavor. And even if someone were to be interested, I suspected that it was most likely that he or she intended to "bias" my votes in his or her favor. So, feeling even more isolated, I dived headfirst into the intricacies of the banking sector, digging into the literature about finance in-depth. Whenever I could, I checked my conclusions with the Chief Financial Officer(CFO), since no one had a better understanding than he did of the models applied to the bank's operations. In an intense and exhausting process, "I learned their language," but our dialogue did not improve. The fact is that I was only able to fully experience and understand the real reasons for this a few years later.**

The feeling of isolation of those professionals who make it to the top of the corporate ladder is a normal topic in coaching sessions: the CEO's loneliness, for example, is already well-known. Although they are the leaders of a team that they have put together and which operates under their unmistakable leadership, CEOs still feel alone in the face of most of the challenges that they face on a daily basis. But what can be said about a member of the board of directors (BoD)? In particular, those who take up a position on a BoD for the very first time tend to suffer from this strange syndrome: feeling lonely while being part of a group, which represents the highest level of power in the organization. Board members may be very well accompanied, but they still feel alone.

When the CEOs feel isolated, there is the possibility – not always real – for them to take that specific issue to discuss with the BoD. However, at a board meeting in which a more complex or sensitive topic is being discussed, who could the board member open up to? Perhaps a better question to ask first would be: when dealing with strategic and often confidential issues, can they really open up to anybody? And if they were to do so, what would be the reaction of the other board members? Often, members of the BoD are appointed by different groups of shareholders – who may or may not be in alignment. This was what happened, for example, at the start of this chapter, in the case reported by the bank's board member. Each person having their own agenda, all of them sitting around the same table and no one being sure just how much they could trust the other people in the group. Another factor that increases the loneliness is the difficulty that some directors (candidly) have in relation to admitting their lack of knowledge or their doubts about a subject. In this case, there is the shame of being viewed by their peers as being ill-equipped to join the BoD and sometimes, also the warranted fear of becoming the subject of ridicule.

---

* The story's conclusion will be presented at the end of this chapter.

The BoD's performance is a result of a combination of various factors such as its structure and composition. But in addition, one also needs to take into account the quality of human interactions at different levels – starting off between the board members themselves and then between the board members and the company's executives. However, before we can analyze these various dynamics, both those within the group of directors as well as outside it, we need to know a little more about the individuals who make up the board: who is the board member as an individual?

The Typical Board Member: A Man and a Former Executive

A white man, aged mid-50s to mid-60s. This is still the predominant profile of board members around the world, despite the winds that are beginning to blow through board rooms. A comparative study carried out on an annual basis by Spencer Stuart among boards in 17 countries,[1] indicates that, in 2019, men continue to dominate board rooms, with a presence equal to or greater than 70% in ten countries, including Canada (70%), the United States (74%), Spain (79%), Brazil (89%) and Russia (92%). With the highest average age, U.S. directors were in the first place with an age of 63 followed by Canada (62) and the Netherlands (61). The countries with the youngest board members were Russia (55), Norway (56) and Italy (57), the same average age bracket as seen in Brazil where 54% of directors were between 50 and 69 years old.[2] In describing the typical profile of a candidate for the board, Forbes lists a set of technical skills and highlights the need for experience as a successful CEO:

> "Companies are highly selective in choosing board members and competition for those spots is fierce. You don't have to be a Fortune 500 CEO[*] to be a candidate (although it helps!), but since for-profit companies have an obligation to deliver a financial return to their shareholders, they need board members with proven expertise starting, running and growing successful businesses."[3]

Naturally, experience as the chief executive is very relevant, but it is important to keep in perspective that this experience may only be necessary on the part of some of the directors. This is because others may have experience in other executive functions or even of a different type, which makes up the set of experience required for a group making joint

---

[*] The Fortune 500 ranking is made up of the 500 companies with the highest annual turnover in the United States.

decisions. Diversity – including in relation to professional background – is the name of the game.

It is also interesting to note that the United States and Canada, where directors have the highest average age, are also ranked first and second in the lengths of their mandates: American directors stay in office for an average of eight years, while Canadians remain in their positions for 7.3 years. Longer terms of office and a higher average age can be indicators of low renewal, which could make it more difficult to increase the diversity in the make-up of BoDs.

The presence of independent directors has gradually increased over the last few decades. However, in the wake of the international financial crisis, it became clear that independence should always go hand-in-hand with the necessary experience and skills required in the company's business. The presence of independent board members can be very high, such as in the case of Switzerland and the Netherlands, which top the survey with figures of 87% and 85%, respectively, while Brazil (39%), Russia (37%) and Turkey (33%) are at the opposite end (see Graph 2.1).

Independent directors: significant global variation

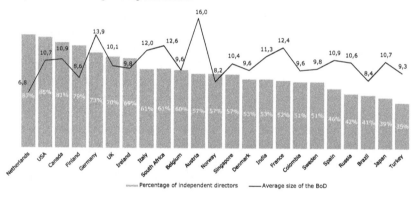

Graph 2.1 Board size and percentage of independent directors.
Source: Spencer Stuart (2020) – sample 23 countries.

Also according to **Spencer Stuart's**[4] international comparative chart, in 2020, the presence of foreigners on BoDs varied from 50.3% (in Denmark) to 4% (in Japan), with the most frequent bracket being between 25% and 40%.

Ethnic Diversity Still a Long Way Off from the Board Rooms

In relation to ethnic and cultural minorities, the Delivering through Diversity report,[5] published in 2018 by McKinsey based on data from

1,007 companies in 12 countries, shows a considerable variation in representation according to the geographic region and the level of leadership surveyed. In the United Kingdom, for example, ethnic minorities represent 13% of the population. Fifty-nine percent of the country's BoDs do not even have a single representative from these segments. In South Africa, where 79% of the country's population is black, most of the domestic and international companies that operate there (69% of the sample) are headed up by white professionals – a reality that results from the impact of the country's complex social history.

Another alarming indicator regarding the low diversity on boards was pointed out by the census of representativeness of minorities, which was carried out in 2018, using the Fortune 500 ranking as the sample. According to this survey, of the 1,033 new seats that were established on the boards of these companies, 80.7% were taken by Caucasians, 59.6% of whom were Caucasian men.[6] The unfortunate episode that led to the death of George Floyd, a 46-year-old black man in the city of Minneapolis, in the State of Minnesota, in 2020, not only angered communities all over the world but exposed top U.S. corporations to criticism for lack of diversity even when they supported the Black Lives Matter movement that gained momentum and public support in its aftermath. Floyd was killed by a white policeman who continued to kneel on Floyd's neck even when he repeatedly pleaded that he could not breathe. It was ironic that the same recognized brands that publicly took a stance on social media and campaigned in relation to the episode in support of social justice themselves had few or no minorities in senior management or on their boards. A number of critics said that a company does not inspire by its posts on social media, but rather by the black faces in its boardrooms, in yet another demonstration that stakeholders are paying attention and demanding consistency from companies. And stakeholders are putting more and more pressure on them so that their statements are aligned with their actions and practices.

In Brazil, a country in which 55.8% declare themselves to be black and brown and roughly 43% consider themselves to be white,[7] the presence of blacks on BoDs is virtually and strikingly non-existent. According to the experienced headhunter, **Fernando Carneiro**[*] "the problem is very serious and will take a relatively long time to be corrected".

---

[*] Fernando Carneiro leads CEO practices in Latin America and Brazil and was a member of Spencer Stuart Global Board. As a recognized expert in corporate governance, he conducted several board searches and board assessment projects for Brazilian and multinational companies. The author interviewed Fernando Carneiro in São Paulo, Brazil, on March 15, 2016.

Women Still in the Minority at the Center of Decision-Making

Over the past few decades, companies around the world have registered a growth in the number of women in their workforce, but when we take a look at the top management levels of organizations, the higher the position, the lower the percentage of women. On a global level, the gender diversity of BoDs is moving forward only slowly and in small steps. In May 2020, the Peterson Institute published data collected between 1997 and 2017 in 58 countries from 62,000 listed companies, which account for 92% of global GDP.[8] No one was surprised by one of the conclusions of this study: if the average annual growth rate remains at 5.2%, gender parity on BoDs will only be achieved in 2045. In Spencer Stuart's analysis of gender diversity in 17 countries, in 2019, female participation on boards varied from 8% to 47%, with the highest percentages in France (47%) and Norway (43%).

In the same study, at the opposite extreme, are Russia, Brazil and Colombia, which have a mere 8%, 11% and 12%, respectively, of women board members. In Brazil, the female presence on BoDs is so lopsided, that it was only in the two-year period from 2019 to 2020 that gender diversity was taken into account for the first time in the data survey for the Corporate Governance Yearbook of Publicly-Held Companies, which analyzes the 150 Brazilian companies whose shares have the highest level of trading on the B3.[9] Out of the total 1,151 board seats analyzed in the sample, only 110 were held by women directors, which translates into a figure of less than one woman per BoD (0.73).

The low gender diversity and the slow progress of this trend on boards are also confirmed in a broader study by **Deloitte**[10] covering 60 countries with data from 2018. Of the 8,648 companies analyzed, the average percentage of seats held by women was one of 16.8%, a mere 1.9% higher than the result obtained two years earlier. Inevitably, this huge discrepancy between the percentage of men and women on BoDs feeds the long-standing and controversial debate regarding the application of gender quotas. After Norway adopted the quota system for state-owned companies in 2003, and later on also for the country's publicly traded companies, the movement toward quotas for women directors picked up momentum and spread across Europe, Asia, Africa and the Middle East. Since then, experts have presented ideas for and against quotas to international public opinion. Among the main arguments against legal mandates is the fact that in emerging markets there are still more men than women with the professional experience required to assume a seat on BoDs. This observation could give rise to negative side effects, such as the concentration of the same women as board members of a number of companies, overboarding them and jeopardizing their performance.

Another side effect raised is the possible devaluation of the female professionals appointed under the quota system, in terms of the actual inclusion in the decision-making process and even in their remuneration, in relation to their male colleagues.[11]

In addition, particularly in countries where there is a concentration of family-controlled companies, female participation on boards should be viewed with caution. And the explanation for this is simple: often, the appointment of women as board members is a family entitlement rather than an achievement. Especially in family businesses, it is not uncommon for the controlling shareholders to give seats on the board to their wives, sisters and daughters, who formally become directors, but who do not always show up at meetings. Preferring not to be identified, in an interview, one independent woman director told of her experience with the family's women on the BoD and was hardly able to suppress a certain tone of indignation:

> I was an independent director for three years at a family-controlled company, and there were two other women with seats on the board, who were the chairman of the BoD's wife and sister. At the only meeting where I saw one of them in the room, we all knew that she was only there to guarantee the voting quorum, due to the fact that other board members were absent. She came in, she voted in line with the president and left. I never ever saw her again.

Among the arguments in favor of gender quotas on BoDs, however, is the fact that legal mandates are indeed increasing – albeit slowly – the presence of women on organizations' boards. In 2019, in **Spencer Stuart**'s comparative study of 17 countries, the percentage of female participation on BoD had risen in France (47%), Sweden (39%), Italy (35%) and the Netherlands (22%), among other countries. According to the survey published in 2020 by **Catalyst**,[12] an American NGO focused on speeding up the inclusion of women in the labor market, despite the fact that they remain underrepresented, 20% of the directors in the 2,765 companies in the sample collected in 47 countries were women – and this percentage represented a slight growth by comparison with the previous year.

This same report concludes that "companies with a woman board chair were more likely to have a larger share of women board members, compared to companies with men board chairs." Analyzing this positive effect in relation to the legal requirement for gender quotas, the researchers found encouraging data: 71.8% of the companies based in countries with established quotas had at least 30% female board members, while in those countries without this legal requirement only 20.3% of the companies had achieved the same percentage of female directors and 23% still had no women on their boards. Also according to this research, to reach "critical mass" in their presence on BoD, women need to occupy at least three seats on each board. This new gender ratio would be able to substantially change the dynamics of board meetings, creating an environment in which there is room for innovative ideas to be expressed, which can lead to the company posting a better financial performance.

In addition to the benefits cited by these studies, the direct perception of players who interact on a daily basis with BoDs is also positive when it comes to the participation of women board members. Fernando Carneiro,* who was a member of Spencer Stuart Global Board, is regularly hired as a headhunter to search for potential directors in the market and is among these enthusiasts. He keeps a close eye on the perception of the other board members and those who hire women directors and makes the argument that the presence of women "improves the interpersonal dynamics among the directors in relation to treatment, objectivity and climate. In addition, it fosters an environment where there is more room for questioning and learning." According to him, women are able to simply say "I don't know," when faced with a question that initially seems more complex. According to **Carneiro**, women directors also encourage a more consistent and persistent focus on issues related to sustainability, human capital, compliance and risk, fostering and perpetuating the commitment to "do the right thing."

As a result of this positive perception regarding the participation of women directors in the business' strategic management, institutional investors are beginning to vote against BoD that are made up exclusively of men. Perhaps this is one of the reasons for the female presence in markets where investors have been more vocal, such as in the United States, for example, where the percentage of women directors on boards jumped from 20.3% in 2016 to 26.1% in 2019, as can be seen in Table 2.1 which shows the evolution of gender diversity in some of the main countries included in **Catalyst**'s survey.

Although the pace of the increase in gender and ethnic diversity has been much lower than desired, a boost may come from the result of a 2019 survey by **PWC**[13] of more than 700 directors in the United States. The research reports a record having been broken: 59% of new independent directors appointed during the period were women or what they categorize as minority men (African American/Black, Asian and Hispanic/Latino). In the previous year, the increase registered was one of just half this amount. The study indicates that the greatest obstacle to changing the picture regarding the make-up of BoD is the low rate of renewal in boards.

---

*   The author interviewed Fernando Carneiro in São Paulo, Brazil, on March 15, 2016.

Table 2.1 Evolution of women's presence on boards of directors. Women's global representation on boards, 2019

Countries	% Women directorships, 2019	% Women directorships, 2016	% With three or more WOB, 2019	% With 1–2 WOB, 2019	% With zero WOB, 2019	Quota and year introduced
Australia	31.2	26.0	58.2	40.3	1.5	No
Canada	29.1	22.8	63.0	35.9	1.1	Pending
France	44.3	37.6	98.6	1.4	0.0	Yes, 2010
Germany	33.3	19.5	81.0	17.2	1.7	Yes, 2015
India	15.9	12.8	21.3	78.8	0.0	Yes, 2013
Japan	8.4	4.8	3.4	63.2	33.4	No
Netherlands	34.0	18.9	65.2	34.8	0.0	Yes, 2013
Sweden	39.6	35.6	96.6	3.4	0.0	Yes, 2016
Switzerland	24.9	17.5	48.8	51.2	0.0	Pending
United Kingdom	31.7	25.3	82.2	17.8	0.0	No
United States	26.1	20.3	56.2	42.8	1.0	CA only, 2018

Source: Catalyst – Women on Corporate Boards: Quick Take, March 2020.

Greater Diversity, Better Performance

Just as disruptive innovations[*] have totally transformed the structure and business models inherited from the 20th century, diversity in the make-up of BoDs – and not just in terms of gender – has become one of the decisive factors that organizations need to revolutionize their decision-making processes. The goal is just one: to add value to the business and at the same time to take into account the interests of an ever more complex and constantly changing society. Ethnic/cultural diversity among the leadership of companies, for example, is already correlated with profitability, according to the study of this question that was carried out by **McKinsey** in 2015 and repeated in 2018.[14] One of the conclusions presented in the most recent report is that "companies with the most ethnically/culturally diverse executive teams – not only in terms of absolute representation but also of the variety or mix of ethnicities – are 33% more likely to outperform their peers on profitability." The document also states that this correlation also occurs in relation to BoDs and concludes that companies with boards with greater ethnic/cultural diversity are up to 43% more likely to present higher profits, as shown in Graph 2.2.

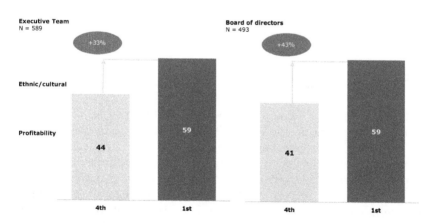

The value of ethnic/cultural diversity on boards and executive teams
Percent

Graph 2.2 Diversity and its correlation with higher profitability for corporations.
Source: McKinsey. Delivering through diversity, January 2018 – sample 12 countries.

---

[*]   Technological and other disruptive factors, such as the COVID 19 pandemic, will be covered in Chapters 3 and 5.

However, diversity does not only produce a greater financial return for companies. With the aim of listing some of the intangible benefits resulting from diversity, **Catalyst** put together a compilation of international studies, under the title *Why Diversity and Inclusion Matter: Quick Take*, which was first published in 2013 and later updated in 2018.[15] The improvements in performance generated by diversity in the make-up of the senior management teams and the board include, among others:

- The companies with the most diverse management teams on average obtain 38% more revenue for their innovative products and services over the course of three years.
- Diversity in terms of gender, country of origin, career trajectory and professional experience are highly linked to innovation among managers.
- The best-placed companies in the ranking of Fortune's most admired companies have twice the percentage of women in senior management as those that are lower down the list.
- BoDs with greater gender diversity are more effective in risk management practices regarding investments in research and development.
- When boards have women directors, more attention is given to the duties of the term of office, such as monitoring and supervising the business' strategy.
- Companies with boards exhibiting greater gender diversity are less likely to engage in controversial corporate practices, such as fraud, corruption, bribery and disputes between shareholders.

Conflicts: Executive Board Member and Autocratic CEO

The classic director – coming from a successful career as an executive and having held the position of CEO – is used to sitting in the front seat, holding the steering wheel firmly and, after making joint decisions with the BoD, driving the car to its destination. In general, they are professionals who are used to flying solo, with the motto "may the best man win". Given their age group, they were most definitely not forged in the team-building culture throughout their careers. Of course, there are cases of specialist professionals, such as lawyers or academics, but they are the exception to the general rule.

This predominance of former executives in the make-up of boards gives the group a unique profile – and can even disrupt the relationship between the BoD and the CEO. And this is because, in addition to it being necessary to find room for a lot of stars around a single table, one can frequently see board members who are focused on operational details: until recently they were in charge of running every detail of the business ventures and handling challenging situations. So, why would they have to abide by that maxim of good governance for board members: "nose in and fingers out"? Now, they are board members who are sitting in the back seat of the car, from where they take part in the decisions – take part, but do not decide by themselves – and have to leave the steering wheel in the hands of the executives led by the CEO. Anyone who is used to being in the driver's seat and sometimes finds himself/herself sitting in the back seat knows that in order to avoid accidents, the recommendation is not to try to show the driver how he/she could drive better. The alternative is to learn to trust and delegate, with proper control mechanisms. And if that doesn't work, there is still the option of changing the driver (more on that in Chapter 3).

However, to operate as a board member previous executive experience is not always a negative factor, but it can offer advantages. In the opinion of an experienced board member, his or her best peers at the board table are often former CEOs:

> In my opinion, having had experience on a number of boards, the best directors are those who have been CEOs. I don't know whether it's a coincidence or because I was also a CEO, but I totally understand how they react to certain issues. Whoever was or is a CEO has a great ability to analyze situations quickly – what are the risks involved and what are the possible alternatives to make the best decision. On the other hand, the CEO is a complex person: he wants to roll up his sleeves, he is the guy who wants to get things done, he did it and, of course, he has a huge ego because he has had a number of successes in his career.

This habit of rolling up sleeves is pointed out as a challenge by the board member of a number of companies and Embraer's board chair, Alexandre Gonçalves Silva,* who acts as a mentor to executives who are newcomers to the board:

> One situation that causes stress at meetings is when you have directors who were executives until recently and who have not yet grasped their new role. They go to board meetings wanting to meddle in management, give orders and enforce their opinion at any cost.

---

* Alexandre Gonçalves Silva is an independent board member and chairman of Embraer's board of directors; he was CEO of General Electric do Brasil between 2001 and 2007 and, since then, has taken part on boards of directors at companies in various of the country's economic sectors. The author interviewed Alexandre Gonçalves Silva in São Paulo, Brazil, on February 19, 2016.

This ability to coexist with his peers is not natural for this executive. He is used to dealing with subordinates or bosses. In general, when you have peers, they are the company's internal competitors, competing for some promotion. On the BoD, everyone is equal and the chairman's vote is also the same. You have to learn to convince others of your ideas using persuasion, using intelligence. You have to be open to changing your opinion and adopting someone else's. All of this is a learning process. However, some people take longer and are still at an executive's pace – which sometimes causes stress at board meetings.

On the other hand, however, some relationship difficulties can be caused by the CEO's own profile. It is not that uncommon to find those who adopt an autocratic and dominant behavior throughout the entire process, from the decision-making stage to implementation, as reported by one interviewee who is very qualified for this view because he has performed both roles. **Sérgio Lires Rial,**[*] who is currently Banco Santander's CEO in Brazil and a member of Delta Airlines' BoD, was the bank's chair when he gave this interview. Rial has substantial experience on other boards both in Brazil as well as abroad:

> Sometimes the BoD has to deal with a domineering CEO, a professional with strong convictions or, as some experts describe it, with a personality bordering on paranoia. Given this CEO profile, board members may feel intimidated. In this case, when the CEO presents a proposition and starts to defend it with his overbearing vehemence, it is necessary to have the courage, within a respectful context, to ask questions. This CEO feels challenged, because he believes that he has already done all the possible and conceivable analysis and thinks he is right – always. What can the board member do to avoid simply being steered to the conclusions desired by the overbearing CEO? The board member does not believe that the proposition put forward is the best one, but it is very hard to stand up to the CEO – because some organizational cultures worship the CEO as if he were a god. The result is an excess of assertiveness and arrogance: the CEO thinks he is the only one who has the necessary knowledge in relation to his propositions, because he is the only one in the board room who is part of the business operation. This is not very smart on the part of the CEO and the board should not fall

[*]   Sérgio Lires Rial, who is currently Banco Santander's CEO in Brazil and a member of Delta Airlines' BoD, was the bank's chairman when he gave this interview. He has substantial experience on other boards both in Brazil as well as abroad. The author interviewed Sérgio Lires Rial in São Paulo, Brazil, on September 11, 2015.

into this trap. But, since in Latin America, the general culture is one of consensus, the board avoids speaking openly and tackling this conflict of closed minds between the board and the autocratic CEO. But, if this situation is not properly discussed, thought through and resolved, it can set the scene for many other problems.

Apparently, this situation results in meetings where the atmosphere is tense, negative and formal, but actually, this is one of the signs that the BoD has a dysfunctional performance. In other words, mutual distrust takes root and the BoD becomes unable to continue to make decisions in the company's best interests. The most classic of corporate governance theories – agency theory – makes the specific argument that executives may make decisions that are more motivated by their own personal interests than those of the company. Forty years ago, **Jensen and Meckling** introduced the concept of managerial behavior to define agency relationships: managers should act as shareholders' agents, being paid to act in the company owners' best interests.[*] Otherwise, they will be expropriating the shareholders' wealth. It is the directors' duty to prevent this from happening.

> "The movement to improve corporate governance evolved in this environment of mistrust among executives, board members, shareholders and investors in the wake of the business and financial scandals that took place at the end of the 20th century and at the start of the 21st century. Stories such as Enron, WorldCom and Tyco were the result of flawed processes based on information asymmetry, difference of interests and misguided intentions, with extra doses of greed and a lack of basic principles of ethical conduct."[16]

There have been a number of cases in which the boards have alleged that they were unaware of the executives' initiatives or even how they used the variable compensation model to fill their pockets, further inflating falsely achieved results. Conclusion: nose in is mandatory!

Way Beyond Technical Skills

It is a big mistake to think that the skills gained from one's experience as an executive will be sufficient to deal with the dilemmas and intricate puzzle of human relationships that is experienced in board rooms.

---

[*] For some time now, the concept contained in agency theory has been questioned by certain groups, who recommend that the directors should serve the interests of the company, rather than just of the shareholders, taking into account the point of view of all its stakeholders.

No matter how broad executives' store of experience seems, in their new role as board members, they will face a lengthy process of learning and continuous improvement, which requires determination and discipline. In the same way as when they were executives, each year they have to look for a personal development program – both in terms of form and content. They need to learn how to create value based on a collective decision-making body as well as to learn even more about those issues that are significant for the boards on which they serve. Content is often more valued by board members, who usually underestimate the form: for most board members, the form just requires the assimilation of a set of rules and processes. However, in order to "drive while sitting in the back seat," it is more important to develop behavioral skills than to gain technical knowledge about the car's engine.

However, valuing behavioral skills does not mean underestimating techniques. **César Souza,**[*] who is a board member, the CEO of Empreenda and who was singled out by the World Economic Forum as one of the 200 Global Leaders for Tomorrow in 1992, thinks that ideally, the minimum make-up of a board should include a variety of technical skills, such as an entrepreneurial profile, a strategist, a finance professional, a human capital specialist, a good legal expert as well as a good communication professional to help the company position itself externally. However, in his interview, he ended up emphasizing that the competencies which are most lacking in boards are really the behavioral ones:

> The thing that is most lacking in boards are more balanced positions between excess assertiveness and the ability to be more flexible. Also in short supply is the skill to negotiate and deal with conflicts. During meetings, before one gets to a stalemate, it is common for the chairman of the board to say: "Ok, let's stop the meeting here, take a break and we'll be back soon: let's cool off." Then, two directors go to one side, three to the other and the rest close themselves off in another room for a few minutes. Matters are not dealt with openly, because conflict is feared. The capacity to anticipate different positions and have the ability to negotiate, see the points of convergence in positions, that sometimes appear to be antagonistic. In addition to being able to negotiate and resolve questions, there is a lack of committed and at the same time flexible positions. At board meetings, I still see creativity and innovation being restricted. There are creative and innovative people among the board members, but they

---

[*]   César Souza – CEO of Empreenda and singled out in 1992 by the World Economic Forum as one of the 200 Global Leaders for Tomorrow, as well as a board member of companies. The author interviewed César Souza in São Paulo, Brazil, on July 22, 2015.

feel self-conscious. When an idea comes up that is a little bit more "out of the box" as it were, there is always someone who says: "Ah, that wouldn't work here" or "it worked for that company because it was in a different sector". And creative people end up losing any interest in bringing up new ideas. Board meetings, which should have a less negative atmosphere, are a bit too formal. But discipline does not mean lack of creativity. Most boards also lack a person who is really competent on the human resources front: a professional who can better understand the behavior of leaders in order to better evaluate them.

Another board member working mostly in family business companies, in turn, states that although the behavioral aspects are essential to the quality of the BoD's dynamics, this set of competences is still undervalued by board members:

> The behavioral approach to corporate governance is still very new. So, in this respect, I do not see many board members who are prepared. You always hear it being said: 100% of board members are hired on account of their CV, due to their technical skills, but 100% of them end up leaving the board on account of the behavioral part. This is what happens: most directors are very well prepared and they also have a lot of experience, but when they sit at the boardroom table, they are not ready in behavioral terms to be there. The gathering of that group of professionals, each with their own success story, the environment, the circumstances of the discussion, the decision process ... I still don't know how to do this, but each board meeting should be structured in such a way as to make sure that all of those present always take the behavioral dimension into account as well.

But, it is not solely the clearly communicated behaviors that work for or against the quality of the dynamics on BoDs. **Thomas Brull**[*] highlights the importance of the emotions that underlie any and all decisions taken by the BoD. In his chapter in the book *Dynamics at Boardroom Level*,[17] he describes his experience as an independent director in a group of companies controlled by two rival families. The conflict was already well-established at board meetings. The family factions[**] only joined

---

[*] Thomas Brull is an independent director at SiemensGamesa Renewable Energies-Brazil and gives courses at the Brazilian Institute of Corporate Governance (Instituto Brasileiro de Governança Corporativa, IBGC) and at the Fundação Dom Cabral (FDC).

[**] Chapter 6 will provide information on the formation of dysfunctional coalitions on boards, regarded as a pathology.

forces when it came to antagonizing the CEO, who, for his part, also had recurring complaints against the board. Despite this intricate network of conflicts, an international fund made an injection of capital into the group, but instituted changes in the governance structure, including the addition of three new members to the BoD. Brull recounts below how he felt and how he began to take a proactive role, acting as a facilitator in resolving these conflicts:

> "In the beginning of the new governance structure, when the three outsiders came in, I felt insecure and less valued, maybe because of a sense of failure, since there was a need to bring new people in. As I understood better what was happening, I tried a more active role by meeting the new members and attempting to be in contact with each other outside the boardroom. As I felt more confident, I also (...) begin a more personal contact with the CEO and now we meet for breakfast once a month. While this gives me new insights and understanding of board dynamic, it enables the CEO to test his feelings and ideas. I have to take care to not disclose inside information of the board and also not to be co-opted by him. (...) I am happy and hope to be part of the solution."[18]

Harmful Behaviors: Excess Vanity

Even though it is not yet something that receives a lot of attention from board members, corporate governance theory and practice have already managed to identify and typify some very frequent harmful behaviors in board rooms. These behaviors may not be the main factor deflecting the decision-making process from the best interest of organizations – but there is no doubt that they play a significant role in this sense. One board member recounts that he recently had the following experience:

> It is not unusual for a group of board members to be against or in favor of a decision merely and simply because there is another group within the board that is regarded as an adversary. So, if one group is against something, the other group is automatically in favor of it. It's like a fight between cliques.* It is very bad. It is vanity speaking louder: it is where one group does not want to "lose" to the other one and the company is the biggest loser. I now remember a situation I experienced: the board decided to make an acquisition. At the meeting, we discussed what our CEO's negotiation strategy would be.

---

*   Chapter 6 will provide information on the formation of dysfunctional coalitions on boards, regarded as a pathology.

Two of the directors wanted to set an upper limit on the amount of the transaction. But the majority voted that the CEO could have a negotiation margin of up to 15% up or down. Well, what happened was that the CEO closed the deal – it was a very important acquisition because we would take over a new market. If we didn't enter, we were afraid that our competitor would make the acquisition – and that would really hamper us a lot. But the CEO, in the middle of the negotiation, instead of going up to the 15% limit, increased the amount by 20%. This had not been approved by the board, but at the meeting he said: "Look, I could either increase the amount by 20% or I would lose the deal..." At the time, those board members, who had already been against the 15% negotiation margin, thought it was absurd that the CEO had exceeded that percentage. They wanted to fire him immediately, claiming that he had closed the deal without consulting the board. But, actually, we realized that they were really feeling offended and that their egos had been hurt. In the CEO's place, perhaps I would have done the same thing: I was not going to lose that deal – because the extra 5% was a negligible amount in view of the entire transaction and the importance of that acquisition. Even though he was not fired, from then on, the CEO was not given any leeway at board meetings, despite the fact that in my opinion, he'd done a great job.

Harmful Behavior: Bullying

Attaching too much value to ego is not the only harmful behavior that runs riot through board rooms. Particularly at meetings where issues will be discussed that are important to the group with more power, board members who have an opinion that is contrary to that of the majority can often be subjected to a number of types of pressure – from jokes and nicknames to intellectual humiliation. This was the case, for example, with the story recounted in Chapter 1. In the hypothetical SanMartín, when the only independent board member was more inquisitive than the others, the board chair intervened: "Relax, you are new to this sector. Just you wait and see the leap that the shares will take at the end of the quarter when the Blue Bird Project is announced." In order to clearly define and identify this specific type of harmful behavior, **César Souza**[*] brought the concept of bullying to board rooms:

There is a system of peer pressure that I have observed since before I was a board member and attended board meetings as a consultant.

[*]   The author interviewed César Souza in São Paulo, Brazil, on July 22, 2015.

It is a type of bullying designed to undermine those who think differently to the group. Sometimes a project gets underway and everyone wants to see the herd effect. Either it is the chairman of the board or it is the majority shareholder or it is the executive who is in charge of the deal: the fact is that he wants the project to be approved – and preferably as soon as possible. Then, someone raises a discordant voice. It is always uncomfortable to ask questions, you are in front of seven or eight experienced and successful individuals. Everything is going fine, and then suddenly, a loner starts to "call attention to something". Maybe it is not the best decision ... and he asks for clarification and wants information. In general, the first reaction, is to try to disqualify that discordant voice. How is this done? It is done by saying something like: "You are not in the business, this item has specific characteristics that you are not noticing". But, if the board member asks what these specific characteristics are, somebody changes the subject. This insinuation is left hanging in the air – that you are not in the business or that you do not have the ability to perceive the nuances or the depth of that project or the business strategy – as if the strategy could possibly be so subtle as to only be perceived and understood by a select few. It is really a type of intellectual bullying to disqualify and embarrass the person, as part of a process, that can even be intimidating sometimes. I mean if the director does not have a well-structured personality, he ends up giving in, because he feels intimidated or because he does not want the inconvenience anymore. Thus, decisions are taken and then there will be a price to pay. I always suggest watching the movie '12 Angry Men'. It's very educational in relation to discordant voices.

With your experience on boards, how should the board member who is confronting this type of bullying react?

In the face of bullying situations, the board member should exercise very good judgment. He or she will need to strike a balance between being firm enough not to give up his or her convictions without becoming too rigid. Because it is not just about being against the majority – asking questions for the sake of it – he or she has to find the necessary flexibility to also continue learning, to understand what may not be noticed, to better understand a subject. However, this flexibility cannot be excessive either ... One cannot simply capitulate and follow the rest of the herd or become someone who goes along with what everyone is doing, like: "I vote in favor, because the pressure from the group is very strong". Since nobody wants to shoot themselves in the foot, it is essential to try and find this balance. You cannot give in to what is inconsistent: board members have to choose their battles. When it is a question of ethics, the practice of values, you cannot avoid these battles. It is a case of zero tolerance. But you cannot be rigid when it comes to matters that are sometimes not essential. To be able to take up a position between firmness and flexibility is a behavioral skill. This is one of the skills that a board member needs to have, and it is not something that you learn in school.

The so-called "bullying" behavior observed by **César Souza** was studied by **Guerra, Barros and Santos'** international research project which was still being concluded when this book was being printed. Three hundred and forty board directors from 40 countries were surveyed with the aim of investigating some of the main challenges faced by BoDs in their quest for effective decision-making. The research project was also designed to map the limitations that harm effective decision-making in groups in general and in BoDs in particular along with the mechanisms that may alleviate these limitations. As far as known, this study was the first attempt to investigate these issues taking a worldwide perspective based on the perceptions of those directly involved in the decision-making of boards. Among the findings of this research is precisely that there is not an insignificant likelihood of a new director being placed in an uncomfortable situation when presenting a totally new and different approach. Only 18% of the directors reported that disregarding ideas suggested by new board members is a non-existent situation in their boards. Graph 2.3 shows the results.

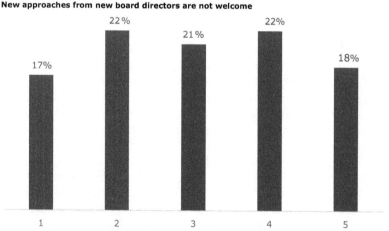

New approaches from new board directors are not welcome

Survey Question: When a new board member or one who has no expertise in the industry puts forward a totally new and different approach or direction to what the industry/company has been doing for years, what is the likelihood that he/she will hear an answer like "you do not know this industry/company. It does not work like that"?
(1) Very high (5) Nonexistent

Graph 2.3 Rejection to new and different approaches.
Source: Guerra, Barros and Santos (2020).[19]

Harmful Behavior: Attachment to One's Own Reputation

There are directors who seem to be more worried about their own reputation and social standing than about the company's results. Sometimes, this is just another example of vanity: one interviewee mentioned the case of a board member, who, on account of his prestige and credibility, was invited to join the board of a company located in a small country town. The board member was from a highly respectable family in the region and was a doctor who had been elected mayor several times. However, soon after he became a board member, the company's business fell apart. Instead of helping to make the necessary – even painful – decisions to try to save the company, the former mayor postponed court-backed debt restructuring as long as possible. He did not want "that failure to tarnish his reputation."

In most cases, however, the attachment to one's own reputation among directors does not manifest itself as clearly in typical episodes of vanity. It is more of a constant, subtle concern that lingers underneath the decisions that they make on the board. For example, they may feel tempted to vote in line with the chair, because they know that this relationship has the potential to deliver more interesting future benefits – or lasting harmful effects. It is not an act of corruption and it does not even represent a conflict of interest: it is simply a permanent willingness to be friendly in order to maintain good relations. This director's mistake may be to take networking too seriously, as **César Souza**[*] explains:

> Sometimes the board member values his relationship capital too much. It's not just proper networking, it goes way beyond that. He has a social relationship with the majority shareholder or is the CEO's friend or the relationship goes beyond the social one: he is a relative of the chairman or has some financial or emotional dependence – on the organization in which he is a board member. As a result, the director begins to attach too much importance to his own reputation; not in the sense of just doing what is right. He wants to make sure that he is well regarded by the people who interest him. He doesn't want them to speak ill of him. If he is very inquisitive, if he does not vote in line with the others, he is afraid that they will say behind his back: "That guy is a pain, that guy asks questions just for the sake of it". It is not easy: sometimes, someone labels a person and very soon the market is repeating that he is a pain. The board member who is overly concerned with his own reputation does not want to miss out, for example, on the chance to be on another board because other people say he is a pain. So, he weighs

[*]   The author interviewed César Souza in São Paulo, Brazil, on July 22, 2015.

things up: "What do I lose if I confront this situation? Am I going to be labeled a pain and will it damage my image?" Or: "Am I going to lose the friendship of this person who is here? Am I going to stop getting on with people well or being heard or being invited to other things?" Deep down, everyone is human and thinks about this a bit – but you can't go overboard on networking.

In a survey carried out by **Guerra and Santos**,[20] 102 Brazilian board members answered which factors are the ones that most cause their peers to deviate from decisions and initiatives that are in the best interests of the organizations (Graph 2.4). Out of the total number of respondents, 72% stated that the board members frequently or very frequently act this way in order "not to damage their social ties with the controlling share-holders," and 56% admitted that frequently or very frequently "their concern for their own reputation is greater than that for the company."

Most frequent factors that cause directors to deviate from the company's best interest

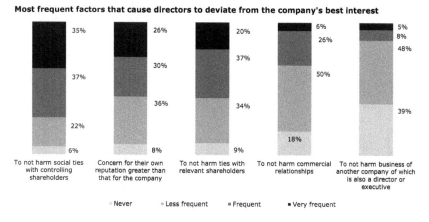

Graph 2.4 The reasons for deviating from the company's interests.
Source: Guerra and Santos (2017).

Harmful Behavior: Lack of Preparation, Not Listening Much or Talking a Lot

In the same survey, when asked about the behavior that causes the greatest disruption to the progress of board meetings and the quality of the decisions, 95% of the 102 respondents highlighted that their peers do not properly prepare themselves. According to this massive majority, this situation hampers or greatly hampers the board's performance. The fact is that they recognize that board members who are not prepared are not in a position to take assertive positions on any subject, because they do not have the full picture. For example, how to ask questions about a project under discussion if the information may be in the material that was previously sent to them – but the directors did not have time to read it? Unfortunately, this type of behavior is far more common than one would like to expect.

On the other hand, there are very qualified board members who prepare very thoroughly. However, in the case of some of these, there tends to be another type of detrimental behavior, they are not good listeners. Board members with this profile are so certain about all things that they do not even bother to listen carefully to their peers or the executives who are presenting a proposal at the board meeting. 86% of the 102 board members interviewed by the **Guerra and Santos'** survey said that the fact that their peers were unable to listen to either hampers or greatly hampers board meetings. Moreover, 76% stated that what hampers or greatly hampers board meetings are those board members who talk too much – which is, in fact, another way of not listening to anyone.[*] The results of **Guerra and Santos'** research regarding what most hampers the performance of boards are shown in Graph 2.5.

Behavior: what prevents the BoD from functioning properly

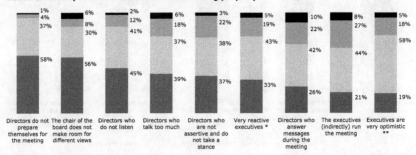

Graph 2.5 Behavioral elements that most hamper the proper functioning of the board.
Source: Guerra and Santos (2017).

The problem with directors who come to board meetings unprepared for making decisions seems to continue. More recent and broader research undertaken by **Guerra, Barros and Santos** indicates that only 22% of the survey respondents believe that directors are often well prepared for board meetings, as shown in Graph 2.6.

---

[*]   On this question in Guerra and Santos' survey, 69 directors selected the fact that the board's chairman is not open to contradictory opinions as being the factor that most hampers the meetings. However, the chairman's role is so relevant that the whole of Chapter 4 is devoted to it.

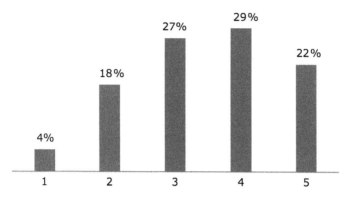

Preparation to board meetings still to be improved

Survey Question: Do you consider that the board members are well prepared/informed when they make decisions at board meetings?
(1) Rarely (5) Often

Graph 2.6 Level of preparation to make decisions.
Source: Guerra, Barros and Santos (2020).[21]

Harmful Behavior: Multitasking and/or Overly Busy Board Member

The typical board member is always super-busy. In general, he (and the majority of directors are still a 'he') serves on several BoDs, has numerous reports to read, training programs to keep up with, goes to the meetings of the committees of the boards on which he serves and still needs to find time to talk individually with the company's executives.[*] It is an almost superhuman volume of activities, but technology is there to help – or to annoy the board chairs, who are responsible for the proper functioning of the body. Prior to the meetings, nobody asks those taking part to turn off their cell phones, tablets and other electronic devices that are connected. It is assumed that everyone around that table knows how to behave, correct? Unfortunately, not all of them. Some directors keep a constant eye on their smartphones, answer emails, type in WhatsApp ... If someone stops talking, waiting for those present to give them their attention, that board member usually says simply – without looking at the person who is speaking: "I am following you. You can go on." One of the directors interviewed for this book recounted the scene she witnessed during a meeting in the middle of a discussion of a very prickly and, at the same time, sensitive issue from an ethical point of view. There was no longer any way to

---

[*]   Chapter 3 explores the concept of overboarded directors.

postpone a decision and, in the end, all of the directors would have to cast their votes on that matter:

> We were in the middle of a meeting, when a cell phone rang with a loud, high-pitched sound. As I have already said, the subject was a very delicate one and the atmosphere was very tense. We were all spooked by that sudden loud ring tone. But what was worse was that our fellow board member, a respectable former minister of the Republic, answered the phone and began talking in a loud voice. From the look in our eyes, he realized he was bothering us. He got up from the table and went over to the window. It didn't help at all. He realized that the conversation would not end soon, so he left the room and stayed outside in the hall for about 15 minutes. I know because we continued to hear him, even outside, with the door to the room closed. How is it possible that a professional of this level does not realize how inappropriate it is to take a call during a board meeting? And, on top of that, to talk with a loud voice, disturbing everyone else? That would already be detrimental enough for the meeting. But it happened at the very worst moment: during our colleague's absence, an even more delicate and essential fact for the issue under analysis was brought up by an executive present at the meeting. No one would ever mention that fact again, because the executive was visibly embarrassed that he had to reveal it. So none of us brought it up again. However, aware of this, everyone's vote could certainly change. The former minister and board member returned to the room, heard the end of the discussion and, finally, cast his vote quietly – totally unaware of that very relevant fact.

Certainly, those directors who adopt this type of detrimental behavior are not aware of the results of the surveys about the human capacity to multitask, in other words, to carry out several tasks simultaneously. In the experiment called the "Invisible Gorilla,"[*] created by **Simon and Chabris,** people watch the video of a basketball match and are required to say afterward how many passes the team in white made. Fully concentrating on the count, most people do not notice a person dressed as a gorilla who appears in the video. An ever-increasing number of studies prove that human beings have a limited level of attention: so, the more tasks that are being carried out by an individual which require attention, the less he or she will be able to perform them properly and correctly. It is

---

[*]   Other concepts are discussed in Chapter 6 based on this experiment developed by Daniel J. Simons and Christopher Chabris in 1999. Video available at: http://www.theinvisiblegorilla.com/videos.html-. Accessed on May 23, 2020.

precisely for this reason that the legislation that prohibits the use of cell phones for drivers who are at the wheel should include speakerphones:

"The problem is with consuming a limited cognitive resource, not with holding the phone. And most important, as the incredulous reactions of our study participants demonstrate, most of us are utterly unaware of this limit on our awareness. Experiment after experiment has shown no benefit whatsoever for hands-free phones over handheld ones. In fact, legislation banning the use of handheld phones might even have the ironic effect of making people more confident that they can safely use a hands-free phone while driving."[22]

Therefore, when that multi-tasking board member says: "I am following you. You can carry on..." science proves otherwise.

More Than a Simple Cluster of Individuals

Given the most typical profiles of white men aged between 55 and 65, with the majority having a background in engineering together with substantial experience in executive positions, it is expected – and befitting – that board members have a high opinion of themselves on account of their career track records. However, despite all their strengths and potential for improvement, when it comes to their performance as a group in boardrooms, they themselves are unsure. A survey that interviewed 182 directors reveals that "90 per cent of directors rate their individual performance as very effective but only 30 per cent rate overall board performance at an equivalent level, exposing a gap that needs to be addressed."[23]

The evolution of corporate governance itself shows that temporarily, some boards seem to be affected by a type of blindness. It is that, as human beings, board members are seized – without realizing it – by a combination of factors: the limits of rationality, the asymmetry of information, cultural and cognitive biases and detrimental behavior, in addition to the specific and very often contrasting interests of the different owners. All of this influences the group's dynamics and can interfere in the decision-making process, causing it to deviate from the company's best interests.

All of these negative factors seemed to be at work in the BoD of La Rochelle, which only managed to avoid missing out on an excellent business opportunity because, by chance, in this particular episode, the specific interests of the majority of the controlling shareholders ended up resulting in the best decision for the bank. However, in a dysfunctional BoD, chance does not always work in one's favor.

A few years after the 2007/2008 international financial crisis, there was still a need to understand all the impacts of the international financial crisis, particularly on banks. As with any other financial institution, at that time at La Rochelle there was special concern regarding the decrease in margins. It was against this backdrop that a proposal to acquire an insurance company with operations in the assets, liabilities and financial risks areas landed on the BoD's table. Although the sector is a highly regulated one and has specific characteristics that could deflect the attention of the bank's CEO – who was already under pressure for results – logic indicated that this was a good opportunity. However, the assessment of this purchase revealed that the attitude of the majority of directors was not focused on what was the best decision for the bank. Instead, each director defended the interests of the shareholder who had elected him.*

As one of the major shareholders was a financial investor, who managed an investment portfolio and was about to do an IPO, that acquisition interested him: it gave an additional glow to his portfolio and could boost investor interest in the initial offering of his shares. Another one already had a business in synergy with the insurance company and, for the first time, was openly and avowedly in favor of a decision. And, last but not least, the third major shareholder, who could be assumed to remain neutral, faced a very difficult situation: its business was going from bad to worse and it needed dividends to deal with a debt; therefore, it was against investing in the purchase of the insurance company. This time, it was the dissenting vote. The majority was in favor of the acquisition, which turned out to be an excellent opportunity for the bank.

A while after this acquisition I stopped being a board member at La Rochelle and, looking back, I can see two aspects that I wasn't able to identify at the time. First of all, obviously I did not get a seat on the bank's board due to my competence (or lack of it) in finance, but rather for my expertise in technology, cybernetics and international experience in different sectors. So that was not what excluded me. It was the unique dynamics of that group of board members. Secondly, if I could have stepped back, at that moment, I would not have accepted the invitation to become a director. At least not in a financial institution of that size, in that context and at that point in my career.

Nowadays, when I talk to executives with the potential to become board members, I say in all honesty: don't overestimate your skills and don't underestimate your limitations, even when you think you've overcome them. Throughout my career, I had improved my interpersonal skills. Okay, it was enough for executive life, but the

---

*   Results of research on coalitions will be presented in Chapter 6.

dynamics on a board of directors are much more complex. On a BoD, it is essential to act as a collective body and, in the group, the power relations and interests are often not all that obvious. Their gaps and expertise will be in interaction with the particular dynamics of that group, bringing out intertwined behavioral equations and unexpected effects. Not even the best CEO is ready to go from executive life onto a BoD without prior preparation, particularly if there is a significant gap in relation to the skills directly linked to the company's business. On the contrary, if you just take the CEO's store of experience, you are likely to have a real mess on your hands. Within a group responsible for decisions at this level of power, making things happen is an art.

Gathered around the BoD's table, the board members are much more than a mere cluster of individuals: they are a group whose performance has a marked impact on the business and the environment in which the company operates. However, there are dynamics within the BoD that can undermine the skills of the most competent and well-intentioned board members and cause dysfunctionalities. Therefore, after identifying the individual profile of directors in this chapter, the focus will then shift to an analysis of the dynamics of the BoD's group of members.

Management of the main tensions (which was already briefly touched on in Chapter 1) that stalk board rooms will be covered in the next chapter, with the emphasis on those tensions that result from two apparent paradoxes in the performance of the directors: the first is caused by the duty on the one hand to criticize and oversee the managers and, at the same time, to be charged with the task of giving them assistance and support, while the second results from the interaction between the board members themselves, as it is essential that there is room for contradictory opinions in the discussions, but also that cohesion should not be lost.

Notes

1 Spencer Stuart Research and Insight. *2019 boards around the world.* Available at https://www.spencerstuart.com/research-and-insight/boards-around-the-world?category=all-board-composition&topic=director-age. Accessed on June 3, 2020.

2 Spencer Stuart. *Brasil, 2019, board index.* Available at https://www.spencerstuart.com/research-and-insight/brasil-board-index. Accessed on June 3, 2020.

3 Forbes. *How to get on a board of directors*, published on September 11, 2017. Available at https://www.forbes.com/sites/nextavenue/2017/09/11/how-to-get-on-a-board-of-directors/#31bd99a51d56. Accessed on June 13, 2020.

4 Spencer Stuart. *Boards Around the World*. Available at: https://www. spencerstuart.com/research-and-insight/boards-around-the-world?category=all-board-composition&topic=independent-directors. Accessed on July 14, 2021.

5 McKinsey. *Delivering through diversity*, January 2018. Available at https://www.mckinsey.com/~/media/McKinsey/Business%20Functions/ Organization/Our%20Insights/Delivering%20through%20diversity/ Delivering-through-diversity_full-report.ashx. Accessed on June 12, 2020.

6 Harvard Law School Forum for Corporate Governance. *Missing pieces report: The 2018 board diversity census of women and minorities on fortune 500 boards*, published on February 5, 2019. Available at https://corpgov. law.harvard.edu/2019/02/05/missing-pieces-report-the-2018-board-diversity-census-of-women-and-minorities-on-fortune-500-boards/#:~:text=In%20the%202018%20census%2C%20representation,held%20 by%20women%20and%20minorities. Accessed on June 12, 2020.

7 Instituto Brasileiro de Geografia e Estatística (IBGE). Síntese de indicadores sociais. Uma análise das condições de vida da população brasileira, 2017. *Estudos & pesquisas. Informação demográfica e socioeconômica nº 35*. Available at https://biblioteca.ibge.gov.br/visualizacao/livros/liv101459.pdf. Accessed on June 6, 2020.

8 Noland, Marcus; Han, Soyoung. *Women scaling the corporate ladder: Progress steady but slow globally*. Peterson Institute for International Economics. May 2020. Available at https://www.piie.com/publications/policy-briefs/women-scaling-corporate-ladder-progress-steady-slow-globally. Accessed on June 7, 2020.

9 Capital Aberto. *Anuário de Governança Corporativa das Companhias Abertas 2019–2020* – As práticas adotadas pelas empresas com ações mais negociadas na B3. Capital Aberto, 11th ed. São Paulo: Editora Capital Aberto, 2020. Available at https://capitalaberto.com.br/edicoes/especial/ anuario-2019-2020/. Accessed on June 3, 2020.

10 Deloitte. *Data-driven change. Women in the boardroom. A global perspective*. 6th ed., 2019. Available at https://www2.deloitte.com/global/en/pages/ risk/articles/women-in-the-boardroom-global-perspective.html.   Accessed on June 14, 2020.

11 IBGC –*Fundamentos para Discussão Sobre Cotas para Mulheres nos Conselhos no Brasil*. 2013. Available at http://www.ibgc.org.br/download/ manifestacao/IBGC_Pesquisa_CotasMulheres.pdf. Accessed on June 13, 2020.

12 Catalyst. *Women on corporate boards: Quick take*, published on March 13, 2020. Available at https://www.catalyst.org/research/women-on-corporate-boards/. Accessed on June 13, 2020.

13 PwC. *2019 Annual corporate directors survey. The collegiality conundrum: Finding balance in the boardroom*. 2019. Available at https://www. pwc.com/us/en/services/governance-insights-center/assets/pwc-2019-annual-corporate-directors-survey-full-report-v2.pdf.pdf.   Accessed   on June 14, 2020.

14 McKinsey. *Delivering through diversity*, January 2018. Available at https://www.mckinsey.com/~/media/McKinsey/Business%20Functions/ Organization/Our%20Insights/Delivering%20through%20diversity/ Delivering-through-diversity_full-report.ashx. Accessed on June 12, 2020.

15 Catalyst. *Why diversity and inclusion matter: Quick take*, published on August 1, 2018. Available at https://www.catalyst.org/research/why-diversity-and-inclusion-matter/. Accessed on June 13, 2020.

16 Guerra, Sandra. Os Papéis do Conselho de Adminstração em Empresas Listadas no Brasil. Master's Thesis. Faculdade de Economia e Administração (FEA)/Universidade de São Paulo(USP), 2009. Available at http://www.teses.usp.br/teses/disponiveis/12/12139/tde-11092009-141955/. Acessed on April, 18, 2021.

17 Brull, Thomas. The Caspian Sea housing company: The role of board member in a two family business. 1st ed. In: Brisset, Leslie; Sher, Mannie; Smith, Tanzi (editors). *Dynamics at boardroom level*. London: Routledge, p. 171-176, 2020.

18 Brull, Thomas. The Caspian Sea Housing Company: the role of board member in a two family business. In: BRISSET, Leslie; SHER, Mannie; SMITH, Tanzi (editors). Dynamics at boardroom level. Routledge, 2020. p. 176.

19 Guerra, Sandra; Barros, Lucas A.; Santos, Rafael L. Decision-making in boards of directors: The roles of meeting dynamics and choice architecture. *Research Project*, 2020.

20 Guerra, Sandra; Santos, Rafael Liza. *Headaches, concerns and regrets: What does the experience of 102 Brazilian directors tell us? Private sector opinion*. Washington, DC: IFC, 2017. Available at https://www.ifc.org/wps/wcm/connect/topics_ext_content/ifc_external_corporate_site/ifc+cg/resources/private+sector+opinion/headaches%2C+concerns%2C+and+regrets+-+what+does+the+experience+of+102+brazilian+directors+tell+us. Accessed on May 21, 2020.

21 Guerra, Sandra; Barros, Lucas A.; Santos, Rafael L. Decision-making in boards of directors: The roles of meeting dynamics and choice architecture. *Research Project*, 2020.

22 Chabris, Christopher; Simons, Daniel. *The invisible gorilla: And other ways our intuitions deceive us*. Broadway Books, 2011. Video available at: http://www.theinvisiblegorilla.com/videos.html. Accessed on May 23, 2020.

23 Pick, Katharina; Merchant, Kenneth A. *Blind spots, biases and other pathologies in the boardroom*. New York: Business Expert Press, 2010.

Chapter 3

Relations under Tension

Chapter Summary

- At the two extremes, both the environment of everlasting fraternization between board members as well as that of open hostility distract the decision-making process from the best interest of the parties and may result in even more serious dysfunctionalities of the board of directors (BoD).
- Diversity in the choice of the profile of the directors is essential in order to help create a balanced environment and ensure that the BoD operates with quality.
- Among other reasons because this performance is already subject to a maze of tensions that occur simultaneously between the directors themselves (within the board) and the interface between the directors and the executives (outside the board).
- The daunting – and contradictory – responsibility of board members to oversee and at the same time support the executives. An enormous and continuous source of tension.
- With Brazilian and international interviewees and a review of the most recent international literature, the internal and external board tensions are identified and analyzed from the point of view of mitigation.
- Real situations experienced by both directors as well as executives are discussed: the executives' resistance to the BoD; the fearsome excessive optimism in relation to the projects' results; the omission of negative information; the lack of time and excess activities; and micro-management or excessive reputational concern, among others.
- Guidance for directors and executives – how to act in order to reduce the tensions in the interface between the board and the management.
- In this chapter caselet, a board director tells how a sympathetic friendship between good friends environment in the boardroom is transformed in a nightmare to him when he was faced by an ethical dilemma.

For 54 years, Hawaii Engineering was a construction company that specialized in large private sector construction projects in our country and abroad and, for 34 years, I was very happy to be working at the company. After I got my law degree, I was invited to join the company's legal department and I built my entire career around the institution. It was vital in shaping my network of professional and personal relationships. In fact, my best friends have always been at the company, including Gabriel, the founder's son and the sole heir to the business. Shortly after his father's death, he took over as Chief Executive Officer (CEO) and quickly began a process of restructuring and professionalizing the company. Asserting that there was a need to make room in management for younger people and those with different experience, Gabriel set up a real board of directors, to which some of the executives at that time migrated. So, in addition to being the CEO, Gabriel also became chairman of the board and appointed me as a director, along with three other engineers, all former executives like me, who had also made a career exclusively at the construction company.

Over the years, our relationship at the board suffered the natural and inevitable wear and tear of everyday professional life, but the atmosphere of camaraderie between us has always been helped by the fact that we have interests in common, especially because we are really keen on the same sport. We were all members of the Yacht Club, we loved sailing together and our wives often came along as well, and they also became good friends. At the BoD's quarterly meetings, the atmosphere was that of a group of friends getting together. There was a lot of talk about family, vacation plans and, particularly sailboats, competitions and the art of sailing. Sometimes, it got the point where I felt that being paid to be a board member seemed like an exaggeration because being part of that group was really satisfying and it was a pleasure.

At most of the meetings, Gabriel mostly spoke about the latest things that had happened in the company, because, since the four of us had already stepped down from the day-to-day management, we were no longer involved in the business. When any topic required real deliberation, it was all done very quickly. The items for discussion would usually be put forward by the new executives, but they were invariably interrupted by Gabriel. With his unwavering smile, he dominated the conversation and enthusiastically outlined why the proposition should be approved. At the end of the chairman's lecture, we, the other four board members, were invariably in agreement. Gabriel's reasoning was always so convincing that there was little debate or questioning at the meetings. Occasionally one of us would make some other comment of agreement, sometimes even in a reverent tone. The truth is that everyone really admired Gabriel, who, in fact, had always shown himself to be a professional with remarkable vision and ability.

In 2015, the chairman of the BoD was very motivated by the federal government's recently launched infrastructure investment program. He wanted a piece of that pie and was convinced that the company was qualified since the company had an impeccable reputation, experience, know-how and efficient processes. So, he put his network of relationships to work and soon mastered an "informal playbook" with a step-by-step guide on how to get into the biggest federal public tenders. At Hawaii Engineering, decisions always followed Gabriel's breakneck pace and the board maintained a friendly atmosphere. However, this environment would soon reveal its consequences...*

As Sir Christopher Hogg** summed up so well, one of the characteristics of a well-functioning Board of Directors (BoD) is that it is certainly not a comfortable place for its members. It is not unusual for directors to feel as though they're "among friends" at board meetings, as illustrated by the story at the start of this chapter. There are a number of factors that can make this so and the first one is structural, in other words, it comes from the very make-up of the board itself. In the previous chapter, when the average profile of board members was discussed, it was stressed that there is normally more similarity than diversity on boards.*** They are typically made up of mature, experienced men, with similar backgrounds and professional experiences, and it is only natural that they should share common interests, in addition to corporate life itself, resulting in the formation or consolidation of good friendships.

Another factor that contributes to this atmosphere of apparent fraternization is that boards of directors are, for the most part, made up of the network of relationships of the controlling shareholder – or of the CEO, in the case of companies that have dispersed ownership. In an unsurprisingly natural way, directors of boards are often chosen from among these people's friends or from their closest business relationships. On top of this, this issue is aggravated, especially when the boards are smaller and there are fewer independent directors, as already shown in Chapter 2.

The most common pretext for favoring the presence of friends on boards of directors is the need for a solid relationship of trust in the business. There is undoubtedly a legitimate concern here regarding the secrecy and confidentiality of the company's strategic matters. Otherwise, how can the board members be given access to the data that is essential

---

* The conclusion of the story will be presented at page 74.

** A quote by Sir Christopher Hogg, former chairman of the UK's Financial Reporting Council (FRC) quoted in Chapter 1: "Good boards are pretty uncomfortable places and that's where they should be."

*** For the statistical figures regarding the profile of the directors, look for pages 36 to 42, in Chapter 2.

for the decision-making process in the BoD? However, this relationship of trust can hide a distortion: one may expect a more complacent and understanding attitude from one's best friends. Even though it is not made explicit and remains in the background, this issue often interferes in the process of choosing directors, as revealed by this episode that was overheard at a party:

> At the head of a conglomerate for decades, the businessman invited an old friend to join his family holding company's board of directors out of the blue. With a reputation for never compromising, the experienced director gave a friendly smile and came out with his most unassuming reply: "I'm sure you wouldn't want a friend who's as critical as I am on your BoD." Everyone around burst out laughing and the uncomfortable situation faded away; the businessman, in turn, changed the subject and never brought up the invitation again. That director was well aware that he would be expected to give in or, at least keep quiet, in the face of the autocratic style of leadership that his old friend stamped on the family business. Otherwise, there was an extremely high risk that their long-standing friendship would quickly turn into something more bitter.

This preference given to a "friend" board member may also have another negative consequence. After all, sharing decisions and – most importantly – sharing power with "strangers" is not something that is ingrained in business culture in countries where the predominant model is that of concentration of ownership. In the specific case of the make-up of boards of directors, the "strangers" are the so-called independent directors. So much so that it is still not commonplace among companies that are less mature on the governance front to use search firms to find directors when assembling or renewing BoD. What probably escapes those who favor friendships is that you don't have to be a friend to act as a responsible and reliable director. In order to avoid the predominance of relationships based on friendship and an overly similar profile in terms of board members, Sir Adrian Cadbury's[*] recommendation was that the choice of a professional to join the board of directors would never be restricted to a single person – whether it be the controlling shareholder, the board chair or the CEO:

> When we were drawing up our code of governance practices, one of our best recommendations was the one against the appointment

---

[*] Sir Adrian Cadbury (1929–2015) was the author of the Cadbury Report, which, in 1992, established corporate governance standards for the United Kingdom. He was also the chair wman of the board of Cadbury Schweppes. The author interviewed Sir Adrian Cadbury's in Dorridge, England, on December 4, 2013.

of directors by the chairman of the board. There were many cases where the chairman simply said, "This is the person I want on the BoD, the one I think is the most valuable and this is the one I pick to be a board member," and the other board members were not consulted. This means that the new director is not in fact independent. Moreover, the danger is that this diminishes the diversity of views on the board. When the majority of the directors have the same background and the same experiences, they tend to think in a similar way, and a BoD should be capable of having a broader view. It should also take into account the opinions of the workforce, the community, the customers and the shareholders. In order to make the group more effective, two points need to be considered: 1) the invitation should be made to the best professionals and 2) the other directors should give their opinion regarding this decision.

An Invisible Tangle of Tensions

Although the atmosphere at the board's meetings may seem friendly and pleasant on the surface, the BoD's dynamics are subject to an invisible tangle of simultaneous tensions – both internal as well as external. There are two main areas, which were briefly touched on in Chapter 1: the first results from the interaction among the board members themselves – both individually and as a group – and these are known as intra-board tensions; the second of these is derived from the relationship between the board members and the executives as well as those resulting from the company's relationship with stakeholders, which although managed by the executives reaches the BoD – these are the extra-board tensions (Figure 3.1).

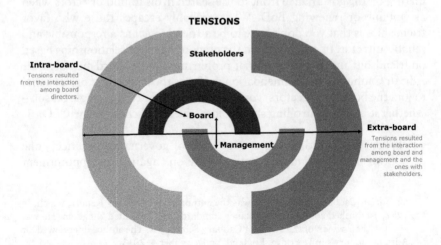

Figure 3.1 Intra-board and extra-board tensions.

The tension in the boardroom is confirmed by the directors participating in a survey of boards in 40 countries. As Graph 3.1 illustrates, only 22% of the 340 directors responded that meetings never take place in a tense atmosphere.

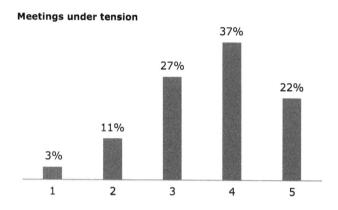

Meetings under tension

Survey Question: Do board meetings take place under a tense atmosphere?
(1) Always (5) Never

Graph 3.1 Tension.
Source: Guerra, Barros and Santos (2020).[25]

Intra-Board Tensions

An apparent paradox is inherent to the dynamics of every group: although there is a need for integration and cohesion, there has to be enough room for contradictory opinions and discussions for productive conflicts of innovation and consistency to emerge during the decision-making process. However, these disagreements can also lead to counterproductive conflicts. For this reason, it is only when it seeks and approaches the equilibrium tension point that the group interacts in conditions to reach its best performance.

Therefore, sitting around the table, the board members are certainly not immune to the tensions that result from the very nature of group dynamics. As such, one of the clearest symptoms of the BoD's dysfunctionality is usually the absence of debate, as can be seen, for example, in the story about Hawaii Engineering (concluded on page 74). On the surface, there seems to be harmony, but the possible conflicts maybe being covered up and anesthetized. This is what **Luiz Carlos Cabrera,**[*]

---

[*] Luiz Carlos Cabrera is the founding partner and CEO of LCabrera Consultants. Former board member of The AESC – Association of Executive Search and Leadership International Board and former chairman of the AESC Brazilian Chapter. The author interviewed Luiz Carlos Cabrera in São Paulo, Brazil, on February 23, 2016.

who is an experienced headhunter of board directors, calls "hypocritical harmony," which, according to him, inevitably leads to wrong decisions that have the potential to destroy the company's value:

> Throughout my experience, I haven't really seen harmony in boards up until now. What can sometimes happen is that there is a hypocritical harmony. One or more of the board members prefer to waive discussions in order to avoid a larger conflict. But even so, the conflict is there, it is known and anticipated. What happens is that, on behalf of different causes – to maintain peace in the family or to preserve friendly relations – the conflict that is there is anesthetized, and this often leads to the wrong decisions. When harmony in the BoD is falsely preserved, the damage to the organization will show up in the short, medium or long term. This reminds me of an old story by Carlos Heitor Cony* in which he describes the coexistence of a group of people, who used to catch the same streetcar every day, at the same time. Despite being strangers, over time, they get to know each other by expression, by face, by the way they dress. Among the directors, particularly when the group is a small one and not that diverse, it is commonplace for something similar to occur. Just a change in the facial expression of one of them leads the other to think: "I am sure of what he's going to say" or "I am sure of what he is thinking". And then the discussions don't take place. And, on a board where there are no productive discussions, the scene is set for the wrong decisions to be made.

How can we prevent this "hypocritical harmony" environment from prevailing?

One of the most frequent solutions has been to invite more than one independent director. But there shouldn't be just one: alone, they will end up frustrated and/or massacred by the hypocritical harmony. Independent board members really help to create or recreate a productive discussion environment, in other words, one that is focused on results. Another point, which is becoming increasingly clear in governance, is that there has to be renewal. In general, these lengthy mandates occur because, when there are shareholder structures that are shared or distributed among different family members, the most important currency is not competence, it is trust. Even in the case of independent directors, once trust has

---

* Carlos Heitor Cony (1926–2018) – Brazilian journalist and writer, who, in 2000, was elected to the Brazilian Academy of Letters.

been acquired, the tendency is to preserve it, clearly transforming the director into a member of the family. The independent board member will be sidetracked to a simpler and more favorable decision-making process, without any discussion – an attempt at cooptation. In order to avoid this, it is best that the mandates be shorter and that the directors can only remain in office for a maximum of two or three terms. This prevents even the independent directors from becoming upset on account of not dissenting or even due to dissenting too much.

Within all and any group, social pressures arise spontaneously and these have a marked influence on individual behavior. They are often so powerful that people even end up choosing to remain silent rather than voicing their wishes or opinion – even when they are formally invited to do so. In many cases, according to researchers, this is just an attempt to avoid the disapproval of others:

> "People might be silent not because they think that they must be wrong ..., but instead to avoid the risk of social punishment of various sorts. In fact, social influences undoubtedly contributed to self-silencing in the Kennedy White House.* Even in societies and organizations that are strongly committed to freedom and honesty, people who defy the dominant position within the group risk a form of disapproval that will lead them to be less trusted, less liked, and less respected in the future."[1]

When, in the interaction among the directors, these social pressures are linked to "Cony's streetcar effect," which was pointed out earlier on by **Cabrera.**** In other words, in the excessively close and lasting coexistence among directors, there may be a loss of quality in the decision process because of what is referred to as groupthink – a concept that will be looked at in greater detail in Chapter 6. **Irving Janis** defines groupthink as follows:

> "(...) refers to a mode of thinking that people engage in when they are deeply involved in a cohesive in-group, when the members' strivings

---

* The researchers refer to the American invasion of Cuba at the Bay of Pigs. The ill-fated invasion, designed to overthrow the revolutionary Cuban government headed by Fidel Castro, went ahead because President Kennedy's advisers said nothing, even when they had reason to believe that the mission would not succeed.

** The author interviewed Luiz Carlos Cabrera in São Paulo, Brazil, on February 23, 2016.

for unanimity override their motivation to realistically appraise alternative courses of action. (...) Groupthink refers to a deterioration of mental efficiency, reality testing and moral judgment that results from the in-group pressures."[2]

A negative consequence of groupthink is that the group's dynamics are susceptible to other anomalies such as conformity and, even more serious, unanimity. These group behavior characteristics have been widely studied and applied specifically to corporate governance, not just because, among other roles, the BoD is the corporate decision-making machine, but also because the pathological interactions between the directors can provoke silent threats. The anomalies are there, but they are not openly acknowledged, and as such end up undermining the board's decision-making process, preventing it from being robust and meticulous and having the necessary thoroughness. Hence, **Katharina Pick** and **Kenneth Merchant**[3] organized intra-board tensions into six different types, which can be summarized as follows:

a. **Social Cohesion Tension:** as a group, the board of directors needs to simultaneously create and avoid social cohesion. There should be common factors – attraction, common interests, cultural similarity, social ties – so that the individuals wish to remain part of the group and this makes interaction more enjoyable, increases motivation and helps to deal politically with internal conflicts. On the other hand, when there is excessive cohesion, it leads to conformity of thought and prevents the emergence of opinions and information that could be very useful to the decision-making process. According to the authors, the choice is not between having or not having cohesion, but rather what is the ideal degree of cohesion and what type of cohesion should exist among the BoD's members.

b. **Dissension Tension:** this tension stems from the continuous search for a balance between enabling and even encouraging contradictory opinions and preventing the emergence of possible conflicts from threatening the group's social cohesion and ending up stalling board meetings. In other words, there should be enough dissension to encourage innovation, but not enough to create chaos. It is the exact measure of what is being called "productive conflict" here.

c. **Psychological-Safety Tension:** the BoD should be a place where the directors feel safe to take risks, share unpopular ideas or admit mistakes. Psychological security is one of the factors that counteracts conformity. However, it can also cause each individual to exert less effort than they could in order to carry out the group's activities. This is what is known as social loafing, a phenomenon of group dynamics, which will be examined in Chapter 6.

d. **Collectivist-Feelings Tension:** it is vital that the board members feel that they belong to the group and that they make up a collective that performs joint activities. However, if this collectivist perception is excessive, it can stifle visibility and individual contribution, becoming one of the factors responsible for unhelpful conformity of thought. For Pick and Merchant, "it is critical to find the balance between being part of and operating as a collective and still valuing and measuring individual contributions."

e. **Diversity-of-Thought Tension:** the main benefit of diversity is to enhance decision-making, enabling board directors to be provided with a number of perspectives, resulting from different genders, ethnicities, cultures, types of knowledge and individual professional and life experiences. Diversity helps prevent polarized discussions. On the other hand, the natural trend among groups is to take into account information that is common to everyone rather than that which is held by just one or two of its members.

f. **Strong-Leader Tension:** the board chairs have a double mission: they need to be able to encourage contradictory opinions, remembering that they are at the head of a "peer group," and, at the same time, make sure that the BoD's operation is in line with the rules and legal compliance. Strong leadership is needed, but not too strong. It is so common for chairs to be misinterpreted in the fulfillment of this dual mission that Chapter 4 will be devoted exclusively to this topic.

These internal tensions which are inherent to the functioning of groups add an extra dose of stress to the already complex decisions made on a daily basis by boards of directors. However, it should be borne in mind that all of this usually occurs in a hidden way, in other words, under the guise of the board's "normal and natural" working. When conflict comes on to the scene – whether openly or in a veiled way, as was the case, for example, at La Rochelle's BoD in Chapter 2 – the destruction of value can become dramatic.

Understood here as "perceived divergence of interest, or a belief that the parties' current aspirations cannot be achieved simultaneously,"[4] conflict has an immediate impact on the behavior of individuals: all that it takes is for someone to "perceive" divergences between the members of the group for them to take steps to defend their interests – even if this just means adopting a concealed defensive attitude. If and when this defensive behavior results in mutual aggression, an empire of hostility is created and the board can simply become toxic, unproductive and paralyzed. The only advantage – if one can regard it as such – is that the verbal war gives off clearer signs of the degree of dysfunctionality that the board of directors has arrived at. The fact is that it is hard for even the most robust and consistent decision-making process to function effectively at any extreme point: whether the decision process happens in the sympathetic friendship between good friends environment or in a situation of an open conflict between the different shareholders' coalitions.

With the exception of cases where dissension reaches the point of exacerbating the conflict, some of the intra-board tensions are exemplified in the episode involving the hypothetical Hawaii Engineering. Under the apparent harmony that exists between the board members, this report shows how the social pressures within the group can lead to a lack of contradictory opinions and, as a consequence, cause very harmful, even disastrous results for the company:

At one of the board's regular meetings (which continued to be held on a quarterly basis), Gabriel gave us the good news: Hawaii Engineering was ready to take part in public tenders for the federal infrastructure program's construction projects. He advised us, however, that there was "a price to enter this club" and reassured: "You can rest easy. Alex, who has just been hired, is our executive who has the most experience in the public sector. He has worked for a number of companies that provide services to government agencies and he knows how it all works". For the first time, as a Hawaii board member, I felt uneasy. I swallowed and was uncomfortable with the implicit proposal placed on the table. But, when I raised a question challenging the idea, Gabriel wound up with his smile and his familiar friendly tone: "You don't want to play innocent, do you? In this country, there is no other way to make things happen!" At the time, I preferred to keep quiet. Once again, Gabriel's decisions were approved unanimously by the BoD. We would only meet again three months later, by which time that day's proposal had already become an irreversible fact.

My discomfort as a director of Hawaii continued. It was as if I could feel the weight of my father's eyes on my shoulders. Back in the 1980s he had been a professor of corporate law and one of the most respected professionals in the country, when it came to the ethical performance of companies. I didn't like having to admit that the professionals I most admired – and who were my best friends – could accept that situation so naturally. And I continued to feel guilty for my silence and omission at that board meeting.

One day, I tried to talk to my wife, Suzy, about this subject: she knew everyone on the board very well and, in addition, was very good friends and a partner with Luiz's wife in a beachwear fashion brand. But she didn't even give me a chance to touch on the ethical issues, which had really been bothering me. When I finished telling her what had happened at the last board meeting, she switched straight over to her own interests: "Please, don't mess things up with them! I am in the middle of getting our brand into the Country Club because of the relationships at the Yacht Club. On top of this, if you create problems for Gabriel, have you thought about what the atmosphere will be like between the two of you in the America's Cup contest in September?" Each one in their own way and for their own reasons, neither Suzy nor Gabriel wanted to hear my questions. I cannot recall many other times when I felt quite so isolated and distressed both on a personal level as well as on a professional one.

I took part in three more Hawaii board meetings, but for me, the pleasant fraternal environment had turned out to be nothing more than a farce: only now did it become clear to me that we were just directors in order to approve the decisions taken by Gabriel, who with his frantic pace trampled on even our most entrenched values. Gabriel did not raise any further discussions regarding the company's participation in public tenders and alleging personal issues, I stepped down as a member of the construction company's board at the start of the following year. That decision made me feel calmer. At the time, it was the best decision I was able to make: even against my ethical convictions, in the name of the friendship, I preferred to keep quiet. Nowadays, as an independent director at a company in another sector, I prefer to avoid sleepless nights: I am always the first one to promote debate on ethical considerations among the BoD.

In 2017, Hawaii Engineering was accused – and eventually found guilty – of paying bribes. Gabriel's name was never directly mentioned either in the courts or by the press. Nevertheless, I found out that the construction company had lost major private contracts both in the country as well as abroad, and there was even talk in the market about a financial restructuring. No matter how big the immediate financial loss is, the destruction of value is undeniable. Lately, the winds have not even been favorable for sailing together.

To finalize this discussion of intra-board tensions, it is fitting to leave behind the realm of fiction, particularly since there is a trend to downplay the damaging effects of excessive conformity in boards of directors. For this reason, it is worth recalling the description of real events made by James Surowiecki in the magazine "The New Yorker" about the performance of the boards of Enron and Tyco. The article argues that, at both companies, the lack of productive debate was what paved the way for disaster:

"On the Enron and Tyco boards, directors consistently deferred to company executives instead of challenging them. They discouraged debate and disagreement instead of cultivating it. In their own worlds, these directors were alpha males and queen bees with strong opinions and a forthright manner. But in a room together they turned into meek conformists, valuing unity over truth. At Enron, for instance, nearly every board vote was unanimous. When Fastow and Skilling[*] proposed the strategies that eventually destroyed the company, board members asked a few cursory questions, then signed off. The directors had forgotten, apparently, that they had the power to say no."[5]

What Enron's board members did not do – but should have done – was to adequately question the model proposed by the executives, even if this caused some degree of tension. After all, this tension between the board and the executives is one of the most common characteristics in the governance environment.

Extra-Board Tensions

The performance of the board members – already immersed in the natural difficulties of the interrelationship between the members of each and every group – is also embroiled in another set of more specific tensions since this one results from the BoD's inevitable interdependence with the managers who are in charge of the business operation. These tensions are inherent in the company's day-to-day management and present a high capacity for value destruction. Even when excessive, these tensions usually go unnoticed, along with other reasons because of the lack of any systemic mechanism to identify the problem, as pointed out by the headhunter Fernando Carneiro[**] who has a lot of experience in putting together boards:

> There is an environment of mutual distrust and, since there is no clarity regarding the separation of the roles of governance and management, personal characteristics end up encouraging conflicts, especially between the chairman of the board and the CEO – not least of all because there is not usually any defined process for identifying and mitigating those tensions.

This climate of mutual distrust between the directors and executives is partly explained by agency theory, which models the relationship

---

[*]   Enron's CFO and CEO.

[**]   Fernando Carneiro leads CEO practices in Latin America and Brazil and was a member of Spencer Stuart Global Board. As a recognized expert in corporate governance, he conducted several board searches and board assessment projects for Brazilian and multinational companies. The author interviewed Fernando Carneiro in São Paulo, Brazil, on March 15, 2016.

between the principal (shareholders) and their agents, those that they hire, and to whom they delegate the company's management. Prevalent in the last two decades of the 20th century as a model for understanding corporate governance, agency theory assumes that executives are the shareholders' (principal) agents, being paid to act in the best interest of the company's owners. However, these managers do not always decide and act exclusively in accordance with this purpose, and the result of this – as shown by the corporate scandals of the late 20th and early 21st centuries – may be the expropriation of wealth from shareholders. For this reason, when it comes to corporate governance, agency conflict is a prime example of this tension: in addition to the relationship of power that the directors have over executives, which would by itself already account for a good deal of tension, there is the permanent feeling that there is a misalignment of interests between the two groups, bearing in mind that the board members are elected by the shareholders.

This tension was initially described in those markets which are dominated by the so-called "true" corporations, in other words, companies without an owner and whose shares are dispersed among numerous investors who trade them on the stock exchange. Over many years, investors have claimed their minority rights and, in the wake of the international financial crisis, have become increasingly vocal and active. Nowadays they seek to engage with the boards of directors of the companies in which they invest for a dialogue regarding the -Environment, Social, Governance (ESG) factors and have stepped up their activism at shareholders' meetings.

In response to increased pressure from activist investors on company boards, a group of 13 CEOs and heads of major US investment companies got together in 2016 to address the trust gap between shareholders and managers and, at the same time, the struggle with what they called the maze of good governance rules. As a result, they developed what they called "Common Sense Corporate Governance Principles," which were seen by the market as investor-friendly propositions.[6]

But agency conflict is not restricted to the world of corporations. In companies where ownership is concentrated, agency conflict exists and can occur in a double way. The controlling shareholder acts as the principal in the relationship with the managers and, in addition, also plays the role of the agent in the relationship with the minority shareholders – who also have the right to question whether the controlling shareholder's decisions and actions are in the best interest of all the shareholders. As activism among minority shareholders is on the increase, with demands for a voice and a seat on the boards of directors, this is yet another factor that generates tension in the BoD's decision-making process. After all, does that helicopter acquired by the company, but which also serves the controlling shareholder's family, add any value to the business and also benefit the minority shareholders? Isn't the excessive salary of the chairperson, who is also a controlling shareholder, a way of expropriating from the minority shareholders? Questions such as these have been increasingly raised by active minority shareholders, who put pressure on boards to exercise their role of guarding the interests of all shareholders and avoiding the potential abuses of the controlling shareholders.

However, on occasion, an opposite and rare situation may arise – minority shareholders are now accused of abuses. In 2016, there was a case in Brazil where significant minority shareholders used a legal device to convene a meeting in an investee company to discuss the company's economic and financial situation and take measures to mitigate what they contended was the possibility of insolvency. The company reacted, claiming that these investors were interested in creating volatility in order to make gains on the company's securities and lodged an appeal with the Brazilian Securities and Exchange Commission (CVM), the capital market's regulatory body.

The company asked for the case to be investigated and obtained an injunction in court to suspend the convening of the meeting. At the same time, a meeting of shareholders was called to propose the removal of the two fund managers who sat on the company's board of directors and fiscal council – a corporate entity in charge of analyzing, reviewing and approving the financial statements and comprised of members elected by the Annual General Meeting (AGM). The allegation was that both of them had failed in their fiduciary duties, as they had requested an excessive amount of data from the company, suggesting that the request was linked to their own interests rather than those of the company.

This type of incident generates a lot of controversy regarding directors' rights to ask executives for information. On that occasion, the then lawyer Marcelo Barbosa, currently president of CVM, said that:

> "directors have a duty to monitor executive management and an exhaustive set of rules should not be created as to how this should be done. Precisely so that each director can decide within reason what he/she wants to have access to."[7]

However, often a board member cannot even ask for the information since the company's rule is that the request has to be evaluated collectively in order to be attended. Mauro Rodrigues da Cunha, a board director of listed companies and who at the time served as president of the **Brazilian Association of Capital Markets Investors (AMEC)**, was categorical in saying that "directors have the right to question executive management on any whatsoever topic and have the right to do so directly, without any need to ask for permission."[8]

Expanded Focus: Beyond the Narrow Interests of the Shareholders

The board's role goes beyond safeguarding the interests of all the shareholders; it also has to pay attention to the interests of the company's other stakeholders. This awareness has become clearer with the increasing questioning of the view that value is created exclusively for shareholders. The concept considers that the company should include the creation of value for its stakeholders that is compatible with that for its shareholders and, in addition, the director's obligation should be to the company as a whole rather than just to its shareholders. In August 2019, the issue gained even greater prominence, when the approximately 200 CEOs, who make up the Business Roundtable (BRT) – an American association created in 1972 – signed and released a Statement on the Purpose of a Corporation, making commitments in relation to the satisfaction and development of customers, employees, suppliers, communities and shareholders. In the end, the statement emphasizes: "Each of our stakeholders is essential. We commit to deliver value to all of them, for the future success of our companies, our communities and our country."[9] In January 2020, in Davos (Switzerland), the manifesto that was released at the end of the World Economic Forum's annual meeting stated that the model focused exclusively on the interests of shareholders is no longer appropriate for the reality of the 21st century, which includes climate change, globalization and digital transformation. In his annual letter to investors in 2020, Larry Fink, CEO of BlackRock, the world's largest asset manager with a total of US$9 trillion in assets under management, reiterated the company's commitment to all stakeholders:

> "We believe that all investors, along with regulators, insurers, and the public, need a clearer picture of how companies are managing sustainability-related questions. This data should extend beyond climate to questions around how each company serves its full set of stakeholders, such as the diversity of its workforce, the sustainability of its supply chain, or how well it protects its customers' data. Each company's prospects for growth are inextricable from its ability to operate sustainably and serve its full set of stakeholders."[10]

The BRT's proposal has been challenged, among others, by academics. One of the most vocal researchers on the subject has been **Lucian A. Bebchuk**. Together with his co-author, **Roberto Tallarita**, he published an article[11] stating that the BRT's statement should be viewed as a public relations exercise rather than the harbinger of a major change. The researchers argue that in addition to being short on details and misleading, the commitments to all stakeholders that were proclaimed do not really replace – as BRT would seek to demonstrate – their previous statements. This is because, in its 1997 statement, the authors argue, BRT preached that the executives' and directors' greatest duty is to the corporation's shareholders and explicitly defends "taking into account the interests of the corporation's other stakeholders."[12] Therefore, the authors' assessment is that there is nothing new in the BRT's new positioning.

The arrival of the COVID-19 pandemic a few months later in 2020 pushed these issues even more into the spotlight and caused the "S" (Social) of ESG (Environmental, Social and Governance) to break down the door of board rooms. In order to ensure their own survival in the short and long term, companies were forced to take a new look at the relationships throughout their value chain with a special focus on customers, employees and suppliers from the sustainability angle. Based on this clearly disruptive situation, ESG issues began to receive a lot more attention in board rooms.

However, since they are potentially controversial, these issues are capable of further increasing the tension between directors and executives. As it is the managers who interact with the other stakeholders, they are also the ones who should know and present these demands to the BoDs. Therefore, regardless of whether the company is a publicly traded one or a private one and whether its control is defined or dispersed, boards of directors have gradually found themselves under pressure to take into account not just shareholders and investors in their decision-making process, but also the multiple voices of other stakeholders.[*]

Together, but often sensing that their objectives are conflicting, directors and executives have, on a daily basis, to try and find a balance between emphasizing the business' financial performance to satisfy shareholders and investors and, at the same time, considering the interests of the other parties that make up the company's environment. Both directors as well as board members should be aware that any slip-up here can be fatal for the company's reputation: it does not take much effort to recall recent episodes that have decimated the value of once-solid brands in the market.

Difficult Balance between Support and Supervision

However, inside the board rooms, this backdrop of tensions is interwoven with other, more pragmatic, but no less important issues. Board members wear a triple hat[13]: in addition to being in charge of the

---

[*] The concept of stakeholders adopted here refers not only to those who are directly involved with the company, such as employees, suppliers, customers, the community and the government, but includes the company's entire value creation chain and actors in the environments in which it operates.

decision-making machine, they also have to exercise the roles of supervising the company's performance along with that of the managers and, at the same time, advise and support them with their projects and initiatives. Oscillating between the opposing attributions of supporting and controlling, directors do not always succeed in finding the right balance. If it is excessively supportive, the board may set the stage for possible management failures. While overly controlling and skeptical, boards tend to stifle executives' initiatives and entrepreneurial vigor, in addition to to making them act less transparently:

> "If you want the CEO to be transparent, (...) then you can't take every little thing that he tells you is wrong in the company and then drill down on it and beat him up on it. That's what gets management sometimes gun-shy about letting boards really know what's going on."[14]

It is important to add to this context the fact that board members should also always be on the lookout to try and check whether the proposal that is on the table in the board room is the result of a collective decision that was made by the executive leadership team,[*] where everyone was able to express their enthusiasm or reservations regarding the proposal. Or, on the other hand, whether the proposal basically expresses the view of a CEO who, is perhaps very centralizing and assertive and usually imposes his/her will on the team.

When Executives Resist the BoD

The board's supervisory role has been gaining ground and relevance ever since the corporate scandals which occurred for the most part in the United States at the start of the 21st century and resulted in the adoption of improved corporate governance practices. The good practices related to this supervisory role have not always helped alleviate the delicate relationship between directors and executives. The CEO in particular tends to view this as a loss of power, according to **Luiz Carlos Cabrera**[**]:

> We are all learning about governance, including executives ... The broader distribution of equity control, the growing complexity of business, in short, everything that has increased the importance of the board of directors ended the direct relationship, the executive's direct

---

[*] The expression executive leadership team is used here to refer to the members of the C-Suite as a collective decision-making body.

[**] The author interviewed Luiz Carlos Cabrera in São Paulo, Brazil, on February 23, 2016.

conversation with the owner. He was used to having this conversation: he used to open the door, he used to talk to the owner, left with the decision made and that was the end of it. His intention is to continue like this, having prior meetings, he wants to talk to the controlling shareholder first. But this is no longer effective, and the executive has to get used to the protocol for presenting things to the board. To identify this problem, when I talk to the CEO, I ask, "How essential is this board to you?" And a lot of them say something along the lines of: "It just tests my patience, it just causes me headaches, I don't see any essential reason for it, if I could have a direct relationship with the controlling shareholder, it would be a lot more effective. We work twenty days a month for the BoD; in fact, I could be doing other things instead of preparing this load of reports for a bunch of directors who don't understand anything about the business". These are the outbursts that I hear every day. In my view, roughly 40% of CEOs still view the board as nothing more than a necessary evil and do not take advantage of the support of the directors. In general, when the CEO can no longer interpret the context the way he used to, instead of realizing that the environment has become much more complex, he blames the board: "Do you see? It is this delay in taking decisions. I had to explain this five times in there".

A survey by **Guerra and Santos**,[15] conducted with 102 directors, confirms this resistance on the part of the managers to the board's supervisory role: 76% of the board members believe that executives react badly to questions and that this attitude hampers or significantly hampers the functioning of boards. Taking an oppositional attitude to the board's work is not the smartest option for a CEO. Nor for the board members, who, in the day-to-day relationship, sometimes find themselves literally in a "tight spot" when they need more information from managers in order to take decisions. In a survey of 45 experienced directors, one of them reported how he/she had to be extremely careful in the face of a group of unfriendly managers:

"When [management] walked in and sat down around the edge of the room, I said, 'Folks, we're very aware of all the work you've done. We've had a great review of all that. But there is an enormous amount of information here. You all, we know, have made very significant decisions to get to the conclusions you've come to. We suspect they are the right decisions. But the only way we will know, and be able to put our judgment on that, is if you'll permit us the opportunity to test you in many ways during the next couple of days of discussions, so that we can get through the same small knotholes and decisions you did, in the same way that you did.

And you're going to need to be patient with us, if you'll do that with us.' They did, we did, and we got to a very common ground. But it took a lot more intense discussion, and an environmental change between the management and the board that says asking questions, probing deeply, is not bad, it's good."[16]

The Dreaded Excessive Optimism

It is undeniable that the ability to head up corporate projects, assessing risks and inspiring confidence in better future results is among the roles expected of a CEO. It is difficult to imagine executives stating that there is a possibility that their plans will not work. In addition, there is a natural tendency to expect past positive circumstances to repeat themselves. The CEO's professional profile is forged by a track record of success and he/she will do everything humanly possible – even maybe a little bit of the impossible – in order to stay ahead of the game. However, together these factors can result in a scenario of excessive optimism, an idea that already puts board members on the alert: this is because high doses of optimism are associated with major corporate catastrophes.

> "The Global Financial Crisis (GFC) personified the optimism of all its players leading into the collapse of Bear Stearns' in early 2008. The collapse of the company was a prelude to the risk management meltdown of the Wall Street investment banking industry in September 2008, and the subsequent GFC and recession. This collapse was one fuelled by optimism and has been documented extensively since 2008."[17]

Following this experience, which is still producing very damaging consequences, it is only natural that caution regarding executives' optimism would contaminate board rooms all over the world. In the **Guerra and Santos** survey, 78% of Brazilian board directors stated that this factor is a critical one, as it impairs or significantly impairs the BoD's performance. There is another important cause for this perception on the part of the directors: a study by **Barros and Di Miceli da Silveira** reveals that companies managed by CEOs who are more optimistic or overconfident have higher debt ratios.[18] To combat CEOs' over-optimism, especially when coupled with possible slip-ups in terms of the manipulation of information, **Alexandre Gonçalves Silva**[*] recommends the definition

---

[*] Alexandre Gonçalves Silva is an independent board member and chairman of the board of directors of Embraer; he was the CEO of General Electric do Brasil between 2001 and 2007 and, since then, has taken part on boards of directors in

of metrics aimed at avoiding mistakes in the executives' performance assessment:

> It is necessary to have well-defined metrics to measure the executives' and the company's performance. I have experienced situations where there are plans and goals for an executive and, when you check at the end of the year vis-à-vis the results, the person registered a score of 90%. But everyone knows that the executive in question performed poorly. When this happens, it is because the metrics were badly specified. There are areas where metrics are difficult – for example, in the legal area, in HR and in customer services. There are many nuances, of course; in production it is easier to measure. Financial results are also easier to measure. But measuring the intangible is very complicated. So, at one of the companies where I was a board member, we spent a lot of time identifying metrics to really be able to monitor performance. On a more complex project, it is necessary to break it down into action plans and define checkpoints to see if everyone is progressing at the same pace. Each of these action plans has to have someone who is responsible, how much he will spend, the timing, the goals, and you have to have metrics to measure everything. If this is done, it gets easier. Otherwise, the board is vulnerable to being manipulated by the CEO, wanting to show that the business is doing fine, when it is not. With metrics, there's no mistaking it. It takes a lot of maturity to adopt these metrics, because even so, there is still a significant part of the person's assessment that is not mathematical, but which is discretionary.

Excessive optimism will be looked at again in Chapter 5, in the context of the most difficult decisions made by directors.

The CEO's Biggest Sin Is Having a "Gift for Deception"

It would be a never-ending exercise to list examples of CEOs who assert that their interests are aligned with those of the organization and those of the shareholders and are committed to managing things in the best way possible firstly on behalf of the collective goals and only secondarily for their own benefit. This detail of the factual reality cannot be denied any more than that people occupying high executive positions often "present the facts in a rose-tinted light" to defend their own interests. Some attitudes toward the board, such as postponing bad news,

---

companies in various of the country's economic sectors. The author interviewed Alexandre Gonçalves Silva in São Paulo, Brazil, on February 19, 2016.

disrespecting the organization's values or sugar-coating figures, really call into question the moral integrity of some CEOs.

In the following two excerpts from interviews, the sources preferred not to be identified, as they had probed deeply into this question of falsifying the information transmitted by the CEO to the directors. The first of them, a former executive in the industrial area, admits that intellectual dishonesty is detrimental in relation to the BoD, but recalls that "there are people who even lie to their shrink."

> One of the biggest sins of CEOs is a lack of honesty, understood here as intellectual dishonesty: incomplete or distorted or error-inducing information. I consider this serious from a moral point of view. There are people who even lie to their psychotherapist, there are people who are in graduate school and who cheat in their exams. I mean, he is no longer a child, he is not at school because his father sent him. It would be better not to go to the therapist and not to do a post-grad course. For me, these are totally incoherent situations, but I've seen CEOs do this.

According to a former CEO from the financial area who was in charge of the management of hedge funds in various European countries and is today a director at a global financial institution, some specific characteristics of the sector itself can also induce the CEO to consciously leave out information for the board of directors:

> First off, it needs to be remembered that I am answering for the specific perspective of someone who worked in the hedge fund industry. In this case, the CEO controls a lot of information, remember that the analyzes and projections are all written in such a way as to immunize the manager of the portfolio from any liability. At the same time, you want a BoD that can give you ideas, make introductions to new and potential investors and help you, as CEO, to make progress on the corporate governance front, to make the processes better. You want the directors to collaborate, but at the same time, you don't want to give them too much information. In my case, half of the board members were also investors in our funds, so we wanted to keep them happy. Moreover, since they were investors, you don't want to show them the weaknesses of your operations or risk controls. You want to develop the best possible risk control and you ask for their help. So, you present everything in a positive light.

> **And now that you are a board member, how do you feel about the CEO?**

> When you're the CEO, you try and show the company's best face to the board. Therefore, they believe and reinforce the fact that you are

a good CEO, that you are doing a good job, and the directors are happy to find more investors for you. On the other hand, now that I'm sitting on the board of directors, I specifically want to know the imperfections in order to be able to help solve problems. For me, this is the most interesting dilemma between being the CEO versus being on the board. One tries to show the best side while the other one tries to look at the underlying.

Although according to the principles of corporate governance, the CEO answers to the board of directors, in practice, there may be an imbalance of power between the parties, particularly when the company's chief executive also holds the position of board chair. In situations such as this, it makes it easier for the executives to exercise their "gift of deceiving." For this reason, it is the other directors, mainly the independent ones, who need to ensure that the board is not under the thumb of the CEO or becomes blind to his failures, limitations and biases – or even possible deviations in his conduct. In cases like this the presence of the Lead Independent Director[*] can prove to be very efficient.

A study published in the **Harvard Business Review** (HBR),[19] analyzed 38 incidents caused by improper behavior on the part of CEOs between 2000 and 2015. According to this study, 34% of the cases revolved around lies told to the BoD about criminal records or falsifying credentials; 21% involved amorous relationships with subordinates, suppliers or consultants; 16% referred to questionable (non-illegal) use of corporate funds and 13% were related to public statements that were offensive to customers or social groups. The researchers reached, among others, the following conclusions: the impact on the company of the CEO's misconduct was significant and long-term, with practical consequences, such as the loss of customers; however, only 58% ended with the executive being fired. In March 2020, another article published in the HBR pointed out: "Inside many companies, it's unclear who manages the CEO. The chief executive reports to the board, but board members aren't inside the company every day, seeing an executive's actions. That's why in the healthiest companies, executives "manage" each other.[20] But what about when there is social pressure within the group of executives that can silence contradictory opinions, as already described above? In this case, who "manages" the CEO?

---

[*] This practice will be looked at in greater detail in Chapter 4.

For **César Souza,**[*] who is an experienced board member, one of the ways to prevent this type of problem is for the directors to get to know "the person" who is the company's CEO better:

> In general, the CEO is evaluated on the basis of the results achieved, but not the person himself. And it is not common to go into his or her merits: they either get rid of him or promote him. In my opinion, this occurs because the board directors do not socialize with the executives; not, at least, at the level of depth they should. It is not about being together on a daily basis, obviously, but finding out a bit more about who the executive is, how he thinks, his values, how he makes decisions, his motivations. Sometimes the director does not know who is a careerist and who is not; who likes the company, who is there because they are passionate about the business or who is simply spending time there to be able to go elsewhere. I mean, without knowing a little, it is hard to assess why certain decisions are proposed. An independent director or one who does not take part in the day-to-day management cannot go a year without having at least two private meetings with the CEO or with one of the other executives. When I talk about a private meeting, what I mean is inviting the person for a conversation, spending two hours, sitting down and talking: "How do you see things, what is your real view of the business?"; "If you were a shareholder, what would you do?"; "If you were in my shoes, what do you think you could do?"; "What is your next career move?"; "Why are you proposing an acquisition, this is the third time that you have proposed an acquisition, what is behind this?"; "What is your strategy for the company?" Or: "Why do you always react?"; "Why do you only value numbers, the quantitative result, rather than the qualitative one?"; "What is your assessment of the company?"; "Which company do you most admire in the market?"; "Who are the business leaders you admire?" The director's role is not just to read the documentation, go to board meetings and then sign the minutes. He is not paid just to attend meetings.

The Best Attitude of Executives

And lastly, two of the interviewees gave their recommendations to help executives become more effective in their relationship with directors,

---

[*] César Souza – CEO of Empreenda and singled out by the World Economic Forum, in 1992, as one of the 200 Global Leaders for Tomorrow, in addition to being a director of companies. The author interviewed César Souza in São Paulo, Brazil, on July 22, 2015.

overcoming the main tensions inside and outside the board on behalf of the business' interests. **Alexandre Gonçalves Silva**, who was a CEO for many years and now serves on boards, suggests maturity, balance and control of one's ego:

> I believe that mature, intelligent executives, who are in control of their egos deal with the BoD very well. They discuss things openly, defend their opinions and listen to the opinions of the board members. The CEO should be open to changing his mind, open to listening to and accepting the board's views. At the same time, he needs to have the guts to defend his position when he thinks he's right. I see exceptional relations between the two parties. Everything will depend on the BoD's maturity, on the governance, on the performance of the committees. I have noticed a substantial improvement in boards. Even at private companies and smaller companies, more importance is being given to boards of directors.

As a way of reducing tensions between the CEO and the directors, **Luiz Carlos Cabrera** believes that the two parties should make a joint effort to build a bridge:

> I have used a metaphor for the CEO who comes up to me and says, "Do you know how I see the board? From my point of view, the BoD is a closed door". Instead of this, I ask him to view the board as a bridge. But on the other side of the bridge there needs to be a chairman of the board or a more skilled director, who can provide assistance, helping to close the gap between the two sides, bringing the CEO closer. However, it is interesting to note that the emphasis in this learning process has been much more focused on correcting errors than on natural interaction. The moment that the CEO is able to recognize: "If it weren't for the board, I would have made a huge mistake" the relationship takes a turn for the better. The door opens when a mistake is avoided in the last minute of the game.

Executives: More Favorable Attitudes in the Relationship with the BoD

- Do not resist the actions of directors whose roles include supervising the performance of managers;
- Do not intend your decisions to be autocratic – discuss proposals with the team of directors first and then accept contributions from the directors;
- Remain open to the directors' contributions;

- Proposals to the BoD should avoid unnecessary details, but be open to questions;
- Never falsify data or put off presenting bad news to the board of directors;
- Be mature, open and keep your ego under control.

Directors Also Sin

In this delicate relationship between directors and executives, up to this point, we have only addressed the main sins committed by the professionals in charge of the company's management. However, board members are not immune to failure (their most detrimental behaviors were addressed in Chapter 2). Occasionally, they also contribute to damaging the level of understanding with managers. Among the specialists interviewed, there was one criticism that was virtually unanimous: some directors, particularly those who used to be or are still executives, are unable to resist interfering in the day-to-day management of the business.

Violation of the traditional maxim about directors, "nose in, fingers out," is one of the biggest causes of friction with managers. When they go beyond their duties and move forward into operational issues, board directors limit the CEO's scope and authority. In **Alexandre Gonçalves Silva's**[*] opinion, the board members cannot get involved in day-to-day matters, give orders or even interact directly with subordinates – with or without the CEO's prior knowledge. He considers this attitude "a mortal sin, a disaster," but he makes a single exception: it is when the board director realizes that he/she can help with some specific point, especially if the CEO is younger and still developing. In this case – and only in this case – he regards the director's direct contribution to the executive as being a mature and positive step, provided that it takes place outside the board meeting.

The same point was brought up for discussion by **Luiz Carlos Cabrera,**[**] but with an even broader perspective. According to him, in addition to overstepping their role, directors – when they are former executives – may even feel somewhat jealous and envious of the CEO's performance. The situation could only be worse, as **Cabrera** highlights, if the executive's performance is exceptionally positive and/or if he/she belongs to one of the shareholder families or controlling group:

> The situation gets even worse when this former executive who has become a director nurtures two dangerous feelings. The first is envy of

---

[*]   The author interviewed Alexandre Gonçalves Silva in São Paulo, Brazil, on February 19, 2016.

[**] The author interviewed Luiz Carlos Cabrera in São Paulo, Brazil, on February 23, 2016.

the CEO's performance. The second is jealousy. It seems interesting that I'm talking about mundane feelings, such as envy and jealousy. But this has a greater impact on the degree of tension than the performance issues themselves. It is more about jealousy and envy than strategic misalignment. The relationship becomes extremely complicated, as the CEO has little room to do better, grow, increase results, diversify and innovate. Often, the conflict reaches a point of dissatisfaction, which results in the CEO leaving the company. And, if you try to point out that what is going on here is connected with envy and jealousy, you will probably hear: "No way, do you think this is what is the real issue? No, the main factor here is this performance problem... "What makes me more optimistic is that, when making a board assessment, I am beginning to hear one or other individual statements – protected by confidentiality rules – that that decision "was not a rational decision, it was a totally emotional one". As in any place, within the BoD, relationships are riddled with emotions. This relationship will only get worse if the CEO is a member of one of the shareholder families.

The topics that will be addressed in Chapters 6 and 7 include how to identify, understand and mitigate the impact of these emotional and behavioral issues on the performance of boards of directors.

Overstretched Board Members

Another point considered critical is the chronic lack of time reported – often without any shame – by some board members. It is not uncommon for a director who takes part in up to six BoDs to also be an investor in some of these companies or to have another professional activity. Without time to look at each of these businesses in-depth, the overstretched and/or overboarded director can barely get himself/herself ready for the meetings, as **César Souza** [*] notes:

Sometimes, I see directors who attend the meeting without knowing what is going on. I mean, the day before they read the documents, on the day of the meeting they go there, then they see the minutes, sometimes they meet the executives. Many board members don't even know the company's operation. There is a factory in a remote location, but the director has never even been there, he doesn't know how things are done, he doesn't know the customers or the competition and he doesn't understand the market. He just follows things based on the reports, what is published in the media and some market research, but he does

[*]   The author interviewed César Souza in São Paulo, Brazil, on July 22, 2015.

not have any personal awareness regarding the life of the company. This is a very big mistake. I think that an independent director should, at very most, sit on three boards. Any more than that and it is very difficult to dedicate yourself with the depth you should.

This realization that board members go to meetings without knowing what is going on is confirmed by the research carried out by **Guerra and Santos**.[21] When asked what is the number one factor that hampers the BoD's proper functioning, 95% of the respondents cited directors who have not prepared themselves for the meetings. This factor can have at least two consequences: (1) when they realize that they are being questioned by a director who has not prepared for the meeting and has not previously read the documentation, it is only understandable that the executives, especially the CEO, feel that they are wasting their time when they are in front of the BoD; (2) without preparation and without any prior in-depth analysis, no director is in any position to contribute to the board's better performance and, therefore, of the business itself.

Guerra, Barros and Santos[22] found that 33% of directors surveyed sit on three or more boards and 24% on three or more board committees. Their research carried out in 2020 with a sample of 340 board directors in 40 countries also found that 30% of the sample do not participate in any committee, as shown in Graphs 3.2 and 3.3 (see following pages).

The amount of time actually needed to take part in a BoD had not been analyzed in any great depth. As of this writing, there was no record of any study detailing how board members spend all the time set aside for performing their role and which also took into account the different types of organizations in which they operate. According to a survey conducted in Brazil by **Better Governance**[*][23] – a consultancy that specializes in corporate governance, which provides support for improving the model and adopting best corporate governance practices – on average board[**] members devote 157 hours a year to their work on the board, while advisory board members spend 131 hours. Out of this total, 46% of the time is devoted to activities outside of board meetings, such as reading material, telephone conversations, individual meetings and interviews. One hypothesis that can be made is that the amount of time that the directors dedicate may be linked to the board's effective role in the company's governance, a topic that will be examined in detail in Chapter 4 in the differentiation between a supporting BoD and a protagonist BoD.

---

[*] The author is the founding partner of Better Governance.

[**] The difference between a board of directors and an advisory board is that the former is legally responsible for effectively taking the decisions within its scope of authority, while an advisory board's role is limited to providing advice and recommendations around decisions that are the BoD's or the management's ultimate responsibility.

Number of board and committee positions

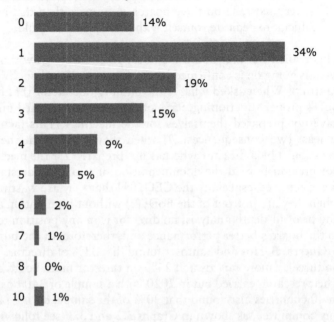

Survey Question: How many boards of directors are you on at the present time?
[number]

Graph 3.2 Number of directorships.
Source: Guerra, Barros and Santos (2020).

Above All Else, One's Own Reputation

If, on the one hand, excessive optimism is a potential slip-up on the part of the executives, on the other, there may also be disproportionate caution on the part of the directors. In a private conversation, a successful CEO, who had experience at a company where there was no defined control, a so-called corporation, highlighted a very distinctive aspect of boards in this shareholding context. Unlike boards where the presence of the owners is significant – and therefore where the entrepreneurial and risk-taker DNA is dominant – a corporation's board may have a very small risk appetite. What is the advantage? On a corporation's BoD, a lack of motivation can befall directors because, after all, they do not gain anything else from the success of an initiative, but failure can cause them some damage, particularly to their reputation.

This experience can also be transferred to another environment where there are a lot of "owners" and no controlling shareholders: that of

Number of board and committee positions

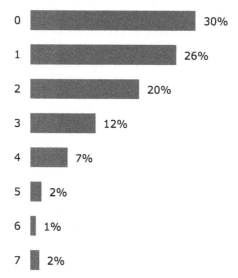

Survey Question: How many board committees are you on at the present time considering all your board seats?

Graph 3.3 Number of committee.
Source: Guerra, Barros and Santos (2020).[26]

non-profit entities. In these organizations, directors may be less inclined to take risks since, in this case, they have more to lose than to gain. One's reputation is all that matters.

Directors: More Favorable Attitudes in the Relationship with the CEO

- Never overstep your duties and invade the CEO's space and authority;
- Do not take part in so many boards that you do not even have the time to prepare for meetings;
- Do not be afraid of business risks, prioritizing only your own reputation;
- Invest time to get to know the executives better;
- Go deeper into issues related to the environment and the operation of the business;
- Never micromanage executives' initiatives.

It Takes Two to Micro-Manage

Another very delicate topic involving the relationship between directors and executives is that of micromanagement. At the heart of the identification of this extremely harmful attitude is the ability to distinguish between what is an unimportant detail and what is a relevant and strategic detail for the business:

> "The difference between micromanaging and appropriate questioning is not always a bright line. What really defines micromanaging is not whether a director is digging into details. It's really a question of which details and for what purpose. Is the director making a small point, like nit-picking expenses? Or is the director drilling down into details that help reveal a higher-level issue – detecting a structural change, getting at the root cause of a problem, or questioning the effectiveness of a process? (...) The key lies in the analytics of working backward to link the operating details with strategic issues. (...) When a director picks up on a small point and challenges it for the sake of showing who is right or what could have been done differently, or when a director attempts to make a decision about operations, or individual people, it's fair to say that person is micromanaging."[24]

Micromanagement is a behavior that can increase irritability levels for both directors and executives. The two sides always have tiresome stories to tell. For example, it is common to see board members barely managing to suppress the look of boredom when their fellow micromanager asks for the floor. Their faces reveal what they are thinking: "Here he/she comes! This executive will redo the accounts for each slide in the presentation!" And what is worse, leaving aside essential questions.

For their part, the executives try to restrain themselves a little more as they know that the more details they bring, the more minutiae will be asked – but are not always successful in this respect. However, they also bear their share of responsibility for the micromanagement of some board members. The CEOs should choose what is relevant to support the directors' decision-making. But, to do that, they should look at the proposition from the director's point of view, not just their own.

One of the directors interviewed recounts the scene she witnessed at a meeting: the CEO began to describe the amount in liters of a substance needed for the operation of the machinery of one of the company's businesses and this triggered a hail of questions from a director who had been a plant manager. The meeting went very well until the CEO set off the micromanager: he was the one who came down from the level of looking at the forest as a whole to looking at the detail of a leaf on the trees. In this case, it is always hard to deter the temptation of those who are operational creatures, who find it hard to forget their origins.

Therefore, it may be not a wise move for executives to make presentations with figures regarding aspects that are highly operational and irrelevant to the BoD. Besides being insignificant in the general reckoning, the excess of details will eventually trigger another onslaught by the micro-manager board member. When it comes to keeping the discussion at a high level at board meetings, the CEO should be able to leave out operational minutiae by focusing on truly strategic issues. And, in order to do this, it is vital that executives are transparent, objective and assertive in their propositions before the BoD.

But, of course, it is not just up to the CEOs and their teams – to prevent, impede or mitigate the micromanaging behavior of one or more board directors. This is just one of the board chair's many duties, which in addition to the usual technical skills, require a great deal of emotional intelligence and sensitivity in relation to the group's internal dynamics and its interactions with executives. Particularly in countries where most companies have defined control, the board chairs' role is often confused with that of the CEO and/or of the controlling shareholders. In these multiple roles, they are often misunderstood in their attempt to fulfill the difficult mission of being at the head of this orchestra which is so difficult to conduct. For this reason, the chair and their responsibilities will be covered in-depth in the next chapter.

Notes

1 Sunstein, Cass R.; Hastie, Reid. *Wiser: Getting beyond groupthink to make groups smarter.* Harvard Business Press, 2015. Available at https://hbr.org/product/wiser-getting-beyond-groupthink-to-make-groups-smarter/2299-HBK-ENG. Accessed on July 6, 2020. Location 448 of 3122.
2 Janis, Irving Lester. *Groupthink: Psychological studies of policy decisions and fiascoes.* Boston: Houghton Mifflin, 1982, p. 9.
3 Pick, Katharina; Merchant, Kenneth. *Recognizing negative boardroom group dynamics.* In: Lorsch, Jay William (editor). *The future of boards: Meeting the governance challenges of the twenty-first century.* Boston: Harvard Business Press, 2012, p. 113–132.
4 Pruitt, Dean G.; Rubin, Jeffrey Z. *Social conflict: Escalation, stalemate, settlement.* New York: Random House. 1986, p. 4.
5 James Surowiecki has been writing the financial column for the magazine *The New Yorker* since 2000 and was previously responsible for Slate maagazine's Moneybox column, having also worked at *Fortune*, the *Wall Street Journal*, *Wired*, *Times* and the *Washington Post*. His column *Board-Stiffs*, from March 8, 2004, can be found at http://www.newyorker.com/magazine/2004/03/08/board-stiffs. Accessed on July 8, 2016.
6 The Washington Post. Article these business titans are teaming up for better corporate governance, de Jena McGregor, published on July 21, 2016. Available at https://www.washingtonpost.com/news/on-leadership/

wp/2016/07/21/these-business-titans-are-teaming-up-for-better-corporate-governance/. Accessed on May 21, 2020.

7   Valenti, Graziella. Acesso de Conselheiro a Dados Gera Debate. *Valor Econômico*, São Paulo, July 20, 2016, p. B2.

8   Ibid.

9   Business Roundtable. Statement on the purpose of c Corporation. Published on August 2019. Available at https://opportunity.businessroundtable.org/ourcommitment/. Accessed on June 8, 2020.

10 Fink, Larry. A fundamental reshaping of finance. Available at https://www.blackrock.com/corporate/investor-relations/larry-fink-ceo-letter. Accessed on June 08, 2020.

11 Bebchuk, Lucian A.; Tallarita, Roberto, The illusory promise of stakeholder governance. February 26, 2020. Forthcoming, *Cornell Law Review*, December 2020, Available at SSRN: https://ssrn.com/abstract=3544978 or http://dx.doi.org/10.2139/ssrn.3544978. Accessed on December 7, 2020.

12 Business Roundtable. Statement on corporate governance. 1997, September. *apud* Bebchuk, Lucian A.; Tallarita, Roberto, The illusory promise of stakeholder governance (February 26, 2020). Forthcoming, *Cornell Law Review*, December 2020, Available at SSRN: https://ssrn.com/abstract=3544978 or http://dx.doi.org/10.2139/ssrn.3544978. Accessed on December 7, 2020.

13 Available at http://www.governanceprinciples.org. Accessed on June 7, 2020.

14 Lorsch, Jay William. *The future of boards: Meeting the governance challenges of the twenty-first century*. Boston: Harvard Business Press, 2012. Available at https://store.hbr.org/product/the-future-of-boards-meeting-the-governance-challenges-of-the-twenty-first-century/10913. Accessed on June 7, 2020. Location: 405 of 2780.

15 Guerra, Sandra; Santos, Rafael Liza. *Headaches, concerns and regrets: What does the experience of 102 Brazilian directors tell us? Private Sector Opinion*. Washington, DC: IFC, 2017. Available at https://www.ifc.org/wps/wcm/connect/topics_ext_content/ifc_external_corporate_site/ifc+cg/resources/private+sector+opinion/headaches%2C+concerns%2C+and+regrets+-+what+does+the+experience+of+102+brazilian+directors+tell+us. Accessed on May 21, 2020.

16 Lorsch, Jay W. *The future of boards: Meeting the governance challenges of the twenty-first century*. Boston: Harvard Business Press, 2012. Available at https://store.hbr.org/product/the-future-of-boards-meeting-the-governance-challenges-of-the-twenty-first-century/10913. Accessed on June 7, 2020. Location 382 of 2780.

17 Thuraisingham, Meena; Lehmacher, Wolfgang. *The secret life of decisions: How unconscious bias subverts your judgement*. Aldershot: Gower Publishing, 2013.

18 The sample is made up of 153 companies whose shares are traded on the São Paulo Stock Exchange and with data available 1998 and 2003. Barros, Lucas A. B. de C. e Da Silveira, Alexandre Di Miceli. Excesso de Confiança, Otimismo Gerencial e os Determinantes da Estrutura de Capital. *Revista Brasileira de Finanças*, v. 6, n. 3, 2008.

19 Larcker, David; Tayan, Brian. We studied 38 incidents of CEO bad behavior and measured their consequences. *Harvard Business Review*, June 9, 2016. Available at https://hbr.org/2016/06/we-studied-38-incidents-of-ceo-bad-behavior-and-measured-their-consequences. Accessed on June 7, 2020.

20 Dabrowski, Wojtek. How companies can keep CEO behavior in check. *Havard Business Review,* March 11, 2020. Available at https://hbr.org/2020/03/how-companies-can-keep-ceo-behavior-in-check Accessed on June 9, 2020.

21 Guerra, Sandra; Santos, Rafael Liza. *Headaches, concerns and regrets: What does the experience of 102 Brazilian directors tell us? Private Sector Opinion.* Washington, DC: IFC, 2017. Available at https://www.ifc.org/wps/wcm/connect/topics_ext_content/ifc_external_corporate_site/ifc+cg/resources/private+sector+opinion/headaches%2C+concerns%2C+and+regrets+-+what+does+the+experience+of+102+brazilian+directors+tell+us. Accessed on May 21, 2020.

22 Guerra, Sandra; Barros, Lucas A.; Santos, Rafael L. Decision-making in boards of directors: The roles of meeting dynamics and choice architecture. *Research Project,* 2020.

23 Better Governance. *Conselheiros: dedicação de tempo dentro e fora das salas de conselho. Pesquisa sobre conselhos de administração e consultivos,* published in June 2020. Available at https://bettergovernance.com.br/2020−06-01-Conselheiros_Pesquisa_Dedicacao_de_Tempo.pdf. Accessed on August 28, 2020.

24 Charan, Ram. *Owning up: The 14 questions every board member needs to ask.* San Francisco: Jossey-Bass, 2009.Available at https://www.wiley.com/en-us/Owning+Up%3A+The+14+Questions+Every+Board+Member+Needs+to+Ask-p-9780470397671. Accessed on June 08, 2020. Digital Edition. Locations: 2507, 2514, 2522 of 3040.

25 Guerra, Sandra; Barros, Lucas A.; Santos, Rafael L. Decision-making in boards of directors: The roles of meeting dynamics and choice architecture. Research Project, 2020.

26 Ibid.

Chapter 4

The Chair of the Board, Too Often Misunderstood

Chapter Summary

- The role of the chair of the board of directors (BoD) is not fully understood – not just by the chair himself but also by all those who interact with him. There is little in the way of literature in relation to the best attributes of the chair of the BoD, whereas there is an abundance of research regarding the Chief Executive Officer's (CEO) skills profile.
- If board members already feel isolated, there are some authors who claim that the chair of the BoD occupies the "loneliest chair in the world." He is responsible for the board, the management and the interaction with shareholders: "The chair of the Board of Directors is totally alone."
- Interviewees and **Guerra and Santos**' research indicate that there is room for improvement in the performance of chair of the BoD. In answer to the survey, 36% said that the chair of the board is not very effective or is ineffective in relation to the planning of the BoD's annual agenda; 26% said that he does not make proper efforts to ensure good governance and 25% said that the chair of the BoD does not ensure that there is room for the expression of different opinions.
- The symbiosis between the chair of the board's style of operation and the operating profile of the BoD (leading actor or supporting actor).
- The chair of the BoD is *primus inter pares* (first among equals) and must act as a facilitator of the board's operations as well as of the decision-making process. He is the one who is responsible, for example, for finding a balance between consensus decisions and the need for an opposite viewpoint or even to reduce tensions between the BoD and management.
- The ten commandments of a good relationship between executives, board members and the chair of the BoD.

- Assessment of the board – internal and/or independent: diagnosis, planning and implementation of solutions.
- The decision of firing a CEO amidst the pressure for an Initial Public Offering (IPO) and in a scenario where biases were haunting the board. The caselet of this chapter brings the account of the board chair on what he did to reach the best decision.

There is very little objectivity and rationality in our opinions, or even in our decisions. We prefer to believe that we are always able to choose what is best for us or for the business. But that's not the way it is. Irrational emotions and feelings get in the way. Our perceptions are rarely based on facts. Once an opinion takes root in our mind, it is hard to change it or at least to find another solution to the same problem. Of course, I do not exclude myself from this: I admit that I have to constantly make an effort to try to keep myself aware of my possible biases. And this discipline has proven very useful for me and for the companies where I serve as a board member.

For example, I was the chairman of the board of a company in the United States in the machine tool sector right after the global financial crisis. After going through a difficult process of insolvency and reorganization, control was acquired by two private equity funds, who elected two directors to the board. As a result, the board now had 13 directors. Once the crisis period was behind us, our strategic objective shifted to restructuring the company in order to carry out an IPO. In the opinion of the two directors elected by the funds, who soon gained the support of another eight directors, our first step to achieving this should be to get rid of Harold, who at the time was our CEO.

In their view, this was the easiest way to move forward with a business that had just narrowly avoided going bankrupt. As for myself, I was convinced that this might be the easiest way, but it was not the one that would produce the best results. I knew our CEO well enough, a man in his 50s who had been with the company for thirty years. His long tenure was one of the reasons why most of the directors believed he was unable to avoid the problems that had recently been faced. It is always possible to hold the leader responsible for everything that happens. But in my opinion, they were being influenced by the new directors who had been appointed by the funds. On top of this, there was a big rush to launch the IPO. And they thought that Harold would not be able to make the company look good to investors and run an effective road show. However, in my opinion, that was not true. I had had the opportunity to see how

decisive Harold had been in getting through that turbulent period.
I was sure that he still had a lot to contribute.

Convinced that the majority were letting themselves get carried
away more by perceptions and biases than by the facts, I made an
attempt to listen to two other directors. I suspected that they were
also not sure that firing Harold was the best way out and also wanted
to bring the debate regarding the possible change of the CEO out
into the open. At that time, some of the directors even said I was be-
ing stubborn. But, as chairman of the board, it was part of my job. I
knew that I had to make sure that the decision-making process was
objective and robust. I admit that it was an uphill task. It required
skills that I wasn't even sure I had developed so well over the years.[*]

When it comes to the role of the chair of the board of directors (BoD),
there is only one point on which there is virtually unanimous agreement,
namely that the chair of the board's role is not fully understood – not just
by the one who holds this position, but also by all those who interact with
her/him. It is very likely that one of the causes of this misunderstanding
is the fact that the chairperson's responsibilities have traditionally been
underestimated and even neglected both inside and outside the corporate world. All one needs to do, for example, is to research just how few
studies there are that are focused on the best competencies of the board
chairs, while experts scrutinize and reconstruct the ideal profile in terms
of the skills of Chief Executive Officers (CEOs). In the board rooms, this
misunderstanding becomes very evident: because the chairs' role is not
well understood, they are often misinterpreted in the performance of
their duties, which increases the level of tension in their interactions with
executives and even with the other directors.

Among the reasons for this biased understanding is that the position
of chair of the board is invested with an aura of supreme power. Within
the company, the chair is seen as the lord of lords, the leader of leaders,
the commander in chief. This hierarchical idol worship becomes clearer
in those economies where the majority of companies exhibit concentrated ownership, due to the fact that, on the whole, the chair was the
founder and/or is perhaps is still one of the main owners of the business.
This is accentuated in Latin culture, where the custom is one of "those
who can, give the orders, and those who are smart, obey them." However, unfortunately, this view centered on the exercise of power does
not always lead the chair to conduct the decision-making process in the
organization's best interest, as was stated by one interviewee:

The chairman of the board does indeed have a lot of power, but
he is not always totally well-intentioned, for example, when he

[*] The conclusion of the story will be presented at the end of this chapter.

steers the discussion toward decisions that are in his interest. Politically speaking, the chairman can steer the decision, ensuring that everything is decided by the sheer force of his power. Or, because a stakeholder who is represented there has a larger equity interest and wants everything to be done his own way. Or, it may even be that the chairman himself has some specific interest in that decision, but that it is not necessarily the best decision for the company. So, the big dilemma for the chairman of the board is to try not to take sides or to steer the process. The chairman has power, but he should not use it to construct a decision in his favor. I think this is the most complex issue in relation to the chairman of the board's role.

It is also true that, to a large extent, the organization's own shareholding structure ends up shaping the chair's operating style. In publicly traded companies and corporations, the chairperson of the board tends to adopt a much more active and diligent approach, as there is no dominant shareholder who is close to the company and keeps a close eye on management. Something very similar occurs at non-profit institutions when there are no predominant members. When it comes to a semi-public or a state-owned entity, the chair is dealing with a strong, active shareholder. This is a very complex context, especially in countries where, although corporate legislation provides for public interest taking precedence over private interest, public sector management has given preference to the interests of governments or political parties. This freak effect of politics sometimes ends up turning the chairs of state-owned companies into real jugglers in many countries. In family-owned businesses or companies where there is defined control, the owner tends to be closer to the business, monitoring management on a daily basis. It is also common that other family members are part of the company's management, a situation that creates even more confusion in relation to the chair's role, as explained by the board director **Alexandre Gonçalves Silva**[*]:

> In companies that have controlling groups or controlling shareholders, these generally appoint the director occupying the position of chair of the board. In this position, since he is also the controlling shareholder, his image is more than that of a simple chair of the BoD. As the controlling shareholder and chair of the board at the same time, he dominates the board and decides what he wants. Sometimes the chair may also have a child who is the CEO or another relative

---

[*] Alexandre Gonçalves Silva is an independent board member and chairman of Embraer's board of directors; he was the CEO of General Electric do Brasil between 2001 and 2007 and, since then, has taken part on boards of directors at companies in various economic sectors of the country. The author interviewed Alexandre Gonçalves Silva in São Paulo, Brazil, on February 19, 2016.

or friend as the CEO, in which case the situation can become very complex indeed.

These ambiguities in the performance of the chair's role, are by no means exclusive to any one country. As well as recognizing that the chair's role is indeed very misunderstood and underappreciated, one of the conclusions of a study[1] with directors and senior executives from more than 12,000 companies located in 17 countries was precisely the following: the positive and/or negative characteristics in relation to the chairperson's role transcend national borders. In other words, the skills that make a chair of the board effective – or ineffective – in the United Kingdom or the United States are the same as those of a chair of the board operating in any of the other countries studied, "despite the cultural, legal and political differences as well as the differences in the structure of boards of directors." The same study also found that the quality of the performance of board chairs varies a great deal even within the same country and highlighted the lack of training and development for directors to assume the position of chair of the board.

However, it does not require such a broad, refined survey to reach the conclusion that the chair's role is truly not understood and that this has detrimental consequences for the performance of the BoD as a whole. All one needs to do is to spend time on a daily basis at board meetings to identify a series of very practical real obstacles. One of them, which was discussed in Chapter 2, is the difficulty that most board members have in making the transition from their former executive roles to their new responsibility to supervise and support the business' current managers. In the case of the business' founder, who previously held the position of CEO, when they migrate to the position of chair of the board, everything becomes even more complex. In order for this transition to be successful, the experienced headhunter of directors, **Luiz Carlos Cabrera**, has observed two interesting phenomena:

> Among the group of controlling shareholders who are board members, when they realize that none of them has the ability to be chairman of the board, I have noticed a trend in the market nowadays to look for a professional chairman, who is capable of inspiring, promoting and coordinating the meeting and the agenda and who can get everyone to make their best contribution. Another phenomenon is when one of the shareholder directors decides to assume the role of chairman and focus exclusively on that, doing an excellent job. I am not going to say that they manage to stop being a shareholder, but they fight against the controlling shareholder attitude and effectively become a driver for the board of directors to give its best performance. The most interesting thing is that the best chairmen that I have seen were owners who became directors and ultimately

became chairmen of the board. They are younger, aged between 40 and 50, and look upon the position of chairman as a new way of contributing to the company, finding pleasure in being the board's chairman, rather than an executive.

And in the case of family companies, when the founder of the business, who becomes the chair, is, for example, the father of the newly appointed CEO?

Ah, that is difficult, but I have seen cases where this transition is successful. When it works, the one who makes the biggest transformation is the one who has been succeeded, not the successor. It is the chairman who changes, not the younger CEO. It is someone who used to be the CEO who decides to assume the role of chairman of the board, taking on new duties, such as being the company's institutional representative. He does not take this responsibility away from the CEO, but rather shares it with him as a facilitator. The secret is to find satisfaction in this new role, the same that he used to have when he ran the business. It is a great challenge, a difficult maturing process. But I have witnessed this metamorphosis: the old CEO, who had everything at his disposal, becomes the chairman and is thoroughly enjoying what he is doing, defining well his set of duties that complement the CEO, who is his son. Sometimes, it takes two or three years to learn not to answer a question with a decision. Since he is no longer the one who decides and performs the job, his contribution becomes to get the best out of what the board and the executive body can give the company.

Before specifically analyzing the performance of boards' chairs, **César Souza** points out that, up until the corporate scandals, the BoD itself played no significant role in organizations. He recalls that in some companies most meetings were held *ad referendum*: the minutes were drawn up and a secretary was entrusted with the task of circulating the document to collect the directors' signatures. It was only after these extremely damaging events that the codes and practices of governance were improved and the need for a separation between the executive power and the power of analysis and deliberation became clear. For **César Souza**, there is a clear evolutionary process underway in relation to the performance of the BoD and that of its chairperson, but we are still a long way off from the ideal point:

The chairs of boards do not yet have a very clear understanding of their role as the coordinator of a collective decision-making body, and they sometimes confuse the chair's role with the power to command decisions regarding what the company needs to do. In my opinion, on a scale from one to five, the chair of the board is still between two and two and a half. He is halfway there, but he still has quite a way to go in order to better understand his role, to exercise the power to better evaluate the executives, to take the lead during board meetings, to try to get the best out of everyone and, in addition, to have the ability to deal with all the stakeholders, rather than just the shareholders. The chairs of boards need to learn to coexist with and cultivate a healthy diversity. Many of them still like yes-men, directors who agree with everything, without any relevant questions... what a waste!

According to the survey by **Guerra and Santos,**[2] there is a lot of room for improvement in the performance of boards' chairs (Graph 4.1). For the 102 directors who answered the survey, the chair of the board is often not that effective or is ineffective in relation to the planning of the board's annual agenda (36%), and moreover his/her work does not achieve the best performance in terms of ensuring good governance (26%) or making sure that there is space for the directors to voice different opinions (25%).

Chair: room for improvement

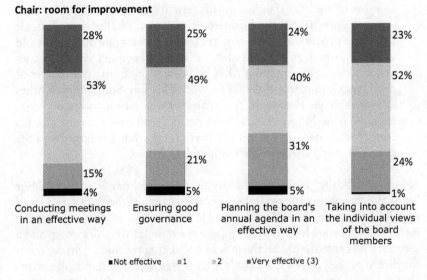

Graph 4.1 Evaluation of the effectiveness of the board chairs.
Source: Guerra and Santos (2017).

Chair of the Board and the BoD Have a Symbiotic Relationship

With consequences that are not always productive, there is a symbiotic relationship between the style of the chair of the board and the type of board itself. Since the performance of both is strongly intertwined, it is not possible to try and understand the chair of the board's role without first analyzing what are the different engagement levels for boards under the different circumstances and points of the business cycle. For example, **Nadler, Behan and Nadler's**[3] model (Figure 4.1) proposes the existence of five BoD archetypes: passive, certifying, engaged, intervening and operating with different degrees of involvement in the decision-making process.

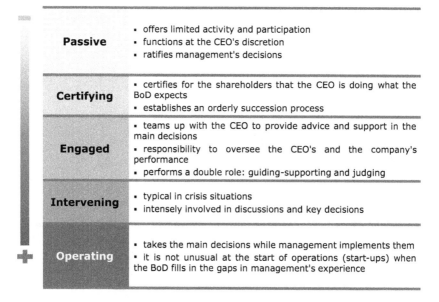

Figure 4.1 **Different degrees of the BoD's engagement according to the circumstances of the business.**
Source: Adapted from Nadler, Behan and Nadler. p. 18.

Regardless of this engagement detailing, however, it is possible to synthesize the profile of the boards into two different categories (Figure 4.2 – see following page). There is the **protagonist board**, one which, in fact, leads the decision-making process, defines strategic guidelines, oversees the business and supports the executives. In contrast, there is the board that plays only a limited **supporting role**, which is one that acts as a sounding board for ideas, an information channel for other relevant shareholders or stakeholders and/or ends up serving merely as an instrument for complying with the legal formality of governance.

All over the world, this limited **supporting role of the boards** of directors is still common, particularly when it comes to family-controlled companies. In the report of its annual survey carried out in more than 50 countries, **PwC**[4] states that family businesses are still unable to make full use of their boards, which should be a lot more than a simple "rubber-stamp" for endorsing decisions, and concludes: "While every family firm will want directors who 'fit,' every business will have different needs when it comes to the selection of the board." Another study[5] that focused on governance practices attempted to identify the adjectives attributed to define the performance profile of the boards of 106 family businesses in Germany, France, Italy and Spain. The result came as no surprise: 53% of the interviewees stated that the BoD has a decision-making profile, while 28% chose the adjective advisory and 19%, informative. In other words, applying the result of this European survey to the Protagonist and Supporting categories, we find that, in those countries, 53% regard the BoD as protagonist, while 47% recognize that the board operates in a supporting role.

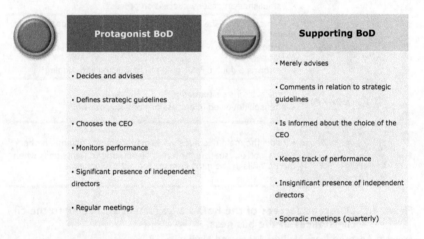

Figure 4.2 Characteristics that differentiate the Protagonist BoD from the Supporting BoD.

It is precisely at this point that the symbiotic relationship between the board's profile and the chair's performance can become counterproductive. It is the chair's mission to support the board's effectiveness, but there is no way to expect him or her to proactively exercise the full range of his or her duties in the face of a board of directors designed to be and to remain in a supporting role in terms of defining the company's strategic direction. Therefore, given this board profile, there is an increased likelihood that the chairpersons are only there to notify the board members regarding what they have already decided and to fill them in regarding their handling in charge of the business. After all, when the BoD limits itself to acting as a "sounding board," there is a high probability that the chair will assume the position of maximum leader of the organization, which expects only and solely advice from its directors. Nothing else.

Chair of the Board: *primus inter pares*

As a way of combating the prevalence of this command and control role, the chairs should assume the leadership of the board as a reincarnation of the Roman concept of *primus inter pares* – the first among equals.[6] The chair of the board's vote should not carry more weight than that of the other directors nor should it be decisive in tied decisions. This is equivalent to saying that the chair's power is no different from or greater than that of the other directors. He/she was only chosen by their peers due to their ability to get the best out of each individual sitting at the table, reconciling interests and organizing the collective decision-making body's work. Their goal should be to guide the BoD's work so as to make the highest governance body truly a decision-making one, in other words, to assume its protagonist character.

Therefore, in order to operate among equals, the chair's vote should not be viewed by the other directors as an influencing factor in the decision-making process. This is the best way to make the other directors' views thrive, as well as to foster a frank and well-informed debate. But nor can the chair of the board neglect his or her responsibilities. So, when can the board's chair express his or her opinion? In pursuit of this balance, with his extensive experience, **Pedro Parente**[*] recommends that the BoD's chair should always be the last one to express his or her opinion. According to him, an exception should only be made when there are a lot of serious risks involved in the decision:

> In general, the chair of the board should be the last one to vote. Usually, as he is the last one to vote, the chair's position does not play a crucial role in the decision taken, it is just one vote, right? This is my view, this is how I play it – except in complex and important situations, when the BoD's chair has to make his position clear. I think it is important for the chair of the board not be remiss in decisions where there are significant risks to any choice that is made, whichever way the decision goes. In this case, he chooses the best moment to let the directors who are going to vote know what his position is. That is the wisdom of knowing when to reveal your vote. Sometimes, if the board's chair expresses his position beforehand it can be an unnecessary constraint for the other directors. But there may be

[*] Pedro Parente, who is the current chairman of BRF's board of directors, was previously the Chair of B3 and the CEO of Petrobras between May 2016 and June 2018. In addition to having held various executive positions and having served as a board director and chairman of the BoD of a number of companies, he was also the Minister of Planning (1999), the Chief of Staff of the Presidency (1999–2002) and the Minister of Mines and Energy (2002) in Brazil. The author interviewed Pedro Parente in São Paulo, Brazil, on September 3, 2015.

situations – just a few – in which, due to the nature of the decision that will be taken, this "constraint" may be necessary.

The Right Moment to Speak

The research undertaken by **Guerra, Barros and Santos,**[7] which was carried out with a sample of 340 board directors acting in 40 countries, indicates that more than half of the directors studied acknowledge that the chairpersons in their boards are almost never the first to express their opinion on a discussion item, as shown in Graph 4.2.

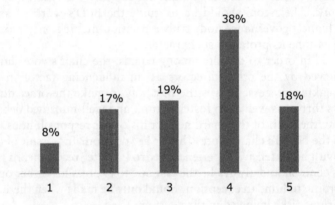

Survey Question: Is the chair of the board one of the first to express his/her opinion when a matter is proposed for discussion or decision?
(1) Always (5) Never

Graph 4.2 Chair: the first to speak.
Source: Guerra, Barros and Santos (2020).

When **Sir Adrian Cadbury**[*] published a book[8] with his personal views on corporate governance, he placed special emphasis on the chair of the board's role, stating that the BoD's chair is the one who is responsible for making the board work and getting the best out of each director. In his opinion, the first step toward achieving this mission is to understand that occupying the position of chair of the BoD does not mean having the right to impose his or her vision and will. Twelve years after writing this book, in an interview given to the author, **Sir Adrian** said he was concerned that the chairperson of the board's role continues to be

---

[*] Sir Adrian Cadbury (1929–2015) was the author of the Cadbury Report, which, in 1992, established corporate governance standards for the United Kingdom. He was also the chairman of the board of Cadbury Schweppes. The author interviewed Sir Adrian Cadbury in Dorridge, England, on December 4, 2013.

underestimated. According to him, the board is not a natural body for the management of the business and, therefore, simply bringing people together is not enough to create an efficient BoD:

> It is the chairman's task to make the board effective and this requires an understanding of the individual board members and, above all, enabling them to work together as a group. As the board's chairman, you need to be aware of the experience and skills of all the directors. You have to understand what each one can offer, what their motivations are, where they're coming from. So, you have to provide a forum, hold meetings where each one of them can express their views and make their contribution. The ability to make it possible for people to give their best requires a personal ability to listen and to understand others. The chairman of the board also has to be ready not to assume the role of leader for himself, but to ensure that the board as a whole takes credit, and that ultimately depends on the people who are on the board. Above all, the chairman should have the ability to assess each director's contribution and their contributions as a collective.

Those who were interviewed for this book were practically unanimous in asserting that, in addition to having the technical skills, in order to perform this role of facilitator the chair of the board needs to know his/her peers. It is necessary to know how each one of them reacts to different situations and, especially, to encourage each member to make their particular contribution. Acknowledging that no leader is blessed with absolute wisdom and that nobody has all the answers, the BoD's chair is equipped to get the best out of the diversity that exists among the directors, as explained by **Alexandre Gonçalves Silva**, who sits on the boards of a number of companies and is the chairman of Embraer's board:

> I think the following is fundamental: the chair has to make room for everyone, listen to everyone's opinion and realize that there are different people – people who are more extroverted, who find it easier to express themselves and there are also others who are quieter. The chair has to endeavor to get the opinion of each person there, because, in general, everyone on the board has a lot of experience. The BoD's chair has to believe that those people there can collaborate. On the board, people bring different experiences, practices and cultures, and the chair has to make the best of this diversity.

The chair of the board must also find the delicate balance between the beauty of collective decisions taken by consensus and the certainty that the proceedings for reaching a resolution remain open to contradictory opinions. A more harmonious decision-making process always seems welcome and well-intentioned. Therefore, there is a tendency to seek consensus as a way of publicly expressing the robustness of the decisions taken by the board. Although not necessarily illegitimate, this trend may be mistaken, bearing in mind the internal social pressures on groups that were discussed in Chapter 3. From this angle, deliberations that always favor consensus may merely reflect the dissension tension: the fear that the emergence of any possible conflicts threatens the group's social cohesion.

On the contrary, in order to prevent an environment among the directors that **Luiz Carlos Cabrera** calls "hypocritical harmony,"[*] it is preferable that the chair of the BoD endeavors to encourage the directors to spell out the differences between them. Only in this way is it possible to ensure that the best decision for the company is adopted in a decision-making process – maybe not always beautiful and perfect –, but which **Pedro Parente**[**] defines as "corporately" healthy:

> In the position of chair of the board, I always make it clear that there is no problem, no problem at all, if the directors spell out a difference. This is extremely healthy, because you can be sure that the issues were discussed to the maximum. It is very important for there to be contradictory opinions, because it is one of the most important factors for decision making. When consensus is sought at any price, there is a big risk of killing off contradictory opinions, and as a result, relevant aspects may be left out of the debate. I not only encourage the others to express dissenting opinions, but I also invite and encourage anyone who voted against the decision to clearly articulate the rationale for dissenting, if they want to add it to the minutes. The assumption is that everyone there is seeking what is best for the company, so I think that on the BoD it is necessary to debunk the need for decisions by consensus.

On the other hand, the chair of the board also has the task of facilitating the decision-making process beforehand behind the scenes, carrying out what may be called "advance discussions" with the directors. There is nothing Machiavellian in this stance, as long as it is not done in the sense of steering the majority's decision in accordance with the chair's interests or opinions. The chair should not use his power to influence decisions. Quite the contrary, these conversations should be a truly genuine inquiry with the aim of having an open and broad dialogue at the board meeting.

[*]   See the concept in Chapter 3.
[**]   The author interviewed Pedro Parente in São Paulo, Brazil, on September 3, 2015.

For this reason, it is the chair's job to talk to each board member beforehand about the topic to be debated, making sure that everyone is fully up to date and the degree of depth of the information shared. Furthermore, in these advance discussions, the chair needs to be fully aware of each director's possible doubts or restrictions. In that case, he/she can recommend an informative chat with an executive or even himself/ herself present new elements that are supplementary to the discussion. The chair's main goal is to optimize and facilitate the running of the meeting, including encouraging the directors who are less assertive, but who have a contribution to make in that specific debate, to take a position.

The chair has the option of postponing that decision in more extreme cases. This can be done, for example, when the chair believes that most of the board members do not have enough information, or have a biased perspective due to a preconceived position (the concept of framings will be discussed in Chapter 6). One of the interviewees explained the situation:

> Sometimes, as chairman of the BoD, you realize that the directors are not prepared to make that decision at the next meeting. So, you should step back, subtly remove that topic from the agenda, without negatively affecting the company. Of course, there are some decisions that cannot be left until later. But on the other hand, as chairman of the board, you realize that there is no advantage in taking the decision forward at that point, because it could lead to a wrong decision, a poorly made decision.

It seems that the majority of boards are not fully using available mechanisms for improving the quality of the board's decision-making. The research project of **Guerra, Barros and Santos**[9] explored three different decision-improvement mechanisms, and the results indicate that they are not that common among boards of directors. Graph 4.3 (see following page) shows that the majority of boards do not adopt the meeting interruption mechanism as suggested by the interviewee above. Further details regarding decision-mechanisms will be presented in Chapter 7.

From time to time, the chair's behind-the-scenes work ranges from "advance discussions" to dealing with a director requesting to change his/her vote on an item considered at an earlier board meeting. Sometimes this occurs for a legitimate reason: the director has just had a little more time to reflect and has changed his/her mind and may even present new items that contribute to the debate. However, on other occasions, the person is not sufficiently assertive at the meeting and afterward passes the problem on to the chair. It is a really sensitive situation. The chair cannot simply overlook the fact of having received this new information from one of the directors; on the other hand, the chair cannot reopen the

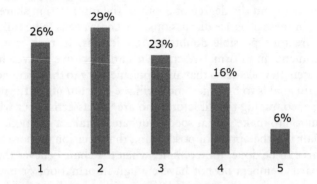

Decision improvement mechanisms not common yet

Survey Question: In order to avoid hasty decisions, does the board use a regular meeting interruption mechanism for coming back to the topic at a later time? (1) Never (5) Always

Graph 4.3 Meeting interruption mechanism adoption.
Source: Guerra, Barros and Santos (2020).

decision-making process for any pretext whatsoever. It is at this point that the chair of the board brings his or her ability to work behind the scenes into play, also after the event, as another interviewee says:

> I experienced this situation on a BoD with seven directors, I carried out a preliminary process to sound out a certain decision. I spoke to the board members individually and we made the decision. Two days later, one of them calls me up and says: "Look, I want to tell you that I have a reservation regarding this decision." At least at that moment I felt that the director regarded that concern as being very relevant. So, instead of presenting him with a counter-argument, I told him that I would hold another round of talks. I chatted with the other five again, calling each one of them, and told them: "We now have additional information to consider, which is of this type..." And all of the others said that they were not prepared to change their vote, as they did not consider the new information to be sufficiently relevant. When I went back to the board member who had presented his reservation, I conveyed everyone else's position, vote by vote, even mentioning a few phrases, but without identifying who said what. Since a few days had already gone by, he seemed to be less worried. The director had even presented me with an alternative, and when I informed him of the position of the others, he was finally convinced. This type of situation uses up a lot of the chairman's energy, but he has to know how to deal with it. It sucks, but it happens.

According to **Katharina Pick**,[10] in addition to offering and seeking input from the directors – both before and after the debate – as well as establishing clear rules for the decision-making process at board meetings, the BoD's chair also shapes the board's processes in order to enable efficient communication between the directors and the executives. The chair also defines his own role in relation to bridging the gap between the BoD and the executives, creating – or failing to create – an area of trust, cooperation and dialogue between the two groups. It is here, heading up the interaction between the board and management, that some of the most prominent tensions fall on the chair's shoulders (see also Chapter 3), without him or her even having the benefit of being able to share and delegate his or her tasks. For this very reason, **Kakabadse and Kakabadse** go so far as to state that the chair of the board occupies the loneliest seat in the world:

> "This may be the loneliest job in the world. Technically, the CEO reports to the chairman. By implication, the CEO discusses his problems with and is counseled by the chairman. The chairman has no such luxury. The chairman is held accountable by the board, by the shareholders and, by implication, by management. The chairman is alone."[11]

Chair of the BoD and CEO: Same Goal, Different Roles

Although most corporate governance codes around the world recommend structural separation between the positions of chair of the board and CEO, there is a heated argument in relation to this question, particularly in the United States, where it is still common for the same person to perform both functions. However, the G20's/OECD's Principles of Corporate Governance, which were revised for the second time in 2015,* make it clear that this separation is a good practice:

> "(…) the objectivity of the board and its independence from management may be strengthened by the separation of the role of chief executive and Chair. Separation of the two posts is generally regarded as good practice, as it can help to achieve an appropriate balance of power, increase accountability and improve the board's capacity for decision making independent of management."[12]

---

* First published in 1999, the G20's/OECD's Corporate Governance Principles have become an international benchmark in corporate governance and have been adopted as one of the Financial Stability Board's main standards for sound financial systems and were endorsed by G20 in 2015.

However, there are also arguments in favor of combining the two positions, including among others, the principle of a single command,[13] which would create better-defined lines of authority to which management (and even the BoD itself) would respond more effectively. **Sir Adrian Cadbury**[14] recalls that the two positions often arise together, given that the founder of a business typically successfully serves as both the chief executive and the chair of the board in its early years. But **Sir Adrian** himself cites the three main reasons for the roles of chair of the board and CEO being separated: (1) each position requires a different set of skills; (2) the chair is responsible for choosing and leading the team of board members, which by itself requires a lot of dedication; and, last but not least, (3) the combination of the two positions held by a single person makes it more difficult for the board to perform its role of supervising management.

Nonetheless, transitional situations may occur where there is a need for a single person to take over the company's helm. However, with the exception of these specific periods, if corporate governance requirements establish two bodies – the BoD and the executive board – what is the real justification for both of them to be headed up by the same person? In other words, what is the justification for such a concentration of power? Besides, despite arising together, as the company grows, the challenges and risks become even more complex and the decision-making process needs to become more robust. It is in this context that the contrast of perspectives made possible by the BoD becomes even more beneficial for mitigating the biases and pitfalls that can blind executives.

If these arguments were not enough, despite recognizing that the chair of the board and the CEO have the same overriding objective of encouraging the best performance of the business, there are other undeniable differences between the two roles. One image that clearly illustrates this difference is that of the CEO as the company's heart, "pumping energy," while the BoD is its soul, as it acts as its "conscience and moral guardian."[15] Another stance is that in well-run businesses there is – and there should be – a certain degree of creative tension between the board and management. "When this tension does not exist, it is a sign that someone is not fulfilling their obligations."[16] This is a point on which **Sir Adrian**, in his interview, also agreed:

> It is essential that the BoD's chairman succeeds in building a relationship with the CEO so that each one clearly understands his role. The chairman should not seek glory for himself, he should be concerned that the executives receive credit. The CEO will fulfill his mission if he can count on clear leadership regarding the company's purpose and strategy. If he gets support when he needs it and is supervised when it is necessary. We saw a good example of an absence

of this role when a number of UK banks faced problems, as the CEOs were allowed to adopt high-risk policies and the board did not fulfill its monitoring role. The CEO needs to know that it is not just the chairman, but that the board as a whole takes responsibility for helping him achieve the success desired by everyone.

For **Pedro Parente,**[*] who has worked in both positions during different periods, there can be tension in the interaction between the chair of the board and the CEO even in the most everyday activities. According to him, when it comes, for example, to the pace of the decision-making process, the CEO tends to favor speedy decisions, while one of the responsibilities of the chair of the BoD is exactly the opposite, in other words, to ensure that the decisions are taken collectively, with extensive discussion and the participation of all the directors:

> Over the course of my career, I was an executive for many years in both the public and private sectors, and it is really a challenge to step down from that position and start to lead a collective body, becoming a chair of the board. As the BoD's chair, first: you will no longer make decisions alone; second: you are not there to rush the decision – the essential thing is that it is made in the amount of time that it needs, after all the directors have expressed their opinions and taken part – in such a way that the best of that set of wisdom and experience is reflected in the decision-making. For me, that is the main difference. I would say that, when acting as the chair of the board, technical knowledge and accumulated experience are as important as the ability to lead a collective. This experience is a very rich one and it's very interesting: you succeed in changing your executive mindset to be the leader of a collective body and start working by influence rather than by imposition.

The Ten Commandments for a Good Relationship between the Executives and the Board and Its Chair

The quality of the interaction between the CEO and the chair of the board sets the tone for the relationship between the board and the entire management. However, the executives should make no mistake: the power is not only in the hands of the board of directors. Executives can play a leading role and make a difference with

[*] The author interviewed Pedro Parente in São Paulo, Brazil, on September 3, 2015.

their attitudes and initiatives, avoiding the need for many relationship discussion sessions so common between couples facing challenges. The following are some commandments to assist executives in building a better relationship with the board:

1. Do not complain too much and do not play the role of victim. In order to exercise influence, be proactive. To do this you need to understand the board's role. It is not a matter of being annoying: the BoD has an obligation to monitor the performance of the business and to oversee the work of the executives. This is beneficial, as it provides an additional element of risk prevention: if management is mistaken, the board is another layer to make decisions more secure.

2. Executives usually think that the board delays the company's operations and increases the amount of bureaucracy. It is necessary to recognize that the BoD is focused on the safest decision and needs inputs in order to take that decision. Since management is in control of all the facts, it can sometimes appear that the board is taking too long to reach a decision. Instead, put yourself in the board's shoes: without all the information you already have about the proposed initiative, would you feel safe in making an immediate decision?

3. Be thoughtful: the best answer may be "I don't know, but I will make an effort to find out." An attitude of honesty builds trust. Attempting to stall or even giving a superficial response will only reduce confidence. Only mature executives and those who are masters of themselves are able to say "I don't know." And this generates even more confidence among the directors. Stalling, not even in the worst of circumstances.

4. Don't fall into the overly operational board member's trap. Don't go into details and instead answer the questions in an objective way. But don't get caught up in an excessive amount of detail. The more details you provide, the more details you will be asked for. So, prior to presentations, review the material. Make sure you do not go beyond the right measurement for a board of directors, which should look at the forest rather than the trees.

5. If you feel that your board is in a bad mood with you, take the initiative: try to have a frank conversation with the BoD's chair, encouraging him to speak openly about what is bothering him/her or what is bothering the board.

6. Invest time and energy to prepare the material for the board. Most executives have not mastered the craft of preparing

well-drafted items for consideration by the board. How do you expect the BoD to approve an investment of hundreds of millions over a period of more than a decade with the information that it is receiving? Put yourself in their shoes. What would you need to know in order to feel comfortable about approving this proposal? Organize the process and surprise the board. The board secretary can be your ally in this undertaking.

7. Would you like to receive 50 pages to learn about something that you will have to decide in two days' time? So, take charge of the process of drawing up materials so that they arrive on average seven days before the BoD's meeting, or, at very least, giving your board members an entire weekend to analyze the material.

8. When you take the lead in preparing good materials in advance, you can afford the luxury of performing an important activity: namely, talking to each director prior to the board meeting. But don't use this conversation to lobby the board member. Use this time in a legitimate way, trying to explain your proposition and listening to any restrictions that the directors may have. And when you listen, you will really pay attention. This proactive approach also allows you to make adjustments to the proposal before the BoD's meeting, saving time and ensuring a more robust and comfortable decision process for everyone involved.

9. Do not underestimate the director who is not an expert on the business and who has no experience in your sector. For this very reason, he/she can bring an out-of-the-box view and identify factors that you – the expert executives – no longer see.

10. The BoD can be your ally. Make use of it, ask it for guidance and even listen to those who have positions that are very different from yours.

The Role of the Lead or Senior Independent Director

The practice of deploying one of the directors to act as the leader of the independent directors has been introduced in the United States and the United Kingdom. This role is given different names in each of these countries: **Lead Independent Director (LID)**, in the US, and **senior independent director (SID)**, in the UK. Although the roles of LIDs and SIDs have been applied in a slightly different way, in both cases the most commonly seen objective is to provide an appropriate balance of power in those cases where the CEO is also the BoD's chair. What is sought by adopting this practice is to preserve the board's independent decision-making capacity. The recommendation of the second revision of the **G20's/OECD's Corporate Governance Principles** is as follows:

> "The designation of a lead director is also regarded as a good practice alternative in some jurisdictions if that role is defined with sufficient authority to lead the board in cases where management has clear conflicts. Such mechanisms can also help to ensure high quality governance of the enterprise and the effective functioning of the board."[17]

In Spain, this goes beyond being mere good practice; Spanish law mandates that when a listed company's chair and CEO are one and the same person, the board must elect a Lead Independent Director. But LIDs/SIDs are not just a good idea in those cases where there is no separation of the roles of CEO and chair. They also can play a critical role, for example, in two other situations. First, when the board chairs are dominant shareholders whose interests may clash with those of other shareholders. One clear instance of this is the setting of remuneration for themselves or for management when members of the controlling family are executives. The second situation that is becoming widespread is the role of the LID/SID in large corporations where the chair, although independent, is so involved with management and the company that in a very short space of time they lose the necessary detachment from management that independent leadership requires. In such corporations, the chairs spend half of their time working at the company in constant interaction with management.

Additionally, the **Lead Independent Director** is responsible for giving voice to the concerns of the independent directors and he/she can also liaise with them, providing room for a more open discussion of their views or for exchanging information in advance. British Petroleum (BP)'s Senior Independent Director (SID) **Paula Rosput Reynolds**[*] offers another argument for **Lead Independent Directors**, noting that SIDs can help in situations of disagreement among directors by bringing another perspective to the table, helping to "ventilate" the sensitive topic. She gives the example of when a fellow director is the only one who is uncomfortable about a decision being endorsed by the chair. The SID can help diffuse

---

[*]   Paula Rosput Reynolds is an Independent Director at BP and non-executive director of BAE Systems plcand General Electric Company. She was the former chair, president and chief executive officer of Safeco Corporation, a Fortune 500 company. The author interviewed Paula Rosput Reynolds, in a virtual internet room, on August 11, 2020.

the dynamic of other board members "ganging up" on the dissenting director and reframe the discussion so that agreement is not capitulation. This intervention can help ensure that the dynamic of what's going on in the boardroom continues to encourage discussion of differences.

Another role for LIDs/SIDs is to interact with the institutional investors' **Environment, Social and Governance (ESG)** teams. It is different from the role played by the Investor Relations Department since the LID satisfies investors expectations of hearing from an independent voice. The topics covered under the so-called "investors engagement" are mostly focused on environment, social and governance concerns. **Paula Rosput Reynolds** explains her view regarding the SID's engagement with investors:

> You're there mostly to listen to people. You're not there to craft or defend the company's position in that discussion. Rather, you're there to act as a trusted, sounding board for shareholders. After I've met with a group of shareholders, I produce a matrix of the issues that shareholders raised. [It is] non-judgmental. It is simply the issues on shareholders' minds and the list is shared with the whole board or the relevant committee. What I think is very important is that the SID is not there to defend the company. The SID is there to be sort of a neutral sounding board and carrying those messages back to the board. The SID role also gives assurance to shareholders that they're not going to be argued out of their position. This neutral stance allows them to articulate their position. And everyone understands that someone from the company may come back to shareholders later and try to change their minds. But in the first instance, the whole encounter is merely to take in the input.

Given all of these circumstances and roles, the role of the LID/SID can be instrumental in ensuring that the BoD achieves its best performance.

The Chair of the BoD and His/Her Faithful Squire

Among good governance practices, there is a function, which can be of great use to assist the chairs of the board of directors in their work, particularly in the case of those (almost all) who have a very busy schedule. It is that of the so-called board secretary, who has also been called the governance secretary in some countries and who can actually become the chair of the BoD's most faithful squire. For this reason, it is recommended that he or she answers directly and exclusively to the chair of the board and that his or her role as a "neutral agent" is made clear to the entire organization.

The function can also encompass other activities and become the governance officer of the firm, being the guardian of its good governance in a broader sense.

The definition of rules about the board secretary's relationship with the chair and the board's members is of utmost importance in order to prevent the board secretary from facing conflicts and problems of delegation – which, in the end, would only increase the points of tension between the chair of the board and the other directors and between the BoD and management. One of the board secretary's goals is just the opposite: to reduce the potential for stress in these interactions. A good definition of a board secretary is "cotton between crystals," which shows that relationship skills and knowing how to navigate the levers of power, where high levels of vanity are not uncommon, is a matter of survival. Together, the chair and the board secretary make board meetings run smoothly and more effectively: "Essentially, the chairman is responsible for the board's functioning and conduct, while the board secretary takes over the mechanisms and processes of governance."[18]

The IBGC's Good Practice Guide for the Governance Department gives a more detailed definition:

> "The board secretary is the professional responsible for directly supporting all activities related to the functioning of the governance system, and it is vital that he operates with autonomy and impartiality in the interactions between the agents and the governance bodies and in the proposing of and/or implementation of processes that promote the best corporate governance practices."[19]

On top of this, the guide also spells out what the chairs' duties are, and what they can – and should – delegate to the board secretary to ensure the quality of the board's and its committees' workings. In addition to ensuring that the governance documents comply with the applicable regulations and legislation, the board secretary takes care of a set of tools with the aim of "guaranteeing agility in communication, providing transparency of information, giving the agenda predictability and facilitating access to governance documents."[20] Among the tools directly related to the BoD's day-to-day functioning, the document emphasizes the following:

Annual calendar of corporate events: Generally approved before the end of each financial year, its purpose is to synchronize the dates of the BoD's, the committees' and the executive board's meetings with those of the shareholders' general meetings, enabling the advance scheduling of all the participants, as well as making it possible to send in advance the information that is necessary for the efficiency of the decision-making process.

Meetings' Agenda and Annual Agenda: With the board secretary's assistance, the BoD's chair draws up the Meetings' Agenda and the topics to be discussed and/or resolved by the directors, in accordance with the executive board's demands and in synch with the shareholders' general meetings. The Annual Agenda's schedule is spread over the months and the board secretary can suggest current topics that are relevant to the strategic business context or to the best governance practices. In addition to disclosing the two agendas internally, the board secretary handles the follow-up of the outstanding issues.

Minutes of the board meetings: The board secretary is responsible for drafting the minutes of the board meetings in a reliable and clear way and these minutes should include the definition of deadlines and those responsible for the initiatives. The minutes of the board meetings are the main record of the BoD's proceedings and include statements, relevant requests and, in particular, dissenting votes and abstentions. On top of drawing up the minutes, the board secretary is also responsible for their internal and external disclosure, when necessary.

Items for consideration: Far from being a bureaucratic procedure, this document registers the topics that will be submitted for approval, demonstrating in an organized and objective way that the decisions are in alignment with the corporate strategy.

Governance portal: The website should provide – in a clear, concise and objective way – a set of information that is relevant to the decision-making process, as well as to the inspection and monitoring of the company's results, with the board secretary being responsible for the administration, maintenance and updating of the content and also for establishing the access profiles.

High Tension: Detrimental Types of Behavior

A number of the interviewees pointed out that, in addition to the natural difference in points of view that exists between the chair of the BoD and the CEO, other factors may end up creating tensions between the directors themselves. For example, one of them recounted the case of a board where the directors tried to build a relationship with the CEO in parallel with the chair's work. In the chair's absence, other directors tried to gain the CEO's sympathy, by making statements such as: "Ah, the chair is a real pain, he is this and that" or else "… yeah, the chair was really overly tough on you today. I don't think he understood your point well…". Obviously, there is no doubt that the CEO can have individual relationships with the other directors. However, everything has to be co-ordinated and trust has to be built up with the chair of the board, within a governance process closely overseen by him or her. The chair should make sure that the relationship between the BoD and management is an extremely professional one.

"Enlisting the CEO's complicity" and/or "speaking badly about the chair behind his back," are just some examples of the more harmful types of behavior that can occur among directors. The bulk of these detrimental attitudes, such as bullying, excessive vanity, parallel conversations, inattention caused by electronic devices and lack of preparation for meetings, have already been discussed in Chapter 2. The issue here is a different one: taking care that these types of behavior do not negatively affect the progress of the meetings is another of the chair of the BoD's tasks, given that this can lead to even more tension in the boardroom, as was the case with an excessively talkative director, according to the report from one of the interviewees:

> Overly talkative directors are a problem, but the chair of the board is the one who has to deal with the situation. It cannot be another board member. In the two cases that happened to me, the first time, I was aware of the windbag. So, I personally went to have an honest and respectful conversation with the chair and said: "Look, I can't make my best contribution and I'm not here to fight for room. I am asking you to see if there is anything you can do. But, if it is not possible, it is a very difficult situation, so, since I cannot contribute the way that I would like to, I would have to resign from the board". Shortly after that, I noticed that the person in question had improved a lot. So, I approached the formerly overly talkative director, I went to have coffee with him and to have a chat, and he relaxed. Sometimes this happens because the person feels insecure. On other occasions, it is because the person in question really is a windbag and thinks that the most intelligent person on that board of directors is the one sitting in his chair. That's a more complicated situation. The second time I faced this situation, I was the chair of the board and a director complained to me about another director's loquacity. At the next meeting, I asked the other directors to participate and I made room for everyone to speak. I tend to operate using this type of indirect hint, unless it reaches a point where it's unbearable. In this case, I give the overly talkative director some direct feedback, especially if there is an evaluation process of the board of directors.

On occasion, as well as concentrating on building the bridge with management and dealing with the sometimes detrimental behavior of the other directors, the chair of the BoD himself is the one who exhibits idiosyncrasies. Perhaps the most common type of misguided behavior among chairs, as already discussed in this chapter, is that of taking advantage of their power and of their leadership role to influence and steer decisions in accordance with their own interests – rather than in the best interest of the company and all its stakeholders. In this case, the chair is usually excessively present and assertive, condemning the board to a supporting role.

At the opposite end of this behavior – but just as harmful – is the case of a board chair who lacks more affirmative positions. For example, he allows the board to be dominated by one of his peers (in all likelihood the most talkative director) or even by the CEO, as a French respondent who experienced this type of situation on a BoD in his own country recounted:

> I have an example of a chairman who did not fulfill his role but allowed himself to be dominated by the CEO. All of the directors complained, as management was not really being challenged. The chairman of the BoD did not allow time for the other board members to express their opinion. He was absent, remiss and did not perform his function. So, the CEO took control, set the agenda and dominated the board.
>
> **What can a director do in the face of this type of behavior by the chair of the Board?**
>
> First of all, get together with the chairman and have a chat. Ask: why? You need to find out if the issue is a lack of experience or shyness or maybe the person does not know the business very well yet. Find out the reasons why and try to help. It is not difficult. I was once a board member where the chairman was like that. After six months, I decided that I should help. We had a meeting at which I explained the chairman of the board's role, how he needed to behave and how I could help. It worked. For example, when someone brought up topics that were off topic, I asked the chairman to summarize the main discussion, bringing him back to his role. At meetings, it is only natural that sometimes there will be parallel conversations, but it is necessary to say: "Okay, let's get back to focus and reach a conclusion before we move on to the next point". This is very important. With my 12 years of experience as an independent director or a consultant at publicly traded or family-owned companies, I know that if there is not good governance, there will not be a good chairman. For me, this is an absolute truth. The chairman of the board has to take the lead and ask the directors to participate, to make them more proactive, become more involved and get ready for

meetings. A board member who is silent is useless. It is interesting to study the chairman of the BoD's role because it is part of the regulations and since he is the one who puts best practices into action. All of this depends on the chairman of the board.

Along with excessively assertive or exaggeratedly negligent behavior, some other sins of board chairs were pointed out by **Sérgio Lires Rial.**[*] In his opinion, one of the ways to prevent or mitigate the most damaging effects of ineffective types of behavior, both on the part of the chair as well as of the other directors, is to adopt a systematic process of evaluation and feedback:

Besides excessive presence, which is capable of hijacking the debate, the chair of the BoD's second capital sin is, at times, being overly concerned with risk mitigation and not promoting the quality of the decision-making process. Another serious flaw is not being concerned with the mix of technical content and diversity within the board. The chair's fundamental role is to look at the board as a team and try to get the best out of it, either individually or on the basis of the group's composition. The fourth sin is a lack of feedback. The chair rarely gives or receives any feedback. I do not think that such feedback should be restricted to an annual assessment. The assessment should not come as a surprise, it needs to be much more dynamic. There need to be other points of contact throughout the year. The chair of the board turns to another director and says: "I felt that, on this issue, you were either not engaged or felt uncomfortable... what happened, what was missing?" Or the chair observes that the board member has not been prepared for the meetings. In the feedback conversation, he may become aware of the individual's specific temporary problematic situation. But if the failure carries on, I think that a good practice is to have a much clearer discussion about the number of boards that this person should take part in. It is best to spell out the criteria before the person joins the board. In my experience, this sort of prior agreement works very well: what are the board's expectations of you and then go on giving systematic feedback. Unfortunately, I have not seen this improvement with continuous assessment.

---

[*] Sérgio Lires Rial has ample experience as an executive and as a director both in Brazil and abroad, he is currently Banco Santander's CEO in Brazil and a member of Delta Airlines' BoD. He was the bank's chairman when he gave this interview. The author interviewed Sérgio Lires Rial in São Paulo, Brazil, on September 11, 2015.

Opening the Black Box: Evaluation of the BoD

The importance of board assessment processes has been recognized and a number of corporate governance (CG) codes already require that a formal review be carried out on a regular basis. In France, the Netherlands and the United Kingdom, for example, the requirement specifies that an assessment of the BoD should be carried out at least every three years with the participation of an independent consultant. By adopting a systematic and independent evaluation process, the board of directors, being the central hub of the organization's governance, sets the example that the willingness to continuously improve is a value to be pursued by all of the company's other levels and instances.

Nevertheless, there are still companies where the main obstacle to the systematization of this initiative is the presence of controlling shareholders, family members, founders or ministers as board members, given that the assessment can be viewed as an embarrassment for them. In his interview, **Pedro Parente**[*] points out that this remains one of the reasons for the continued resistance in relation to board assessments:

> If there was a prior declaration: "Don't worry, we will carry out an assessment, but the assessment will be positive", every company would evaluate the board. But since there is always the possibility of a negative assessment – and, if there is no possibility of this, then there is no point whatsoever in carrying out the assessment – there is resistance. Sometimes, among the directors there is a lack of humility to accept being evaluated: "Look, we are the company's highest body. So, by definition, we are excellence personified. Why carry out an assessment if we already know that this is an excellent board?" The view is that if they have been invited to sit on a board of directors, the question of their performance or suitability has already been settled. That is why, once again, the chair of the BoD's role and the way in which the evaluation is carried out is very important. The sensitivity and ability of those who deliver the results individually to each director has to be very refined. You need to have what we call an honest but respectful conversation.

Whether for this reason or for another, **Guerra, Barros and Santos'** research shows the existence of a certain polarization in relation to the periodic assessment of boards: while 36% of the 340 board directors acting in 40 countries state that their BoDs never carry out periodic assessments or that they do so at intervals of more than three years,

---

[*]   The author interviewed Pedro Parente in São Paulo, Brazil, on September 3, 2015.

another 44% declare that the practice is carried out on an annual basis for their boards, as shown in Graph 4.4.

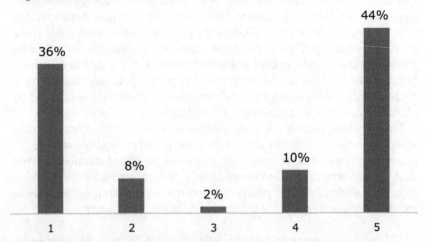

Regular evaluation of BoDs is not yet a common practice

Survey Question: The board carries out a regular evaluation of its performance

1 (never)
2 (at less frequent intervals)
3 (every three years)
4 (every two years)
5 (annually)

Graph 4.4 Board evaluation existence.
Source: Guerra, Barros and Santos (2020).

Even though there is still some resistance – explicit or veiled – in relation to board assessment processes, at least among the world's largest corporations, this practice is increasingly being adopted, as is revealed by an analysis of the proxy statements of the companies that make up the Fortune 100[*] ranking that was carried out in 2019. Published in the **Harvard Law School Forum of Corporate Governance**, the study was designed to examine how the leading companies in the United States are improving and communicating the assessment process of their boards of directors to the stakeholders. Of the total of this select sample, 73% carried out an assessment of their BoDs last year and 27% used or considered using independent third parties to facilitate the process. According to this task, investors, regulators, CG experts and other stakeholders

---

[*]   The Fortune 100 sample includes the 100 North American publicly-held companies, which occupy the top of the Fortune 500 ranking, which is made up of the 500 companies with the highest annual turnover in the United States.

are continually challenging organizations to examine and explain the performance and composition of their boards. According to the authors, we are seeing the emergence of a new corporate mantra:

> "Indeed, many stakeholders note board effectiveness and composition as a top priority and foundation for long-term value creation and sustainability. Boards are listening. They are enhancing their evaluation practices, addressing the need for increased board diversity, expertise and effectiveness, and better communicating their work to investors and other stakeholders. Continuous improvement is the new mantra—for boards, and also management, talent and companies themselves. Boards should embody—and their disclosures should reflect—this mantra."[21]

It is also the case that most of the companies that adopt the process of assessing their boards end up recognizing that they benefit from this move. In a study carried out by **Deloitte** with 271 directors,[22] 81% of them agreed with the statement that the board performance assessment influences future changes. In the report of **PwC**'s annual survey with the chairpersons of boards,[23] 57% of them stated that, as a result of the issues identified in the board's assessment, steps were taken over the next period that improved the BoD's performance. Among the main changes made are: seeking experts with complementary skills to join the board (35%), changing the composition of the committees (30%), increasing the BoD's diversity (17%) and changing the board's composition, in other words, not reappointing one of the directors for the next period. Although it is not the most common development, this can actually occur, as one of the interviewees with international experience on boards recounts:

> In the "360-degree" assessment, as we were getting close to the end of the BoD's term of office, in my role as chair of the board, I asked for a specific individual performance assessment question to be included. Each of the directors had to answer whether or not each of the others should remain according to his or her perception of their performance. The first time we did this, there was no indication of any problem. Because, as chair, if one or two point out an issue, I also assess whether or not that is part of the tensions resulting from the interactions. But the second time we did it, when half of the board pointed out the same problem in relation to the same director, then I knew that an issue had been identified and that I needed to take action. The feedback session with him was not easy. At first, he seemed shocked because he would not be reappointed to the board. But afterwards he acted normally, completed his term of office and even contributed again. It was an excellent learning experience for the group.

Although the results are not always so drastic, **Luiz Carlos Cabrera** states that the assessment of the board, when supported by individual feedback, also proves to be very useful in behavioral changes. According to him, in this area, the most common failures are long-windedness, a lack of preparation for meetings and the excessive anxiety of the directors, particularly the chair of the board. However, the assessment process can make the group more cohesive and even enable one director to support the other:

> Normally, protocol requires the BoD's chair to provide feedback, but some chairs ask the consultant to take part in order to ease the situation. The most common corrections I have seen are regarding long-windedness – there are some people who love the sound of their own voices, any question is transformed into a dissertation for a master's degree. The second type of behavior that changes the most is the lack of prior preparation. I experienced a very awkward situation in relation to this. I was assessing a chair, who was the company's founder and its majority shareholder, and I asked: "Do you arrive prepared for the meetings?" And he said, "I am prepared. It is not that I prepare for the meeting, I am already prepared." So, when the behavior is one of arrogance, the board member is god's teacher, then it is more difficult to change. There is also the anxious type, who cannot wait for his moment to speak and ends up almost revealing his own decision before listening to others. This is a defect that is easier to deal with than that of arrogance. In the case of anxiety, I suggest, for example, that the person choose a guardian on the BoD. When he begins to exhibit the inappropriate behavior, the other person just puts his hand on his arm and the individual becomes aware that he is anxious. It helps in making the change, I've seen it change a person. It was a tip from an English director, who told me: "The person who can most help a director is another director". Because, sometimes, the consultant helps the person to become aware of inappropriate behavior, but he will not be there at the time to help with the mechanics of avoiding the behavior.

The assessment of the BoD can be carried out in four dimensions – separately or simultaneously (see the box) – with multiple combinations appropriate to the context or situation being experienced at that time by the BoD. Depending to a large degree on the stage of maturity of governance, the assessment may be restricted to the members of the board or it may also include the external view of the members of the committees (who are not directors) as well as that of the executives. It is still very rare, but it is possible – and, at times, desirable – to give investors a voice as well so that they can state their opinions regarding the performance of a certain company's board of directors as shown in Graph 4.5.

Outsiders not yet heard in the evaluation process:

35%	17%	7%	41%
Just the board members	Board members and executive officers	Board members, executive officers and other stakeholders investors or other interested parties	Not applicable

Survey Question: Indicate who the evaluators are:
Just the board members
Board members and executive officers
Board members, executive officers and other stakeholders (investors or other interested parties)

Graph 4.5 Board evaluators.
Source: Guerra, Barros and Santos (2020).

The specific characteristics of the model adopted are not paramount. However, two common points are essential. Firstly, the involvement of an external independent professional ensures the impartiality, confidentiality and objectivity of the process. And secondly, as **Alexandre Gonçalves Silva**[*] says, we should not lose sight of the fact that the assessment is a tool for improving governance:

> After doing three or four assessments, the people who remain on the board become more objective. They state what really matters to improve the group or the person. It is not criticizing for the sake of criticizing, the aim is to improve. Furthermore, I think that the assessment should always be done by an external consultant, because in the conversation between the consultant and the individual there is greater freedom, a better environment. I have seen many directors change as a result of the assessment. I remember a board member who was the leader of a committee, who was criticized as a committee leader, not as a board member. In the committee, he did not provide much room for discussion and wanted to resolve matters in his own way.

[*]   The author interviewed Alexandre Gonçalves Silva in São Paulo, Brazil, on February 19, 2016.

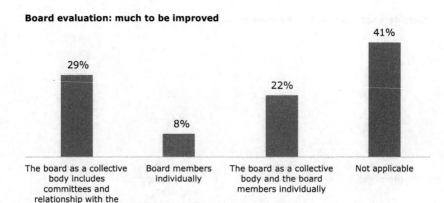

Board evaluation: much to be improved

Survey Question: Indicate what the subject of the evaluation is:
• The board as a collective body (includes committees and relationship with the executive board)
• Board members individually
• The board as a collective body and the board members individually

Graph 4.6 Board evaluation scope.

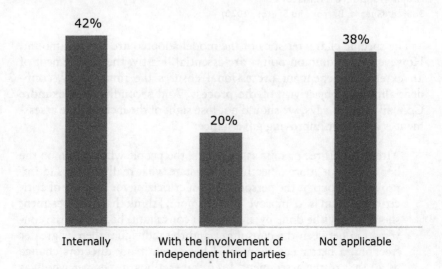

Survey Question: Indicate how the evaluation is done:
• Internally
• With the involvement of independent third parties

Graph 4.7 Board evaluation method.
Source: Guerra, Barros and Santos (2020).

At the next committee meeting, he talked openly with staff about it and dealt with the issue with incredible maturity. I think the board's assessment is an excellent tool to help the BoD mature. Otherwise, it does not mature. When you are not made to face the problems, you do not learn. Difficulties are the things that teach us the most.

Board Assessment: How, Who, Why?

1. What are the main drivers of the BoD's assessment process?

   As the organization's central governance body, the BoD should be seen as an example of the search for continuous improvement, but there are more specific objectives such as:

   - To make the decision-making process robust and, therefore, reduce the risks of the decisions adopted;
   - To align the BoD's structure with the strategy, recognizing the transformations required to continue on the right path;
   - To harmonize the relationship between the BoD and management, increasing efficiency by identifying synergies;
   - To improve the BoD's interactions with committees, investors and other stakeholders;
   - To create value through governance, increasing internal efficiency and improving external perception.

2. What can be included in the assessment process – together or separately?

   Board, as a collective body:
   - Structure and composition;
   - Roles;
   - Functioning: processes and governance department;
   - Dynamics;
   - Interface between the board and committees;
   - Interface between the board and management;
   - Behavioral aspects involved in the BoD's performance;
   - Chairmanship of the board.

   Committees:

   - Structure and composition;
   - Roles;
   - Functioning: processes and governance department;
   - Dynamics;
   - Interface between committees and the board;

- Interface between committees and management;
- Coordination of the committee.

Board Members:

- Individual self-assessment;
- Peer review;
- Skills, characteristics and attributes.

Benchmark:

- Comparison of selected practices with best practices;
- Comparison with national and international peers from the same industry and/or that are admired.

3. Who participates in the board's assessment process?

Depending on the context of the business and the level of governance maturity, the following may take part:

- Just the directors;
- Committee members who are not directors;
- Executives;
- It is still rare to include investors' views and expectations in relation to the BoD and the company's governance.

4. How is the board's assessment process carried out?

Two tools are most often used in the assessments: (1) electronic surveys and (2) personal and confidential interviews in which each interviewee has the opportunity to spell out his or her opinions and perceptions about each topic.

It is in these personal interviews, taking advantage of the confidentiality guaranteed by someone who is independent, that the board members open up and discuss the most critical points experienced on the BoD, suggesting possible opportunities for improvement.

At the end of the assessment process, the board should hold an in-depth discussion regarding its results and draw up an action plan with deadlines and the assignment of responsibilities. The chair of the BoD is responsible for monitoring the plan's implementation and providing the board of directors with feedback in relation to the progress of the proposed improvements over the following year. In addition, if necessary, with the support of an external professional, the chair provides feedback to the individual directors. This is also an opportunity for him to receive more detailed feedback from his peers.

The BoD's assessment processes, especially those whose model involves a 360-degree evaluation among the board members, can also be of great use to help the board's chair mature. According to a survey,[24] the development of boards' chairs involves three alternatives: feedback from the board, regular participation in networks of chairpersons and opportunistic learning. However, the study acknowledges that out of the three the development tool that has the greatest impact is that of peer feedback.

It is in this equal exchange with their peers that the BoD's chairs help – and are supported – in the construction of a favorable environment so that everyone – directors and executives – can make their best contribution to the sustainability of the business. Because this is a cooperative cause, **Sir Adrian** even compares the board's chair to a conductor – he is the one who conducts and orchestrates the means for the group to achieve its best performance. But he recalls that, besides being a conductor, "chairs have to be their own composers and they cannot be sure in advance what tunes their soloists will play or whether they will perform at all."[25]

Perhaps that is why some prefer to compare the chair of the board to a jazz musician – one who is capable of creating the best improvisations, based on the deepest technical knowledge mastered by the group of musicians.[26] Orchestra conductor or jazz musician, the trait that best characterizes his performance at the head of the board is the ability to lead and get the very most out of the group – either under ideal conditions of conformity or in the most critical moments of disruption. Therefore, in addition to occupying the loneliest seat in the world, one study[27] points out that in the face of potentially disruptive events, it is also the BoD's chairperson who is often "(...) the catalyst for boards to 'call out the issue' and has a critical role in maintaining strategic leadership and alignment in times of discontinuity and uncertainty." But, far beyond the disruptive moments, most of the day-to-day events in the business' management are already enough to keep the chairperson of the board and the other directors awake at night, as will be seen in the next chapter.

Now the chair of the board from the case at the start of this chapter explains how he managed to come up with a decision that ended up satisfying everyone:

> *One of the points that made me resist the decision to fire the CEO was precisely my assessment that a number of directors had made a hasty and superficial judgment. Harold had well above average technical skills in the sector, had strategic vision, management skills and was really well liked and respected by the company's team of employees. The context experienced by the company had been very*

unfavorable. Would another CEO have achieved the same result as Harold?

I didn't want to impose my vision, but I knew that, as the BoD's chairman, I had a particularly important role in that difficult situation. I had to ensure that we made the best decision, whatever that may be. I looked for a decision process to address the issue in an objective and in-depth way. Instead of looking at our CEO as an isolated problem, I tried to introduce the search for strengths and weaknesses into the discussion dynamics and address each of the limitations identified in the CEO one-by-one. By this means, I got the board to exhaustively consider the possibilities to compensate for his shortcomings. Otherwise, as the majority of the board of directors already intended, the only solution would be to replace him. But if that turned out to be its ultimate decision, we would know that it had been taken after an exhaustive process in which all prospects and possibilities had been considered.

So, he wasn't the best in the financial area. Did that alone disqualify him? Was there anything that could be done to compensate for this limitation? More than presenting answers, as the chairman of the board, I conducted a questioning process, attempting to extract the answers from the directors. One of them suggested hiring the best finance executive to mentor Harold. The questioning also led to the conclusion that he was very good in the technical area, but he was overstretched. In this case, immediately, one of the directors presented a proposal: "Okay, so we will hire someone to provide him with more support in this area." He needs to be a more assertive leader, to communicate better and to make his strategy clearer? Okay, so let's find the best coach for him. This detailed analysis of Harold's limitations as well as of his strengths and potentials ended up leading the BoD to the decision to renew its bet on his performance.

In this way we evolved throughout the process until the first positive results began to emerge and the BoD's confidence in Harold started to recover. He even gained the trust of one of the representatives of the private equity funds, who was able to overcome his initial negative perception. Instead of simply discarding him, we addressed his limitations over a period of two years. In the process the board realized that the set of qualities that enabled Harold to achieve important results in the past were worth hanging on to. In 2017, when we finally carried out the IPO, the stock was quoted at $ 30, and three years later it had increased to $ 120. It's amazing how much value Harold was able to generate both for himself and the shareholders. When he retired last year, no one else remembered the former criticism of his performance. As a chairman of the *board, this was an important learning experience for me on how to shape the decision process to make it much more objective, always recognizing the fact that the board may be hijacked by distorted views or become prey to situations where rationality does not rule.*

Notes

1 Kakabadse, Andrew; Kakabadse, Nada. *Leading the board. The six disciplines of world-class chairmen.* Nova York: Palgrave MacMillan, 2008.

2 Guerra, Sandra; Santos, Rafael Liza. *Headaches, concerns and regrets: What does the experience of 102 Brazilian directors tell us? Private sector opinion 39.* Washington, DC: IFC, 2017. Available at https://www.ifc.org/wps/wcm/connect/topics_ext_content/ifc_external_corporate_site/ifc+cg/resources/private+sector+opinion/headaches%2C+concerns%2C+and+regrets+-+what+does+the+experience+of+102+brazilian+directors+tell+us. Accessed on May 21, 2020.

3 Nadler, David A.; Behan, Beverly A.; Nadler, Mark B. *Building better boards: A blueprint for effective governance.* São Francisco: Jossey-Bass, 2006 *apud* Guerra, Sandra. *Os papéis do CA em empresas listadas no Brasil.* Master's Thesis in AdministrationFaculdade de Economia e Administração (FEA)/University of São Paulo (USP). 2009. Available at http://www.teses.usp.br/teses/disponiveis/12/12139/tde-11092009-141955/. Accessed on April 18, 2021.

4 PwC. The 'missing middle': Bridging the strategy gap in family firms, 2016. Available at https://www.pwc.com/gx/en/family-business-services/global-family-business-survey-2016/pwc-global-family-business-survey-2016-the-missing-middle.pdf. Accessed on June 25, 2020.

5 Russel Reynolds and Associates together with the IESE business school – survey of corporate governance practices in European family businesses, Summer 2014. Available at http://www.russellreynolds.com/sites/default/files/europeanfamilybusinesspaper.pdf. Accessed on August 4, 2016.

6 Lechem, Brian Chairman of the Board. *A practical guide.* Hoboken: John Wiley & Sons, 2002.

7 Guerra, Sandra; Barros, Lucas A.; Santos, Rafael L. Decision-making in boards of directors: The roles of meeting dynamics and choice architecture. *Research Project,* 2020.

8 Cadbury, Adrian. *Corporate governance and chairmanship – a personal view.* Oxford: Oxford University Press, 2002.

9 Guerra, Sandra; Barros, Lucas A.; Santos, Rafael L. Decision-making in boards of directors: The roles of meeting dynamics and choice architecture. *Research Project,* 2020.

10 Pick, Katharina. Around the boardroom table-interactional aspects of governance, PhD Thesis in Organizational Behavior, Harvard University, 2007.

11 Kakabadse, Andrew; Kakabadse, Nada. *Leading the board. The six disciplines of world-class chairmen.* New York: Palgrave MacMillan, 2008, p. 15.

12 G20's/OECD's Corporate Governance Principles. Available at https://www.oecd-ilibrary.org/governance/g20-oecd-principles-of-corporate-governance-2015_9789264236882-en. Accessed on June 10, 2020.

13 Leblanc, Richard; Pick, Katharina. Separation of chair and CEO roles. Importance of industry knowledge, leadership skills, and attention to board process – director notes, August 2011. Available at http://www.yorku.ca/rleblanc/publish/Aug2011_Leblanc_TCB.pdf. Accessed on August 24, 2016.

14 Cadbury, Adrian. *Corporate governance and chairmanship – a personal view*. Oxford: Oxford University Press, 2002.

15 Kakabadse, Andrew; Kakabadse, Nada. *Leading the board. The six disciplines of world-class chairmen*. Nova York: Palgrave MacMillan, 2008.

16 Lechem, Brian Chairman of the board. *A Practical Guide*. Hoboken: John Wiley & Sons, 2002.

17 G20's/OECD's Corporate Governance Principles. Available at https://www.oecd-ilibrary.org/governance/g20-oecd-principles-of-corporate-governance-2015_9789264236882-en Accessed on June 10, 2020. p.51

18 Harper, John – Chairing the Board. *A practical guide to activities and responsibilities – institute of directors*. London: Kogan Page, 2010.

19 Instituto Brasileiro de Governança Corporativa (IBGC). *Boas Práticas para Secretaria de Governança*. São Paulo, 2015. Available at https://conhecimento.ibgc.org.br/Paginas/Publicacao.aspx?PubId=20996 Accessed on May 21, 2020.

20 Ibid.

21 Klemash, Steve W.; Rani, Doyle. *Evolving board evaluations and disclosures*, published on October 2, 2019. Available at https://corpgov.law.harvard.edu/2019/10/02/evolving-board-evaluations-and-disclosures/. Accessed on June 26, 2020.

22 Emea-Deloitte – 360 Boardroom Survey. Agenda priorities across the region — Study carried out with 271 directors from 20 countries in Europe, the Middle East and Africa, June 2016. Available at https://www2.deloitte.com/content/dam/Deloitte/ch/Documents/audit/ch-en-emea-360-boardroom-survey-agenda-intercative.pdf. Accessed on August 30, 2020.

23 PWC. Boards confront an evolving landscape – PwC's annual corporate directors survey 2013. Available at https://corpgov.law.harvard.edu/2013/10/11/directors-survey-boards-confront-an-evolving-landscape/. Accessed on August 30, 2020.

24 Kakabadse, Andrew; Kakabadse, Nada. *Leading the board. The six disciplines of world-class chairmen*. Nova York: Palgrave MacMillan, 2008. This study involved directors and senior executives from more than 12 thousand companies situated in 17 countries.

25 Cadbury, Adrian. *Corporate governance and chairmanship – a personal view*. Oxford: Oxford University Press, 2002, p. 79.

26 Coutu, Diane. Why teams don't work. An interview with J Richard Hackman. In: *HBR's 10 must reads on teams*. Boston: Harvard Business School Publishing Corporation, p. 21–34, 2013.

27 Henley Business School; Alvarez & Marsal. *Boards in challenging times: Extraordinary disruptions leading through complex and discontinuous challenges*. Available at http://www.alvarezandmarsal.com/sites/default/files/am_boards_in_challenging_times_research.pdf. p. 9. Accessed on July 14, 2016.

Chapter 5

What Keeps Board Members Awake at Night?

Chapter Summary

- Directors are permanently immersed in a context of serious decisions that are often made in environments of great uncertainty and/or ongoing attempts to reduce risks.
- Although it may be viewed as a "decision-making machine," this process in the board of directors (BoD) is also subject to human beings' inability to think and act in an exclusively rational way.
- Guerra and Santos' research highlights the decisions that most frequently cause directors to lose sleep, including among others, particularly those related to the hiring and firing of Chief Executive Officers (CEOs) and transactions involving the company's sale, merger and acquisition.
- Based on interviews and market studies along with more recent academic studies, an examination is made of the various aspects of these decisions and other factors of influence, such as low objectivity due to overenthusiasm regarding the propositions.
- Do's and Don'ts with guidelines for dealing with excess optimism on the part of both executives as well as directors.
- Another major cause of insomnia are ethical issues, which are discussed with the interviewees, who recalled some illustrative cases.
- The chapter starts off with discussions based on the following topics: What corporate challenges and dilemmas will we face over the next few years in light of the increasingly unstable and changing outlook? What are the potentially disruptive events that represent the greatest threat to the continuity of the business? What will be the role of board members in this future scenario?
- This chapter caselet covers the tension and uncertainty of taking one of the most difficult decisions of a board: firing the CEO when all is well with the company, except for the CEO's behavior.

One of the most complex and difficult situations I have ever faced as a director was the sacking of a CEO. This is never a simple decision ... There are always a lot of factors involved. The worst nightmare is the possibility that you fire one CEO and you end up hiring another one with even more disappointing results than the first. So, try and imagine what it is like to discuss sacking a CEO who has achieved excellent results in terms of running the business. There were 11 of us who had a seat on the board of a listed US food corporation that had only recently made an impressive turnaround after a long period of stagnation and losses.

Already a veteran executive and having been with us for just under two years, the CEO was heading up the company's turnaround process. Phillip acted quickly and did what needed to be done: cutting and downsizing the cost structure, selling off the less profitable businesses to boost cash and invest in the more successful enterprises. Operationally, he was very good and his management, in addition to bringing a breath of fresh air to the company's administration and renewing it, was well received by investors. Those last two years had seen an increase in trading volume and in the value of our shares on the New York Stock Exchange (NYSE).

Everything was fine, except for one detail. Those of us who were on the board had already noted that our CEO demonstrated a very unclear boundary between his personal interests and those of the company. Without projecting the slightest sense of discomfort, he made it clear that most of his focus was on his own compensation. Since the business was well on the way to recovery and doing so at a rapid pace, he made it clear that he wanted the biggest possible bonus – no matter the cost. In addition, the way he used the company's money contravened our expenses policy. He seemed to think that the rules that all the rest of us followed did not apply to him. It was as if he was saying: "I am saving the company US$ 100 million. Who cares if I travel first class?"

In the United States, you have to disclose the CEO's remuneration and, if he infringes the company's policies, and if he authorizes unjustified expenses, this amount has to be disclosed. You cannot make exceptions. At first, we assumed that he might not have properly understood that the rules applied to everyone and that, therefore, the board should clarify the behavior that it expected from him in the future. Even when the situation became a recurring one, the board members were still divided: some of them thought that it might be possible to make an exception, to sweep the whole thing under the carpet. This group was concerned about one thing above all. They felt that the market would not react well to the announcement of the CEO being sacked. Were we giving up on the turnaround? Who fires a CEO who achieves such positive results?

However, others – and I included myself among this group – were of the opinion that, by overlooking the CEO's transgressions, in addition to being complicit with the CEO's breaking the rules, we would be sending the wrong signal: "When you are caught doing something wrong in this company, the board members look the other way." The BoD's silence would encourage unethical and even illegal behavior by other employees. And it could make the CEO even more aggressive in his demands: "I am this company's savior and the board of directors needs me so much that it is willing to ignore the rules. What else would the directors overlook in order to keep me here?" As far as I was concerned, this was the sort of responsibility that we faced. Our decision revolved around our CEO's integrity.

*While we spent months on end on an inconclusive debate, new facts suddenly caught us by surprise. The board received a very specific anonymous internal tip-off: the CEO had traveled first class again, this time to Paris. There, under the pretense of a business engagement, he had met up with a personal friend and paid the entire cost of a very sophisticated dinner – In excess of US$ 50,000, including all the travel expenses – which was unjustifiable under the company's policy. All the employees knew the rules. When you are the CEO, you live in a house with a glass ceiling and glass walls. That was a concrete sign regarding our CEO's integrity. And the report was a very detailed one. It was already known in-house that he was practically stealing from the company. At that point, the issue became a priority; it was necessary to put an end to our sleepless nights and resolve that dilemma very quickly.**

If there is one of the board of directors' (BoD) duties that best exemplifies its performance, it is the responsibility for making strategic decisions in the organization. Without a doubt, the BoD is the corporate decision-making machine, and a large part of the success – or failure – of companies, lies in this process. Awareness of the relevance of this everyday responsibility for business results would, by itself, be reason enough to cause a good deal of stress. However, this strain is magnified by the fact that the decision-making process is always wrapped up in a scenario of internal and external uncertainties – both for the company as well as for the individuals themselves. A number of researchers have already tried to address this issue, including among others, **Thuraisingham and**

---

* The conclusion of this story will be presented on page 155 of this chapter.

Lehmacher, who argue that the decision-making process is always very imprecise because:

> "We are not as skilled in decision making as we like to believe we are. Besides while we would like to believe that organisations are largely built on ideas of rationality, they in fact operate in irrational ways because it is people that are tasked with making organisations work, and people bring emotions with them. However even when people appear to act in irrational ways, they are generally irrational in a systematic way, that is ways that are related to their thinking habits. This is why decisions make for fertile ground for much to go wrong –one's personal filters, bias, preferences, values and beliefs get in the way and result in decisions that may not be as skillful as they could be."[1]

Permanently submerged in this context of serious decisions taken in very uncertain environments, sleepless nights seem to be a common factor in board members' stories. In a survey conducted by **Guerra and Santos**[2] with 102 Brazilian directors, the interviewees listed the main factors keeping them awake at night (Graph 5.1) and then described the most difficult decisions they had dealt with at the meetings of the boards on which they serve (Graph 5.2).

Main reasons why board members experience sleepless nights

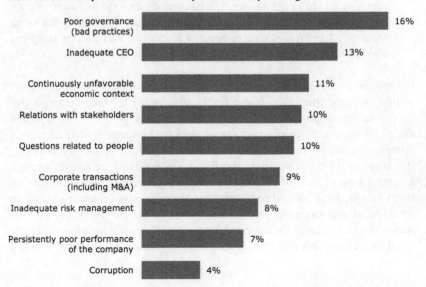

Graph 5.1 The issues that keep board members awake at night: top nine answers representing 88% of those chosen from 13 alternatives.
Source: Guerra and Santos (2017).

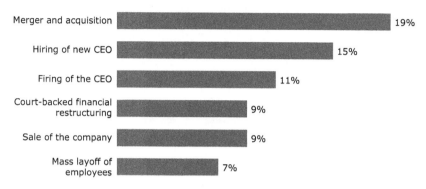

Most difficult decisions taken as a board member

Graph 5.2 The most difficult decisions: top six answers representing 70% of those chosen from 15 alternatives.
Source: Guerra and Santos (2017).

In the following two graphs (Graphs 5.3 and 5.4 – see following page), it is interesting to note a slight variation in the answers to the same question, according to gender and the degree of independence declared by the board members themselves. For example, among independent directors, the most difficult decision is usually related to the sale of the company (77.8%), while for non-independent directors the most sleepless nights are caused when mass layoffs are being discussed by the board (75%). The main causes of concern among male directors were split between hiring/firing the CEO (37%) and mergers and acquisitions (23%). Among female directors, the biggest headache is usually caused by merger and acquisition processes (38%).

A research project conducted by **Guerra, Barros and Santos,**[3] in 2020 among 340 directors from 40 countries, found that, although the uncertainties and complexity of the business environment continue to grow and at an ever-faster pace, 82% of those interviewed admit that the decision-making process usually involves a certain degree of resistance to different approaches presented by new board members. Furthermore, Graph 5.5 (see page 143) indicates that 30% of them stated that when they are dealing with complex issues, their BoDs do not come up with creative and innovative solutions, while 35% are neutral.

In addition to board meetings often being stuck in a rigid ritual of routines,[*] the board may get bogged down on operational issues and the past. The survey *Directors: dedication of time inside and outside*

---

[*] The concept of "habitual routines" developed by Gersick and Hackman will be covered in Chapter 6.

Most difficult decisions according to gender and independence

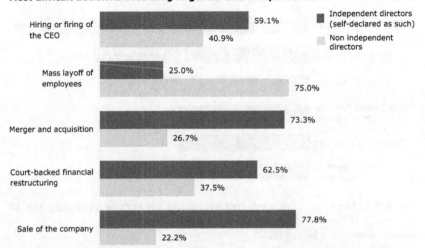

Graph 5.3 The most difficult decisions according to director independence: top five answers chosen from 15 alternatives.

Source: Guerra and Santos (2017).

Most difficult decisions according to gender and independence

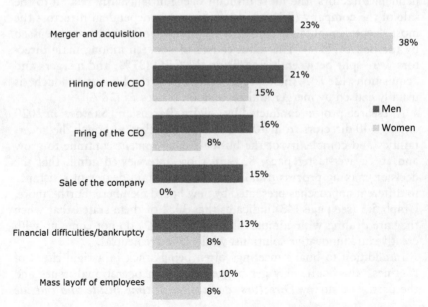

Graph 5.4 The decisions regarded as most difficult according to gender: top six answers chosen from 15 alternatives.

Source: Guerra and Santos (2017).

Quality of board decisions

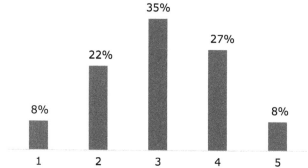

Survey Question: When it addresses complex issues, the board usually comes up with creative and innovative solutions
(1) I totally disagree (5) I totally agree

Graph 5.5 Creativity and innovation.
Source: Guerra, Barros and Santos (2020).

boardrooms,[4] published in 2020 by **Better Governance**[*] collected responses from 103 members of 238 boards. These revealed that 46% of board meetings' time was focused more on analyzing the past than on the vision of the company's future. Almost half of the board members (47%) admitted that 30% of the time for discussions at meetings was spent on topics that should be restricted to management.

M&A[**]: More Adrenaline Than Results?

Anyone who has attended meetings that precede major merger and acquisition transactions knows that the atmosphere is dominated by a huge amount of tension and emotion. On those occasions, all the adrenaline released in the final contest of any sporting event can be easily raised to the umpteenth power. Face to face at the conference room table, those dozen or so bankers and lawyers experience hours at a stretch of all the things that are part of an exciting film – only in real life. It is a mixture of emotion, fear, competition and anticipation of the thrill of a possible victory. Perhaps this explains the willingness of these professionals to work non-stop on an agreement for up to 48 hours, without returning home. Sometimes without even stopping to eat. This sea of adrenaline,

---

[*] A consulting firm specialized in corporate governance that provides support for the improvement of the CG model and adoption of the best CG practices. The author is a founding partner of Better Governance.
[**] Mergers and Acquisitions.

of course, affects both the managers of the acquiring company and those of the company being sold, including the executives and board members. Those who buy relive the feeling of history's conquerors, with the exquisite pleasure of the business world. Even if this is never spelt out, buying is winning the battle and subjugating the party purchased.

But, certainly, by itself, this overdose of adrenaline would not be able to justify the accelerated growth in M&A activity all over the world. The justification behind M&A activity is usually based on a list of factors, including among others the expectation of a rapid acceleration of business growth, cost reduction, gains of scale, conquest of new markets and increased offerings of products and services. This is the rational explanation for why, in 2018, global M&A transactions totaled US$ 4.1 trillion and, in the following year – despite registering a slight decline – JP Morgan's Global M&A Outlook report assessed the level of activity in this market as follows: "Despite increased concerns of an economic slowdown (...) the appetite for large transformative deals overall was still strong among corporates in 2019."[5]

However, what raises the suspicion that there are other reasons – besides rational ones – to foster the continuous growth of merger and acquisition activity is the fact that traditionally these transactions have registered dubious results. The story is already an old one: with regard to M&A transactions, back in in 1981, in the annual report of his company Berkshire Hathaway Inc., the legendary investor **Warren Buffett** stated:

> "Many managements apparently were overexposed in impressionable childhood years to the story in which the imprisoned handsome prince is released from a toad's body by a kiss from a beautiful princess. Consequently, they are certain their managerial kiss will do wonders for the profitability of Company [Target]... We've observed many kisses but very few miracles. Nevertheless, many managerial princesses remain serenely confident about the future potency of their kisses-even after their corporate backyards are knee-deep in unresponsive toads."[6]

Another pioneering assessment of a sample of 107 companies from around the world that had closed the 700 largest M&A deals between 1996 and 1998, indicated that success and the perception of success can be different. One year after the transaction, 82% of the respondents were convinced that the deal had been a success. However, upon a deeper investigation, it became clear that 45% of those transactions had not been formally reassessed during that period. Therefore, that initial positive response was more reflective of an individual's feelings than of an objective fact. The same study applied an objective criterion for measuring results and came to the following conclusion: 83% of the M&A operations had failed to generate more value for shareholders. This negative effect was later confirmed by a number of other studies; with one of these studies reaffirming that 60% of mergers and acquisitions do not succeed in delivering the promised value.[7]

However, in 2020 a number of studies already pointed to a slightly less optimistic tendency – or, at least, a somewhat more balanced one – on the part of the executives and a more proactive role of the directors in supervising M&A transactions. The seventh annual study into M&A trends published by **Deloitte** in 2020 analyzed responses from 1,000 executives of North American companies and private equity investment (PEI) firms. Among those who were interviewed, 82% said that their BoDs actively supervised M&A negotiations, but only 4% expressed an expectation that there would be a decrease in the pace of mergers and acquisitions. Nevertheless, almost half of them admitted that the most recent transactions had not generated the expected value, as per the report *The state of the deal: M&A trends 2020*:

> "Despite general optimism for M&A in the year ahead, challenges remain as dealmakers faced diminishing ROI on transactions in recent years. Of all dealmakers, 46% say that less than half of their transactions over the last two years have generated the expected value or return on investment."[8]

Among the external causes of this failure, executives cited economic (32%) and market forces (30%) and, among the internal reasons, they pointed to the fact that sales (30%) and profitability expectations (28%) were not met, as well as, among others, failures in due diligence (24%) and the inability to align the organizational cultures (20%). Among the factors that, according to them, boosted the success of the M&As, are: effective integration (20%), accurate assessment of the target company's value (20%) and consistent due diligence process (13%).[9]

One of the hypotheses to explain the continued pace of M&A deals, despite the considerable historical record of failures, is excess pride (the hubris hypothesis[10]): the executives of the acquiring company regard themselves as being more competent than those of the acquiree. Arrogantly, they nourish the mistaken belief that they will manage and maximize the assets of the acquired company better than its current managers. Fortunately, this is not always the overwhelming factor, as narrated by one of the directors interviewed:

> In an acquisition proposition, there was an obvious opportunity to generate value, but there was also a clear doubt regarding the integrity and ethics of the company that was being purchased. The business was in another country, with another culture and other values. There were 12 directors, six of whom were independent, and there was a clear difference of opinions. The financial opportunity

was obvious, mathematically demonstrated on a spreadsheet. On the other hand, there was the incalculable; it was the lack of cultural fit between the two companies. If we didn't make the purchase, the money would be on the table. At the start, the group of directors linked to the controlling shareholder and the CEO thought the acquisition should be made. The rational argument was that those who buy can quickly impose their culture, their values and change the people. You can do whatever is necessary to achieve conformity with what you think is right. For me and three other directors, this view underestimated the cultural complexity of the acquired company. The idea is you will send an army, you will put a brigade inside the acquired company and you will be able to solve everything. That is not the way things work. From the moment the acquisition is made, the buyer's reputation is at stake. The one who ended up playing a decisive role in the process, was the CEO who changed his view during the process ... Despite being on the side of the controlling block of shareholders, he was very assertive and took a firm stand against the purchase. I mean, with all those ethical and reputational doubts, to go ahead and make the acquisition with the board split was, at the very least, very, very risky. And that ended up being the right decision.

Too Much Enthusiasm, Too Little Objectivity

Even so, the CEO described in the previous account can be considered as the exception that proves the rule. In most of the M&A proposals presented to BoDs, linked to the hypothesis of pride, the trend among executives tends to veer more toward excess optimism and confidence, overestimating their own ability to generate high returns. Researchers argue that one of the characteristics of overconfident CEOs is that they keep their stock options until the expiry date. As they don't diversify their own portfolio, they trust in the quality of potential merger projects.[11] In this case, on average, they are more likely to propose M&As that increase the business' diversification, particularly if the company can finance the acquisition internally and/or has untapped credit capacity.

This was the conclusion of a study that was carried out in the United States,[12] which analyzed M&A decisions made between 1980 and 1994 by Forbes 500 companies. This result was very similar to the one obtained by the study that was conducted in Brazil by **Barros and Da Silveira**. According to the two researchers, extremely confident and optimistic CEOs have a greater tendency to:[13]

- invest more;
- carry out more mergers and acquisitions;
- accept projects with a lower expected profitability and, therefore, undertake worse mergers and acquisitions.

As a consequence, Barros and Da Silveira also point out four other characteristics resulting from the excess optimism of these CEOs:

- greater indebtedness of the company;
- payment of lower dividends;
- preference for variable compensation;
- frequent buyback of the company's own shares.

On the other hand, it is only natural when proposing an M&A deal to the board of directors for the CEOs to be enthusiastic: obviously, they would not put a proposition before the board that they did not trust. However, it is also natural that the directors are expected to put a limit on this optimism. It is necessary to be aware of executives' biases and to maintain objectivity. "Don't fall in love with the idea", as one experienced board member usually recommends. The category of overconfidence biases and the impacts of optimism will be covered in Chapter 6, and how to deal with these, in Chapter 7.

M&A: Warning Signs

Thuraisingham and Lehmacher identified what they call "warning signs," indicating that excess optimism had gained a seat on the board table. According to these authors, biases of enthusiasm are jeopardizing the quality of the decision-making process in a merger and acquisition process, when:

- there is unanimous agreement without much debate;
- there is a forecast of remarkably high growth;
- there is a lack of systematic risk assessment, particularly of the intangibles;
- the decision-making timetable is a short one;
- there is a marked emphasis on the positive aspects of the M& A deal;
- there is euphoria surrounding a large transaction;
- the due diligence process was rushed and insufficient;
- the risk approach is inconsistent.[14]

It is important that the board and management establish ex ante criteria that need to be met in order for the transaction to qualify for consideration. This initiative will maintain the necessary level of rationality as it becomes crystal clear to all the actors involved what the parameters and limits are that need to be considered. The clarity in the kick-off analysis process prevents each proposal from being treated as an exercise in opportunism, rather than a rational consideration of the transaction in light of the company's strategic goals and the likely totality of other transactions that the company might pursue. Approving a well-articulated set of criteria that has to be met before anything else is probably the greatest contribution the board can make to ensure that management acts in line with the strategic drivers increasing the success of an M&A deal.

One of the recommendations of the **National Association of Corporate Directors (NACD)**[15] for dealing with very optimistic CEOs is to ensure that the debate is based on objective and factual data. In addition, it is very "important to understand if value creation is realistic based on market conditions." These objective contributions built on each director's expertise add a multifaceted perspective to the discussion. Productive debate emerges in this space open to contradictory opinions, and the best decisions become possible. Which is exactly what happened on a BoD which altered – with success – the course of an acquisition, as a director recalls:

> I prefer not to go into specifics as to exactly what the deal was, but we were making an investment, a very important acquisition. At the board meeting at which the proposal was initially presented, the CEO and the chairman of the board, who is also the controlling shareholder, were enthusiastic. For them, at that point, the transaction was practically already a done deal. The board had six members, four internal directors and two independent ones. And one of the independent directors, who had experience in the capital market, made the following proposal: "Look, why not change the outline of the deal, why not change the shareholding structure that the company will have in the target company?" The initial reaction was neither negative nor immediate assimilation. The reaction was not like, "OK, your contribution is accepted." It was more like, "Let's see if there is any merit to what he is proposing". Then there was what I call the "political canvassing" stage. Our CEO often uses this mechanism. During the pre-deliberation phase, he talks with and listens to the board members a lot. All informally, like: "This is the direction we are going in... We are thinking about doing this ... this, this and that." When the director who is an expert in the capital market made this point at the meeting, one of the internal board members also wanted to talk, and a debate got underway, because he had other comments to make. So, for the acquisition that was going to have structure X, the directors proposed structure Y and Z and, after the in-house debate, it was not X or Y ... It ended up being XYXZ, which was a hybrid based on our conversations and debates. Then the deal moved forward and has now been presented more formally to the BoD. All inputs were taken into account and a path was constructed – and they were very relevant aspects, they were important additions to the discussion.

Board Members: How to Deal with Excessive Managerial Optimism

In order for board members to be able to deal more effectively with the excess optimism of executives, in addition to the set of behavioral resources and tools that will be presented in Chapter 7, there are some good recommendations that can be put into practice immediately. The following suggestions were developed by **Professor Lucas Barros** for the purpose of promoting objectivity in the relationship between the BoD and the CEO and can be applied particularly during the prior discussion stage and shortly after a merger or acquisition has been carried out:

During the proposal's deliberation, it is recommended that the directors:

- Counteract the risks to the manager's optimism;
- Request more detailed and substantiated studies;
- Exercise skepticism, consistently asking questions;
- Consider the possibility that the CEO may have his/her own biases;
- Make sure that collective decisions are less affected by biases;
- Challenge the propositions in a constructive way;
- Select projects carefully so that they are aligned with the shareholders' interests;
- Ensure a safer decision-making process.[16]

In the implementation of the project, the directors assume the roles of supervision and support:

- Monitor the project's implementation: exercise stricter supervision, if the manager's performance is biased;
- Make sure that there are no relevant changes without further ratification by the BoD;
- Inform the manager in a clear and timely fashion of any concerns and provide advice.[17]

Executives: How to Limit Their Own Excess Optimism

The directors are not the only ones who have to tackle excess optimism in the board rooms. All the suggestions made up to this point also serve as points for CEOs to consider. In addition to these and a set of resources addressed later on in Chapter 7, there are also some other more specific recommendations that can be implemented so that the executives themselves can avoid the blindness caused by the rush of enthusiasm. These suggestions are not mutually exclusive; on the contrary, they can – and should – be implemented simultaneously:

- The CEOs should make sure that the proposals put before the board are the result of collective perspectives on the part of the executive board. Each executive has his/her own expertise and contribution to make, and the CEO's role is to listen and mull things over. To remain sincerely open to the contributions from the team itself and then to practice the same listening skills at the BoD meetings. And the CEO is the one who should make sure that it is a collective decision.

- The CEOs should frequently – and honestly – ask themselves the following questions: "Is there room for all the executive officers to put forward contradictory opinions?"; "Am I in the habit of allowing and also encouraging the executive officers to make their contribution openly, even when it is contrary to my view?"; and last but not least: "Do I keep myself open to questions from both the executive officers as well as the board members?"

- It is healthy to practice what one of the directors interviewed in this chapter referred to as "political canvassing": pre-deliberation conversations between the CEO and the directors – on a one-to-one basis. These are discussions aimed at the exchange of ideas and the identification of possible contributions. Conducting "political canvassing" doesn't mean the CEO is organizing some sort of plot or exerting pressure to get a favorable vote for the project. The "political canvassing" is an open conversation between the CEO and each of the directors aimed at designing the best project and reaching the best decision with everyone's contribution. It is a dialogue, not a monologue.

- After the "political canvassing," the CEOs can still fall back on the **"devil's advocate"** exercise. They present the board members' contributions to their team and designate one of the executive officers to get ready to "attack" the project. Meanwhile, the others look for arguments to support the position in favor of the proposition. At the end of this exercise, it is possible that the team of executives, instead of feeling overly proud and optimistic, will be thinking more clearly when it forwards the proposal to the BoD.

CEO: Hard to Hire, Assess and Sack

Adding together the second and third place responses to the **Guerra and Santos'** survey[18] (hiring the CEO: 15% + sacking the CEO: 11%) put the overall topic of replacing the company's main executive in the first place, with 26% – ahead of M&A (19%). It's no wonder. The board members' most important task is to ensure that the organization is under the leadership of the right CEO since this decision has a direct – as well as indirect – impact on all the business areas and dimensions.

For this reason, choosing a CEO, planning his/her succession or finding an emergency replacement has been the constant cause of a lot of headaches for board members. It must be precisely for this reason that 52% of the 783 directors interviewed in **PwC**'s survey,[19] declared that the CEO's succession should be given even more attention by their BoDs. Although it involves uncertainties and can be a painful process for the parties involved, changing the CEO has gradually become more frequent. According to the CEO transitions report by **Spencer Stuart**,[20] between 2009 and 2019, the total annual number of CEO transitions among the 500 companies that make up the S&P500[*] rose from 46 to 56, an increase of almost 22%, with the highest incidence occurring among the companies that are included in the S&P100[**] (25%).

Boards experience considerable uncertainty surrounding the CEO's replacement even when an agreed succession plan is in place. No matter how well planned and anticipated, this decision faces a number of difficulties: some of which are more objective, such as issues related to compensation, while others are more subjective. Some are even downright emotional, as will be seen below in the accounts of some respondents. The complications start off with the traits of the leader's profile: no matter how diverse and fine-tuned the assessment tools that already exist, there is no way to avoid a significant degree of subjectivity in this process. Dilemma: how to identify the right CEO for that specific moment of the business cycle and who also matches the company's particular cultural characteristics? The best fit between CEO and company involves factors that are neither objective nor measurable.

It is commonplace for questions and dilemmas of another type to arise at board meetings when discussing the performance of a CEO who has been in charge of the operation for some years. For example, the board may have identified areas where the executive needs to improve his/her performance. Dilemma: in that case, should time and money be invested in

---

[*] Standard and Poor's 500 (S&P 500) – the stock market index that includes the world's 500 largest companies that are listed on the United States' main stock exchanges, the NYSE and the Nasdaq.

[**] S&P100 – the index that brings together the S&P500's 100 largest companies.

the CEO's development or will the board regret in a year's time that it has put off the decision to replace him/her? Another possible situation is that of the CEO who does not produce extraordinary results but has an average performance track record. Dilemma: since the process of selecting and choosing a new CEO is a complex and subjective one, isn't there always the chance that the next one will also have a below-average performance?

When Family Is Involved, Everything Becomes Even More Complex

To make all of this even more complicated, complex and subjective, there are circumstances where in addition to all these questions and dilemmas you have emotional factors. The directors realize that the sacking of the CEO will be one of the hardest blows of that professional's career; this decision is never cold-blooded and of course a rational one. As it is common that the years of coexistence create affective ties, it is usual for this decision to be put off for as long as possible. They are all waiting for an assurance that they will never have, since, by its very nature, this is a decision that is surrounded by uncertainty.

These emotional issues become even greater in family businesses, as one director recounts, also showing a real situation of a lack of fit between the company's profile and that of the CEO – no matter how good their skills may be:

The company had just implemented corporate governance practices ... And, on the board of that family business, I and another independent director began to speed up decisions, we structured the processes better with strategic planning, budgets ... and then the business started to grow faster than the CEO could keep up with. He was 54 at the time. He was the founder's son and he held the position of CEO and chairman of the BoD. This stage was not even the most complex one: it was not that hard to convince him to continue just with the board of directors. As there were no successors ready among the third generation, our idea was to bring someone in from outside. Initially, there was marked resistance from the entire family: "How can we have a stranger as the group's CEO, heading up family members who are executives and being subordinate to the chairman, who is the former CEO?" The selection took a long time. The other independent director and I were leading the process; we didn't want to make any mistakes. The person chosen was an excellent executive with international experience. And to sum up a long story in a nutshell, the first year was brilliant; but in the second year, things began to fall apart ... The new CEO lost his enthusiasm. Looking back, I think that maybe this was our mistake: we hired a very competent

CEO, with an excellent resumé, who had already worked outside the country, but who had no experience whatsoever with a family business. We, the independent directors, even tried to give him more room, but we were unable to avoid the family's involvement in the day-to-day routine. Sometimes, there was even interference by the chairman of the BoD, who had previously been the CEO ...

What was it like until you reached the decision to fire that CEO?

It was very complex. It took up a lot of our agenda ... There were so many other issues to discuss at the BoD, but it turned out that this was what most took up our time – not just at the meetings, but also outside of them. When we spoke to the family about the need to change the CEO again, their first reaction was a negative one: "Can't you help him? He is serious, honest, hardworking. It was so hard to find one... Now we don't want to fire him. We trust him, we even have a certain fondness for him." Then, when the external scenario deteriorated, the results got even worse ... until the day when sacking him could not be put off any longer.

Was he replaced by another outside executive?

No, the family wouldn't accept another outsider. So, this second phase, after sacking the CEO, was even more difficult, much more complex. It was necessary to manage the family by returning to management. The new CEO was one of the third generation of the family and skipped development stages. But, amazing as it seems, it turned out to be a good solution. Since the biggest risk was his professional immaturity, we decided to hire two coaches. Why two? One for the behavioral aspects and the other one for the technical ones. And it was very good. He responded very well, he wanted to prove that he was the right CEO for the family's business. He proved to be, but it took time.

For this reason, over and above technical competencies, **Ira Millstein**[*] emphasizes the qualities of the human being as those that make the greatest contribution to the best performance as a CEO or a board member (also see Chapter 1). In **Millstein**'s view, the first requirement is that, in addition to having the ability to distinguish what is right, the person has the courage and the willingness to act in accordance with his/her values. To give an example of this, **Ira** recalled an episode from the early 1990s,

---

[*]   Ira Millstein, corporate lawyer and a senior partner at Weil, Gotshal & Manges, is one of the most highly regarded corporate governance experts in the United States and headed up the committee that drafted the OECD's – Organization for Economic Cooperation and Development's – Corporate Governance Principles. The author interviewed Ira Millstein in New York, United States, on March 31, 2014.

when General Motors' board of directors publicly replaced its CEO, at a time when this sort of public decision was nearly unprecedented:

> General Motors had a typical big company public board comprised of highly regarded individuals who were leaders in their fields. Following with the customs of the times, however, they did what other boards were also doing – which was, in general, to defer to management. Accordingly, when they confronted a crisis, following tradition, they mostly followed management's advice. This time, however, the crisis seemed to threaten the whole company and the board realized that it might well be time to change management and find a new direction. Yet, they were confronted by the fact that boards didn't publicly dismiss large public companies CEOs. Even a dramatic changing of management was usually accompanied by nice words and a handsome package. I don't remember at the time instances where it became publicly known that management was not performing and had to be changed. This time, the board knew that the time for change had come and they went about what was, for them, the unpleasant prospect of publicly bringing in new management so that the departure of the old was rather obvious. For them, this was unchartered waters and quite a break from tradition, especially for one of the largest corporations in the United States. They recognized that it would create a public stir and that they might well be criticized, but they did it courageously.

This GM episode was a milestone and it became a textbook case in corporate governance, since, from that point onwards, the process of changing the CEO began to be seen as something legitimate and even expected from BoDs when the CEO's performance is poor. This concept also applies when there is a mismatch between his strategic view and that of the shareholders or even when there is a slip in relation to the practice of values. Of the 56 CEOs who were replaced in 2019 among S&P500[21] companies, 13% of them resigned under pressure. Therefore, although it is complex, painful and still gives directors a lot of sleepless nights, the discussion about the possibility of replacing the CEO is becoming increasingly common in board rooms. **Robert Monks,**[*] who has always been critical of the performance of BoDs in the United States, is of the opinion, particularly in times of crisis, that the decision should not be postponed:

---

[*]   Robert Monks is a co-founder of Institutional Shareholders Services and the author of books such as *Corpocracy* and *Watching the Watchers*. The author interviewed Robert Monks in Pelican Hill, Newport Coast, California, United States, on September 13, 2013.

When performance is poor, in an emergency situation, what can the board members do? They cannot manage the company, they cannot hire a person who will magickly will fix everything ... What they can do is go to the managers and say: "Your performance is bad and we are losing shareholder value". It is necessary to make a decision, even if it is to liquidate the business. The managers have to hear the words: "We are going to suggest to the shareholders that the company be closed down." This is what can clear everyone's mind.

However, the conclusion of the episode that began in this chapter indicates that, no matter how complex it may be, it is better to deal with the dilemma and take a decision regarding the CEO – even if the company is performing well under his/her leadership, such as in Philip's case:

After receiving the internal tip-off, our first step was to hire a law firm to investigate the expense reports submitted by Phillip since he was first hired. Everything was passed on. A thorough investigation of the trip to Paris was carried out. We had to protect ourselves against any future lawsuit by him against the company. The CEO's dismissal had to be substantiated and documented. One of the lawyers managed to talk to the guest at that dinner in Paris, and not even he regarded the event as a professional engagement. Unfortunately, Phillip had made his expense report and presented it to the company as such. It was proven that this was not a one-off misappropriation, it was a pattern of behavior.

Based on this evidence, the directors' main focus of concern shifted to the market. We knew that we would be harshly criticized for firing a successful CEO. Without openly discussing the question of integrity, which we did not intend to do in order to preserve the individual's reputation, the market would not understand our reasons. The stock's price would drop sharply. In the opinion of the investors, we should be severely punished for letting go of that manager. The impact of that sacking could put a heavy strain on the board.

There were many direct and indirect negative consequences. To support us in this, we hired a corporate communication consultancy. The CEO's integrity would not be called into question. The company focused the announcement on the best angle: the dismissal did not involve differences in the business strategy. In addition, management was not willing to backtrack on the company's turnaround, which was not yet complete and would continue with another CEO. At the same time, we had also hired a search firm to start the selection process for a new executive as soon as possible.

Having taken all the precautions and with the help of our lawyers, we had a meeting with Phillip. The facts revealed by the investigation were presented, including the testimony of his friend, stating that he did not consider that dinner in Paris as being part of any business dealings. Of course, he insisted otherwise, but our lawyers immediately moved on to the details of the termination agreement. We didn't pay him much, in fact; we even managed to get him to return some money from unjustified expenses. As far as the market was concerned, there was no question in relation to Phillip's integrity. A mutual agreement was reached and the process was announced regarding the hiring a new CEO. Even so, as the board of directors, we were severely criticized and the share price registered a significant drop. That was a very difficult decision, but the board has to be ready to do what is right. Eventually, after a few months, with the company's performance continuing to be on track and showing good results, the stock rebounded and even began to climb again. The company's strategic restructuring continued to be successful even without Phillip.

Independence and Ethics Go Hand-in-Hand

As harsh as it may seem, **Monks'** suggestion that there should be strict transparency in the relationship between the directors and the CEO can pave the way, precisely, for very positive attitudes. **Mervyn King**[*] recalled the episode of a CEO who, when faced with a necessary – and painful – decision, demonstrated absolute independence of conscience. It was a global textile company's subsidiary in the southern hemisphere that was not coping with the Asian competition. It would have to be closed down, the losses would have to be covered, the creditors would have to be paid off and 3,700 people would have to be fired, including the CEO. According to **King**, the CEO insisted on being present and taking a stance at the board meeting in favor of closing the factory, explaining that he himself saw no alternative for the operation:

> On that day, I learned that independence is more a state of mind than any other factor. At the meeting, that CEO managed to be more motivating and positive than anyone else. That was when I learned that we have to be aware of our own interests in order to exclude them from the focus. You have to go into the board room with a clear mind.

---

[*]   Mervyn King is chairman emeritus of the GRI (Global Reporting Initiative). King, who is a South African with a distinguished career as a supreme court judge in that country, chaired the King Committee on Corporate Governance, which produced South Africa's governance code. The code, the King Report on Corporate Governance is an international reference already in its 4th edition. The author interviewed Mervyn King in New York, United States, on April 1, 2014.

In addition to the historic change of GM's CEO in the 1990s, **Ira Mill-stein**, in his interview, recalled two other occasions on which the decisions made by the boards of directors became paradigms. Apparently, initially, it would even be possible to conclude that the directors were making a decision against the company's own financial interests. One such episode was the recall of Tylenol* by Johnson & Johnson. In addition to the high cost, there was also a risk that removing Tylenol from supermarkets and pharmacies might damage the image of the company's other products on the shelves. However, J&J's board of directors preferred not to give priority to reputational risks at that time In the end, this decision reinforced the brand's positive perception for the future. Another example he cited was the decision to stop selling cigarettes by the CVS** chain, with hundreds of pharmacies spread throughout the United States. In **Ira**'s opinion, even if CVS lost money in the short term, abandoning the sale of tobacco products was the right thing to do:

> In business, there is always a day when a big problem arises, and you have to act, or not. At this point, you depend on knowing how to identify what is right and taking action. This requires that the board has independent directors who understand the nature of the business. Good directors need to have an in-depth knowledge of who the stakeholders are, appreciate the nuances of the business, be independent and, at meetings, pay close attention and dedicate the time needed to lead. If you could ask Adrian [Cadbury], I'm quite sure he would say the same thing. Everything I said beforehand is a necessary prerequisite, but the only decisive factor is being able to take the right action when the time comes.

At board meetings, exercising independence requires that board members have a "backbone," in other words, they are able to express themselves firmly, even if this is uncomfortable or even if there is a risk of losing their seats on that board, as one of the board members who was interviewed in the United States explained. According to him/her, to lead is "to make decisions guided by what is right, but with the flexibility of those who know that they are not always right." With this in mind, the director is in a better position to choose which battles are worth fighting, as another interviewee explained:

---

* In 1982, in the Chicago area, seven Americans died after taking Tylenol pills that had been maliciously poisoned. J&J voluntarily recalled the drug in the United States and later re-launched the product with safer packaging.

** When it announced in 2014 that it was permanently discontinuing the sale of cigarettes at its pharmacy chain, CVS lost estimated annual revenue of US$ 1.5 billion. This decision took seven years to be taken and implemented.

One of the worst battles I faced as a board member involved ethical issues. An acquisition proposal to expand the business was presented to the BoD which had 11 directors – two of whom were independent, including myself. In my view, the source of funds for this investment was not completely clear and transparent. I mean, it was not obvious to me that everything was absolutely crystal clear and correct, both in terms of the source of the funds as well as the investment in the new project itself. Then, the proposal was discussed a number of times and, as far as I was concerned, the answers were never satisfactory. I asked for further studies to better support the decision. But the board did not want to accept dissent, it wanted the decision to be unanimous. Then the second internal relationship problem arose in the BoD. I was independent and represented minority shareholders, yet the majority demanded that the decision in favor of the deal be unanimous. Then, they registered the minutes saying that it had been a unanimous decision. I didn't sign them. I demanded that the minutes be altered. Either they were altered and my reservations would be included in the minutes, or I would not sign them. They altered the minutes because I stuck to my guns: they didn't want to pay the price of me making my disagreement public, or resigning from my position on the board and explaining the reasons. I most definitely was not going to sign those minutes under any circumstances. There are some battles that, when the subject involves ethics and values, it is not possible to go along with things, it is zero tolerance. You have to fight and not compromise …

There was another independent director, what stance did he take?

Yes, there was another independent director… sometimes, we managed to align ourselves, work together on the issues, but in this specific case, he capitulated. On a BoD of 11 directors with only two being independent ones, it is very hard not to be alone. When you have three or four, the situation changes a bit. My recommendation is that at least a third of the directors on the BoD should be independent ones. And that this one third of independent board members also come together to form a position of mutual support. It is not to set up a scheme, it is to make it possible for the board to be more than just a channel for approving decisions. The point of the BoD is to discuss and seek the best decision. And, in order to make the best decision, the voices have to be active. A good director has to be firm enough, but also flexible when it is necessary.

There are times when very personal – even intimate – issues come into play in the decisions taken in the board room. An American who was interviewed told the story of a director who was forced to step down

from the BoD of an insurance company because he had aggressive behavior with his family and he hid it. There was a meeting which that
board member had to attend by phone and everyone noticed that he was
more aggressive than usual. That evening, the CEO, who also held the
position of board chair, saw media reports that the board member had
been arrested for abusing his wife. This explained his physical absence
from the meeting. After some debate, a decision was made to ask him to
step down from the board: "He had the opportunity to tell us what had
happened, but he chose to hide the truth. The trust was broken. It was
not possible to keep him on as a director."

Undoubtedly, this is an extreme case: the issues of the board member's
personal life had to be debated by the BoD in order to make a decision
regarding the integrity of his behavior – current and future. However,
there are circumstances in which the director may find himself/herself in
a stalemate position in the decision-making process – when the director's
personal beliefs come into direct conflict with the most logical analysis.
A good example of this situation is narrated below, involving a board
of directors 70% of whom were young professionals, representatives of
investment funds in the business:

> The proposal involved the purchase of a large area where the com-
> pany had previously invested $9 million. What was being decided
> was the continuity of the project. On the BoD, on one side there were
> the entrepreneurs who had created the business. And on the other
> side, as the majority shareholders, there were the directors who rep-
> resented the funds. There was nothing illegal, no doubt in terms of
> compliance in relation to the investment. It was an extremely poor
> region. The project would bring in more than $ 110 million and
> could lead to significant positive social changes. But it was also an
> ecosystem that was already degraded, which was at the start of a
> recovery phase. That was the doubt. There was no way to measure
> and assess whether the project would produce socio-economic devel-
> opment for the local population in the future or whether there could
> be more environmental damage.
>
> The founders wanted to get out of the investment, realizing the
> losses. But, for the funds, the deal was interesting for the return, with
> a remote prospect in of reputational risk. To stop at that point would
> mean losing the money that had already been invested there. The
> most likely outcome was that there would be a conflict, setting out
> the difference in worldview between the entrepreneur board members
> and the board members representing the funds. However, one dis-
> tinct factor steered this decision-making process in a different direc-
> tion. Most of the directors elected by the investors were very young,
> around 30 or 35, and were raising families with small children.

They brought to the discussion their personal views in favor of preserving the environment: despite the preferences of the funds, they voted against the new investment and the continuity of the project. Among these young board members, the individual's view, their conscience prevailed. So, the company divested, decided to get out of the region and realized the loss. Despite the fact that financial logic indicated the opposite. The victory was that of the view of the younger board members who were concerned regarding environmental issues and with the legacy for their children, but targeting the future of all children. The fund's immediate return came in second place. Conscience won the day. The environmental concern was stronger among these young directors, who did not even prioritize the potential positive externality that the project would generate on the social front, benefiting the local population with the investment. So, at the end of the day, I still can't say: "Regarding that project we did the best." It may still be that we will regret that decision one day. ...

Decisions involving ethical issues and the practice of individual values are certainly among the most complex ones made by board directors. However, the survey by **Guerra, Barros and Santos,**[22] that was carried out in 2020 in 40 countries, indicated that most of the directors (66%) believe that the boards on which they serve have never made any ethically questionable decisions, but 34% of them do not have this same degree of comfort and expressed having some degree of ethical disagreement in the decision-making process, according to the figures shown in Graph 5.6.

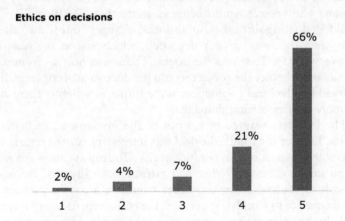

Ethics on decisions

Survey Question: Do you think the board makes decisions that, from your point of view, are ethically questionable?
1 (often) 5 (never)

Graph 5.6 **Ethically questionable decisions.**
Source: Guerra, Barros and Santos (2020).

Even Worse Is Regretting the Decision

Regret for decisions made is not such an unusual sentiment in board-rooms. According to **Guerra and Santos'** survey,[23] in relation to the same five decisions that respondents considered to be the most diffi-cult (M&A, hiring a CEO, firing a CEO, mass layoffs and sale of the company – Graph 5.1), they were asked if, after knowing the impact of their decisions, they would take another approach if they had it to do all over again. In answer to this question, just 36% of the directors stated that they would not do anything different (Graph 5.7), with 38.9% of the board members admitting that they would have taken a different approach today (Graph 5.7).

Out of the group of 102 directors, the decisions that most of-ten resulted in some degree of regret were those related to the hir-ing of the CEO and the sale of the company, followed by M&A, the sacking of the CEO and the mass layoff of employees (Graph 5.7).

What would the directors have done differently in the most difficult decisions?

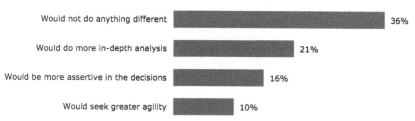

Would not do anything different — 36%
Would do more in-depth analysis — 21%
Would be more assertive in the decisions — 16%
Would seek greater agility — 10%

Graph 5.7 Regret for more difficult decisions and other possible approaches: the four top answers from 58 directors, representing 83% of the responses.
Source: Guerra and Santos (2017).

Among the different approaches that board members would currently adopt in relation to the decisions they regretted are: carrying out more in-depth analysis, being more assertive in their decisions and seeking greater agility in the decision-making process.

There are even cases of regret after the director took an excessively assertive position – for or against – a proposal presented to the board. In a retrospective assessment, one of the interviewees admitted that now he would have taken a more flexible approach to a decision in relation to dividends in a family business at which he was an inde-pendent director. According to him, it is likely that, at that time, his behavior was a reaction to the "atomic bomb" that the board's chair put on the table:

> It's been a long time, I am not going to remember many of the de-tails, but it was a decision regarding dividends. The controlling

Women are more likely to admit they would take a different approach now that they know the results

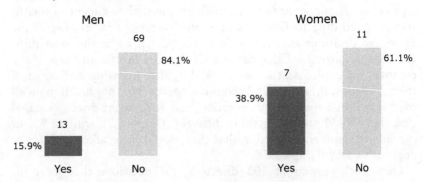

Graph 5.8 Regret varies according to gender: the absolute number above each bar indicates the total number of yes/no answers in the sample by gender. The percentages below the bar indicate the percentage of men or women who answered yes or no to the question.

Source: Guerra and Santos (2017).

What are the decisions that cause the greatest regret among board members

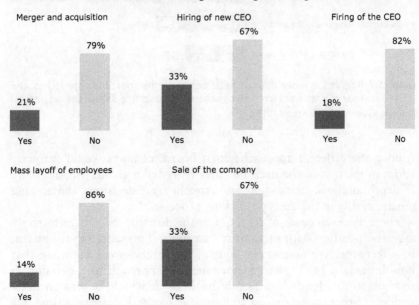

Graph 5.9 Degree of regret in the five decisions regarded as the most difficult ones: the five top ones chosen out of a total of 15 alternatives.

Source: Guerra and Santos (2017).

shareholder was the chairman of the board and he dropped the proposal on the BoD as an atomic bomb. That's how he wanted it and he set out the details ... He took everything for granted, as if the board of directors was there to approve it. But there was also a relevant discussion by the board of directors about the difficult macroeconomic situation that the country was experiencing. I therefore argued that the company should be more conservative with regard to dividend distribution. The argument was intense ... Then, when the chairman realized that the other independents were siding with me and the situation was moving in the direction of the board being convinced, he said: "No. My position must prevail", and I asked: "But why must it prevail"? In addition to dropping the bomb, the chairman also insisted: "Because at some point being the owner has to be worth something." When it came to the crunch, what was seen was that the chairman, in fact, was not prepared for a decision according to governance, which was contrary to what he intended to do. There was a very significant amount of unproductive discomfort. Nowadays I tend to encourage prior conversations, a lot of dialogue in order to understand all the possible angles. Perhaps this would have prevented me from taking such an active stand against the chairman. Particularly because the distribution of dividends, which ended up being made along the lines intended by him, did not cause any major damage to the company. Even with the macro scenario remaining negative for the next two years. In other words, nothing that a good prior conversation could not have aligned the positions between us.

This director who was interviewed clearly demonstrates what is the board's role in approving the distribution of dividends. Strangely, however, in many boards where there is a controlling shareholder, the board members minimize the behavior expected from the board. In most cases, they understand that dividends merely refer to complying with the law in some jurisdictions and the company's policies. But, as the diligent board member explains above, this is indeed the role of the board, which acts as a protagonist and decides in accordance with the company's context and its current and future needs. The other shareholders outside the company, if there are any, rely on the board to perform this role. And, when there are no other shareholders or quotaholders, it is the employees and the other stakeholders who expect the BoD to carry out a real annual analysis, rather than just a formal one.

In the survey by **Guerra, Barros and Santos,**[24] the vast majority of the respondents (55%) consider the quality of the performance of their boards to be good or very good and, for 83% of them, the level of satisfaction with the decision-making process ranges from medium to high, as shown in Graphs 5.10 and 5.11.

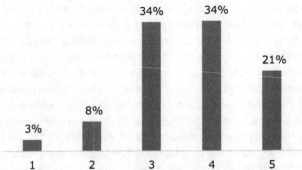

Perception on the board's performance

Survey Question: How do you assess the overall quality of the board's performance?
(1) Very poor (5) Very good

Graph 5.10 The board's performance.

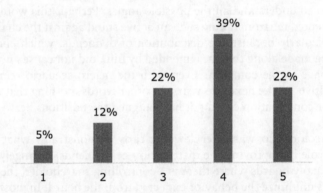

Survey Question: On average, do you feel satisfied or frustrated with the decisions made by your board?
1 (frustrated) 5 (satisfied)

Graph 5.11 Level of satisfaction with decisions.
Source: Guerra, Barros and Santos (2020).

Decisions in a Disruptive World

Since the 17th century,* when the first commercial companies appeared where the owner was no longer also the manager of the venture, all the decisions covered up to this point are absolutely

---

* Story of Governance is covered in Chapter 1.

intrinsic to the business – although they still cause insomnia, a lot of discussion and even some regrets for board members as well as for the executives. In other words, for four centuries, all these sleepless nights have been caused by business as usual... So what can we say about the future of decision-making at companies? What will be the corporate challenges and dilemmas faced in the coming years in the face of an increasingly unstable and ever-changing scenario? What are the possible disruptive events that represent the greatest threat to the continuity of business?

In 2016, the **World Economic Forum**'s report[25] already identified some of the main geopolitical and social risks for the next decade, which will have a direct impact on the management of domestic and global businesses. Undoubtedly, there was not – and there is not any way to remain immune to the consequences of a crisis in the supply of drinking water, food or to climate change and extreme temperatures in summer or winter. Nevertheless, at the time of writing this edition, there was a resounding – and not so unforeseen[*] – impact of the COVID-19 pandemic that, starting in February 2020, infected millions and caused the death of more than 4 million[**] people:

> "In the span of a few months, what started as a global health crisis has also morphed into an economic crisis. It's been more than a century since the world has seen these two forces so intertwined. As economies the world over seek to reopen, businesses are keenly interested in the interplay between personal safety and economic behavior."[26]

Globally, all sectors of economic activity have been affected, with increases in layoffs and a drop in revenues being registered in different degrees of intensity – from the most affected sectors, such as the airlines and the global tourism and hotel sector chain, to those, such as consumer goods e-commerce platforms, as well as digital delivery services

---

[*] For the past two decades, Microsoft's founder, Bill Gates, has, together with his wife Melinda, dedicated himself to global health issues. Since 2015, he has been warning of the potential risk of a pandemic: "So this is a serious problem. We should be concerned. But in fact, we can build a really good response system. We have the benefits of all the science and technology that we talk about here. We've got cell phones to get information from the public and get information out to them. We have satellite maps where we can see where people are and where they're moving. We have advances in biology that should dramatically change the turnaround time to look at a pathogen and be able to make drugs and vaccines that fit for that pathogen. So we can have tools, but those tools need to be put into an overall global health system. And we need preparedness" (available at: https://www.ted.com/talks/bill_gates_the_next_outbreak_we_re_not_ready/transcript?language=pt-br#t-56107).

[**] At time of publication, the death rate from COVID-19 was still rising significantly.

and suppliers of ready-made meals,[27] which, shortly afterward, ended up getting a boost from the compulsory social distancing to avoid contagion by the virus. Ill-equipped to come up with an immediate response to the depth of the crisis, companies – more than ever before – looked to their boards of directors for guidelines to speed up the recovery:

> "None of us can predict the true impact of the pandemic on the global economy, but at this pivotal moment, there are clear choices to be made. The way in which boards do their work at this time will be a critical factor in an organization's ability to emerge from the current crisis and push forward into a new era of economic recovery and opportunity for the benefit of all stakeholders."[28]

Amid the profusion of reports, surveys and articles published in relation to the management of business during and after the pandemic, the **World Economic Forum** consulted 350 of the world's leading experts in risk analysis, who prioritized four points of concern: (1) a prolonged economic recession; (2) possible obstacles to investments in sustainability; (3) increased level of social anxiety; and (4) the emergence of new risks due to the abrupt adoption of new technologies. However, according to these experts, companies' should not be blinded by the consequences of COVID-19, other risks, including cyber risks are increasing: "Couple these with concern of another infectious disease outbreak, an {the risk of an} increase in cybercrime and the breakdown of IT infrastructure and networks, and the outlook fuels pessimism."[29]

Like Bill Gates who predicted the pandemic, **Linda Parker Hudson,**[*] CEO of the Cardea Group and the first woman to head up global corporation in the defense and security area, has been warning at least since 2015 that boards of directors need to pay more attention to cyber risks and prepare their companies for an IT crisis. According to **Hudson**, it is just a matter of time:

> I believe that cyber risk is the biggest one that corporations face today and I do not think that boards of directors are giving the issue the proper attention. It affects everything, not just your computer system, but the basic business, supply chain, communications. It can turn the company's structure upside down. It is not something you can lock in the back room and not worry about. There can be huge losses for companies, and if we are not prepared to deal with cyber risk, it will

---

[*]   Linda Parker Hudson was the CEO of the North American subsidiary of BAE System between 2009 and 2014, becoming the first woman at the helm of a global aerospace defense and security company. She currently serves as CEO and chairperson of the board at the Cardea Group, in addition to being a board member of Bank of America and Ingersoll Rand. The author interviewed Linda Parker Hudson in Washington, D.C., United States, on April 16, 2015.

be our fault [of the boards]. It is not a question of "if it happens one day...". It is a question of "when will it happen" ... And it is already happening on a daily basis with all of us. It cannot be put on boards' agendas when the damage occurs. It is necessary to find a way to measure this, even if it is a score card. Think about if a terrorist or a hacker destroys confidence in the electronic banking system. What will happen to the global economy? We are always talking about infrastructure issues. What would happen without drinking water or a major problem in the transport system, but cyber risk would have far worse consequences. It is difficult to figure out how to translate such sophisticated technical issues into terms that boards of directors can understand. Most directors are not able to do this, but they need to know at least that the right system is being used. That is why professionals with my type of background are being brought on to boards. I come from the national security area, I worked in the field of aerospace defense for 42 years, I know that this is a threat to national security and that the average person has no idea how vulnerable businesses and organizations are on the cybersecurity front. For boards of directors, the first step is to recognize that the topic needs to be included in the agenda and then to start discussing the alternatives that may or may not work. We are just beginning to take cyber risk into account.

To identify the potentially disruptive risks for business, **Henley Business School**[30] conducted a study with 70 directors from 50 companies with revenues of around £1 billion. The result pinpointed four types of events capable of making the decision-making process of companies even more complex. From the in-depth interviews with the board members, a matrix emerged intersecting disruption scenarios with planned and unplanned causes and/or causes arising from internal or external situations (Figure 5.1 – see following page).

Three very relevant conclusions were drawn from this study by **Henley Business School**. First off, CG codes and practices were not established to deal with disruption. On the contrary, they are governance guidelines defined for incremental corporate scenarios and, therefore, in times of extraordinary crisis, like what occurred during and after the COVID-19 pandemic or one that may be caused by cyber risks, they may be of very little help to managers. The second and third conclusions are directly related to the board's actions. Exactly as **Linda P. Hudson**[*] pointed out previously, it is the BoD's responsibility to identify and bring up the greatest risks faced by the business discussion for discussion beforehand and early on.

[*] The author interviewed Linda Parker Hudson in Washington, D.C., United States, on April 16, 2015.

Four types of disruption facing BoDs

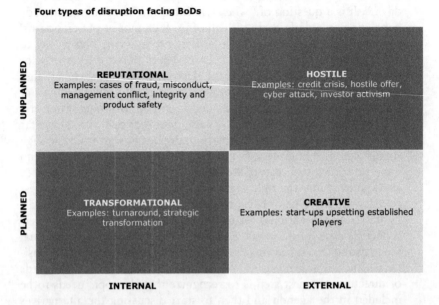

Figure 5.1 Events with the potential to make the decision-making process even more complex.

Source: Henley Business School, Alvarez and Marsal. Joint Research Programme on Board Leadership Report. Boards in Challenging Times: Extraordinary Disruption. Leading through complex and discontinuous challenges. 2016.

Up until Chapter 5, the discussion has been of the performance of BoD. Its operating structure was presented, along with the tensions that arose inside and outside of board rooms, the most detrimental types of behavior resulting from the interactions among the directors themselves and with the managers, the complexity of the decision-making process and its possible defects. All of this wrapped up in a scenario whose evolution carries more threats to the quality of management than an effective contribution and in which the actions of the board members are essential in order to face and overcome the possible disruptive business events.

In practice, despite the advances and improvements in corporate governance, what has been seen is a history of inefficiencies and failures that have led to corporate scandals. In theory, experts demonstrate that the set of – objective and rational – administrative tools – which were applied up until then was insufficient to prevent, deter or mitigate the corporate crises that originated in mistaken decision-making processes. How, then, to deal with this sum of factors deviating from the best decision, the one capable of generating more value for stakeholders? If rationality is *not* enough to manage the business well, what is there besides rationality. This will be covered in Chapter 6.

Notes

1 Thuraisingham, Meena and Lehmacher, Wolfgang. *The secret life of decisions: How unconscious bias subverts your judgement.* Aldershot: Gower Publishing, 2013.

2 Guerra, Sandra; Santos, Rafael Liza. *Headaches, concerns and regrets: What does the experience of 102 Brazilian directors tell us? Private sector opinion.* Washington, DC: IFC, 2017. Available at https://www.ifc.org/wps/wcm/connect/topics_ext_content/ifc_external_corporate_site/ifc+cg/resources/private+sector+opinion/headaches%2C+concerns%2C+and+regrets+-+what+does+the+experience+of+102+brazilian+directors+tell+us. Accessed on May 21, 2020.

3 Guerra, Sandra; Barros, Lucas A.; Santos, Rafael L. Decision-making in boards of directors: The roles of meeting dynamics and choice architecture. *Research Project*, 2020.

4 Better Governance. *Conselheiros: dedicação de tempo dentro e fora das salas de conselho. Pesquisa sobre conselhos de administração e consultivos*, published in June 2020. Available at https://bettergovernance.com.br/2020–06-01-Conselheiros_Pesquisa_Dedicacao_de_Tempo.pdf. Accessed on August 28, 2020.

5 J.P.Morgan. *2020 global M&A outlook.* Available at https://www.jpmorgan.com/jpmpdf/1320748081210.pdf. Accessed on July 13, 2020.

6 Malmendier, Ulrike; Tate, Geoffrey. Who makes acquisitions? CEO overconfidence and the market's reaction. *Journal of Financial Economics*, v. 89, July, 2008. Available at http://www.sciencedirect.com/science/article/pii/S0304405X08000251. Accessed on July 21, 2016.

7 Thuraisingham, Meena; Lehmacher, Wolfgang. *The secret life of decisions: How unconscious bias subverts your judgement.* England: Gower Publishing, 2013.

8 Deloitte. *The state of the deal: M&A trends 2020.* Figures available at https://www2.deloitte.com/us/en/pages/mergers-and-acquisitions/articles/m-a-trends-report.html. Accessed on July 13, 2020.

9 Ibid.

10 Kahneman, Daniel. *Thinking, fast and slow.* New York: Farrar, Straus and Giroux, 2011.

11 Malmendier, Ulrike; Tate, Geoffrey. Who makes acquisitions? CEO overconfidence and the market's reaction. *Journal of Financial Economics*, v. 89, July, 2008. Available at http://www.sciencedirect.com/science/article/pii/S0304405X08000251. Accessed on August 04, 2020.

12 Ibid.

13 Barros, Lucas A.; Da Silveira, Alexandre Di Miceli. Excesso de Confiança, Otimismo Gerencial e os Determinantes da Estrutura de Capital. *Revista Brasileira de Finanças*, v. 6, n. 3, 2008.

14 Thuraisingham, Meen; Lehmacher, Wolfgang. *The secret life of decisions: How unconscious bias subverts your judgement.* England: Gower Publishing, 2013.

15 National Association of Corporate Directors (NACD). *Governance challenges 2016: M&A oversight.* Available at https://www.nacdonline.org/Resources/Article.cfm?ItemNumber=27364. Accessed on July 21, 2016.

16 Barros, Lucas A. Vieses Gerenciais e o Conselho de Administração. 4° Curso Avançado de Conselheiro de Administração. IBGC, June 2010.

17 Ibid.

18 Guerra, Sandra; Santos, Rafael Liza. *Headaches, concerns and regrets: What does the experience of 102 Brazilian directors tell us? Private sector opinion.* Washington, DC: IFC, 2017. Available at https://www.ifc.org/wps/wcm/connect/topics_ext_content/ifc_external_corporate_site/ifc+cg/

resources/private+sector+opinion/headaches%2C+concerns%2C+and+regrets+-+what+does+the+experience+of+102+brazilian+directors+tell+us. Accessed on May 21, 2020.

19 PwC. *Governing for the long term: Looking down the road with an eye on the rear-view mirror*. Annual Corporate Directors Survey, PwC, 2015. Available at https://www.pwc.ie/publications/2015/annual-corporate-directors-survey.pdf. Accessed on July 15, 2020.

20 Spencer Stuart. *CEO transitions 2019*. Available at https://www.spencerstuart.com/research-and-insight/ceo-transitions-2019. Accessed on July 15, 2020.

21 Ibid.

22 Guerra, Sandra; Barros, Lucas A.; Santos, Rafael L. Decision-making in boards of directors: The roles of meeting dynamics and choice architecture. *Research Project*, 2020.

23 Guerra, Sandra; Santos, Rafael Liza. *Headaches, concerns and regrets: What does the experience of 102 Brazilian directors tell us? Private sector opinion*. Washington, DC: IFC, 2017. Available at https://www.ifc.org/wps/wcm/connect/topics_ext_content/ifc_external_corporate_site/ifc+cg/resources/private+sector+opinion/headaches%2C+concerns%2C+and+regrets+-+what+does+the+experience+of+102+brazilian+directors+tell+us. Accessed on May 21, 2020.

24 Guerra, Sandra; Barros, Lucas A.; Santos, Rafael L. Decision-making in boards of directors: The roles of meeting dynamics and choice architecture. *Research Project*, 2020.

25 World Economic Forum's Global Risks Report 2015. *Governing the global company. Oversight of complexity*. Robyn Bew, from the National Association of Corporate Directors (NACD) and Lucy Nottingham, from the Marsh & McLennan Companies. Available at: https://www.mmc.com/content/dam/mmc-web/Global-Risk-Center/Files/governing-the-global-company.pdf. Accessed on July 20, 2020.

26 Deloitte. *In the throes of a dual-front crisis. Establishing the road to a global consumer recovery*. Available at https://www2.deloitte.com/us/en/insights/industry/retail-distribution/consumer-behavior-trends-state-of-the-consumer-tracker/covid-19-recovery/04–29–2020.html. Accessed on July 17, 2020.

27 KPMG. *Impactos e respostas aos efeitos do COVID-19*, April 2020. Available at KPMG_abril 2020_Covid19_PoV_Advisory_Deck geral – final (003). pdf. Accessed on July 16, 2020.

28 Deloitte. *COVID-19 and the board A chair's point of view*. Available at https://www2.deloitte.com/global/en/pages/about-deloitte/articles/covid-19/covid-19-and-the-board-a-chairs-point-of-view.html. Accessed on July 17, 2020.

29 World Economic Forum. *COVID-19 risks outlook: A preliminary mapping and its implications*. Available at https://www.weforum.org/reports/covid-19-risks-outlook-a-preliminary-mapping-and-its-implications. Accessed on July 17, 2020.

30 Henley Business School; Alvarez & Marsal. *Boards in challenging times: Extraordinary disruptions leading through complex and discontinuous challenges*. Available at http://www.alvarezandmarsal.com/sites/default/files/am_boards_in_challenging_times_research.pdf. Accessed on July 14, 2016.

Part II

Thinking Outside
the Box

Chapter 6

The Myth of Corporate Rationality

Chapter Summary

- Particularly in the wake of the succession of corporate scandals of the late 20th century, governance policies and practices are continually being improved, but the boards of directors (BoDs) state of the art are still a source of inspiration. The performance of boards of directors cannot yet be regarded as a paragon. Why?

- The limits of human rationality proposed by two winners of the Nobel Prize for Economics: **Herbert Simon** (1978) for proposing that human behavior is intentional, but its rationality is limited; and **Daniel Kahneman** (2002), who again applied these concepts to the organizational decision-making process and brought to light the influence of cognitive biases.

- According to **Kahneman**, human beings have a limited attention span and their behavior is triggered by two systems, being subject to failures: **System 1** is fast, automatic and works without attention, while **System 2** is slower, more reflective and carries out activities that require focused attention.

- In the integrated action between **System 1** and **System 2**, systemic failures, called cognitive biases, can occur.

- The influence of the cognitive biases on the behavior of the individual and of groups.

- How cognitive biases can distance the decision-making process of boards of directors from the best interests of the parties.

- The group biases described in this chapter are illuminated with the results of an international research with 360 respondents. Research participants are from 40 countries, and being more representative in the sample are Brazil, Colombia, Peru, Philippines and the United States. Respondents are from 21 different industries, 132 of them being board directors from closed companies, 112 from listed companies, 44 from not for profit and 4 from cooperatives.

- The detrimental effect of an internal dispute in the board is just the the peak of the iceberg of this chapter's caselet. But there is much more to be unveiled when a director too influencial to be challenged is too protective of the CEO.

As a board director, I have always tried to base my positions on logical and objective analysis. For me, as a trained engineer and a former executive in the infrastructure sector, reason has to prevail in business decisions. I didn't even consider that other factors could actually end up playing an important role – until I witnessed a process that made me realize that some factors can indeed overcome rationality and have a negative impact on the group's behavior and on the board's decisions.

One of the BoDs on which I served was a holding company that managed an extensive investment portfolio. Since Mergers and Acquisitions (M&A) transactions took place on a frequent basis, there was a committee dedicated exclusively to the analysis of new investments. The Chief Executive Officer (CEO) had been at the helm of the holding company for many years and knew how to consolidate his internal relationships. Highly skillful, he got along very well with investors, with the executives of the investee companies, and moved easily within the BoD. When proposing acquisitions, the CEO relied heavily on a director, Lucas, who was an expert in the M&A area and who headed up the investment committee. He had a lot of experience in the sector and already had more than a hundred corporate transactions under his belt. On account of this, he was well known and respected – even revered by the market.

As far as all the directors were concerned, the CEO's constructive dialog with the members of the investment committee and in particular with Lucas appeared to be very positive. The process of analyzing, debating and deciding on acquisitions and mergers usually went very smoothly. There was an apparent harmony that made us believe that the whole process was a very objective and efficient one. However, last year the board began to become aware of a rather widespread dissatisfaction on the part of a group of shareholders in relation to the investment portfolio's results. Soon afterward, the annoyed shareholders succeeded in electing a new board member, Oscar, who was a finance specialist and who came from the banking sector.

Right from the very first meeting, behind the conversations and pleasant smiles, it was clear that Lucas and Oscar were not getting along. Always very talkative, the latter emphatically opened the debate regarding the performance of the investment portfolio. According to him, "the result was mediocre and was way below the potential both in terms of the existing operations as well as of the new investments." There could be some other factor that was wrong in the implementation of the investments, but based on his skeptical view as an investment analyst, Oscar did not rule out the possibility *that part of the problem lay in the choice of investments. At some meetings, when the CEO was asked to take part, Oscar questioned the expected profitability of the proposed operations and it was very clear that he was not satisfied with the answers. It was obvious that the director, who had very extensive experience in financial analysis of transactions, was not satisfied with the methods that the CEO used to select and prioritize the various investment opportunities.*

In his role on the investment committee, Lucas had taken part in the decisions of most of the past transactions and had detailed knowledge of every deal. In addition, there was a visible affectionate, almost paternal stance in relation to the CEO. A master in the art of relationships and of the right age to be Lucas's son, the CEO shared his apprehensions and the hardships imposed on him by the board. Lucas was totally sympathetic to the CEO and often stood up for him at the BoD. For Lucas, "the portfolio's results were above average in M&A" and the CEO was definitely doing his best. The CEO continually asked the board for more resources to perform his role, but the BoD was of the opinion that it had hired a very experienced CEO: he should be able to handle the search for new investments and oversee three small operations, headed by hired executives, without any problems.

But Oscar maintained an excessively critical position both in relation to the investment analysis model he encountered upon his arrival as well as in relation to the CEO himself, who was the one who selected the investments and argued in favor of one as opposed to the other. Oscar was surprised that all his questions did not result in anything. The investment analysis model was not reviewed and neither was the CEO's performance. What the finance expert did not know was that, outside the boardroom, his colleague Lucas, was making every effort to "fault the critical board member". Over a cup of coffee, at lunches, at all and any formal or informal meetings where Oscar was not present, we – and even the CEO – were treated to comments such as: "Oscar has very strong opinions, despite the fact that he is not exactly an expert in mergers and acquisitions, notwithstanding his knowledge of financial models" or "The argument he made is irrelevant. We make use of a methodology that he doesn't know" or "Why is he always against the CEO?". He left the question hanging in the air: "Was Oscar jealous or, deep down, was he competing with the CEO and would he really like to be sitting in his chair?"

These comments occupied the minds of all the directors, and the group started to analyze the situation based on these reports, which made us wonder about and doubt the motivation of the actions of the new director Oscar. Was he really jealous of the CEO or want his position? Was he really overly critical and unable to appreciate the CEO's significant efforts? After all, Lucas had an incredible amount of experience in M&A and should be respected for his analysis. Being a born skeptic as I always was, I even suspected that there might be some sense in Oscar's arguments. But questioning Lucas head-on was no insignificant matter: he was so influential that we knew that nothing good would come for anyone who questioned his ideas. After all, it was inevitable that we would meet him outside the board; Lucas was simply too influential. But for now, those were my suppositions. I did not yet have any idea as to what it all really meant. The dynamics of the events, which I witnessed, were still rather hazy and I could not anticipate the dire consequences of those conversations in the hallway. *

The successive corporate scandals over the last few decades have kept boards of directors under scrutiny: "What are the directors doing while the company undergoes a marked destruction of value with profound and irreversible social and/or environmental losses?" In order to prevent – or at least mitigate – the occurrence of these disasters, corporate governance (CG) specialists from all over the world in the public and private sectors strive to review the performance of boards from a wide range of angles, such as structure, composition, interaction with committees, processes, quality of information provided to the directors. Bearing in mind that all of these aspects have been thoroughly analyzed and continuously improved since the start of the 21st century, shouldn't we able by now to count on truly excellent BoDs? Why can't we have boards that are more efficient and effective, in addition to being capable of ensuring the creation of sustainable value? In all honestly, it has to be admitted that the day is still a long way off when boards of directors will be able to fully perform all of these roles, attributes and capabilities. In other words, when it comes to the workings of BoDs, the state of the art is still an aspiration.

At the same time as all the policies, rules, practices, mechanisms and processes that have been adopted, even on those boards that are regarded as being among the "best in class," the behavioral aspect of the decision-making processes is a factor that has not yet received the proper attention – whether in relation to the individual or to the group. In order to try and explain why these aspects have been continually overlooked in the assessment of BoDs, perhaps the best starting point is the excessive importance that is still attached to human rationality and the ability to make objective decisions – particularly in the business environment. Introduced by classical economists, it took some time for the premise of human rationality in the decision-making process to be challenged by modern concepts of psychology and sociology. And even after having been scientifically discredited, the idea remains an ingrained one today, since human beings tenaciously insist on believing that they make their decisions solely on the basis of reason.

---

* The conclusion of the story will be presented at the end of this chapter.

One of the first to question this concept was **Herbert Simon**, winner of the Nobel Prize in Economics in 1978 for his pioneering research into the decision-making process within organizations. **Simon**[1] was already arguing back in 1947 that in relation to human rationality, the social sciences suffered from acute schizophrenia: on the one hand, "economic man" was considered absolutely rational and all-knowing, while on the other, the tendency of social psychology was to reduce knowledge to affectivity and demonstrate that man was not as rational as he would like to be.[2] Between these two currents, Simon balanced himself on a new proposition. In his opinion, "human behavior is intendedly rational, but only boundedly so." This concept of bounded rationality opened up a totally innovative perspective in the field of management, recognizing human limits in terms of processing information and, therefore, the consequent inability of managers to make optimal decisions in an economically rational way.[3] Therefore, in order to analyze what the boundaries are that can limit human rationality, this chapter discusses the behavioral approach: firstly, from an individual point of view and then from a group perspective. The next chapter will cover the instruments already available to align corporate decisions more closely with rationality and their application in boards of directors.

Limited Attention Span

Daniel Kahneman, another winner of the Nobel Prize in Economics in 2002 for the theory of decision-making, started from the concept of rationality to devise, together with **Amos Tversky**[*], an approach to the human cognitive process, explaining its systematic failures. In his book *Thinking Fast and Slow*, **Kahneman** adopts a terminology already established by psychology, – **System 1** and **System 2** of the cognitive process. According to him, **System 1** is responsible for automatic and quick actions, those attitudes adopted without effort and attention, even involuntarily. **System 2** is the conscious and reasoning self, the one that controls those actions that require attention and which are more complex. Among the abilities included in **System 1** are those that are innate as well as those that are learned, which become fast and automatic, due to a great deal of practice. Those in **System 2** are discretionary and require full attention, ceasing to be carried out as soon as the focus is shifted. For example, **System 1** can't help but know what 2 + 2 is or fail to understand a simple sentence in its own language, since this type of knowledge is stored in memory and is accessed without intention and effort.

---

[*] Amos Nathan Tversky (1937–1996) – Israeli psychologist, one of the pioneers of cognitive science, died before his theories received recognition with the Nobel Prize, which was awarded to Kahneman in 2002.

Control of attention is shared by the two systems, and **System 2** has some control over **System 1**'s functioning because it can reprogram the attention and memory functions. For example, when a tourist rents a car in London, they have to make an effort and pay extra attention to driving on the left side of the road. Instead of driving the car almost on autopilot as they usually do in their own towns, **System 2** helps tourists make a continuous effort to drive correctly during their stay in London. In short, **System 1** handles common activities quickly and automatically until some variation in the routine appears, and then **System 2**'s attention and reflection ability is called upon to take control (Figure 6.1).

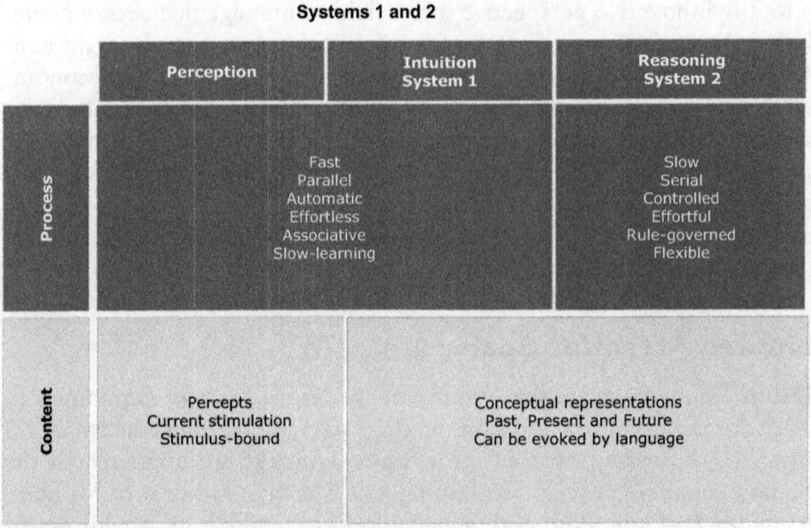

Systems 1 and 2

	Perception	Intuition System 1	Reasoning System 2
Process		Fast Parallel Automatic Effortless Associative Slow-learning	Slow Serial Controlled Effortful Rule-governed Flexible
Content	Percepts Current stimulation Stimulus-bound	Conceptual representations Past, Present and Future Can be evoked by language	

Figure 6.1 Division of activities between System 1 and System 2.
Source: Kahneman, Daniel. Maps of bounded rationality: a perspective on intuitive judgment and choice. Nobel Prize Lecture. 2002.

It is precisely in the sharing of control of attention that the first limitation of human rationality can arise. As Kahneman points out, **System 1** is capable of performing several tasks simultaneously, whereas **System 2** does not have this ability:

"[When] you are asked to do something that does not come naturally, (...) you will find that the consistent maintenance of a set requires continuous exertion of at least some effort. The often-used phrase 'pay attention' is apt: you dispose of a limited budget of attention that you can allocate to activities, and if you try to go beyond your budget, you will fail. It is the mark of effortful activities that they interfere with each other, which is why it is difficult or impossible to conduct several at once. You could not compute the product of 17×24 while making a left turn into dense traffic, and you certainly should not try. You can do several things at once, but only if they are easy and undemanding. You are probably safe carrying on a conversation with a passenger while driving on an empty highway, and many parents have discovered, perhaps with some guilt, that they can read a story to a child while thinking of something else."[4]

The exhaustion of this "attention budget" is exactly what happens with the participants of the so-called Invisible Gorilla experiment:[5] people watch the video of a basketball game and, in the end, they are required to state the total number of passes made by the team dressed in white. Their attention is so concentrated on the task of counting that most of them do not realize that someone dressed as a gorilla crosses the court. According to **Guerra and Santos**'[6] research, one of the harmful behaviors at board meetings is that of directors who multitask: they try, for example, to split their "attention budget" between talking on their cell phones, answering e-mails and, at the same time, listening to the latest proposition presented to the board by the CEO. What is the likelihood that something relevant will escape them? As the gorilla experiment proves, the chances are high.

In boardrooms, the intense focus of attention devoted to just one aspect of an issue can make the directors fail to see "the gorilla" – not least of all because there is also a tendency toward over-optimism, which has already been pointed out in Chapter 3. Of course, the facts tend to be more subtle and complex, and for that reason, it is possible that blindness produces even more dramatic results. Who has not heard of a board that was totally won over by an acquisition with high potential for gain and was blind to the huge difference in culture between the acquired company and the acquirer? The day after the deal was closed, the huge contingents of personnel on both sides began to (mis)understand each other just like a person who lives in Greenland and a nomad from the Sahara. The most serious thing, as **Kahneman** states, is that, in addition to being blind to the obvious, it is also possible to be blind of one's own blindness.

Origin of Cognitive Biases

The division of labor between **System 1** and **System 2** normally works very well. While **System 1** reacts rapidly to familiar situations, using accurate models and short-term forecasts, **System 2** remains comfortably at rest. This partnership is an efficient one as it minimizes effort and optimizes performance. However, it turns out that **System 1**, in addition to never being turned off, has little in terms of logical understanding. For this reason, its response model – fast and unthinking – can potentially "contaminate" the process. **Kahneman** refers to this process by the apparently sophisticated term "heuristic,"[*7] but its meaning is pretty easy to understand: it is a simple tactic of the mind, which helps with finding suitable, even if not perfect, answers. And this contamination is the result of cognition biases, as Kahneman explains:

> "System 1 continuously generates suggestions for System 2: impressions, intuitions, intentions, and feelings. If endorsed by System 2, impressions and intuitions turn into beliefs, and impulses turn into voluntary actions. When all goes smoothly, which is most of the time, System 2 adopts the suggestions of System 1 with little or no modification. You generally believe your impressions and act on your desires, and that is fine – usually. (...) The arrangement works well most of the time because System 1 is generally very good at what it does: its models of familiar situations are accurate, its short-term predictions are usually accurate as well, and its initial reactions to challenges are swift and generally appropriate. System 1 has biases, however, systematic errors that it is prone to make in specified circumstances."[8]

Were it not for the limited ability to focus attention and the vulnerability to biases, the human capacity to make decisions would be closer to rationality. However, being under the influence of **System 1** round-the-clock, the individual believes he/she is making a totally rational decision, when, in fact, he/she is the victim of a misperception, "suggested" by the possible cognitive biases. For **Kahneman and Tversky,**[9] any activity that involves some kind of prediction involves a significant component of judgment, intuition and educated guesswork, which leads to the following conclusions:

- More than random, errors of judgment are systematic: in the same way as there is myopia, there is also mental astigmatism.
- Like all mortals, no technical expert, physicist or intelligence analyst is absolutely immune to their own cognitive biases. Therefore, statistical experts are also subject to the so-called "statistical biases," as will be seen below.
- Mistaken intuitions are such as optical illusions: attractive even when the person is fully aware of his or her nature.

As an example of the vulnerability to perception: even being totally focused on seeing the vase in Figure 6.2, the person sees the faces on the sides of the figure, even without wanting to. The reverse is also applicable.

---

* According to Kahneman, "heuristics is a simple procedure that helps find adequate, though often imperfect, answers to difficult questions. The word comes from the same root as eureka".

Not every blind person knows he/she is blind

Figure 6.2 Intuitions and optical illusions have a strong attraction: what did you see first, the faces or the vase?

If all of this were not enough, human beings are also more prone to identifying other people's errors than their own, as the report of an independent board director regarding the case of an entrepreneur in the alternative energy value chain sector makes clear. After carrying out a successful **Initial Public Offering (IPO)**, a series of minor mistakes made by the controlling shareholder ended up driving the company to disaster:

> The company went public during an IPO window and it was very successful. The CEO, who was also the founding entrepreneur and controlling shareholder of the business, was so excited about the success with international investors that he decided to assume the IR (Investor Relations) functions as well. This, on the eve of 2008, when the global economy began its meltdown. At that point his first mistake was the decision to replace his CFO, who did not speak English, because he wanted to have a more sophisticated professional. He had a point: 70% of the new investors were foreigners. But the previous CFO had a firm grasp of the company, understood the business model, had good control over liquidity and kept the treasury position. The new one came from a multinational and was unfamiliar with the business. Shortly before the end of that year, he made a presentation to the board, showing that everything was going well.

With the scenario that was approaching, I had already been very vocal with the CEO that leverage should be kept at a maximum of 2.5 x EBITDA. However, when I returned from the end of the year break, he called me for a private chat: he said he had reached the conclusion that the figures presented earlier were wrong and he asked me to suggest a new CFO. On top of this, he mentioned that a debenture issue had been made, which had increased leverage to 4.5. The board had never been consulted about this issue. We immediately looked into how it was possible to issue debentures without the board's knowledge and truly all the governance documents were silent regarding this matter. At that point the crisis was already upon us. For the CEO, the question was whether to use the company's available cash to pay off the first tranche of the debenture or to maintain investments required in order to start offering energy in accordance with regulatory requirements. For me, there was no doubt: as a publicly-held company, if we did not comply with the regulations, the Federal Prosecutor would be all over our operation. It was necessary to continue with the investment and to negotiate with the banks.

At that time, I assumed that the crisis was still manageable. I thought it would be possible to reprofile the debt with the creditors and move on. But, shortly afterwards, the investment bank came to the conclusion that not even renegotiating 100% of the debt ... To overcome that level of leverage would require an equity solution, a new capital contribution. Unfortunately, since the global financial market was already in meltdown, an organized sale of assets had to be made, the creditors were paid and the company ceased to exist.

In retrospect, it is now possible to ask why this entrepreneurial CEO increased leverage to 4.5 x EBITDA. My opinion is that there was a blindness caused by a certain degree of amateurism and excitement vis-á-vis the international investors. In 2006, in order to get the IPO done, he told a story of a successful strategy and made a commitment to a revenue of $ 1 billion at the end of 2007. The thing is, in order to achieve this, the business had specific characteristics that indeed required very high investments in advance. With the disruption of the global financial sector, he could have reached out to investors and simply said, "Look, the world has changed over the last 12 months and the company's goals have also changed." But he insisted on fulfilling the commitment he had given and the company became excessively leveraged. Among other reasons, because he intended to do a follow-up to the IPO ... Every CEO, particularly those who are entrepreneurs/the founder of the business, have some undeniable behavioral characteristics: a great deal of self-confidence, an exaggerated self-esteem as well as the mythical vision of building an empire. There is nothing wrong with this, as long as they are not blinded by it ...

Scientific demonstrations regarding the flaws – inevitable – in decision-making processes tend to leave board directors with their hair standing on end, particularly those who are more confident about their rationality and objectivity, like that which was described in the story at the start of this chapter. "Where will the gorillas be?", they fret. Even the most capable and senior of all directors can be subject to cognitive biases: the alternative is to mitigate them. However, prior to this, it is essential to understand them and admit that they exist and have an influence on human behavior.

Biases and Their Cognitive Traps

Operating continuously in an uncertain environment, directors try to base their decisions on objective, technically sound data: the various probabilities are turned inside out and the forecasters have the nerve to present the figures down to the cents. All of this can give the impression that the decision will be based exclusively on objective information and with the highest degree of rationality. Nevertheless, all evaluations, judgments and choices are subject to cognitive biases that are capable of undermining the quality of the decisions, causing them to stray from rationality. Therefore, every decision will only prove correct if and when the assumptions – which seemed to be so sound! – prove to be real.

> "It ain't what you don't know that gets you into trouble. It's what you know for sure that just ain't so."[*]

The controversy that arose on the internet in connection with this phrase placed at the start of the film *The Big Short*, attributed to the American writer Mark Twain, ended up being subtly ironic: did the film, which addresses one of the greatest moments of collective blindness in the US financial market, have an incorrect quote as its starting point? Did the screenwriter and director trip over some cognitive bias? Or was it just a trick to see who was really paying attention? Who let the "gorilla" slip by unnoticed? The fact is that there are many biases and they always seem to be lurking, ready to interfere with human rationality.

---

[*] *The Big Short* (2015), a film directed by Adam McKay and based on the book by Michael Lewis, recounts the explosion of the subprime mortgage bubble in the United States in 2007/2008 and how a group of investors profited by "seeing" what no one saw or didn't want to believe was true.

When they demonstrated the existence and influence of cognitive biases in decision-making processes, **Kahneman and Tversky** made a generic classification, forming three major groups: (1) availability, (2) representativeness and (3) anchoring and adjustment. And based on this new thinking, a number of researchers began to navigate the world of bias, which can be classified in an infinite number of ways. This book uses the detailed cognitive bias description constructed by **David Arnott**,[10] an expert in decision support systems. He studied the various researchers who threw themselves into the field of cognitive biases and identified 37 important biases, which he organized into six categories:

1. Memory;
2. Statistical;
3. Confidence;
4. Adjustment;
5. Presentation;
6. Situation.

This grouping, which makes it easier to the variety and categories of biases, is described in Table 6.1 merely as an illustration. Not always easy to distinguish, it is also possible that various biases overlap, making the decision process even more complex. For simplicity, from here onward, this book will focus on the six categories of biases, which will be applied in practical situations to help identify them.

Table 6.1 Individual cognitive biases grouped into six categories

Category	Type of bias	Description
Memory	Hindsight	In retrospect, the degree to which an event could be predicted is often overestimated.
	Imaginability	An event may be judged more probably if it can be easily imagined.
	Recall	An event or class may appear more numerous or frequent if its instances are more easily recalled than other equally probable events.
	Search	An event may seem more frequent because of the effectiveness of the search strategy.
	Similarity	The likelihood of an event occurring may be judged by the degree of similarity with the class it is perceived to belong to.
	Testimony	The inability to recall details of an event may lead to seemingly logical reconstructions that may be inaccurate.

Statistical	Base rate	Base rate data tends to be ignored when other data are available.
	Chance	A sequence of random events can be mistaken for an essential characteristic of a process.
	Conjunction	Probability is often overestimated in compound conjunctive problems.
	Correlation	The probability of two events occurring together can be overestimated if they have co-occurred in the past.
	Disjunction	Probability is often underestimated in compound disjunctive problems.
	Sample	The size of a sample is often ignored in judging its predictive power.
	Subset	A conjunction or subset is often judged more probable than its set.
Confidence	Completeness	The perception of an apparently complete or logical data presentation can stop the search for omissions.
	Control	A poor decision may lead to a good outcome, inducing a false feeling of control over the judgment situation.
	Confirmation	Often decision-makers seek confirmatory evidence and do not search for disconfirming information.
	Desire	The probability of desired outcomes may be inaccurately assessed as being greater.
	Overconfidence	The ability to solve difficult or novel problems is often overestimated.
	Redundancy	The more redundant and voluminous the data, the more confidence may be expressed in its accuracy and importance.
	Selectivity	Expectation of the nature of an event can bias what information is thought to be relevant.
	Success	Often failure is associated with poor luck, and success, with the abilities of the decision-maker.
	Test	Some aspects and outcomes of choice cannot be tested, leading to unrealistic confidence in judgment.
Adjustment	Anchoring and adjustment	Adjustments from an initial position are usually insufficient.
	Conservatism	Often estimates are not revised appropriately on the receipt of significant new data.
	Reference	The establishment of a reference point or anchor can be a random or distorted act.
	Regression	That events will tend to regress toward the mean on subsequent trial is often not allowed for in judgment.

(Continued)

Category	Type of bias	Description
Presentation	Framing	Events framed as either losses or gains may be evaluated differently.
	Linear	Decision-makers are often unable to extrapolate a non-linear growth process.
	Mode	The mode and mixture of presentation can influence the perceived value of data.
	Order	The first or last item presented may be overweighted in judgment.
	Scale	The perceived variability of data can be affected by the scale of the data.
Situation	Attenuation	A decision-making situation can be simplified by ignoring or significantly discounting the level of uncertainty.
	Complexity	Time pressure, information overload and other environmental factors can increase the perceived complexity of a task.
	Escalation	Often decision-makers commit to follow or escalate a previous unsatisfactory course of action.
	Habit	An alternative may be chosen only because it was used before.
	Inconsistency	Often a consistent judgment strategy is not applied to an identical repetitive set of cases.
	Rule	The wrong decision rule may be used.

Source: David Arnott, Cognitive bases and decision support systems development (2006).

Memory

One of the main discoveries of **Hermann Ebbinghaus** (1850 – 1909), a German psychologist who was a pioneer in the empirical study of human memory, was precisely in relation to the process of forgetting. According to him, after the first recollection of an event, there is an abrupt initial decline in memory, followed by a gradual and continuous forgetting. More recently, other studies have shown that memory is made up of vivid flashes, forming a reconstruction that does not always need every event experienced.

Based on the **Ebbinghaus** forgetting curve, cognitive scientists came up with an experiment to check the degree of memory of a group of people in the light of three tragic events in the United States: the assassination of John Kennedy (1963), the explosion of the space shuttle Challenger (1986) and the attack on the Twin Towers (2001). First, the participants' memory was tested at shorter regular intervals and then, after a period of three years. The results revealed that only 7% of people had memories that were in line with what actually happened; 50% were wrong in 2/3 of their statements about the events and 25% were wrong in every detail recalled.

The flaws in the recall process are no different with everyday memories or with accumulated knowledge, as in the episode experienced by General Matthew Broderick during the rescue of the victims of Hurricane Katrina:

"On Monday August 29, 2005, Hurricane Katrina hit the south coast of America, 55 miles south of New Orleans – a heavily populated city much of which was below sea level.

General Matthew Broderick, Director of the 300 staff-strong Homeland Security Operations Center, Washington DC (which was the clearing hub for intelligence from the ground on major domestic disasters before passing it on to the White House) was an experienced man in charge at the time of Katrina. He had 30 years of experience running the Operations Centre of the Marine Corps including the evacuation of Saigon and Phnom Penh. If anyone was qualified to sift good information from bad, Broderick was. However, his long experience had told him that first reports are often inaccurate and exaggerated. So, he spent that Monday trying to get confirmation from reliable reports on whether the levies of New Orleans had been breached. Reports were coming in thick and fast and by the end of the day he had many reports, some of which were conflicting, and he had to decide the reliability of those reports. That evening he went home after reassuring the White House that there was no substantial breach of New Orleans levies. It was not until late morning on the August 30 when he informed the White House that levies had been breached and much of New Orleans was already under water. This delayed the federal response by 24 hours causing the death of 1,800 people and hundreds and thousands to lose their homes and livelihoods. Katrina was a disaster that cost the US Federal Government US$86 billion.

In that critical 24-hour period after the hurricane had hit the south coast, Broderick had listened to those reports carefully, selectively picking a few that appeared to him as less exaggerated, all the time applying his recollection of how the first reports of previous events he had managed had been exaggerated. He failed to notice the one to two reports that held the truth of what was unfolding.

'It's my responsibility ... to inform these key personnel,' Broderick told a Senate panel investigating the Katrina response. 'If they did not receive... information, it was my responsibility and my fault.' He later resigned citing family reasons."[11]

The above account by **Thuraisingham and Lehmacher** reveals a cognitive bias in the Memory category, that of similarity. General Broderick evaluated the information he received immediately about the damage caused by Katrina, looking for similarities with his previous experience, which had shown him that the initial data for an event "was generally" exaggerated. On the other hand, still analyzing from the perspective of cognitive biases, it is likely that, at the same time, the general was also the victim of the selectivity bias, in the Confidence category, which occurs when expectations about the nature of an event can influence what information is regarded as relevant, which leads the person to only select the elements that confirm his/her reasoning or evaluation. Bearing in mind that a large part of the assessments and decisions taken in business management are based on the directors' and executives' accumulated knowledge and expertise, it is therefore always recommended to make room for doubt and contradictory opinions. So, the next time your colleague on the board fiercely advocates following a certain path, giving vivid details from his/her memory about previous situations where a similar initiative was successful, you should take it with a grain of salt: everyone is subject to **memory biases** – and, possibly, aggravated by other biases, such as selectivity.

Statistical

Numbers have the power to give the appearance of objectivity to the most unlikely analyses. **Kahneman**[12] states that human beings have a tendency to process information following a reasoning that is contrary to the principles of probability theory. In **Guerra and Santos'**[13] research, board members claim that the three main factors for their wrong decisions include risks and costs minimized by a project's proponents (Graph 6.1). These directors may have overlooked the chances that the executives are also acting under the influence of **statistical cognitive biases** presented before the board. One of them is precisely to ignore statistical data and relevant and available projections and base the reasoning on a simplifying heuristic, such as associations created intuitively by similarity.

To give an example of such bias, **Kahneman** describes a boy named Steve who is "very shy and withdrawn, invariably helpful, but with little interest in people or in the world of reality. A meek and tidy soul, he has a need for order and structure and a passion for detail." And he then asks what, in your opinion is more likely: Is Steve a librarian or a farmer? Solemnly neglecting the relevant statistical data that in the United States there are more than 20 male farmers for each man who is employed as a librarian, most people respond based on the profession's stereotyped personality – and predictably get it wrong: Steve is a farmer, not a librarian. To summarize why intuition prevails over relevant data, **Kahneman** created the acronym **WYSIATI**:

> "Jumping to conclusions on the basis of limited evidence is so important to an understanding of intuitive thinking (...), that I will use a

cumbersome abbreviation for it: WYSIATI, which stands for 'what you see is all there is.' System 1 is radically insensitive to both the quality and the quantity of the information that gives rise to impressions and intuitions."[14]

Other studies conducted by researchers at the **University of Colorado**[15] demonstrate yet another form of bias: even the composition of the sample can influence decision makers. In three experiments, professional selection processes were simulated, producing different combinations of gender and ethnic minorities in the group of four finalist candidates. Regarding the hiring of men and women, the results were as follows: (1) when there is just one woman among the four finalist candidates, her probability of being hired is 0%; (2) when the four finalists include two men and two women, the chances that one of the females is selected rises to 50% (in addition to the probabilistic increase expected due to the fact that there are now two women finalists); and (3) when the group of finalists consists of three women and one man, the chances that one of the females will be selected rises to 67%. The results in relation to ethnicity followed the same trend. According to the researchers, this suggests that the bias in favor of maintaining the status quo can be changed by a real change in the status quo:

> "(...) when we created a new status quo among the finalist candidates by adding just one more woman or minority candidate, the decision makers actually considered hiring a woman or minority candidate. (...) Managers need to know that working to get one woman or minority considered for a position might be futile, because the odds are likely slim if they are the lone woman or nonwhite candidate. But if managers can change the status quo of the finalist pool by including two women, then the women have a fighting chance."[16]

Confidence

The negative effects of over-optimism on decision-making have already been discussed in Chapters 3 and 5, and come back into the picture as **confidence biases**. These usually occur, for example, when the degree of confidence in one's own decision-making ability is so great that it prevents the search for new information for the best risk assessment. Or when more information is sought to support a proposition's assumptions, without paying attention to those that show a possible error. Furthermore, according to **Kahneman**, there is a tendency to overestimate what is already known and to underestimate coincidence:

> "(...) a puzzling limitation of our mind: our excessive confidence in what we believe we know, and our apparent inability to acknowledge

the full extent of our ignorance and the uncertainty of the world we live in. We are prone to overestimate how much we understand about the world and to underestimate the role of chance in events. Overconfidence is fed by the illusory certainty of hindsight."[17]

To get back to real situations, all that you need is one initial question: in your experience as a board director or executive, how many times did a budget which seemed plausible when approved, end up becoming a piece of fiction? Overconfidence is likely to have indicated more favorable winds than those which actually occurred. In **Guerra and Santos'**[18] research, the 102 directors interviewed admitted that overconfidence was the most frequently-cited reason for making wrong decisions.

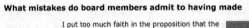

What mistakes do board members admit to having made

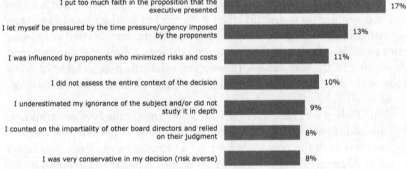

I put too much faith in the proposition that the executive presented	17%
I let myself be pressured by the time pressure/urgency imposed by the proponents	13%
I was influenced by proponents who minimized risks and costs	11%
I did not assess the entire context of the decision	10%
I underestimated my ignorance of the subject and/or did not study it in depth	9%
I counted on the impartiality of other board directors and relied on their judgment	8%
I was very conservative in my decision (risk averse)	8%

Graph 6.1 Main causes of mistakes in the decision-making process: the seven main answers represent 76% of the total answers. Total of 11 possible alternatives.
Source: Guerra and Santos (2017).

The overconfidence that prevails in boardrooms was also confirmed in a more recent survey by **Guerra, Barros and Santos,**[19] of 340 directors serving on boards in 40 countries. Fifty-seven percent reported a high level of confidence among the board of directors and executives, while 25% remained neutral and 18% disagreed that there is this excessive confidence.

Adjustment

Another mistake that can also be triggered by numerical information, are adjustment biases, the classic example of which is **anchoring**. This bias is generated by two different mechanisms: one is related to **System 2** and occurs by means of a deliberate adjustment process, while the other, which is related to the speed and automatism of **System 1**, results from a **priming effect**, where simple exposure to one or another word can cause immediate and measurable changes in the association with other meanings.[20] One example of an **anchoring effect** given by **Kahneman** is the individual answer to questions such as: "Was Gandhi about 144 when he died? How old was Gandhi when he died?" The starting point of the answer is already suggested by the proposition or formulation of the question itself. In different circumstances, this **anchoring bias** causes the person to make an initial estimate that is **adjusted** to move closer to the final answer, but which is always influenced by the initial proposition.[21]

The anchoring that results from the priming is a suggestion that selectively evokes compatible evidence. According to **Kahneman** himself, it was the German psychologists **Thomas Mussweiller and Fritz Strack** who most convincingly demonstrated the role of associative coherence in **anchoring**:

> "In one experiment, they asked an anchoring question about temperature: 'Is the annual mean temperature in Germany higher or lower than 20°C (68°F)?' or 'Is the annual mean temperature in Germany higher or lower than 5°C (41°F)?' All participants were then briefly shown words that they were asked to identify. The researchers found that 68°F made it easier to recognize summer words (like sun and beach), and 40°F facilitated winter words (like frost and ski). The selective activation of compatible memories explains anchoring: the high and the low numbers activate different sets of ideas in memory. The estimates of annual temperature draw on these biased samples of ideas and are therefore biased as well."[22]

Presentation

Among the cognitive biases are those that are related to the way information is presented. It is even considered natural, for example, when someone chooses a food that is 90% fat-free instead of one that presents itself as having only 10% fat. The two statements are absolutely equivalent in terms of content, but the way of presenting them is decisive for the consumers to make their choices. In other circumstances, the presentation of a figure involves emotions more directly. The patient, who is going to undergo surgery, probably prefers to hear that, after one month, his/her chances of survival are 90% instead of being informed by the doctor that the mortality rate up to 30 days after surgery is 10%.

Among **presentation biases, framing** can be identified by those who witness decision-making processes on boards on a daily basis. **Framing bias** results from the form or even the order in which each piece of information is perceived and processed. For example, the first person to speak up about an issue is more likely to define the views of the others, in other words, to frame the others' perspective. It is for this reason that, in Chapter 4, a number of the directors interviewed, including **Pedro Parente**,[*] recommend that the board chair should always be the last one to express his/her opinion regarding a proposal. Another interviewee reported the following typical case of the negative effect of a **framing bias**:

> For the first time, we had managed to hire an external consultant to carry out an assessment of the board. For three months, time and money were invested to conduct an in-depth assignment. Board directors, executives and even some shareholders were interviewed in order to identify points for improvement in the board of directors. I monitored it closely and was very optimistic in relation to the opportunity for improvement. A meeting was scheduled to present the results of the assessment and, subsequently, to define a plan of action. But as soon as the consultant presented the results, the first board director to speak up, after saying that the assessment had been done well, put a real damper on the whole thing. At least, for those who were eager to discover the outcome of the assessment. He argued that, instead of wasting time on formalities, such as the action plan resulting from the board's annual assessment, the board should concentrate more on analyzing the business' strategic issues. The others immediately embraced this perspective, which, furthermore, seemed to be much more interesting than scheduling their own homework to improve the BoD and the board directors themselves. The plan of action from the assessment of the board of directors came to be viewed as an unnecessary formality. There was no way to redirect the discussion, in other words, to reframe everyone's understanding. Not even when I myself argued that one of the points identified for improvement was specifically the board's going into greater depth on strategic issues. Unfortunately to a great extent the assessment of the board of directors ended up being a wasted opportunity, since its conclusions had no effect and since we did not have a systematic action plan of improvement, we were also unable to focus the board's discussions on the company's strategy, which the board director so compellingly argued for. He wanted to achieve the same objective, but he attacked the means, showing a lack of

---

[*] Pedro Parente, who is the current chairman of BRF's board of directors, was previously the Chair of B3 and the CEO of Petrobras between May 2016 and June 2018. In addition to having held various executive positions and having served as a board director and chairman of the BoD of a number of companies, he was also the Minister of Planning (1999), the Chief of Staff of the Presidency (1999–2002) and the Minister of Mines and Energy (2002) of Brazil. The author interviewed Pedro Parente in São Paulo, Brazil, on September 3, 2015.

knowledge and a certain degree of arrogance. I have seen the first opinion "contaminate" the perception of others a number of times. It is not impossible to reframe the discussion, but it can be difficult, depending upon the context.

The example given at the start of this chapter clearly demonstrates **framing bias** with the overlap of the **halo effect**, that is, the tendency to like (or dislike) everything related to a person, including things that have not even been empirically verified yet. In the case initially reported, Lucas, the director who was an expert on mergers and acquisitions, was influenced by the **halo effect** when standing up for the CEO against Oscar, the new board member who was a finance expert, without even being able to objectively analyze his considerations and demands regarding the new merger proposal.

Another director interviewed recounts an episode in which recognizing the role of **framing** made it possible for the members of a board to become aware and accept new perspectives, which were supported by an external consultant:

> Anyone who thinks that biases do not exist is not being realistic about life. When you become emotionally attached to a decision and passionately pursue a goal, you are subject to blind spots. This certainly happens to me and to everybody. But I believe that there are sinister biases and positive biases. I once had to draw up a succession plan on our board. All of us already had our opinions as to who the next CEO should be. We worked for almost nine months, however, with a consultant, a professional who systematized the succession process without making it overly bureaucratic. It was interesting to observe people's reaction. In the end, an executive who we had initially regarded as being in third or fourth place for the succession ended up being chosen as the new CEO. And that only happened because of the new ideas presented and the methodology used by the consultant. So, in order to identify the bias, it is important to have the right person with the courage to raise the issue, not just for choosing the CEO, but for every type of decision made in the boardroom. It may be good for the organization to have someone who goes against the flow.

Situation

Excessive amounts of information can add even more tension and pressure to the decision-making process and distract the board's focus from what is relevant – or irrelevant – when evaluating a proposal before it. This is the case, for example, of the board director with a tendency to micromanage, which was discussed in Chapter 3: immersed in details, the director increases the risk of letting the "gorilla" slip past.

The directors who responded to **Guerra and Santos'**[23] survey (Graph 6.1) identified **time pressure** as one of the three main causes for their mistakes in boardrooms. Executives may routinely cite short windows of opportunity due to competitive pressures or expiration of exclusivity periods as leaving the Board no alternative but to quickly consider the available information and make a decision. presented by the executives, which requires a quick reaction or that the competition does not wait or even an offer to acquire a business, of which the exclusivity term is running out. These situations appear to be frequent in various parts of the world. In **Guerra, Barros and Santos'** latest research,[24] only 12% of board directors say that board meetings never take place under time pressure or pressure from a deadline in relation to taking a decision. Along the same lines, a mere 15% of directors state that the time available for the BoD to reach a decision is never less than the amount of time needed, as shown in the results in Graphs 6.2 and 6.3.

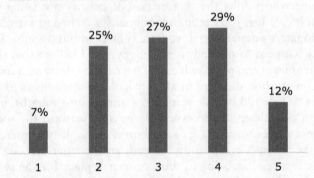

Insufficient time in boardrooms

Survey Question: Do the board meetings take place under time pressure or pressure in terms of deadline for decision making?
(1) Always (5) Never

Graph 6.2 Time pressure.
Source: Guerra, Barros and Santos (2020).

Time pressure, however, can have impacts that go beyond those observed in the decision-making process itself, influencing behavior in an unexpected way, as shown by the classic experiment performed by Princeton researchers in 1973.[25] Separated into small groups, students were invited to give a presentation on the biblical parable of the Good Samaritan, the man who helps a wounded and abandoned victim of thieves on the road between Jerusalem and Jericho. In the experiment, as students were supposed to go from one building to another in order to make their presentation, the researchers planted a mugging "victim" in rags on the route.

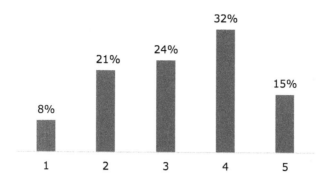

Survey Question: Do you get the feeling that the amount of time that the board has to produce decisions is less than the amount of time it needs? (1) Always (5) Never

Graph 6.3 Time availability.
Source: Guerra, Barros and Santos (2020).

The researchers noted that the influence of time pressure on behavior was unmistakable: in the group that was instructed to proceed to the other building as quickly as possible only 10% of students helped the "victim," while 90% simply ignored the person. Furthermore, there were even some who virtually trod on the "victim" because of the rush. Among the students in the group that was given the least degree of time pressure, 63% stopped to help.

The conclusion of this experiment can certainly make a board director think twice before accepting **time pressure** imposed on complex and risky decisions, "because an excellent opportunity will be lost forever." A refusal to submit to **time pressure** is not always well understood by fellow directors, as one of the interviewees recounts:

As the chair of a non-profit organization's board, I experience time stress with a different focus than in companies. For example, at the charity a very delicate issue arose and I wanted to resolve it by consensus. So, I scheduled another meeting with the executive committee, which was smaller, and we began the meeting at five in order to finish it at seven. Around half past six, one of the vice-presidents intervened, saying: "I think we have already discussed this topic a lot. Most of us agree with you and the matter is resolved, we have other items on the agenda. Let's move on, otherwise the meeting won't end at seven." Silence. As the chair, I replied: "No, no. Let's continue, the topic is a delicate one and it is not finished." The vice-president was shocked and uneasy. At a certain point, another board member changed his mind, then another one went on to accept … and slowly we arrived at a consensus at half past eight. The atmosphere was a bit tense between the two of us until the vice-president invited me for coffee, he wanted to clear up the situation with me. I took the opportunity and presented my position as chairman of the board: "I am going to say two things and then you will end up agreeing with me. The first is: the people who are on that body are not earning any money, they are donating their time. They are all CEOs of large companies and I do not think that I have the right to impose my will or the will of the majority forcing it down the throats of a minority without the matter being discussed until exhaustion. Therefore, I strove for consensus and I will continue to seek consensus, except as a last resort. The other point is this: as chairman of the board, my vote is the same as everyone else's, but the one who changes the agenda topic is the chairman. The chairman is in charge of the agenda." At that moment he ended up laughing and acknowledged that putting time pressure on the chairman does not help.

Whether due to the attempt to build a consensus or on account of some dysfunctionality in the board, meetings really can seem endless, making the directors tired adding even more **complexity** to the decision-making process, and introducing situation biases. For 68% of the board directors who answered a survey conducted in 2020 in 40 countries,[26] fatigue contributes to hasty decisions, as shown in Graph 6.4.

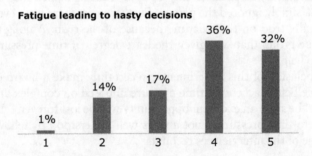

Fatigue leading to hasty decisions

Survey Question: Does fatigue/tiredness among the board members during meetings contribute to the body making hasty decisions?
(1) Always (5) Never

Graph 6.4 Fatigue.
Source: Guerra, Barros and Santos (2020).

Another significant **situation bias** is **attenuation** when the context of decision-making is simplified, overlooking or minimizing uncertainties. For **Arnott**,[27] the "crudest way to cope with an uncertain decision environment is to simply consider them as certain." Although it can have dramatic consequences, mitigating or underestimating impacts or innovations that have appeared on the scene is not an uncommon corporate behavior. For example, who would have said at the start of the 21st century that the largest taxi networks in the world would not own a single car? Or that the accommodation sector would be revolutionized by digital platforms that have no real estate assets? Furthermore, that after having achieved a resounding success, these same innovative business models, which became symbols, were themselves threatened by a totally unexpected disruptive factor: the COVID-19 pandemic? For many players in these sectors, the emergence of these business models is a clear demonstration that **attenuation** in relation to innovations – particularly those which, at first glance, seem too far out of the box – may have detrimental consequences for more traditional companies. If these examples are still not enough, all you need to do is to remember the Swiss watches rejecting digital technology or Kodak, which invented the digital camera but did not back its development so as not to rival its main product: film. The history narrated in the wake of the pandemic tends to demonstrate more than ever that one needs to be permanently on alert not to be caught off guard by the **attenuation bias:** everything can change. And the impossible – going through the door without prior notification.

In Addition to Biases, There Are Dysfunctional Behaviors

Occurring separately or overlapping, the set of cognitive biases identified and described by researchers helps explain just how hard it is for decision-makers to act exclusively within the frame of rationality: the human propensity to irrationality is now a solidly studied concept.[28] It is not only cognitive biases, however, that cause individual board directors to stray from their most objective and rational decisions. **Dysfunctional behaviors**[*] exhibited in boardrooms can be so commonplace that they contaminate the performance of the collective body as a whole. For this reason, based on a study of boards of directors carried out in Canada, **Leblanc and Gillies**[29] outlined a basic typology of the behavioral profile of dysfunctional directors:

Types of Dysfunctional Board Directors

- "Caretaker" chairs – are unable to effectively run board meetings, do not deal with interpersonal conflicts and disagreements, and do not relate well with the other directors, the CEO and the executive team. They should be replaced if they do not improve.
- "Controllers" – dominate the functioning of the board by competence, diplomacy, humor or anger. They are very dangerous, especially when the board includes dysfunctional directors who are unable to neutralize them.

---

[*] See also the most harmful behaviors described in Chapter 2.

- **"Conformists"** – are board directors who do not collaborate and do not perform, who support the status quo and are rarely prepared for any serious discussion. They tend to be liked on account of past successes or relationships and may have been CEOs or politicians who now enjoy limited credibility.
- **"Cheerleaders"** – are "enthusiastic amateurs" who constantly praise the directors, the CEO and the executive team, but are unprepared for meetings, heedless of the strategic issues faced by the company and usually ask stupid questions. At worst, they are viewed with contempt, at best, they are known as "sleepers," "non-performers" or "ineffective."
- **"Critics"** – are constantly criticizing and complaining in an aggressive tone of voice and with harsh words. The other board directors refer to them as "manipulative" or "sneaky." In addition, they lack the ability to dissent in a constructive way, which is a characteristic of challengers or change agents.

The authors of this typology stress that, particularly in the case of people carrying out their responsibilities often in complex circumstances, no classification should be written in stone. They state that, in specific situations, it is possible for individuals to act differently than they would under "normal" circumstances. Therefore, in a situation of greater stress, a habitually dysfunctional board director may come up with exceptional ideas, while another can cause surprise by his or her lack of effectiveness. In other words, a dysfunctional director can start to behave in a functional way and vice versa. However, **Leblanc and Gillies** concluded that these behavioral characteristics of the individual often serve as a good indicator of a board member's future performance.

Up to this point, this chapter has discussed the influence of cognitive biases and the constraints on human rationality from the point of view of the individual. However, when people come together in a group, as is the case with boards of directors, there is an increase in the complexity of interpersonal dynamics and this can produce even more complex dysfunctionalities. Therefore, gradually, the role of behavioral factors on the quality of the decision-making process in organizations has been gaining the proper visibility and importance.

According to researchers,[30] one of the main sources of problems in interpersonal relationships within groups is **social pressure**, the fear of public disapproval (which can lead to bullying*) or damage to their good relationships with people considered to be more important or powerful. In **Guerra and Santos'** survey[31] of 102 directors, the vast majority stated that concern not to damage social ties with the controlling shareholders (72%) or with the most important shareholders (57%) is a frequent or

---

* See also the most harmful behaviors described in Chapter 2.

very frequent reason that sidetracks them from making decisions that are in the company's best interest. **Pedro Parente**[*] who is an experienced chair and has had a consistent career as a CEO, highlights that throughout his career he has seen this social pressure be transformed into omission and frustration at board meetings, especially when the board plays only a supporting role, as described in Chapter 4:

> The greatest obstacle to more assertive behavior by board directors – even independent ones – is undoubtedly the position of the chairperson and the owners, if they are present at meetings. It is the main constraint factor. I have seen the simple exercise of a contradictory opinion result in intolerance and then the removal of directors. I often see frustrated people, especially when the board is a pro forma one, for appearance's sake. Unfortunately, it is more common than it should be. I have no statistics regarding this point, it is my observation. But it is not unusual for there to be directors who are truly remiss. The board member's independence is an assumption, which needs to be confirmed in the board's practice. And if, despite being technically independent according to legal requirements and definitions, that board director does not speak up, does not behave as such, the company no longer benefits from his or her contribution.

When added together within the group, individual biases generate a series of obstacles and deviations in the decision-making process, making the board as a whole more vulnerable to the suppression of dissenting opinions, the misperception of risks or the wasting of time, while important activities await a decision. These are just some of the factors that – potentially – are capable of causing the board to make decisions that none of the directors would take individually (notwithstanding their own biases!). Being for the most part unconscious, biases move through boardrooms like lost souls, terrifying those who can see them and destroying the purported rationality of decisions. In an attempt to at least reduce this negative influence on the group, a number of authors have attempted to identify these group biases and have created classifications, which can be summarized as follows:

Cognitive Biases Active in Group Dynamics

Herd effect – some directors (usually without enough information) tend to get carried away by the opinions of their peers, resulting in a decision that was not properly thought through/discussed.

---

[*] The author interviewed Pedro Parente in São Paulo, Brazil, on September 3, 2015.

Group thinking – the formation of homogeneous groups, with a similar style of thinking, which tends to avoid conflict and seek consensus at any cost, ignoring external information.

False consensus – the trend among some individuals to think that their opinions and assumptions are always correct, overestimating the probability that the other directors will agree with their point of view.

In-group favoritism – the tendency to support the opinions of the company's directors and executives and to reject suggestions from outsiders, disregarding views from outside the organization that could be relevant.

Self-serving – the proneness to attribute success to internal characteristics and failure to external or exogenous influences (attribution of blame to third parties).

When asked about how often they saw these group biases occur inside the boardroom, the directors researched in **Guerra and Santos'** survey[32] identified the ghosts that rage out of control inside the "black box."

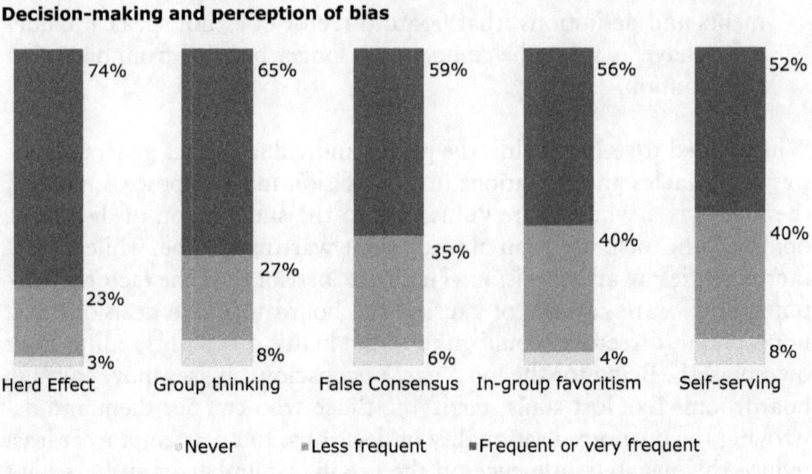

Decision-making and perception of bias

	Herd Effect	Group thinking	False Consensus	In-group favoritism	Self-serving
Frequent or very frequent	74%	65%	59%	56%	52%
Less frequent	23%	27%	35%	40%	40%
Never	3%	8%	6%	4%	8%

Never   ▪Less frequent   ▪Frequent or very frequent

Graph 6.5 Group cognitive biases most present in boardrooms.
Source: Guerra and Santos (2017).

Pathologies: In Groups, the Biases Add Up and Increase

It is essential to note that the biases inherent to the group's dynamics occur at the same time – often unconsciously – as the series of intra-board and extra-board tensions that have already been detailed in Chapter 3.

At meetings and in the decision-making process, this combination can lead to such serious dysfunctionalities that Pick and Merchant[33] actually preferred to classify them as pathologies, describing them in the following way.

Excessive Conformity

Generally characterized by a **lack of diversity**,[*] the environment of BoD is a breeding ground for **excess conformity**, which can gradually shape and standardize the behavior and opinions of the directors. The group's feeling of cohesion is welcome, as it increases the perception of satisfaction with the jointly carried out activities, reduces the inclination to leave and increases the level of engagement as well as a commitment to the business' goals and results. But what one has to be careful with here is the degree of cohesion.[34] **Pick and Merchant**[35] point out that research has already demonstrated that, on boards where there is room for the contradictory opinion of the minority to be heard, the decision-making process is more robust and the group is able to arrive at more creative and innovative solutions.

All these factors related to cohesion, therefore, are very positive until the point at which they weaken the debate within the BoD and become pathological, causing **three typical behaviors of excess conformity**, which result from group thinking:

1. a sense of invulnerability based on successful initiatives in the past;
2. questioning and/or self-defense in the face of information contrary to the group's perspective;
3. loyalty to the group and its survival creates strong social pressure for the point of view of the majority to always prevail.

According to the survey by **Guerra, Barros and Santos** (2020), excess conformity, does indeed still seem to be predominant in boardrooms, with room to increase the level of comfort for disagreements and the level of dissension among directors, as shown in Graphs 6.6 and 6.7 (see following page).

The question, which gives rise to all the problems related to excess conformity, is well summarized in a phrase by the American writer Mark Twain: "*When you find yourself on the side of the majority, it's time to pause and reflect.*"[36]

---

[*] The typical profile of board directors has already been covered in Chapter 2: a man in his mid-50s, usually a former CEO with similar values and beliefs.

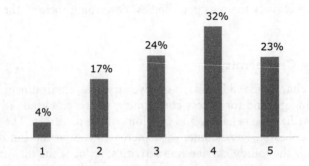

Comfort to disagree and level of dissension: it could still be better

Survey Question: The level of comfort for board members to disagree with
those who have the most power in the organization is:
(1) Nonexistent (5) Very good

Graph 6.6 Comfort to disagree.

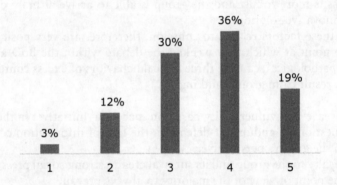

Survey Question: The level of dissension at board meetings – free debate with
the expression of contrasting views – is:
(1) Nonexistent (5) Very pronounced

Graph 6.7 Level of dissension.
Source: Guerra, Barros and Santos (2020).

Negative Group Conflict

Bringing different professional backgrounds to the board, it is natural –
and even desirable – for there to be differences of opinion among the directors in their assessment of the proposals. This is what researchers call
cognitive conflict:[37] the ability to disagree respectfully, contributing to the
debate leads to the best-combined solution. In previous chapters, experts
and board directors who were interviewed, such as **Luiz Carlos Cabrera
and César Souza,** differentiated between productive and counterproductive conflicts. The question here, however, is how to maintain the right

level of cohesion: not so comfortable that the directors hesitate to put forward a contradictory opinion for fear of damaging social ties and not so uncomfortable as to cause inaction due to fear of disapproval public. The pendulum of discord needs to find a balance, because **negative conflicts** can deeply corrode the board's work, with harmful consequences not just for the board's performance but also for the company and its stakeholders.

Assessing the degree and quality of the conflict in boardrooms, in the survey by **Guerra, Barros and Santos,**[38] more than half of the directors feel that the level is appropriate, while just 21% state that it goes beyond the limit, ceasing to be productive and beneficial, as shown in Graph 6.8.

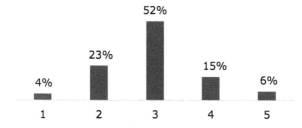

Conflict: majority feel that it is at the right point

Survey Question: How would you rate the level of conflict in your board?
1 (there is never any conflict)
3 (there is the right amount of conflict to allow free discussion of ideas)
5 (there is a lot of conflict, to the point where the conflict becomes negative)

Graph 6.8 Level of conflict on boards.
Source: Guerra, Barros and Santos (2020).

Another study carried out by the **International Finance Corporation (IFC)** and the **Center for Effective Dispute Resolution (CEDR)** with 191 directors and executives of companies of various sizes, investigated what, in their opinion, were the most frequent causes of counterproductive conflicts in boardrooms, as shown in Table 6.2 (see following page).

It is interesting to note the prominence of behavioral factors directly involved among the main reasons for counterproductive conflicts experienced within boards of directors, such as the personal attitudes of the directors (38.4%) and the involvement of shareholders or family members in the business (21.7%). In the most common shareholding context, with control by business families or control shared between business groups and funds – some of these negative conflicts are recurring, particularly when it comes to family-controlled organizations, as **Luiz Carlos Cabrera**[*] explains:

[*] Luiz Carlos Cabrera is the founding partner and CEO of LCabrera Consultants. Former board member of the AESC – Association of Executive Search and

Table 6.2 Behavioral aspects are among the main causes of conflict on boards

Financial, structural or procedural workings of the organization	40.3%[a]
Personal behavior and attitudes of directors	38.4%
Strategy development, including mergers and acquisitions	37.2%
Risk appetite and risk management	31.3%
Change and crisis management	30.6%
Audit findings	29.9%
Board process issues, such as structure of meetings, schedules, etc.	29.4%
Management oversight	28.4%
Composition of the board and senior management	24.7%
Involvement in the business of shareholders/owners' family in business	21.7%

a The percentage indicates whether the topic of the dispute is frequent or very frequent.
Source: IFC-CEDR.[39]

From my observation, negative conflict is usually more serious when a family member is the chief executive – even if he is not a shareholder. Because there is no shame. When it is just one family, you already have conflict, and it gets much worse in companies that are controlled by two or three families. Conflicts are sometimes over petty matters. The worst times are when discussing the remuneration of a family CEO with the rest of the family. There was one that said to me: "What I earn is an allowance, it is not the salary of a CEO of a high-performance business!" You cannot let a rift occur, so what you do nowadays is arbitrate. You call in a specialized consultancy to present the remuneration of other equivalent CEOs. It is necessary to substantiate the proposal to be discussed by the family. Another mission, one of the most difficult ones, is the hiring of the first non-shareholder CEO. This happens because there are no people with the necessary abilities in the family for the position or because the conflict within the family or between the controlling shareholders is already so great that it is preferable to bring someone in from outside. Even so, it is difficult to get past the conflict that has already taken root.

And in companies with shared control, what do you notice in relation to counterproductive conflicts?

Leadership International Board and former chairman of the AESC Brazilian Chapter. He was awarded the Gardner W. Heidrick award, which is given annually by the AESC, to which he made a notable contribution to the executive search consultancy activity. The author interviewed Luiz Carlos Cabrera in São Paulo, Brazil, on February 23, 2016.

Shared control is also an ideal environment for negative conflict. Once again, I stress the independent director's role. He needs to be very mature to know how to exercise his role. Why? In shared control there is often an attempt to avoid conflict by holding a prior meeting and then arriving at the board meeting with the decisions already made.* Then they ask the independent director: "And what do you think?" There is no point in saying what he thinks, because if he doesn't agree, it's already too late. The decision has already been made. Very often, not all the controlling shareholders gave their opinions at the prior meeting, and, when the matter comes before the board, the discussion can become very bitter. This controlling shareholder will try to reverse the previous decision of the other, seeking an alliance with the independent director, who did not take part in anything earlier on and who does not have all the information. At that point, there is a very quick attempt at cooptation and the conflict just gets worse, because now the independent also has to position himself. So, one of the tensest moments is the rediscussion of a topic with the participation of the independent directors, who were left out of the advance discussions. Over the last few years corporate governance has begun to play a more active role, and companies are gradually learning to rely more on the contribution of independent directors. In regions where almost all boards have one representative who is linked to the shareholders, the conflict is inherent.

Even when they do not get to the point of causing the company to break down or to disintegrate, counterproductive conflicts can cause tangible damage to the business, as revealed by the **IFC-CEDR** survey. Table 6.3 presents the main negative impacts of the disputes according to the 191 directors and executives who responded:

Table 6.3 Main damage caused to the business by counterproductive conflicts

Wasting management time	49.3%[a]
Distracting from core business priorities	44.9%
Reducing trust among board members	42.8%
Affecting the functioning of the board	42.1%
Affecting the efficiency of the organization	38.3%
Negatively affecting relationships within the organization	32.4%
Costing the company money	29.5%
Damaging long-term business performance/profitability	26.8%
Affecting the reputation of the organization	23.7%

a Percentages stating the item had a "significant" or "very significant" impact.
Source: IFC-CEDR, 2014.[40]

---

* This is the opposite behavior to what, in Chapter 4, was called "advance discussions," when the chair has talks in advance with the directors to encourage everyone to be in a position to make their best possible contribution and not hesitate to bring contradictory opinions to the debate.

Dysfunctional Coalition

If, on the one hand, excessive social cohesion can lead to conformity and group thinking, on the other, when cohesion is very weak, it can contribute to the formation of dysfunctional coalitions, which only protect their own interests. It is not unusual for this to happen, particularly if the composition of the board of directors includes distinct groups, each representing a different family or shareholder. In this case, alliances can be forged and, even when the subgroup seeks specific, temporary goals, the polarization and breakdown become definitive.

Another factor that favors this type of internal coalition is the leadership style exercised by the board's chairperson. If they are very strong and assertive, they may end up arrogating to themselves the power to lead by using manipulation and blindsiding. On the other hand, where there is a leadership vacuum on the part of the chair it will contribute to the other directors exercising power in a more subversive way in order – sometimes with the best of intentions – to make the board play its role.[41] Individually or together, these circumstances facilitate the emergence of real warring factions within the board, resulting in harmful consequences,[42] including among others:

- Discouraging contradictory opinions within the coalition, alliance or faction (whatever one prefers to call it);
- The coalition rationalizes disregarding facts and data that are not in line with the thinking of that internal subgroup of the BoD;
- The coalition competes with other directors as if they were rivals, ignoring the board's common objective, which is the strategic management of the business;
- Within the coalition there is a strong pressure to reach and maintain consensus;
- Other directors may self-censor in order to avoid conflicts with the coalition;
- These disputes do not only occur between the directors, but also against other specific subgroups such as shareholders, executives and other stakeholders.

When they looked into the frequency of coalitions in boardrooms among the 340 directors from 40 countries they surveyed, **Guerra, Barros and Santos**[43] discovered that 63% of the sample has at least one coalition, as shown in the figures in Graph 6.9 (see following page).

In addition to demonstrating the **framing bias** and the **halo effect**, the case presented at the start of this chapter is also an example of

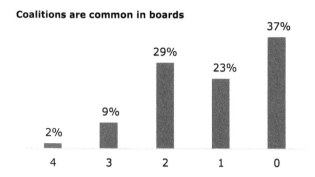

Coalitions are common in boards

Survey Question: Does your board have coalitions (groups that seek to exert political/social influence on the board)? How many coalitions can you identify? (4 = 4 coalitions or more); (3 = 3 coalitions); (2 = 2 coalitions); (1 = 1 coalition) or (0 = There are no coalitions).

Graph 6.9 Level of coalitions.
Source: Guerra, Barros and Santos (2020).[53]

the formation of a coalition. Although unconsciously, a subgroup of directors aligned themselves with Lucas, the investment committee's coordinator and a mergers and acquisitions expert who stood up for the CEO and failed to consider the observations and demands of the director who pointed out the fallacies of the proposed transaction in an objective way. This shows how, as tension and polarization between the subgroups increase, the BoD gradually becomes less effective, ceasing to perform its functions, among them, as in this case, that of objectively monitoring the performance of the CEO and the results that he/she delivers.

Habitual Routines

Everybody wants a board that works well, but it is the chairperson who is responsible for enforcing the rules and ensuring the efficiency of the BoD's operating processes. However, in exercising this role, there is a risk that board meetings will become excessively routine and bureaucratic, which makes the board members less inclined to offer their best contribution. While the **habitual routines**[*44] follow their inflexible

---

*   According to Gersick and Hackman, the so-called habitual **routines** occur when "a group repeatedly exhibits a functionally similar pattern of behavior in a given stimulus situation without explicitly selecting it over alternative ways of behaving."

rhythm, they are there, physically present, but, dominated by **System 1**, the mind does not pick up on the issues that could be more important. Graph 6.10 shows how often board meetings get bogged down with habitual routines, which are capable of hijacking the effectiveness of the decision-making process.

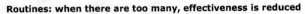

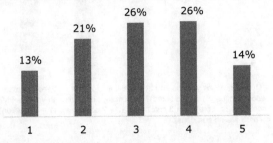

Survey Question: The board is stuck in habitual routines that shape the way it works (absence of a flexible dynamic) reducing its effectiveness:
(1) I totally agree (5) I totally disagree

Graph 6.10 Habitual routines.
Source: Guerra, Barros and Santos (2020).[54]

One example of a situation in which boards are usually hijacked by routine is the very common habit of starting meetings by analyzing the results of the period prior to the board's meeting. The justification given for sticking to this routine seems convincing: after all, the board needs to base its discussions on what is – or is not and should be – happening. Isn't this merely fulfilling the BoD's role of monitoring the company's performance and its results? On the other hand, this routine practice can be very inefficient: the directors use up the "prime time" of the meeting, when everyone is rested and full of energy, to look at the past – rather than at what still needs to be done and what is urgent. Another negative is that the discussion of past results may end up reducing the amount of time available for matters that are strategic or of key importance to the company, as described by a director who was interviewed for this book:

> We have a monthly meeting of about four hours and our chairperson insists on starting off by analyzing the previous month's results. Normally, 45 minutes are reserved for this agenda item, but it is quite common for us to spend half the meeting – and sometimes even more – on this discussion. What happens is that all the board directors end up wanting to make individual comments about one fact or

another. We often discuss details of the operation that we shouldn't be looking at. When one of us points out that we are frittering away time that could be used for very important topics, there is always the argument that what we are discussing is very important and that it is pointless to move forward without resolving the issue in question. I have noticed that this is also a way – whether consciously or not – of avoiding discussing other issues in depth.

It is as if there is a mental block. Too much time is spent analyzing the result for the period and no time is spent talking, for example, about the lack of a holistic model for risk management or about the need to change the CEO. He has been with the company for 13 years and is way too old. He is no longer able to meet the business' present needs, much less its needs for the future. This routine restricts the board's dynamics. I wonder whether the analysis of the previous period's results could not be an essential part of the pre-meeting reading material, and if and when there was any deviation from what was planned – that deserved discussion – the topic would be given more time on the agenda. But even so, the start of the meeting would be reserved for the major topics planned for that day instead of for the monitoring of performance.

Shared Information

In addition to rigid routines that fritter away the board directors' precious time, there is the **shared information** bias, which can contribute to the group failing to take into account data that is relevant to the decision-making process. This cognitive misunderstanding involves various aspects of group dynamics, including what **Sunstein and Hastie** call informational signals. According to them, the person "perceives" a signal in his or her fellow board member and fails to share information or opinions that would be relevant to taking a decision. For example,

> "In the federal government, (…) people might silence themselves because they think that an official who does not share their views and who has his own information must be right. If the secretary of defense has a strong conviction about whether military intervention is a good idea, the people who work for the secretary might shut up, not because they agree, but because they think that the secretary probably knows what he is doing."[45]

According to the **IFC-CEDR**[46] study, the BoD can exhaust itself discussing at great length information that is already known to everyone, instead of dedicating itself to sharing the data that only one or two members of the board have. Group dynamics are subject to a series of factors that increase this inappropriately shared information bias, including among others:

- The desire to reach closure instead of prioritizing the construction of the best possible decision, gathering new information;
- In more ambiguous and judgment-oriented tasks, the group places a greater value on the search for consensus rather than for the best solution;
- When analyzing in advance just the information that is already available to the majority, the directors arrive at the meeting with pre-judgments. When the discussion starts in the group, directors are more inclined to bring up only that data which confirms their previous evaluation;
- In order to form or maintain their reputation, preserve bonds of friendship or win the competition with other directors, the person seeks the group's support for their personal opinions;
- The group usually considers the person who repeats information that is already shared by the majority as being more capable rather than someone who brings new data to the discussion (Graph 6.11).

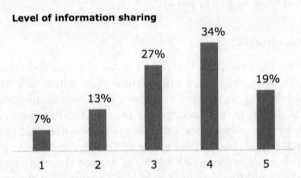

Level of information sharing

Survey Question: When making important decisions, did the board members share information that only they had, even if it seemed obvious and already known to everyone?
1 (individual information sharing was selective and very limited)
5 (individual information sharing was very pronounced)

Graph 6.11 Information sharing.
Source: Guerra, Barros and Santos (2020).[55]

Pluralistic Ignorance

Especially when the board's leadership is weak, the group's members may have different opinions, but refrain from expressing them because they believe they do not coincide with those of their colleagues. This leaves little room for productive conflict. **Pick and Merchant** would say that such boards suffer from **pluralist ignorance bias**. This bias adds harmful consequences to the mistakes from information sharing that have already been described. Fearing the group's social pressure and not feeling psychologically secure, one – or more – board directors may avoid voicing opinions, which they believe are at odds with the majority. Even on BoDs where there is more room for dissent and more psychological security, it takes a lot of backbone to bring a major problem that the board possibly does not want to see. The situation only gets worse if there are public implications, which, in the case of a company with shares listed on the stock exchange, is no trifling matter.

In addition to courage, to embark on a task of this kind, the directors will have to invest time to satisfy themselves in relation to what they intend to expose to the board. This was the case, for example, with this member of an audit committee because of his literacy as a seasoned accountant, but who was not a member of the Board, which can be the case in some countries:

> This was the tensest, most stressful moment that I have ever experienced on an audit committee. I was called with three other professionals to take part in a preparatory committee for the future audit committee of a company that was going to do an IPO. When I come on board, I'm a real doubting Thomas. I go through the whole thing to see what's going on, I want to make sure that the picture they give me is a true representation of the situation. This company, due to the nature of the business, is totally dependent on the quality of information technology (IT) for two basic functions: risk management and information security management. Two months before the audit committee's first report was published, at a strategic planning meeting, one of the directors openly questioned me as to what I thought of the company's IT structure. Everyone was in the room, including the IT director, and I replied, "In terms of internal controls and processes, the situation can be compared to a Ferrari without brakes. It has a very powerful engine, a fantastic execution capacity, it has competent people, but the IT systems are worse than appalling. If it isn't fixed, everything that you are planning for the company's future will be built on shaky ground." And I detailed the reasons, including the result – which was very bad – of some tests that I had already carried out. People started muttering nervously, but that's as far as it went.
>
> Some time went by and, when discussing the draft of the audit committee's report, I have another ritual that I follow: I hold a meeting with the members of the committee and we go over the report item by item, word by word. And in the conclusions, we decided to put a qualification regarding the quality of the internal controls

in IT. And that was how the document went forward to the board meeting, which I was not present at because I was not invited and I was not a director.* At the meeting one of them raised the point: "Did you read this here? The audit committee is saying that our IT system is a mess!" Obviously, that was not the word, but that is how the BoD interpreted it. Another director rang me and turned on the speakerphone: "Look, this sentence here, we wanted to look into the possibility of you removing it." My answer was immediate: "Gentlemen, I cannot do that, because the decision to include it was not mine, it was the decision of the committee's members. I don't have the authority to remove a sentence that I didn't put in alone. So, if you want to be justified in asking for it to be removed, I will ask you for half an hour, I will get in touch with the other members of the committee and we will resume the call with everyone."

After about forty minutes, we were back on the phone, but the position we took was a joint one: "We do not feel like minimizing the forcefulness of something that needs to be brought to the market's attention in an explicit way. We are not going to find the solution to this problem by removing the information or softening the words." The CEO then had a brilliant insight and proposed a conversation between himself and the members of the audit committee. Five minutes later he put us all on a conference call, because he had realized that in that collective discussion someone would end up adopting a radical position. One of the committee members ended up making a conciliatory proposal: "Instead of leaving the qualification in the conclusion, how about we put the same sentence in the report's initial part? This way it presents the issue in the proper light and then the reader will have the entire document to put things in context." All the members agreed and the audit committee, having stuck firm to its position of not excluding important information that would become public, ended up gaining a respectability that it did not have beforehand. To conclude, soon after that, the IT director left the company and I am still part of the committee today, almost ten years later.

Unfortunately, the feeling that you get when moving around boardrooms is that there are more examples that are the opposite of the one which has just been described: not even slightly unpleasant matters are brought up. The invisible barrier of silence – as thick as the walls of a fortress – remains

---

*   In some countries it is possible – and sometimes even commonplace – for the audit committees to include experts who are independent but who are not members of the full board. This is the case in this account.

unbroken. Inertia is not vanquished in order not to break the climate of harmony, not to contradict those in power or, simply, not to create embarrassing situations. How many times did the directors of the companies involved in the various cases examined by investigations of wrongdoings remain silent even in matters of such ethical significance, not to mention the legal concerns? In these cases, this synthesis of **Dante Alighieri**'s verses fits like a glove: "*The darkest places in hell are reserved for those who maintain their neutrality in times of moral crisis.*"[*]

Social Loafing

Operating in a collective body can also hide another pathology, which is the phenomenon known as **social loafing**.[47] A study carried out more than 130 years ago by the French agricultural engineer **Max Ringelmann**[48] ended up leading to an unexpected conclusion: he asked a group of workers to pull a rope with as much force as possible; first, individually, and then together. **Ringelmann** measured the strength exerted by each person and then measured the strength performed by the group. **Ringlemann**'s measurements revealed the sum of the effort expended individually was greater than the force exerted collectively by the group of workers pulling together. This could only have one meaning: the human tendency to exert oneself less when one's effort is not clearly identifiable in the group. This phenomenon was called **social opportunism**[49] in the 1970s.

This is a scary finding for boards of directors. After all, the directors do not just work side by side, most of their activities are performed in a collective and interdependent way. Therefore, if the sum of the professional backgrounds, experiences and training of the directors is less in their work on the board than it would be individually, then the companies are really losing a valuable contribution by having brought them together as a group.[50] This was exactly what was verified in 2020 in the research carried out by **Guerra, Barros and Santos**, as shown in the figures presented in Graph 6.12 (see following page).

Polarization

Lastly, another bias that can arise in groups is **polarization**. In this context, polarization refers, not to the character of debate between the

---

[*]   As a matter of fact, this phrase attributed to Dante and which was one of American President John F. Kennedy's favorites, summarizes a long series of verses from Canto III of Hell in The Divine Comedy. Available at https://www.jfklibrary.org/Research/Research-Aids/Ready-Reference/JFK-Fast-Facts/Dante.aspx. Accessed on July 26, 2020.

Social loafing: board members who contribute less

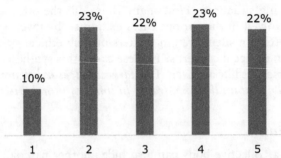

Survey Question: Some of the members on your board of directors collaborated
less than they could have done because the work is collective and individual
efforts are not always identified:
1 (I totally agree)
5 (I totally disagree)

Graph 6.12 Social loafing.
Source: Guerra, Barros and Santos (2020).[56]

board directors, but as a tendency for the collective body to adopt more
extreme positions and make more extreme decisions. Individually, the
person analyzes an issue and takes his/her opinion to the group, where
he/she will hear new arguments, being subject to give in to his/her desire
for acceptance by the group or to the more persuasive proposals from his/
her peers. This being the case, at the end of the discussion, the tendency
is for the decision to be in the initial direction defined individually, but a
little more extreme. In other words, groups made up of individuals who
are more willing to take risks will end up assuming riskier positions,
while those that bring together people who are more risk-averse will tend
to make more cautious decisions. This bias tends to manifest itself more
frequently on boards where there is less room for contradictory opinions,
with low psychological security, little diversity and weak leadership.[51]

Polarization was also observed in **Guerra, Barros and Santos'** research.
Out of the 340 directors who responded, 44% were of the opinion that
the BoDs on which they served tend to make more conservative decisions
than those that would be adopted individually and, at the opposite extreme, 16% stated that the boards end up assuming a higher degree of
risk when making a decision collectively, as shown in Graph 6.13 (see
following page).

Even Flawed, Boards of Directors Make a Valuable Contribution

Despite being continually subjected to so many uncertainties, paradoxes,
internal and external tensions, as well as all these individual and

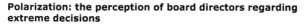

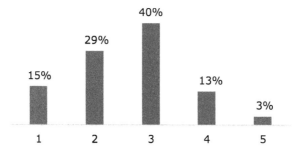

Survey Question: In your opinion, does your board make more extreme decisions (riskier or more conservative) than the board members would make individually?

1 (the board's decisions tend to be more conservative than those that would be made individually)

3 (the board's decisions tend to be the same as those that would be made individually)

5 (the board's decisions tend to be riskier than those that would be made individually

Graph 6.13 Polarization of decisions.
Source: Guerra, Barros and Santos (2020).[57]

group cognitive biases, it is vital to admit that the simple existence of boards of directors, as the highest governance body, is strongly rooted, as **Forbes and Milliken**[52] would say, in the "wise belief that the effective oversight of an organization exceeds the capabilities of any individual and that collective knowledge and deliberation are better suited to this task." On the other hand, it is impossible to fail to observe that BoDs were created in the vain hope that the group – by itself – would act to correct or, at least reduce individual errors. The bad news, as this chapter has shown, is that group interaction boosts and amplifies the occurrence and consequences of individual biases. The good news is that, becoming aware of the existence of biases in the human cognition process, individuals have become able to develop instruments to mitigate the negative effects of group action. Unfortunately, this was not the case recounted by the board director at the start of this chapter. He began to suspect that Lucas might be failing to be objective and that those conversations in the hallway could have really detrimental effects:

> *But everything became much clearer when the CEO presented a new merger proposal to the directors. I remember that it was at that moment that I began to detect the internal dispute that was making the board dysfunctional. During the various rounds of discussion, the debate was polarized between Lucas, with all of his skill in M&A, and Oscar, with his unquestionable experience in finance and his*

*assertive and critical stance. The rest of the board members –
including myself – remained silent. First of all, because none of us
had their level of expertise, and secondly, because Lucas was too
influential to be challenged. More than just respected, he was even
revered by the market; he had excellent relations and a recommendation from him had the power to open or close a lot of doors. So,
nobody wanted to take sides in what might appear to observers to
be a struggle of egos. But, sitting in a privileged vantage point, I
wondered about the reasons for Lucas' defense of this merger: was
it really a business opportunity that could not be missed out on or
was he unconsciously being biased, trying to protect the CEO in a
paternalistic way?*

*That was, until in one of the discussions about the new invest-
ment, Oscar brought up two arguments that seemed to me very
relevant and objective. Before the vote was taken, he wanted two assessments to be made which, according to him, were not being taken
into account by the regular due diligence process, adopted in the
company's model: (1) as there were changes and greater complexity
in the regulatory environment, he would like to get the opinion of a
tax expert to assess the legal risks of that specific transaction; and
(2) since the two companies had totally different cultures, he would
like to get an independent consultant to carry out an assessment
regarding this aspect to assess the risks in the merger process, which
would also be useful in guiding the subsequent merger process, if it
was confirmed. At the end, Oscar stressed that he was not a priori
against the merger, he just wanted to have more objective tools for
its analysis. At that meeting, he was not challenged – not even by
Lucas with all of his expertise in merger operations.*

*For two months, the matter was not brought up in the BoD. It
was not known on the board whether the requested due diligence
was being carried out or not. Everything was quiet until we received
the final material regarding the acquisition without the two reports
that had been requested by Oscar. The meeting for the final decision would be in a week's time, just within the exclusivity period of
the negotiations. Absolutely calm, Oscar pointed out that he was
perceiving an ineffective dynamic in the board: "Nobody adopts a
clear position and then, my request for opinions is simply ignored."
He voted against the proposal. This time, I was the only one to
speak out in favor of the opinions requested by Oscar as fundamental to decision-making and, so I also voted against it. But we were
defeated by the majority who were in favor of the transaction. At
the end of the meeting, when we talked, Oscar commented: "My
disappointment is not that this merger was approved. We are systematically failing to use tools for more objective business analysis.*

If we continue along the lines of the current portfolio, no one will gain value from it." Nobody could demonstrate that Oscar had a second agenda to position himself critically in relation to the CEO and the quality of the management of the investment portfolio. On the other hand, Lucas's indulgence of the CEO hung in the air, without it ever being brought out into the open.

I will need to wait a few more years to see if Oscar's predictions in relation to the future of those transactions actually occurs. However, my suspicion is that those businesses will add very little value over time, not to mention the exposure to risks minimized at source. And what was all of this about? Different views of two experts? Predominance of egos? Or the blindness resulting from the protective and paternalistic attitude of one expert towards the CEO, when he is the one that you most expect to have an impartial, technical and rational opinion? What is certain is that I learned that, paraphrasing Hamlet, there is much more between heaven and earth in the decision-making process of boards of directors than our vain and pretentious business rationality might suppose.

In order to offer tools and paths for all those who depend on the decisions of BoDs and for the directors themselves, as described in this case, the next chapter will present a guide for navigating the world of limited rationality which is also fertile for biases. And, in this way, the chapter will get the best from the existence of a collective decision-making body.

Notes

1 Simon, Herbert Alexander. *Administrative behavior; A study of decision-making processes in administrative organization.* New York: Free Press, 1976.
2 Balestrin, Alsones. Uma análise da contribuição de Herbert Simon para as teorias organizacionais. *Revista Eletrônica de Administração (REAd)*, v. 08, 2002, Escola de Administração — Universidade Federal do Rio Grande do Sul — UFRGS. Available at http://seer.ufrgs.br/index.php/read/article/view/44111. Accessed on June 14, 2020.
3 Arnott, David; Pervan, Graham. A critical analysis of decision support systems research revisited: The rise of design science. 4 ed. *Journal of Information Technology*, London: Palgrave Macmillan, v. 29, p. 269–293, 2014.
4 Kahneman, Daniel. *Thinking, fast and slow.* New York: Farrar, Straus and Giroux, 2011. Location 462 of 10934.
5 This experiment, which was mentioned in Chapter 2, was developed by Daniel J. Simons and Christopher Chabris in 1999 and the video is available at: http://www.theinvisiblegorilla.com/videos.html. Accessed on May 13, 2020.
6 Guerra, Sandra; Santos, Rafael Liza. *Headaches, concerns and regrets: What does the experience of 102 Brazilian directors tell us? Private sector opinion.* Washington, DC: IFC, 2017. Available at https://www.ifc.org/

wps/wcm/connect/topics_ext_content/ifc_external_corporate_site/ifc+cg/
resources/private+sector+opinion/headaches%2C+concerns%2C+and+
regrets+-+what+does+the+experience+of+102+brazilian+directors+tell+us.
Accessed on May 21, 2020.

7 Kahneman, Daniel. *Thinking, fast and slow.* New York: Farrar, Straus and Giroux, 2011. Location 1607 of 9418.

8 Ibid. Location 331 of 9418.

9 Kahneman, Daniel; Tversky, Amos. *Intuitive prediction: Biases and corrective procedures,* 1977. Available at https://www.researchgate.net/publication/235103436_Intuitive_Prediction_Biases_and_Corrective_Procedures. Accessed on October, 1, 2016.

10 Arnott, David. Cognitive biases and decision support systems development: a design science approach. *Information Systems Journal,* v. 16, n. 1, p. 55–78, 2006. Available at https://www.researchgate.net/publication/220356732_Cognitive_biases_and_decision_support_systems_development_A_design_science_approach. Accessed on October 18, 2016.

11 Thuraisingham, Meena; Lehmacher, Wolfgang. *The Secret Life of Decisions: How Unconscious Bias Subverts Your Judgement.* England: Gower Publishing, 2013. Location 186 of 3405.

12 Kahneman, Daniel. *Thinking, fast and slow.* New York: Farrar, Straus and Giroux, 2011.

13 Guerra, Sandra; Santos, Rafael Liza. *Headaches, concerns and regrets: What does the experience of 102 Brazilian directors tell us? Private sector opinion.* Washington, DC: IFC, 2017. Available at https://www.ifc.org/wps/wcm/connect/topics_ext_content/ifc_external_corporate_site/ifc+cg/resources/private+sector+opinion/headaches%2C+concerns%2C+and+regrets+-+what+does+the+experience+of+102+brazilian+directors+tell+us. Accessed on May 21, 2020.

14 Kahneman, Daniel. *Thinking, fast and slow.* New York: Farrar, Straus and Giroux, 2011. Location 1422 of 9418.

15 Johnson, Stefanie K.; Hekman, David R.; Chan Elsa T. If there's only one woman in your candidate pool, there's statistically no chance she'll be hired. *Harvard Business Review,* April 26, 2016. https://www.researchgate.net/profile/David_Hekman3/publication/303003812_If_There's_Only_One_Woman_in_Your_Candidate_Pool_There's_Statistically_No_Chance_She'll_Be_Hired/links/575eea9908ae9a9c955f8e2c/If-Theres-Only-One-Woman-in-Your-Candidate-Pool-Theres-Statistically-No-Chance-Shell-Be-Hired.pdf. Accessed on July 26, 2020.

16 Ibid.

17 Kahneman, Daniel. *Thinking, fast and slow.* New York: Farrar, Straus and Giroux, 2011. Location 217 of 9418.

18 Guerra, Sandra; Santos, Rafael Liza. *Headaches, concerns and regrets: What does the experience of 102 Brazilian directors tell us? Private sector opinion.* Washington, DC: IFC, 2017. Available at https://www.ifc.org/wps/wcm/connect/topics_ext_content/ifc_external_corporate_site/ifc+cg/resources/private+sector+opinion/headaches%2C+concerns%2C+and+regrets+-+what+does+the+experience+of+102+brazilian+directors+tell+us. Accessed on May 21, 2020.

19 Guerra, Sandra; Barros, Lucas A.; Santos, Rafael L. Decision-making in boards of directors: The roles of meeting dynamics and choice architecture. *Research Project,* 2020.

20 Kahneman, Daniel. *Thinking, fast and slow.* New York: Farrar, Straus and Giroux, 2011.

21 Tversky, Amos; Kahneman, Daniel. *Judgment under uncertainty: Heuristics and biases.* Oregon Research Institute. Technical Report. 1973. Available at file:///C:/Users/user/Documents/arquivo%20indicado%20cap%20 6%20SG.pdf. Accessed on October 14, 2016.

22 Kahneman, Daniel. *Thinking, fast and slow.* New York: Farrar, Straus and Giroux, 2011. Location 2001 of 9418.

23 Guerra, Sandra; Santos, Rafael Liza. *Headaches, concerns rnd Regrets: What does the experience of 102 Brazilian directors tell us? Private sector opinion.* Washington, DC: IFC, 2017. Available at https://www.ifc.org/ wps/wcm/connect/topics_ext_content/ifc_external_corporate_site/ifc+cg/ resources/private+sector+opinion/headaches%2C+concerns%2C+and+ regrets+-+what+does+the+experience+of+102+brazilian+directors+tell+us. Accessed on May 21, 2020.

24 Guerra, Sandra; Barros, Lucas A.; Santos, Rafael L. Decision-making in boards of directors: The roles of meeting dynamics and choice architecture. *Research Project,* 2020.

25 Darley, John M.; Batson, C. Daniel. From Jerusalem to Jericho: A study of situational and dispositional variables in helping behavior. *Journal of Personality and Social Psychology,* v. 27, n. 1, 1973. Available at https://www. researchgate.net/publication/232591736_From_Jerusalem_to_Jericho_A_ study_of_situational_and_dispositional_variables_in_helping_behavior. Accessed on October 16, 2016.

26 Guerra, Sandra; Barros, Lucas A.; Santos, Rafael L. Decision-making in boards of directors: The roles of meeting dynamics and choice architecture. *Research Project,* 2020.

27 Arnott, David. *A taxonomy of decision biases.* Monash University, School of Information Management and Systems, Caulfield, 1998. Available at https:// www.semanticscholar.org/paper/A-Taxonomy-of-Decision-Biases-Arnott/ c58cca5c8e8774eb5b17ac3159914d1f1357a014. Accessed on May 21, 2020.

28 Arnott, David. Cognitive biases and decision support systems development: a design science approach. *Information Systems Journal,* v. 16, n. 1, p. 55–78, 2006. Available at https://www.researchgate.net/publication/ 220356732_Cognitive_biases_and_decision_support_systems_development_ A_design_science_approach. Accessed on July 26, 2020.

29 Leblanc, Richard; Gillies, James. *Inside the boardroom: How boards really work and the coming revolution in corporate governance.* Mississauga: John Wiley & Sons: 2005.

30 Sunstein, Cass R.; Hastie, Reid —*Wiser: Getting beyond groupthink to make groups smarter.* Harvard Business Press, 2015. Available at https://hbr. org/product/wiser-getting-beyond-groupthink-to-make-groups-smarter/ 2299-HBK-ENG. Localization 260 of 3122. Accessed on June 7, 2020.

31 Guerra, Sandra; Santos, Rafael Liza. *Headaches, concerns and regrets: What does the experience of 102 Brazilian directors tell us? Private sector opinion.* Washington, DC: IFC, 2017. Available at https://www.ifc.org/ wps/wcm/connect/topics_ext_content/ifc_external_corporate_site/ifc+cg/ resources/private+sector+opinion/headaches%2C+concerns%2C+and+ regrets+-+what+does+the+experience+of+102+brazilian+directors+tell+us. Accessed on May 21, 2020.

32 Ibid.

33 Pick, Katharina; Merchant, Kenneth. Recognizing negative boardroom group dynamics. In: Lorsch, Jay William (editor). *The future of boards: Meeting the governance challenges of the twenty-first century.* Boston: Harvard Business Press, p. 113–132, 2012.

34 Katzenbach, Jon; Smith, R.; Douglas, K. The discipline of teams. In: *HBR's 10 must reads on teams*. Boston: Harvard Business School Publishing Corporation, p. 35–53, 2013.

35 Pick, Katharina; Merchant, Kenneth A. *Blind spots, biases and other pathologies in the boardroom*. New York: Business Expert Press, 2010.

36 Source: http://www.twainquotes.com/Majority.html. Accessed on July 28, 2020.

37 Torchia, Mariateresa; Calabrò, Andrea; Morner, Michèle. Board of directors' diversity, creativity, and cognitive conflict: The role of board members' interaction. *International Studies of Management & Organization*. London: Routledge, v. 45, n. 1, p. 6–24, 2015.

38 Guerra, Sandra; Barros, Lucas A.; Santos, Rafael L. Decision-making in boards of directors: The roles of meeting dynamics and choice architecture. *Research Project*, 2020.

39 IFC — International Finance Corporation e CEDR — Centre for Effective Dispute Resolution. Conflicts in the Boardroom Survey. Results and Analysis 2014. p.7 Available at https://www.ifc.org/wps/wcm/connect/topics_ext_content/ifc_external_corporate_site/ifc+cg/resources/guidelines_reviews+and+case+studies/conflicts+in+the+boardroom+-+survey+2013. Accessed on July 26, 2020.

40 Ibid.

41 Pick, Katharina; Merchant, Kenneth. Recognizing negative boardroom group dynamics. In: Lorsch, Jay William. The future of boards: Meeting the governance challenges of the twenty-first century. Boston: Harvard Business Press, p. 113-132, 2012.

42 IFC – International Finance Corporation; CEDR – Centre for Effective Dispute Resolution. Managing conflicts and difficult conversations on the board. Interactive Training. Background Reading Material, 2016.

43 Guerra, Sandra; Barros, Lucas A.; Santos, Rafael L. Decision-making in boards of directors: The roles of meeting dynamics and choice architecture. *Research Project*, 2020.

44 Gersick, Connie J.G.; Hackman, J. Richard. Habitual routines in task-performing groups. *Organizational Behavior and Human Decision Processes*, v. 47, n. 1, p. 65–97, 1990.

45 Sunstein, Cass R.; Hastie, Reid. *Wiser: Getting beyond groupthink to make groups smarter*. Harvard Business Press, 2015. Available at https://hbr.org/product/wiser-getting-beyond-groupthink-to-make-groups-smarter/2299-HBK-ENG. Localization 260 of 3122. Accessed on June 7, 2020.

46 IFC – International Finance Corporation; CEDR – Centre for Effective Dispute Resolution. Managing Conflicts and Difficult Conversations on the Board. Interactive Training. Background Reading Material, 2016.

47 Thompson, Leigh. Desenvolvendo a criatividade dos grupos de trabalho organizacionais. *GVexecutivo: Revista de Estratégia e Gestão. Fundação Getúlio Vargas*, New York: Academy of Management, v. 2, n. 3, p. 63–81, 2003.

48 Kravitz, David A.; Martin, Barbara. Ringelmann rediscovered: The original article, 1986.

49 Latané, Bibb; Williams, Kipling; Harkins, Stephen. Many hands make light the work: The causes and consequences of social loafing. *Journal of Personality and Social Psychology*, v. 37, n. 6, p. 822, 1979.

50 Pick, Katharina; Merchant, Kenneth A. *Blind spots, biases and other pathologies in the boardroom*. New York: Business Expert Press, 2010.

51 Pick, Katharina; Merchant, Kenneth. Recognizing negative boardroom group dynamics. In: Lorsch, Jay William (editor). *The future of boards: Meeting the governance challenges of the twenty-first century.* Boston: Harvard Business Press, p. 113-132, 2012.

52 Forbes, Daniel P.; Milliken, Frances J. *Cognition and corporate governance: Understanding boards of directors as strategic decision-making groups.* Academy of management review, v. 24, n, 3, p. 489-505, 1999.

53 Guerra, Sandra; Barros, Lucas A.; Santos, Rafael L. Decision-making in boards of directors: The roles of meeting dynamics and choice architecture. *Research Project,* 2020.

54 Guerra, Sandra; Barros, Lucas A.; Santos, Rafael L. Decision-making in boards of directors: The roles of meeting dynamics and choice architecture. Research Project, 2020.

55 Guerra, Sandra; Barros, Lucas A.; Santos, Rafael L. Decision-making in boards of directors: The roles of meeting dynamics and choice architecture. *Research Project,* 2020.

56 Guerra, Sandra; Barros, Lucas A.; Santos, Rafael L. Decision-making in boards of directors: The roles of meeting dynamics and choice architecture. *Research Project,* 2020.

57 Guerra, Sandra; Barros, Lucas A.; Santos, Rafael L. Decision-making in boards of directors: The roles of meeting dynamics and choice architecture. *Research Project,* 2020.

Chapter 7

The Behavioral Compass

Chapter Summary

- Opening with an extract from **Mervyn King**'s interview in which he defines the board of directors (BoD) as a "collective mind."
- The directors who were interviewed were encouraged to think about the BoD and about their own performance as the main object of their aspirations: what and how could be the board of the future – that of our best aspirations? What would be the profile of the directors for this new board?
- The behavioral approach is put forward as an instrument for closing the gap between reality and this idealization.
- A guide so that all those professionals who attend boardrooms (board members, executives and all the others that interact with boards) can navigate more calmly and confidently between the behavioral traps, perfecting the interactive process and increasing decision-making efficiency.
- The behavioral tools available and how to apply them.

BoD: A "Collective Mind"

The board of directors is a collective mind. When a BoD makes a decision, it is a group of 12 people, but like one mind – even when something goes wrong, and, based on the odds, something always goes wrong. The board has a duty to take risks for the good of the company and, therefore, is constantly dealing with uncertain events in the future, such as making business judgment calls based on facts, without having all the information available at that point in time, and they are not going to get it right one hundred percent of the time. That's not possible. (...) The board's mind has to be consolidated. Pragmatically, how can this be achieved? Nowadays, most boards have a fragmented collective mind: there is no unanimity regarding the values that drive the business or about who the stakeholders are, or what the needs, interests and expectations of shareholders are.

So, I think an important exercise for all boards is that each director should write down in one sentence what is the purpose of the company's business. So, you need to make sure that everyone agrees regarding the purpose. The next question is about character, which is a better word than organizational culture. Character refers to attributes, it is specific, while culture is a very vague concept. Everyone should write down what the company's character is, but there has to be unanimity, because the board will make collective decisions that will have to fit in with that character. Otherwise, the company will go downhill or its character will have to be changed. The next question involves the company's three main value drivers. The values should be written down and discussed until an agreement is reached regarding them. And these agreed values need to take account of who the company's main shareholders are.

You may find that the perspectives are surprisingly different, but try and align yourselves in relation to these issues. Then write down a sentence or two about the legitimate interests and expectations of the stakeholders. You make all of this visible to everyone and you have to come to an agreement on all these elements. This is a critical exercise for a board to achieve a unified collective mind. This is one of the most important points for BoDs nowadays; the directors have to realize that they need to function as a unified collective mind. At present, boards are thinking on a fragmented basis. When a decision is being made about a specific topic, I am basing my position on one value and you are thinking of another; I am thinking of one stakeholder's expectations and you are thinking of another's; we need this thinking to be unified.

Mervyn King,
Chairman Emeritus of the International
Integrated Reporting Council[*]

The exercise proposed by this renowned guru and pioneer in relation to the concept of **ESG (Environment, Social and Governance)** could not be more practical or simple to execute. There are no pyrotechnics or sophistication, but instead a straightforward activity of aligning what is essential to everything else that a board has to do. The board's collective mind is what will govern an organization. But how can this unified thinking

---

[*] Professor Mervyn King is the chair of the International Integrated Reporting Council (IIRC). He is also chairman emeritus of the GRI (Global Reporting Initiative). King, who is a South African with a distinguished career as a supreme court judge in that country, chaired the King Committee on Corporate Governance, which produced South Africa's governance code. The code, the King Report on Corporate Governance is an international reference already in its 4th edition. The author interviewed Mervyn King in New York, United States, on April 1, 2014.

be achieved, when there are still so many behavioral aspects that are not recognized and directly addressed on boards?

The first step in navigating this still-underexplored behavioral world of boards appears simplistic, but actually, it is just simple: recognizing that the behavioral aspects that are inherent to individuals and groups play a key role in boardrooms. Although it may seem that this is already widely acknowledged, the fact is that, although it is generally accepted, it is not yet given much consideration in the concrete and everyday situations of boards. Furthermore, when a behavioral factor is recognized in an attitude or position, it is usually observed in the other person and not in oneself.

Nothing out of the ordinary. As already mentioned in Chapter 6, in addition to the fact that individuals do not perceive their own biases, there is a tendency to notice other people's limitations more than one's own – which only intensifies the problem. And these biases push the decision further away from rationality, undermining the quality of the decision process, which, in itself, is already imprecise. Given that the level of irrationality that can take over human reasoning is underestimated – even if it seems to be based on rock-solid assumptions – it paves the way for unwanted and unconscious interference in the decision. When it comes to the performance of executives and board members, especially those professionals who have hardly ever ventured outside their own areas of expertise, the likelihood is that the biases resulting from this specialization will be more visible:

> "(...) when making decisions, individually or even in teams, we are likely to view the world from our own functional or expert filter – a product of what we have been exposed to and learned from. This can result in an executive failing to see past the walls of their respective disciplines, biasing their judgement and ultimately impacting the level of collaboration between silos and limiting organizational creativity and agility."[1]

Based on this human dynamic, the conclusion is that groups, such as boards or executive leadership teams,* are fertile ground for the interference of behavioral factors. But this does not mean that making decisions in a group is bad. As researchers along with experts and experienced board directors have already noted: there is no better solution than a board for mitigating the risk of the individual decision, nor any process that is as potent as a result of the different perspectives involved. Perfect? No.

---

* The expression executive leadership teams is used here to refer to the members of the C-Suite taking decisions and operating in a collegial manner.

For sure, it always falls short. But there is still no better option, as illustrated by **Sir Adrian Cadbury**, quoting a phrase from the Roman playwright Plautus:

> "Boards of directors as governing bodies owe their existence to experience over the centuries, not to statute. Their greatest advantage was summed up by a classical author in around 200 B.C., who wrote: "Nemo solis satus sapit". In English, less polished than the Latin, it means that no one on their own is wise enough. To the benefits of collective wisdom can be added those of the need to avoid too great concentrations of power and to share the burden of responsibility at the head of an enterprise.
>
> Boards provide a means of bringing a range of minds and of viewpoints, backed by a variety of experience, to bear on the issues which confront companies. Boards are deliberative bodies and their meetings' ideas are formed and turned into policies and plans of action, through debate. They are a resource to which those who have the executive responsibility for running a company can turn. They are also the source of authority of the executives. Their authority in publicly quoted companies is legitimized, because the board which appoints them to their executive positions has in turn (with all its limitations) been elected by, and derives its authority from, the shareholders."[2]

Therefore, in order to reduce the risk that the decision-making process in boards is adversely affected by cognitive biases or pathologies resulting from the human condition, the secret is to adopt methods and tactics that address these factors. The first step to achieving this is to become aware that individual and group behaviors can have detrimental effects. But the biggest difficulty with this, as has been argued, is that people cannot see their own biases, although they recognize them in others. That's where things get complicated. **Soll, Milkman and Payne**, who worked on a guide to debiasing, argue that "when attributing bias to the person, one implicitly assumes that the situation is more or less fixed, and therefore the best approach is to provide people with some combination of training, knowledge, and tools to help overcome their limitations and dispositions. [The researchers] dub this approach "modify the decision-maker."[3] The other approach they proposed is to "modify the environment", which seeks to change the environment to offer a better match for the thinking or even to encourage a better way of thinking. This means adapting the environment to tackle the biases, in other words, debias them.

These same authors state that the conditions under which decisions are made require even more attention. They address the concept of "decision-ready," when **System 2** covered in Chapter 6 properly performs its role of monitoring, halting decisions and correcting judgments. The authors consider three factors that determine whether the person is decision ready or not:

- **Fatigue and distraction**: the decision process requires effort and attention, so when the person is fatigued or distracted or enters this state during the meeting, their readiness for the decision will weaken.
- **Visceral influences**: although visceral reactions are essential for human survival, strong emotions can negatively affect decisions.
- **Individual differences**: we are different in a number of ways, including in intelligence and ways of thinking. Some biases may be related to cognitive ability – overconfidence and hindsight – while others are not – anchoring, for example.

The argument that changing the person in order to avoid bias is not always effective has gained strength in the so-called "**nudge**" literature. The term is part of the title of a book written by professors **Thaler and Sunstein**,[4] which has had a great deal of impact and which analyzes interventions that they refer to as "**choice architecture.**" This attempt to influence choices is designed to prevent people from making bad decisions on account of a lack of attention, lack of information or limited cognitive abilities.

> "A nudge (…) is any aspect of the choice architecture that alters people's behavior in a predictable way without forbidding any options or significantly changing their economic incentives. To count as a mere nudge, the intervention must be easy and cheap to avoid."[5]

Choice architecture has been widely used in public and private policies in an attempt to make people's lives better. A good example is putting fruit at eye level in a school restaurant instead of simply banning junk food. Foods full of harmful substances may continue to be offered, but the students will be gently "**nudged**" and encouraged – due to their convenience and closeness – to choose the foods that are good for them. **Choice architecture** can also be applied to groups, for example in processes that lead to better decision-making.

Before tackling the detrimental effects of group behaviors, this chapter starts off with the individual ones, covering mechanisms that help prevent decisions from being contaminated by biases that, although individual, are interwoven with those of the group.

To Mitigate Individual Biases

Just as biases may show up one at a time or in different combinations, so too the most appropriate resources for tackling them should be viewed as tools that can be used, on a case-by-case basis, either by themselves or in combination to achieve the best mitigating effects.

Memory

Memories are flawed and recollections fade over time, despite the conviction that we remember the situations experienced in detail. The risk is of falling victim to the certainty that our memory is infallible or at least very accurate.

First of all, like any other, the biases of the **memory** category need to be spelled out. If the individual or group recognizes that the limitations of memory may be mixed in with the decision equation, it is already a start. Some approaches are particularly useful in order to avoid falling into this trap:

- Make sure that, prior to the discussion and debate, the material that will brief the board regarding a specific proposition provides **objective indicators to be taken into account that may contrast with the past experiences** that directors will also bring with them into the boardroom. As noted, memory is fallible and the past experiences of board members can provide at best only a part of the bases for the full analysis of the decision that is on the table.
- **Lovallo and Sibony**[6] indicate how to counter the risk of misinterpreting conceptual relationships based on pattern recognition biases, which can give greater weight to more important or more memorable events. They assert that the best thing to do is to **change the viewing angle** and test alternative hypotheses for the facts: **visits to the field or to clients** are examples put forward by the authors. They also recommend techniques such as **reframing or role reversal** with the aim of encouraging decision-makers to come up with an alternative explanation for the facts presented to them.
- If a person's memory can be flawed, exchanging ideas with others, at least, serves to question its accuracy. Therefore, sharing information is a good exercise, but it should be borne in mind that since groups initially exchange information that everyone knows, one alternative is to use a **questioning process to get from each board member what they alone know.** Open-ended questions, where each one of the directors is asked to think about whether there is something that they know and that they have not yet shared because they think it is

known to everyone, or for any other reason, may help new information to emerge. This issue will be covered again later in this chapter, under the **shared information bias** in the section on **pathology**.

- **Questions**, by the way, are always very important tools for guiding the decision towards a healthier path:
  - Are we analyzing this situation in isolation or incorporating past experiences, which may not be comparable with this context? Are these experiences really comparable?
  - Do we remember (or do I remember) all the difficulties and negative consequences of a past situation or are we just retaining the positive side of that decision in our memory?

Statistical

Impressions can deceive us and as a result the likelihood that something will happen, or not happen, may be overestimated or underestimated. And these are just two of the possible statistical biases. Important: despite their knowledge and apparent scientific impartiality, even statisticians – and even scientists – are not immune to this category of bias and are liable to jump to conclusions based on limited evidence.

The kingdom of quantitative models, which serves as the basis for the proposals with a high economic and financial impact that are presented to boards, may include an even greater threat than that from the biases of the **memory** category. Clad in apparent objectivity and rationality, spreadsheets can hide serious errors in terms of assumptions and even biases that occurred at the start of the analysis, which are more difficult to detect in the overall proposition (refer to the category of **presentation biases** that indicate how the form and order of presentation influence the conclusions).

Like an illusionist, the biases assembled in the **statistical** category are able to deflect our attention from where the proposition's false or flawed element may be. We are so focused on the complexity of the numbers and on the model that we fail to see that the error is in an element that is so simple that it would be seen with the naked eye – by anyone, just using common sense – if all the attention were not focused on the complexity.

Dealing with this type of bias requires:

- One attitude that is recommended is **skepticism**. Faced with something that is backed up by a sophisticated financial and economic model, be even more disbelieving than usual, as it can hide flawed assumptions.

- In fact, before savoring the potential results, it is wise to question the model's assumptions. What samples are used? What is the time interval analyzed? What variables are contained in each of the scenarios presented? Who said that this growth rate is actually achievable?
- **Red alert.** Press the alarm button for yourself and for the group, whenever the analysis is overly complex. It seems obvious, but it is not. This tool can be extremely powerful for board members to navigate the deceptive world of biases. And, in the case of statistical biases, it is very appropriate. Naturally, the board devotes more time to understanding the complexity, but that is not what the proposition is about. Since they are engaged in understanding the complexity, it is quite possible that this distracts the directors from the obvious – something very simple, which is not always correct.
- The debate should be based on simple logic, which is capable of being understood by a young professional who is still inexperienced. The board – and its chair plays a relevant role in this type of dynamic – can, prior to any discussion of the sophistication and complexity surrounding the proposal, ask those who are presenting it, to describe it in a simplified way so that any unqualified person listening can understand it. Sophisticated speech, which is so common in boardrooms, may hide factors that, to the contrary, should be highlighted. More than that: if the board of directors is supposed to be diverse and include different specialties and experiences, a good board – by definition – is made up of people who know a lot about certain topics, but a great deal less about others. Therefore, sophisticated jargon, whether it be in relation to finance, accounting, personnel, technology, or whatever, should in principle be limited in boardrooms. Who is interested in a demonstration of knowledge about a given topic? On the other hand, those directors who do not have in-depth knowledge of a subject under discussion nonetheless need to be able to present their doubts with ease and without the slightest awkwardness. This attitude is still an exception in a world where people do not like to admit ignorance, even if it is entirely justified.

At a company that specializes in IT solutions, when the concept of BPO (Business Process Outsourcing) was still really an innovation, the CEO called attention to a blatant misuse of technical jargon. After a discussion of almost half an hour in relation to BPO solutions in front of the entire executive leadership team, which included the executive officers for marketing, finance, human resources and other areas who were not specialists in technology, he asked: "Stop a sec... what does BPO mean?" And, actually, at that time, only specialists in the IT services area knew what this new development actually was. As an experienced professional in the IT area himself and holding the highest position among those sitting at that collective decision-making body's table, he was the one who candidly asked the question – which, certainly, should have been asked beforehand by any professional finding himself in the middle of a discussion full of technical jargon that was both sophisticated as well as mysterious.

- The **Red Alert** practice should precede the **discussion of what the substance of the proposal really is,** its risk elements and its favorable points, even before the pyrotechnic presentations are outlined and hypnotize the board.
- Separate objective and measurable indicators of what is just an estimate or even an expression of desire: a careful analysis of the assumptions used and the **awareness of how the proponent's desire is capable of making him/her short-sighted** are good examples of attitudes of caution and attention on the part of the director or of the executive at a meeting.

Confidence

Excessive confidence can inflate the chance of success, obscuring the capacity for judgment and even causing what only confirms the initial reasoning or intention to be pursued. And take care: desire shapes reality.

The name of this category of bias – **confidence** – can give the wrong impression. Obviously, confidence is good. The problem is when confidence is so great that it leads to short-sightedness and, why not, to complete blindness. This idea alludes to the concept proposed by **José Ernesto Beni Bologna**[*]:

"Is it possible, in the contract of reason, where rhetoric gains a clear rational dimension, for us to exhaust the problem of desires and intentions? Of course not. (...) The world is not governed by reason. The world is governed by desires, which vary a great deal and can cause distortions even in the reason expressed in the contracts (...) In the 1980s, when humanists were asked to contribute to corporate governance in the United States, it was because there was a strong

---

[*] José Ernesto Beni Bologna, founding president of Ethos Desenvolvimento Humano e Organizacional, is a psychologist and board director and was one of the speakers invited at the 17th IBGC Congress, the central theme of which was the expression "Essence and Appearance".

perception that the concealment of desires and the policies that operate in the underground of the discourse of reason undoubtedly play a fundamental role in corporate scandals (...) when desire supplants the moral nature of the contract."*[7]

This being the case, since they are strongly motivated by their desires, human beings see reality through lenses that lead to their realization, which can cause important omissions to be overlooked or even lead to a feeling of control of the assessed situation. When desire dominates the mind, we are only able to see the evidence that confirms it, ignoring everything else. There are some good tools available for dealing with this type of bias:

- **Becoming aware of the desire** is the starting point. This awareness can be brought to the surface by a brief conversation session in the board of directors, which spells out the desires and intentions of managers, the shareholders and the directors themselves.
- When the desires and intentions of these various groups are absolutely coincident, which is positive as alignment avoids conflicts, an additional question is required: bearing in mind that we are all in alignment, is our common desire clouding our vision? The next step is to consider **how this desire interferes with the decision's objectivity and rationality.** Becoming aware of the desire is a preventive measure and establishes a safer environment for discussion.
- Since the order of presentation of the factors influences understanding and reasoning, as will be seen below in the presentation bias, **starting off with the contradictory or minority view** may provide a chance for the excessive confidence to be questioned.
- Compare the desired proposition with other possibilities. For a proposal to allocate capital, for example, it is always a good idea to compare it with other alternatives for using the same capital on other projects. It should not be assumed that this always happens on BoDs. It is surprising how it is still not clear to some managers that any investment proposal should answer the question: is this really the best way for me to invest the shareholders' money and is it in line with their vision of what is value creation over the course of time? And in order to answer this question, **comparing the proposed investment with other alternatives can prevent**

---

* In his talk, Bologna also stressed that the 2016 Nobel Prize for Economics was awarded to Oliver Hart and Bengt Holmström, precisely for their contribution to the theory of contracts, recognizing that "not a thousand pages of a contract expressed through reason would be capable of encompassing all the factors related to the human interactions".

misunderstandings by avoiding the excessive enthusiasm of those who propose the project. The systematic adoption of this type of process ends up creating continuous attention to the possible existence of biases, thus countering them and creating a stronger culture for dealing with them.

- **Opinions of truly independent third parties who disagree with the proposition** may get on the nerves of those who are the most convinced of the way forward, but it will certainly make the final decision more robust. The point that has to be borne in mind is that the independent third party – who is often a consultant, a lawyer or an auditor – may also model the issues within the **framework** of his or her professional vision (see **presentation biases**).

- The director can make an **individual reflection: where do I stand in relation to this topic?** What do I want the final result of this decision to be? What are my reasons? How does that make me lose my impartiality regarding this decision? Based on this sincere conversation with himself or herself, the board member can be open-minded in relation to those opinions that are contrary to his or her and even make an effort to ensure that the decision-making process includes these views.

- It is advisable to place an **increased warning sign for all proposals where an excessive level of confidence is identified,** amending the assessment with a search for all contradictory points of view that, potentially, might be right. The researchers **Thuraisingham and Lehmacher's**[8] recommendation is that every issue where there is a 90% confidence level in the answer should be treated as if it had a 70% to 75% assurance level.

Adjustment

Reasoning can be importantly influenced by the parameters included in the question one is asked to consider. When it is a question of a quantity, for example, the values initially presented dominate the judgment. Another example is when we are governed by a first impression about someone and then fail to adjust that opinion by taking into account things we subsequently learn about the person which may run contrary to our first impression. In other words, our mind adjusts to what it receives as initial information, embracing it as being true.

One of the **adjustment biases,** namely that of **anchoring,** was also a topic of research by **Guerra and Santos,**[9] who surveyed 102 board members in order to identify the main obstacles to the best decision-making process on BoDs. The result of this question revealed that 64% of the directors believe that anchoring bias occurs in boardrooms with a high or medium frequency (Graph 7.1), although the difficulty involved in identifying it may mean that this figure is understated:

Perceptions about decision-making processes based on preconceived beliefs or views

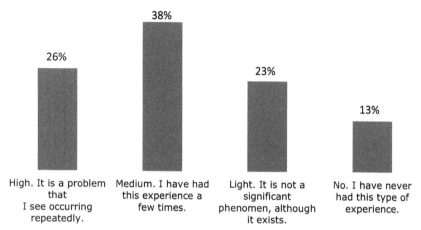

Graph 7.1 The frequency of anchoring bias in boardrooms varies from medium to high.
Source: Guerra and Santos (2017).

One of the challenges in relation to **adjustment biases** is, precisely, to identify that our vision has been captured by an anchor and our reasoning can only look at that situation or person through the aforesaid anchor. In order to address the negative effects of these biases, the following tactics can be used:

- Hold a **discussion based on "out of the box" thinking where there are no limits and make an effort to leave out preconceived views.** This would be a warm-up for the decision-making process itself, which, instead of being based on the anchors embedded in the proposition, would get underway with a broad, open view.
- Request that the **initiative's proponents put forward different and assorted scenarios which should be of a sufficient number and variety to limit the anchor's power.** For example, if the decision is in connection with choosing a CEO, make sure that the list of finalists not only offers diversity in terms of alternatives but also analyzes each candidate from different points of view. In addition, the process for arriving at this final list should incorporate the views of various people who have analyzed the candidates and, pay attention: it is necessary for the different opinions to be presented to the board.

- **Practice scenarios.** If the situation were different or contrary to the one presented, what would be the implications? A hypothetical discussion about a different picture can uncover anchors, which are leading to a biased view.
  - What factors do we not know that could give us more support and what factors do we know that are contrary to the direction that the anchor seems to indicate?
  - Pay special attention to propositions that promise extraordinary gains or warn of irreparable losses: they can put us in a position where we are oscillating between the extremes of greed and fear.

Presentation

The form or order of presentation of the facts or ideas has the power to bias the processing of the information and the resulting conclusion. The form "frames" the reasoning.

Although the term **"presentation biases"** is just an ironic coincidence, the board's decision-making process can actually find itself hijacked by the endless, ingenious presentations made by executives in PowerPoint or Keynote. Apart from spending time just on receiving information rather than using it for an in-depth discussion of each proposition, this is a further cause of concern for directors: it is possible that the way in which the executives structure their presentations **frames** the vision. This is the **framing effect**. If the BoD receives one piece of information before another, that order also has an influence on reasoning and judgment. The biases of the **presentation** category can be counteracted, by paying special attention to elements such as form, order, and scale, along with others:

- The materials that support the board's decisions should be viewed in a different light. The board's chair, with the help of the board secretary, can minimize the **framing effect** by seeking to guide **managers to improve these materials, keeping a careful eye out so that they do not lead to the framing of the reasoning.** On the contrary, these materials should place the proposition in an open and broad framework, which protects against any restrictions on reasoning.
- The dynamics of the discussion by the board and the steps taken are important. Their sequence should ensure that **contradictory views and the different lines of thought have been interspersed since the start** of the process and that there is no excessive influence of one or the other.
- Here, too, the **board chair plays a key role**: if there are different factions or views among the directors, the chair has to make sure that

the order in which they speak maintains this diversity. Ideally, one favorable position should always be followed by another one that contradicts it, and so on until the end. If there is only a minority who hold a different view, it should be spelled out during the initial phase rather than being left to the end of the line, when everyone has already begun to consolidate their decision. If there is just a single board member who has a contradictory position and, particularly, if it seems preposterous to the others, the chair may consider instructing another director to present arguments, which would justify the contradictory position, with the aim of attempting to dismantle or even to verify whether the group is stuck in a **framing effect**.

- When a high-impact decision is made, it **should be dissected in such a way as to ascertain whether or not it was subject to framing** during one of its stages. Even the visual framing of a figure is capable of altering the perception of reality and negatively affecting the choice of the best decision. For example: in which of the central squares in Figure 7.1 is the gray darkest?

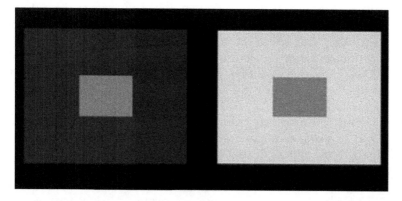

Figure 7.1 Although equal, the background suggests that there is a difference between the two tones of grey.

Situation

The situation and context may jeopardize the decision. Time pressure or understatement of the degree of risk or impact, for instance, can cloud the vision and alter the outcome of a decision.

Chapter 6 described the experiment on the students who were invited to a seminar on the parable of the Good Samaritan.[*] The behavior of the

---

[*] The account of this experiment is on page 194 of Chapter 6.

group under time pressure, ignoring the alleged "victim" and some even step over the person, speaks volumes about the powerful effect of this type of bias. **Time pressure** is one of the most commonly encountered contextual factors of **situation biases**, especially in the decision-making process of organizations. Another bias that is widely found in boards is **attenuation**. For this reason, this chapter gives priority to ways of mitigating these two biases:

Time Pressure

"The window of opportunity for a share issue will close at the end of the quarter", or: "The bidding will end soon", or even: "We have a short period before the seller withdraws the purchase exclusivity." Experienced directors are often subjected to this type of context – sometimes even more than one at a time. Time pressure, however, is not fit for the company boardrooms and it is necessary to use all possible means to avoid it:

- When a board member receives information that a certain decision is extremely urgent, he/she should immediately press the **red alert button** (already mentioned in this chapter). But, unlike the ambulance siren that opens the path for everyone to get out of the way or to move along even quicker, this **red alert should arouse the directors increased attention**: how to get to the hospital without any dead or injured, either inside or outside the ambulance, not now or in the future?
- First off, it is necessary to **understand the rush and its motivation in order to make a careful assessment: what are the associated risks**, apart from the loss of that opportunity? With all this haste, what can confuse individual and collective judgment? Is it really worth taking this decision where there is so much at risk in a situation like this? Under the claim of time pressure, cautious risk analysis was the very thing that was not undertaken in the following case, recounted by one of the directors interviewed:

In an infrastructure services company, prior to taking up this position, the BoD's chairman had acted as an executive who looked for and negotiated new service projects throughout his career and still identified more closely with the role of manager than that of a director. Therefore, the chairman was what could be called a fox taking care of the henhouse with regard of supervising the executives. Everyone was very enthusiastic about quickly closing a deal on an overseas project, which seemed to be in line with the business's growth and geographic diversification goals. The project envisaged the purchase of a closed package of contracts, in fact, a complete basket where there could be some good opportunities lost in the middle together potentially with a lot of bad contracts. In addition, it entailed working with a local partner about whom we knew next to nothing. There was a natural enthusiasm regarding the first international project and intense bullying began of the independent directors who had no specific experience in the company's type of services and projects. When one of us questioned the risks, asking: 'Are we going to take on a twenty-year commitment, in a scenario ridden with doubts, without even knowing much about our partner and just dive straight in? Without even checking if the oxygen cylinder is suitable for diving?' Instead of trying to be objective, the answers were just about the pressure of time: 'You don't understand... The projects in this sector are always like this... There is no other way or we will miss out on the opportunity!' It may seem incredible, but it was just like that. It was impossible to get more time for analysis, and the international project deal was closed. Needless to say, this company is now in a very difficult situation, with a high level of debt that is increasing and, on top of this, it is finding it hard to sell its assets. Now, nobody wants to buy 'the package' of contracts; they just want to cherry pick the best ones.

- There are companies where the culture itself assumes that decisions should always be made at a moment's notice. There is a permanent sense of urgency, which in many cases is associated with an endemic lack of planning or ineffective leadership. Everything is decided at the last minute. In this case, **the BoD's role, over the course of time, is to make its "signatory power" prevail and to limit the rushed approach to decision-making in an educational way.** When management realizes that the board will no longer consider decisions in a hurry – unless it is clearly necessary – the culture begins to change. Often, the entire board gets into a feverish rush, and a single director insists that there is something the board may not be seeing. Although it is the dissenting vote, if the decision really has a material impact, the only recourse is for the director to opt to use **their individual signatory power.** It is necessary to face the discomfort and to insist on registering their vote against or even that the rushed process does not allow a more thoughtful vote. But it is important for the directors to register the justification for their view and all the alternatives they put forward in order for the decision's outcome to be different or at least to be the same, but after having been discussed in greater depth.
- And if the urgency really is necessary, **how can the BoD deal with the pressure of such a short timeframe and try to maintain the rationality and depth required in order to examine the issue? By using dynamics**

different from the normal ones. Exceptional situations require exceptional measures, to be triggered by the board's chair, including:

- To charge a board working group or even an existing committee with carrying out additional analyzes, providing support for the process.
- Directors can be called on individually to undertake an analysis or to arrive at a deeper understanding and then afterward share it with the group.
- Instruct management regarding the additional elements of analysis and other information that the board needs in order to make a decision in a rush.
- Extra meetings are always a problem, given the board members' overloaded agenda, but should not be ruled out. If the process of making a hasty decision is already a riskier one, allowing the decision in relation to a complex and high-impact issue to be concluded via e-mail is reckless. The triviality with which this procedure is adopted is worrying, wrapping up the decision-making process via e-mail when all the pertinent issues haven't really been settled. The normal justification given on these occasions is that all that remains is to confirm rate X or contractual condition Y and that everything else has already been covered and explored with the proper depth. Is this really the case? Or is this simply part of the strategy of those who are in a rush or who are not all that keen on the inconvenience of an extra meeting? Yes, a board of director's decision-making process can be concluded by e-mail, but this only applies to a few situations – after a vigorous discussion in which all the elements have been thoroughly debated.

Attenuation

Phrases such as: "This will never happen in our sector" or: "For decades, the market has only purchased products or services with this characteristic", or even: "This will not even change in the next fifty years" should sound alarm bells, and the director should immediately press the **red alert button.** In covering the decision-making process in a disruptive world in Chapter 5,[*] mention was already made of the **World Economic Forum's** 2020 report, in which 350 global risk analysis experts warn that, in addition to the lasting consequences produced by the COVID-19 pandemic, companies cannot remain blind to the assortment of other risks that are emerging, such as cyber fraud or the collapse of IT

---

* The section *Decisions in a Disruptive World* is on page 164 of Chapter 5.

infrastructure. Then, in Chapter 6, when presenting the **attenuation bias**,[*] examples were given of sectors and organizations that succumbed to their own blindness, assuming certainties and failing to consider future possibilities – probable and improbable. Frequent and repeated, the detrimental effects of **attenuation bias** are nothing new in the post-pandemic and technological disruption world. In 1960, **Theodore Levitt**, in his classic article *Myopia in Marketing*, gave an example of how the attenuation bias almost destroyed the film industry after the emergence of television:

> "Hollywood barely escaped being totally ravished by television. Actually, all the established film companies went through drastic reorganizations. Some simply disappeared. All of them got into trouble not because of TV's inroads but because of their own myopia. (...) Hollywood defined its business incorrectly. It thought it was in the movie business when it was actually in the entertainment business. 'Movies' implied a specific, limited product. This produced a fatuous contentment which from the beginning led producers to view TV as a threat. Hollywood scorned and rejected TV when it should have welcomed it as an opportunity – an opportunity to expand the entertainment business."[10]

Nevertheless, the attenuation of an opportunity or a risk can be countered with the powerful **"What if...?" exercise**. When the board allows a dynamic in which seemingly preposterous ideas are analyzed, taking into account what would happen if the assumptions of the business, services or the market were altered to a marked degree, the room for innovation and the level of preparedness for disruptive transformations soar to a new level.

The **"What if...?"** is designed to shake up current thinking and make room for the new. "No, the risk is not that great and our teams are fully trained to identify, prevent and take action, if the risk should materialize." Does this phrase sound familiar? The director may already have heard it and, afterward, come across a very clear demonstration that not everything was under control. Moreover, often this stance is not only found among executives but is also predominant on the board. For this reason, it is necessary to tackle **deadly attenuations and certainties**, using the following solutions:

- The board's chair appoints one or more directors for specific roles – and in the absence of the chair taking steps, the initiative may come

---

[*] Attenuation bias is presented on page 186 of Chapter 6.

from a director. For example, one director adopts **the approach of an investigative journalist, who is always curious and on the lookout for alternatives that have not yet been considered.** While another board member may play the **role of the devil's advocate,**[*] a **practice that is already well established in vigorous, high-impact decision-making processes.** Much more than mere simulation, these roles are an intellectual challenge and should not be viewed as an exercise that is below the seniority level of such highly ranked professionals. Used on a regular basis, this initiative is a worthy one and has the power to begin to change the board's culture, making it more alert and less vulnerable. However, care should be taken that the **devil's advocate** does not "play" the role falsely, which would probably cause the group to attach less importance to his or her arguments. The role of the devil's advocate should be assumed by a strong figure, who is recognized by the group for this characteristic. **The solution may be to choose someone who has already shown a certain skepticism regarding the attenuation, or to bring in a third party with contradictory convictions to perform this role:**

"The concept of a devil's advocate originated in the Roman Catholic Church's canonization process, in which a lawyer is appointed to argue against the canonization of a candidate – even the most apparently saintly. Similarly, in law, each side files its own brief; the defense doesn't simply respond off-the-cuff to the plaintiff's argument. In business, however, an advocate for a particular option typically delivers a presentation that may contain some discussion of risk but remains entirely the work of someone who is sold on the idea. Members of the executive team are expected to agree with the business case or attack it, although they may have seen it only a few days before the meeting and thus have no way of producing an equally detailed rebuttal or offering solid alternatives."[11]

- Over time, this attitude will spread among management itself, which starts to challenge proposals and assumptions already within the scope of the executives, modeling themselves on what they see the board of directors doing. As a result, the decision-making process gets closer to rationality and there is a reduction in the power of bias and other constraints.
- Also applicable for dealing with attenuation bias is the use of the technique to extract information held by some of the decision-makers but not normally shared, as has already been mentioned in

[*] This practice has already been covered in Chapter 5, on page 150.

the section on **memory biases**. The essential thing is the question: What does someone know which is not being mentioned, but which could make the board view the situation differently than it is being seen right now?

In a Group, Exacerbated Biases

Individual biases rarely occur by themselves in boardrooms. Rather, as was discussed earlier, they blend with those of groups as well as the tense intra- and extra-board interactions. This can make the group's dynamics become even more complex or, possibly, even preposterous.

After researching 1,048 decisions, **Lovallo and Sibony**[12] found that 53% of decision-making effectiveness (considering revenue, profitability, market share and productivity) is explained by the quality of the process to exploit analysis and reach the decision. The inclusion of perspectives that contradict the senior leader's point of view, allowing participation in discussion by skill and experience rather than by rank was cited as a process quality element. Even more interesting: the authors assert that process matters more than analysis. They were not implying that analysis is not important, quite the contrary. But they argue that even superb analysis is useless unless the decision process gives it a fair hearing.

Since many of the tactics already presented for combatting individual biases can be used to reduce the detrimental effects of this combination, specific solutions for group biases will be presented here.

Herd Effect

> In general, because they assume that they have less information than the others, the person allows themself to be led by the opinion of the majority and expresses a decision equal to that of their peers without giving the matter the proper consideration.

Economists have long recorded and studied the behavior of economic agents who, instead of making decisions based on rationality, copy the choice made by the majority because they think that they lack information and/or because they regard the others as being better informed. Have you grown tired of seeing this in speculative bubbles? Because of this **herd effect**, a lot of money has been lost on the stock market, the currency market, the futures market and even in the real estate sector. It is no different on boards of directors: feeling that they lack the proper conditions to make a decision, the board members follow those who appear to be better-informed or, simply, the majority.

But the **herd effect** is tricky. What is the factor which at last causes the animals to break away, skedaddling at full speed to anywhere else?

It can even be a sensible, respected or very powerful voice which, right at the start of the conversation, steers everyone's thinking in the same direction. Then, when the autopsy of the bad choice or the bad deal is carried out, no one remembers that it was that so "reasonable" position that made it impossible for the discussion to take another, perhaps more questioning, direction. In the **Guerra and Santos'** survey,[13] for example, the **herd effect** was the bias most mentioned by the board members as being detrimental to the decision-making process (74%).

But after all, why are humans so easily nudged by other humans? **Thaler and Sunstein** argue that one of the reasons is that people like to conform and they cite an experiment:

> "In the 1950s Solomon Asch (1995), a brilliant social psychologist, conducted a series of experiments in just this vein. When asked to decide on their own, without seeing judgments from others, people almost never erred, since the test was easy. But when everyone else gave an incorrect answer, people erred more than one-third of the time. Indeed, in a series of twelve questions, nearly three-quarters of people went along with the group at least once, defying the evidence of their own senses."[14]

The danger is clear and that is why it is necessary to pay extra care, especially in the case of companies with defined control, where there may be a greater frequency of the **herd effect** in the decision-making process, since the owners are identified by everyone as being the greatest source of power and, more than this, usually have a seat on the BOD. In this case, these owners may end up playing the role of the lion approaching the sheep, scaring the group and making them run at full speed in the same direction – without even knowing why or where. In order to try to prevent this bias from leading the board to the wrong decisions, it is recommended that the following resources be applied:

- The first step is **to become aware that the herd effect is a problem.** According to the results of **Guerra and Santos'** survey,[15] the **herd effect** is the most prevalent bias found on boards.
- Bearing in mind that the herd effect occurs when the agents involved do not have enough information to take a decision, it may seem obvious what needs to be done to prevent it:
  - Make sure that prior reading material is provided to the board of directors, which not only describes the proposal but also takes into account its contours, risks and opportunities. More than that, when preparing the reading material, it is suggested that the executives put themselves in the director's chair: what do I know that the directors also need to know in order to make this decision?

What do they not know? Moreover, the materials should contain the right amount of information, without any excess.

- The objective of this material is to equalize the information on the topic among all the directors. It is hard to apply this practice to all decisions, but it can be used, at least, for those that have a high impact: having an advance discussion – a simple phone conversation, for example – in order to find out what each board member knows and understands about the proposal. The very questions they ask will be a good indicator of what needs to be included or highlighted in the material. Take care: as was already mentioned in Chapter 4, the purpose of this "advance discussion" is not to promote their own interests or persuade the director. If the board member realizes that there is a hidden agenda in this advance discussion, he or she may be overly on their guard.
- This prior view regarding each director's individual understanding of the matter will also make it a lot easier for the board's chair to perform their role.

- During the board meeting itself, special attention needs to be paid to **three types of behavior, which can trigger the herd effect** among the other participants, not always just directors. This is the anticipated or emphatic display by:
  - **Those who have more power** or are perceived by others as having more power. This behavior can even have a detrimental impact if it comes from those who do not have the power to make the decision but will be responsible for implementing it.
  - **Those who are experts** on the subject and/or are recognized by the group as being the ones who have the most knowledge about the subject.
  - **Those who, although not experts on the subject, have recognition and respectability** in the group due to their position, experience or even their popularity.
- Individually, **the directors should reflect on whether they fit into these categories. If so, they should resist the temptation to speak first.** The weight of their opinion is so great that the other voices may become silent – either out of respect or discretion.

Lovallo and Sibony[16] confirm the trend for us to conform to the dominant views of the group and its leader. Although many techniques to stimulate the debate can be used, the authors argue that the use of tools alone will not resolve the issue given that it is a matter of behavior. **Diversity in the backgrounds and personalities** of the decision-makers, a climate of trust, and a **culture where the discussions are depersonalized** are factors presented by the authors as being fundamental. Moreover, **leaders who really believe in collective intelligence are indispensable.**

These same recommendations apply to the groupthink bias, which will be discussed below.

- When the directors described in the three categories above are unable to resist the temptation to speak first, **the chair of the board needs to lead the process and ensure a dynamic in which everyone feels comfortable to set out their views by speaking before experts and the ones with more power or influence in the room.** It is the chair's responsibility to stress that in-depth knowledge and expertise are the primary sources for guiding a decision-making process, but it is precisely there that the **memory or confidence biases** may also be found. In Chapter 4, a number of interviewees provided examples of similar situations and recommended that the board chair should always be the last one to give his or her opinion, precisely in order to avoid the herd effect in the decision-making process. However, **Guerra, Barros and Santos'** research project[17] that was conducted with a sample of 340 directors working in 40 countries shows that this practice is little used. Sixty percent of the interviewees stated that, on the BoDs on which they serve, **experts** are always or almost always the first ones to give their opinion when their area of specialty comes up for debate (Graph 7.2).

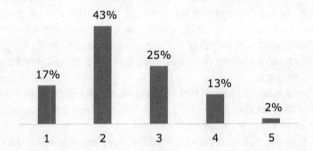

Survey Question: Is the expert on the subject one of the first to express his/her opinion when a matter is proposed for discussion or decision?
(1) Always (5) Never

Graph 7.2 Expert: first to express.
Source: Guerra, Barros and Santos (2020).

Groupthink

In order to avoid conflicts, very homogeneous and cohesive groups tend to seek consensus to an exaggerated degree, shielding themselves from contradictory and external information.

An exhaustive analysis of a series of military fiascos in the history of the United States led **Irving L. Janis**[18] to invent the concept of groupthink, which came in second place in **Guerra and Santos'** survey[19] of the most frequent causes of wrong decisions taken by boards of directors (65%). **The more uniform and less diverse the BoD, the greater the need for tactics to prevent groupthink bias, which can lead to excessive conformity.** Taking into account that the majority profile of a director[*] is still that of a white man, with substantial experience as a former executive, aged mid-50s to mid-60s, it is almost impossible to think differently in such a homogeneous group. This fact was confirmed in the research by **Guerra, Barros and Santos.**[20] Only 8% of the 340 board members interviewed stated that the debate of ideas and positions are characterized as very heterogeneous on their BoDs and 42% of them considered that the differences among the perspectives is average, as shown in Graph 7.3.

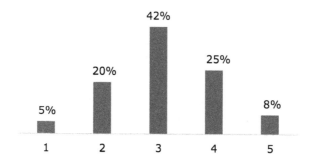

Survey Question: With regard to the discussion of ideas and positions, how would you rate your board?
1 (very homogeneous - everyone thinks alike)
5 (very heterogeneous - the great majority have very different perspectives

Graph 7.3 Level of debate.
Source: Guerra, Barros and Santos (2020).

There are numerous tactics for preventing **groupthink bias**. What follows is not intended to list them all. A number of those discussed here are multi-purpose instruments, that can also be applied to address various other dysfunctionalities and **pathologies** that plague boards of directors:

- **Diverse board.** In its broadest sense, diversity is a great safeguard against this bias, as it ensures that the BoD is made up of people with different backgrounds, professional positions held, knowledge, experience, geographical origin, gender, age, ethnicity and

---

[*]   International research regarding the typical profile of directors and the low diversity in the make-up of boards of directors was presented in Chapter 2.

style. Yes, behavioral style. There will be a lot more development in this field before the style of decision-making becomes an important element for the composition of the BoD. But while we are still struggling to at least increase professional and gender diversity, the sophistication in terms of taking into account behavioral and personality styles is still very limited, although there are already numerous studies demonstrating that the deeper the level of diversity in the BoD's make-up, the greater its creativity and speed in terms of solving problems. International studies have pointed out that:

- Teams that include different viewpoints or thinking styles (cognitive diversity) solve problems faster.[21]
- ..."deep-level diversity" (i.e., differences in background, personality and values) contributed to a higher degree of creativity.[22]

Deep and surface-level diversity will be touched on again in the section **Panaceas.**

- **Allow time for uncertainty.** It is common for boards to be uncomfortable admitting uncertainty, because, at that level of seniority, it is as if there is no longer any room for doubts. **Lovallo and Sibony**[23] agree with this danger, affirming that the culture of many organizations suppresses recognition of uncertainty and rewards behavior that ignores it. As an example, they cite companies where an executive who appears to have greater confidence in a plan tends to have a better chance of seeing it approved than one who highlights the risks and uncertainties in relation to it. And herein lies the danger: it is precisely **out of uncertainty that more robust and even more innovative solutions will emerge.** The board has to allow itself to navigate through the uncertainties and momentary questions so that there is an in-depth examination of the topic and all the opinions are set out, even those of the least assertive or talkative individuals. **Lovallo and Sibony** state that a superior decision-making process counterattacks biases that result from a situation where there is an urge to take action. This is done by promoting the recognition of uncertainty. As examples of this counterattack, the authors say that **leaders should embrace uncertainty while encouraging dissent and suggest tools such as: scenario planning decision trees, premortem** (this latter tool will be presented in the **self-serving** bias tools section).
- The chair of the board or of a committee may formally appoint some members of the board **to play the roles of the devil's advocate and investigative journalist**[*] **with the aim of causing a disruptive effect**

---

[*] See the section on mitigation bias in this chapter in which these techniques have already been addressed.

on the predominant thinking. Having the role formally assigned, the director will be more at ease to exercise it.

- When they are not an expert or when their opinion runs counter to the predominant thinking, not all board members feel confident enough to express their ideas, which can result in the board's decision-making process being contaminated by those voices with more experience, knowledge and power.

- The use of technology to sound out the positions of the directors can be considered as an instrument in the decision process. **Digital survey tools, for example, can bring to the surface the diversity of individual views.** For example, upon listening to the others, the board member changes his/her position and fails to express his/her reservations which could lead everyone to look at other perspectives that were not considered. This process does not necessarily have to be digital. An example of the result of this resource can be seen in a survey[24] undertaken with business administration students where they were presented with a list of goals for choosing a summer internship, a very important choice at that stage of their lives. The average student listed 15 goals, of which only roughly half were self-generated. They recognized the value in the goals cited by their colleagues – without this guidance, they would have made defining decisions in their lives without taking these options into account.

- Another rationale for the adoption of the techniques mentioned above is that the decision-making process contains two very important initial steps: the identification and then after this the selection of alternatives, whether it be of investments, market tactics or the choice of people. The processes used to identify and select these possibilities reduce biases, as this distinction "can help people to improve group processes of all kinds by **dividing decisions or problem-solving tasks into a creative, divergent-thinking stage and a critical, solution-integration stage.**"[25] This proposition is in line with the concept that preferences should be aired during the initial phase of the decision process and, that based on this, the group can focus better on the discussion.[26] For the board's chair, it can be of enormous value to have a prior view of where each director stands in relation to a certain topic. Of course, it is crucial to make it clear that these are initial and early expressions of view and not votes. No one should be bound to their initial views. With this general view understood in advance, the chair will be able to recognize the level of agreement in a given direction, the level of lack of knowledge and even recognize a deadlock or **polarization**[*] in relation to the topic.

---

[*] The polarization phenomenon was covered in "Pathologies", in Chapter 6, page 213, and the ways to mitigate it will be dealt with later on in this same chapter.

Taking into account that almost the entire corporate decision-making process starts off with management, **the executive team can even ensure that certain relevant and risky proposals are also subjected to this type of mechanism** before forwarding them to the BoD. The case presented by **Bob Frisch** in a Harvard Business Review collection is a good example of how this mechanism, along with offering alternatives, provides more time to be invested in those options which show themselves to be better throughout the process:

"A global credit card company was deciding where to invest in growth. Ordinarily, executive team members would have embarked on an open-ended discussion in which numerous countries would be under consideration; that tactic would have invited the possibility of multiple majorities. Instead, they conducted a straw poll, quickly eliminating the countries that attracted no votes and focusing their subsequent discussion on the two places where there was the most agreement."[27]

Although, in this case, the technique has been applied to executive teams, boards can also benefit from similar mechanisms, which consider a larger universe of alternatives before narrowing down the thinking, applying the directors' scarce time on the best-positioned options. However, apart from digital media, there are other resources to ensure that the individual view of the directors guides the first stages of the decision-making process.

- Another very simple possibility, as well as the use of virtual polls, is that each director writes down one or two paragraphs regarding their view on the topic, or even answer one or two questions in writing and bring it to the meeting, reading out the result of their individual reflection. Thus, the various individual views can be heard without the "contagion" of the others. In this manner, one does not lose a view silenced by the power of the other voices.
- A safe environment for contradictory opinions is not just one where questioning is allowed. It is one that offers psychological security to disagree with even the most powerful person in the room. In fact, the most powerful person's role is to behave in such a way that molds the BoD's culture to be open to contradictory opinions, but protected from negative conflicts (described in Chapter 6). Unfortunately, it is common for the board's chairs themselves to inhibit the expression of dissenting ideas – even without realizing it, as one of the directors interviewed described:

In this company where I was an independent director for three years, the BoD's chair went as far as publicly bragging that, on the 'board of his company', everyone could freely express their opinions, and that there was an open stance in relation to contradictory opinions. But in practice, that wasn't exactly how it was: at every board meeting, he started off telling what had happened during the period, but he already gave his own interpretation of everything. And when he presented a proposition for consideration, he did the same thing. Among the independents, there were even those who took a stand and gave their own opinion, even if it was different from the chair's. I get the feeling that he didn't even realize how his power steered the group's thinking in a certain direction. In other words, in the direction of his opinion. Although the chair himself believed otherwise, that board's environment did not really provide room for consideration and debate of contradictory opinions and, undoubtedly a great many reservations, criticisms and questions ended up being left out.

- **Red alert for the strong leader.** In the case described above, it becomes clear how an excessively strong leader's behavior can contribute to groupthink.
- **Like a Trojan horse, groupthink enters the BoD in disguise, since the propositions made by the CEO typically result from the executive leadership team's joint choices and perspectives.** So even before the board is involved, the decision- making process can be highly contaminated by groupthink among the executives, so it is advisable to adopt two preventive measures:
  - The golden rule is to ask: did the executives share the same view regarding the topic under discussion from the beginning? The more impactful propositions should **be the result of a collective decision-making process at the executive leadership level.** The project's proponent – very often, the CEO – **should be encouraged to talk about points of controversy or restrictions during the decision-making process with the leadership team.** If there was no questioning among the executives, then another question remains: was the process at the executive level sufficiently open to contradictory opinions?
  - **Make every effort to understand and find out whether the executive leadership team actually acts as a collective decision-making body.** Over the course of the team's meetings, it is possible to take a poll among the various executives who show up there. But the individual conversations that the board members can have over time with the executives can be much more productive. Of course, every care should be taken so that these conversations are not viewed as an intervention or even as an attempt to bypass the CEO. Moreover, both the CEO and the board's chair need to be informed in advance of these conversations. A more formal path, which, for this very reason, may not be available in smaller

organizations or even with a less mature governance model, is **to adopt a charter or internal regulations for, and record the minutes of formal executive leadership team meetings.** There are companies that already do this. Nevertheless, the directors do not always read these minutes – even if it is to check whether or not there are dissenting or contradictory opinions among the executives.

- **Particularly in the case of more critical and high-impact topics,** the BoD needs to be careful **not to have the CEO as the only source of information,** or only those consultants who may be loyal to him/her or even do not intend to challenge his/her proposition. It is essential that, in critical cases, the directors do not feel isolated, being exposed to a single perspective. The following example, narrated by an experienced board member, shows how a technical, specialized and totally independent view has value:

Although I am an engineer, my specialty is not the civil area, so I don't know how to assess complex infrastructure works projects. But when the board went, at my request, to visit an important project that used sophisticated techniques and bold engineering solutions, I felt uncomfortable. I wasn't sure why, but that construction project which was full of innovations put me on my guard, especially in terms of safety. Something there didn't feel quite right. I didn't say anything at the time, but when we returned from the visit, I made an appointment with the CEO, after notifying the chairman of the board, and said that I wanted the opinion of an independent third party. I even had in mind which consultancy it would be – it was a company with a high level of expertise and technical quality and one in which I had confidence. The CEO ended up accepting and the consultancy I suggested was hired. It identified a series of risks in the project related to some of the bold solutions utilized. The CEO was convinced and the consultancy's recommendations were adopted. Later, there was an accident at the construction site. We could see that if it had not been for the changes identified by the external experts, the disaster would have had devastating consequences, not just from an economic point of view, but possibly with fatalities.

False Consensus

Some individuals, especially strong leaders, tend to always assume that they are right, overestimating the likelihood that others in the group will agree with them.

One of the damaging consequences of false consensus is the isolation on the board of those individuals who have – or could have – a differentiated contribution to offer to the decision-making process. Among the directors surveyed in the **Guerra and Santos** survey,[28] 59% were of the opinion that false consensus occurs in boardrooms frequently or very frequently. In order to prevent and mitigate its most harmful effects, particularly the isolation of the board members who are most qualified to present contradictory opinions, many of the practices already mentioned in relation to trust, **herd effect** and **groupthink** biases can be applied as well as these more specific solutions:

- **Red alert triggered for decisions reached very quickly.** Nobody wants – or should – waste time, but it is better to look at the impact, complexity and risks involved in that decision and ask yourself honestly: what is missing here? Did we analyze a sufficient number of alternatives? Did we make room for contradictory opinions?
- Here once again, **the role of the devil's advocate has the potential to bring hidden fears to the surface.** Always emphasizing that in order to be credible the dissent resulting from the exercise of this role should be genuine: what can go wrong? What are the consequences that are not foreseen, but which can occur?

In-Group Favoritism

The most cohesive and homogeneous groups can allow themselves to be favorably influenced by the company's internal views, rejecting different and/or openly contradictory opinions.

This behavior of openly favoring ideas presented by their peers or the propositions presented by the company's executives is so common that it is regarded as being natural. Among the directors in the survey carried out by **Guerra and Santos**,[29] this favoritism is the fourth most frequently seen bias in boardrooms (56%). In addition to some that have already been mentioned, among the mechanisms that can be applied against this bias are the following:

- **Adopt a stance whereby the expression of dogmatic and ingrained internal convictions and certainties is questioned.** Phrases such as: "In our sector, it doesn't work like that ..." should be challenged with a constructive attitude, which, over time, is incorporated into the decision-making process in order to increase the protection against the damaging influence of the biases.
- **Getting out of the boardroom or bringing views into it from outside.** For this purpose, the BoD can, for example, receive guests, inviting a customer for lunch before the board meeting, at which part of the menu will be the expectations and concerns of that specific

stakeholder. The same format applies to other stakeholders. Another possibility is **to invite specialists or consultants at the start of the debate in relation to a more critical topic.** Also to get away from internal views, which may be biased and not take into account relevant factors, another possibility is, occasionally, for the directors **to take a break from the routine of board meetings in order to visit a customer,** check out a plant or an operation, visit points of sale, attend a meeting with a relevant stakeholder, or even take part in a meeting with investors' analysts, in the case of a listed company which discloses results on a quarterly basis. This type of measure against favoritism bias was strongly recommended by one of the board members interviewed:

I think that it's very important to get out of the boardroom. The contact with reality, real experience, going there, seeing, feeling, this makes a lot of difference. The director now has a better perception of the context in which the company operates. It is not just a two-hour visit; it is going out into the field in order to experience what is really going on. I think that this also has the effect of bringing the directors closer together, and everyone starts to interact within a more human dimension. As I admit the limitation of human rationality, I think that it's difficult to always make the right decision. But by getting out of the boardroom and going out into the field, at least, we have a slightly more informed decision, a little bit more informed than we would get by simply staying with the theory of what is put before the BoD in the form of PowerPoint presentations.

- When it is suspected that there is misalignment between the different types of shareholders or between the BoD and management, **the reasons for these different perspectives can be analyzed more carefully.** Rather than directly taking a defensive stance or creating paths to get around the contradictory view, the gain would be to understand why the contradictory view exists. For example, instead of regarding a minority shareholder's demand for greater visibility in relation to the risk management model as pure excess detail, the board would benefit if it tried to better understand what is actually behind the request. Why is the minority shareholder uncomfortable or suspicious about the risk model adopted? Are they seeing something we don't see or are we just failing to get across the message that our risk model is solid? **Demands from outside may bring up an important issue that the board has not yet identified on its own.**

Self-Serving

This is the tendency to attribute success to internal players and any eventual failure, to external factors or as being the responsibility of third parties.

In other words, this group bias can be translated as "putting the blame on others." In the **Guerra and Santos'** survey,[30] self-serving bias was one of the factors identified as most often causing boards of directors to deviate from the best decisions (52%). The first step to prevent this bias is **awareness**. In addition, as it usually exhibits relevant associations with the **confidence bias**, some of the solutions presented there are valid in this case. There are also other more specific mitigating measures, such as:

- The board should make it a practice **to choose from a wide range of alternatives.** The main benefit here is that the comparison of a number of alternatives generally helps to spell out the flaws and limitations of the internal view.
- To tackle the self-serving bias, the board may apply – separately or together with the CEO and/or the executives – the technique that **Gary Klein, Daniel Kahneman**'s collaborator, calls **premortem**. Before formalizing a decision, the group should hold a quick meeting at which each participant takes a maximum of ten minutes to describe **in writing** what may be **the worst result** of that choice in a year's time. Ideally, the exercise should be done anonymously. This way all the visions are pulled out without potential "censorship" deriving from any sort of pressure. The benefits of this practice are: (1) it helps to overcome a powerful combination of biases, such as **groupthink, self-serving bias and excessive confidence and cohesion**, where any dissenting opinion is often regarded as a lack of loyalty; and (2) to bring to the surface doubts and risks, which remained hidden by these biases. According to **Kahneman** himself, the premortem technique has generated enthusiastic reactions:

"Gary Klein's idea of the premortem usually evokes immediate enthusiasm. After I described it casually at a session in Davos, someone behind me muttered, "It was worth coming to Davos just for this!" (I later noticed that the speaker was the CEO of a major international corporation.) (...) The main virtue of the premortem is that it legitimizes doubts. Furthermore, it encourages even supporters of the decision to search for possible threats that they had not considered earlier. The premortem is not a panacea and does not provide complete protection against nasty surprises, but it goes some way toward reducing the damage of plans that are subject to the biases of WYSIATI* and uncritical optimism."[31]

In fact, over time frank, well-informed debate, without polarization of ideas or predominance of the view of some of the group's members, has proven itself to be the safest and most effective way to tackle the distortions caused by behavioral biases in the organizational decision-making process. Interviewed in a survey conducted by **McKinsey**,[32] 2,200 executives from the most varied sectors, regions and technical specialties considered that the best results are obtained from decision-making processes that include the following factors: meticulous and objective review of the business plan even when senior executives were strongly in favor of the proposition (65%); decision based on a consistent factual scenario (60%); ample opportunity for dissenting voices to speak out (58%) and a proactive search for evidence that contradicts the initial plan and its inclusion in the decision-making process (43%). However, this degree of awareness does not seem to be reflected in decision-making processes at companies' highest deliberative level. In **Guerra, Barros and Santos'** international research project,[33] which interviewed 340 directors, only 4% stated that the BoD on which they work always uses clear mechanisms to expand the alternatives in decision making and just 5% said that the board's chair always applies techniques in order to avoid over-optimism, such as the premortem and the **devil's advocate,** as presented, respectively, in Graphs 7.4 and 7.5.

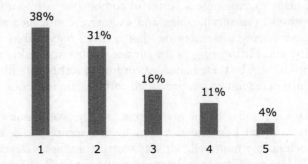

Survey Question: Before or during the meeting, the board employs explicit mechanisms or rules to increase the diversity of decision alternatives (such as checklists, decision trees, and brainstorming or scenario planning techniques) 1 (Never) 5 (Always)

Graph 7.4 **Diversity of decision alternatives.**

*   WYSIATI – What you see is all there is.

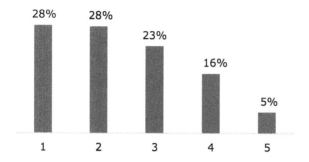

Survey Question: During board meetings, does the chair use regular processes to avoid excessive optimism, such as a pre-mortem or devil's advocate, among other alternatives?
(1) Never (5) Always

Graph 7.5 Generating alternatives.
Source: Guerra, Barros and Santos (2020).

Pathologies

As already discussed in the previous chapter the interference of cognitive biases in the dynamics of groups can occur in a combined way, resulting in such severe dysfunctionalities that the researchers **Pick and Merchant**[34] prefer to classify them as **pathologies**. Avoiding these pathologies requires preventive measures, and one must remain on constant alert to prevent their detrimental influence from overwhelming the board or infecting specific decision-making processes.

Excessive Conformity

This pathology mainly manifests itself when there is a lack of diversity in the make-up of the board and/or when the environment is not conducive to contradictory opinions, as a result of excessive cohesion. The prophylactic treatment methods for this ailment are those that have already been described for tackling biases, in particular, the individual biases of the **situation (confidence and attenuation)** and group biases, such as **groupthink** and also **herd effect**.

Negative Conflict

At the other extreme from excessive cohesion are conflicts that go well beyond the limit of what is healthy. In countries, including those of Latin or Asian origin, for instance, where the predominant culture is that of avoiding disagreements or even touching on delicate issues, dealing with dissent becomes even more complex, as the common tendency

is to smooth things over – even when the disagreement is constructive. However, many studies indicate that there are two prerequisites
for the solution or mitigation of counterproductive conflicts: identifying
the style with which the most sensitive issues are usually dealt with by
the group and the type of origin of these conflicts, which can be personal, structural or business-related, as shown in Figure 7.2.[35]

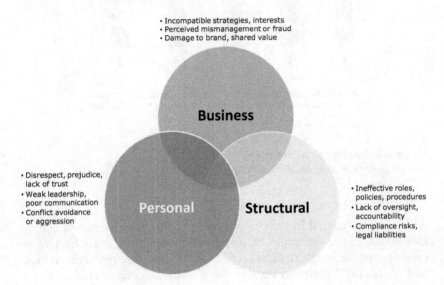

• Incompatible strategies, interests
• Perceived mismanagement or fraud
• Damage to brand, shared value

Business

• Disrespect, prejudice,
  lack of trust
• Weak leadership,
  poor communication
• Conflict avoidance
  or aggression

Personal   **Structural**

• Ineffective roles,
  policies, procedures
• Lack of oversight,
  accountability
• Compliance risks,
  legal liabilities

Figure 7.2 Identification of the possible origin of the conflicts among the
board members.
Source: IFC-CEDR.[36]

Among the possible measures that can be taken to correct really
counterproductive disputes between the BoD's members, **Pick and Merchant**[37] list the following:

• The board's chair should encourage internal confidence in the group,
  **creating strong norms about open disagreement and dissent. This
  will ensure room for differences** and even inviting contradictory
  opinions to be expressed on certain occasions.
• The board chair should foster an **environment that offers psychological safety** to the directors.
• During the conduct of joint activities, make **productive conflict part
  of the work routine.**
• **Deliberately stimulating productive conflict by use of the role of
  "devil's advocate."**
• Anticipate and/or **identify the potential conflict as quickly as possible
  in order to frame it constructively.** In this way, a misunderstanding

related to the performance of an activity or a process will not degenerate into a relationship conflict.

• Over time, **by not ignoring disagreements, the perception develops that the group is capable of efficiently resolving its own conflicts.**

The governance experts, **Masters and Rudnick,**[38] recommend that **Alternative Dispute Resolution (ADR) techniques be applied to boards of directors.** They believe that mediation and arbitration practices can be adapted to the dynamics of BoDs:

• Identify opposing interests rather than conflicting positions;
• Bring to the surface the emotional or factual issues that are involved in the disputes or potential disputes;
• Support the parties so that the focus is maintained on long-term goals and interests;
• Use procedures that encourage collaboration and emphasize flexibility;
• Foster discussion and provide incentives for the free flow of ideas;
• Highlight information about the problem and, therefore, about its solution;
• Facilitate the development of solutions by the parties in a collaborative way instead of imposing solutions;
• When appropriate, use a third party to facilitate and mediate the communication process.

Dysfunctional Coalition

I was an independent board member, but it was impossible to objectively assess any proposal put before the board. The environment was damaged. The two business groups who came together in an innovative business made up the board with three directors representing one side and two for the other side, along with two independent directors. Instead of dealing with the common goals, the focus of the two groups of shareholders was tied to their own interests. It was almost unbelievable: at every debate, even when the two sides came up with similar arguments for or against a decision, neither side wanted to agree with the other. The dominant factor was the atmosphere of dispute. The discussions were much more than heated: everything broke down and ended up in a fight. When one of the shareholder directors tried to reach a compromise, someone soon demanded loyalty. I don't know how they managed to get to this point, what I do know is that the business that seemed very promising at the outset didn't even manage to get as far as having a complete structure. The entire initial investment was lost.

Although it may not be commonplace, the story told by this interviewee does not represent a strange or very rare situation on boards of directors. A number of studies regarding the dynamics of groups indicate the possibility of the formation of hostile subgroups, called coalitions or factions, which have the power to make the board's functioning pathological, against the interests of all parties, not just against the interests of the owners.

As well as making it impossible to have objectivity in the board's decision-making process, these damaging disputes can also occur among other specific subgroups, such as shareholders, executives and other stakeholders. And for that very reason, it is vital to immediately take steps to get the counterproductive conflict back to the level of healthy, constructive differences. In order to deal with this serious problem, the different techniques and tools that have already been explored in this chapter are very useful, such as **exercise of contradictory opinions; openness to questioning; expansion of the alternatives examined;** in the debate phase, **alternating contradictory and favorable positions;** or the proposition for each coalition to carry out the **premortem exercise.** In addition, there are other resources available to mitigate this dysfunctionality:

- **Place coalition members in different subgroups to play new roles, separately from their traditional "allies."** A little-used resource in boards – but one that can address this and other behavioral challenges – is the formation, for example, of two groups (the number of subgroups depends on the size of the BoD and the number of existing coalitions). Before the formal meeting to discuss a given subject, the goal of these new subgroups is to spend half an hour exchanging ideas about that specific topic. It is when they are separated that the members of a coalition will see their ideas and assumptions being challenged by other forms of reasoning and, even better, they will not be under the continuous influence of the members of their own faction. Another possibility with this same technique is **to merge subgroups that are antagonistic in relation to a given issue:** for example, the members of two board committees that have fallen out over the analysis of a proposal can benefit from this technique, bringing the debate out into the open and, consequently, minimizing the effects of the coalition.
- When coalitions exist, **the role of the board's chair is of vital importance,** with the chair's greatest contribution being to the maintenance of his or her neutrality and impartiality. **When it is clear that they have an attachment to one of the factions, one option that can be considered is for the chair to transfer the handling of that specific debate to someone who is more neutral. The Lead Independent Director (LID)** introduced in Chapter 4 would be one option;

otherwise, an independent director who has not yet become close to or is identified with any of the coalitions may serve this role.

- **Encourage the feeling among the directors of belonging to the group,** viewing the board as a collective body that has a common task to be performed. The board's chair is the one who, over the course of time, has to construct the environment of psychological safety that stimulates the perception of belonging among the board members. In order to help the group focus on the points that the directors have in common, it is recommended that exercises be carried out which are similar to the one proposed by **Professor Mervyn King**[*] at the start of this chapter.

One of the forerunners of the behavioral vision applied to boards of directors, **Morten Huse**[39] states that one of the origins of coalition conflicts on the BoD may be the definition of the business' strategic goals. In this case, he points out that the conflict is usually better resolved with political bargaining than with objective alignment around economic incentives. For him, the conflict in relation to the definition of goals drives the search for additional information and new knowledge. This should be seen as an opportunity for learning and not as an obstacle to organizational development.

Habitual Routines[**]

As already covered in Chapter 6, routines are comforting, because, according to **Kahneman**,[40] it is only when contexts show evidence of getting away from the habitual that the individual also brings **System 2** into action; while routines remain intact, human behavior is guided automatically just by **System 1**,[***] which is quick and unthinking. For this reason, routines can also make us shortsighted. The tools to avoid falling into the **pathology** of **habitual routines** are virtually intuitive:

- Although **the BoD's regular rules and dynamics** should be maintained, **they need to be broken occasionally** in order to create a new context in which attention is no longer contaminated and directed by the monotony of rituals.
- **This type of change can be applied to almost everything:** from the order in which the committees religiously make their reports to the

---

[*]   The author interviewed Mervyn King in New York, United States, on April 1, 2014.
[**]   According to Gersick and Hackman, the so-called **habitual routines** occur when "a group repeatedly exhibits a functionally similar pattern of behavior in a given stimulus situation without explicitly selecting it over alternative ways of behaving."
[***] Kahneman's Systems 1 and 2 are described in Chapter 6.

board, to the CEO's repeated presentation of the period's results at each meeting, and even the arrangement of who-sits-where-in-the-boardroom. A simple change of location in the room, for example sitting in front of rather than next to someone, can reveal the person's reactions that one was earlier unaware of. The same goes for the person's proximity, sitting closer to someone increases the possibilities for more direct interaction. This is one of those small changes that are difficult to implement, given the high level of entrenchment in the territoriality of various animals, including *homo sapiens*.

- Other ways to break routines are suggested by **Thuraisingham and Lehmacher**, including among others:
- identifying and revealing unnoticed routines;
- assigning people to activities that are not tied to their traditional loyalties;
- asking a less senior employee to defend the CEO's or the business owner's point of view; and
- reviewing every task in order to challenge routinized thinking.[41]

Shared Information

In addition to confusing information-gathering with data analysis, groups tend to invest more time in debating what the majority already knows rather than concentrating on bringing to the surface knowledge that is under control of the minority, preventing valuable details from being taken into account in the decision-making process. Among the most effective recommendations for avoiding this bias are:

- Avoiding the time pressure bias in the decision-making process also helps to prevent the debate from being restricted to information already shared by the majority. This is yet another reason **to extend the time dedicated to debate**, encouraging the emergence of knowledge that is only within the domain of one or more directors.
- In order to prevent data collection from being confused with assessment, as a facilitator, the board's chair should **first** get the group **to gather all the information and only then start to debate** a specific proposition, particularly the most critical ones and that have the greatest impact on the business.
- One solution that has already been put forward for other biases is **to increase the number of opinions available** in the group, including inviting **third parties to take part in the debate**. This initiative helps the directors avoid becoming attached to generic discussions.

- For the same reason, the **board's chair can encourage less senior professionals to present their views to the board**, recognizing that those with higher status tend to dominate discussions.
- It is also recommended here to use **information technologies to structure the decision-making process**, cataloging and organizing the data available for the decision, with this measure also facilitating the communication between board members.[42]

Pluralistic Ignorance

The pathology of **pluralist ignorance** usually happens when one – or even more than one – director submits to the social pressure from the group and fails to express opinions that are contrary to those of the majority. As paradoxical as it may seem, this problem is more frequent on boards with greater diversity and high social cohesion. **Diversity,** particularly with respect to work experience and gender, can cause the board member to fail to understand the position of the others and, therefore, to prefer to keep quiet or agree with the others. Some of the possible remedies have already been mentioned, but there are also more specific techniques, such as:

- The board chair should promote the **creation of a culture** in which no matter is considered to be beyond discussion.
- **Disagreement,** always in a constructive way, should be seen by all the board members **as an obligation.**
- Foster **renewal on the board,** considering shorter terms given that the pluralistic ignorance bias is less present in BoDs which have a shorter mandate. This is because the shorter mandate prevents directors from getting too attached to a set of rules and to the organizational belief system. Furthermore, new board members bring in new ideas and ask new questions, which overturns the *status quo.*[43]

Social Loafing

The research developed more than 130 years ago by the French agricultural engineer **Max Ringelmann**[44] and reported in Chapter 6, inspired the studies about social loafing: the tendency for individuals to exhibit a sizable decrease in individual effort when performing in groups as compared to when they perform alone.[45] In other words, the individuals in a group make less effort than when performing a task individually. This phenomenon enables us to ask how much is lost in terms of the contribution of those directors who, "cloaked" in the group, do not give the best of themselves. Since the frequency with which this phenomenon occurs is significant, among the tools that can be used to reduce the problem, are the following:

- Individually, **the board members must believe that their contributions are unique** and that they will be considered in the decision-making process. The board chair creates this culture, at regular intervals asking each director to express their opinion on a certain debate and even making it clear, right from the board member selection interview stage, how individual contribution is important to the best decision.
- **Increase the activities carried out in committees,** because the smaller the group, the harder it is for the director to remain anonymous in the result achieved by the team. In addition to the BoD's support committees, it is possible to set up other groups on a temporary basis to tackle specific issues that are more critical or strategic.
- The board's chair should institute **a systematic evaluation process whereby the roles and expectations in relation to the director's individual performance are made clear and rigorously examined,** preferably by his or her peers as well as by the chair. According to **Pick and Merchant,**[46] many psychologists believe that the simple creation of the possibility of individual contributions offered to the group being assessed can already eliminate a large part of social loafing.

Polarization

When they get together in a group, there is a tendency for board members to make more extreme decisions than would be the individual inclination of each director. Whether out of a desire for acceptance or because they have actually been exposed to persuasive arguments, the directors tend to go one step further when they are in the group – either by assuming more risk or by maintaining an even more conservative view. How can falling into the trap of group **polarization** be avoided?

- **A prior poll of the individual opinions and an attempt to increase the diversity in the board's make-up,** which have already been mentioned as mechanisms that can be used against other biases, may also reduce the negative effects of group **polarization.** Moreover, **Kahneman** suggests that each director write down his opinion before the conclusion of the debate, and explains the reason:

"A simple rule can help: before an issue is discussed, all members of the committee should be asked to write a very brief summary of their position. This procedure makes good use of the value of the diversity of knowledge and opinion in the group. The standard practice of open discussion gives too much weight to the opinions of those who speak early and assertively, causing others to line up behind them."[47]

- Alexandre Gonçalves Silva[*] indicates that the **board chair can guide the committees' chairs to bring the diversity of views discussed** to the board meetings. He related his positive experience when the work of the committees helped to avoid polarization on the board:

  Differences of opinion are normal and a good board should have an atmosphere that is favorable to the diversity of views, with the issues being discussed openly and the directors having enough time to fully discuss the issue and to seek a consensus. The board chair has an important role in this respect, trying to make the group be productive, work well as a team, know how to discuss matters and how to deal with differences of opinion ... For example, one good practice is to get the committee that deals with the topic to present the board with different perspectives: 'Look, there are six of us here on the committee and on this subject we had three people who had strong opinion X and three people who had different opinions: Y, Z and H.' I've seen it happen and it's very positive. And I have also seen the following: two opinions were put before the board, which discussed the matter and then decided by consensus, taking into account further information presented by other directors. It was by means of measures as simple as these that polarization was avoided.

Panaceas[**]: Basic Kit for All Routes

Although techniques can be employed to prevent or even resolve each of the cognitive biases – individual or group – and the dysfunctionalities caused by them in the performance of BoDs, there are practices that

---

[*]   Alexandre Gonçalves Silva is an independent board member and chairman of Embraer's board of directors. He was CEO of General Electric do Brasil between 2001 and 2007 and, since then, has served on boards of directors at companies in various economic sectors. The author interviewed Alexandre Gonçalves Silva in São Paulo, Brazil, on February 19, 2016.

[**] The word panacea comes from Greek mythology and refers to a remedy for all illnesses. Outside of the medical context, the term is often used to refer to something that will solve all problems. Panacea, as used in this book, is not intended to imply that the practices and techniques discussed here can resolve all the behavioral challenges boards face, but rather that they are multipurpose solutions with general application to the variety of biases presented earlier.

can reduce a number of behavioral problems simultaneously. These are a panacea for all behavioral ills, which therefore make great travel companions, whether by land, sea or air for navigating this still-unexplored behavioral world of boards.

Diversity and Independence

The diversity and systematic renewal of the composition of the BoD are crucial factors since they minimize the likelihood that the group of directors will become prey to biases, short-sightedness and pathologies. To function effectively the decision-making process must include different views that are expressed with the independence of conscience. This encourages a vigorous debate in which the agents, with a variety of experiences and skills, get the chance to challenge the proposals presented to the board from different perspectives, moving away from a possible initial consensus – which is more subject to cognitive biases.

With regard to diversity, a number of experts[48,49] stress that, in addition to the more visible attributes, such as gender, ethnicity and age (so-called **"superficial level diversity"**), it is important that the board's composition also makes room for what they call **"deep-level diversity"**, which refers to heterogeneity in relation to personality, backgrounds, attitudes, beliefs and values. Using a sample of 385 Norwegian companies, **Torchia, Calobrò and Morner** found that "deep-level diversity (...) impact positively and significantly on the level of cognitive conflict and creativity."[50] In more practical terms, since the composition of boards is still very homogeneous,[*] seeking diversity becomes an even more urgent matter, even if it is in relation to the more visible attributes, according to one interviewee, who argued in favor of the inclusion of younger directors in the make-up of BoDs. In the interview, he mentions a situation in which entrepreneurial board members share decisions with young directors appointed by funds that are invested in the venture:

> Now, you brought up another point – the role of young people. I think that a bit of what we were talking about is the importance of having on the board this diversity in terms of a more holistic view, of you being able to have a dimension that is not a trivial one, which is not that expected from a director/ So what books did the analysts read? They read the compliance book, the risk analysis book, the finance book. That's what they learn from. In a way, entrepreneurs are almost blind to what is outside their world. They believe so much in the business that there is no way they can have an unbiased view.

---

[*]   The typical profile of directors was outlined in Chapter 2.

But that is the entrepreneur's role. If they analyze a lot they may not even be able to do their job.

Therefore, the BoD has to broaden the analytical perspective. But how to enhance boards, how to bring into the team members who are detached both from the financial framework and risk analysis as well as from the entrepreneur's dream? Obviously, this is where young people can play a very strong role. When I say this, someone always makes the case that young people are not yet mature enough to be directors. But that is the whole point: we don't need more maturity. Enough of maturity! There is already a lot of it on BoDs. Be it formal maturity or the maturity of the "old young man". What you need is for the young director to be connected to the world, linked to these new movements and to be able to bring this revamped vision to the environment of the board. Does this mean that the young person's immaturity will take precedence? No. What it means is that that the young person will broaden the board's view, for example, in relation to sustainability, and will also take a more detached stance vis-à-vis the traditional perspective as well as in relation to the vision of the founders of the business.

In relation to the participation of women, as has already been described in Chapter 2, it is undeniable that since 2003, when Norway was the pioneer in adopting quotas for female directors, there has been some quantitative advance. But in qualitative terms, the majority group – white men, ex-CEOs and aged mid-50s to mid-60s – continues to exert social pressure to maintain its status, as an American female director who was interviewed illustrated. After a long and successful career, she rose to the position of CEO of a company in the high-tech sector and afterward became a board member. Right from the start, due to being the only woman on that BoD, the board chair systematically ignored her opinions: "It was as if I had gone back to the 1970s, when I was the only electronic engineer working at the company." Either the chair was alerted by someone that he had "skipped" her turn or she had to take a stand in order to voice her opinions. However, thanks to more recent pressure from some large investors, the make-up of the board has become more diverse, paving the way for two more women. It is the interviewee herself who reports the benefits obtained as a result of this:

Today the board is extraordinarily diverse in terms of gender, ethnicity and age and I see that no one is imposing anything on us. For the first time, I can see the benefits of having different points of view around the table. There are now three of us women, and although the chair remains the same, he can no longer ignore us. I note that women make the decision-making process more structured and we tend to take a more balanced stance in relation to risks. We do not get caught up in the mood of the moment and, for this reason, we are not swayed by reckless propositions. Not only in relation to women, but diversity really does generate a better decision-making process; I have witnessed this in the changing dynamics in the boardroom.

With regard to diversity in the make-up of boards of directors, a North American director points out that, even in the United States, where the governance requirements for companies, particularly those that are listed, are more stringent, the tendency is still for there to be a lot of homogeneity among the board members. According to **Herman Bulls,**[*] preference is given to those with a generalist background, when, in fact, it is the diversity of expertise among the directors that makes it possible to reach more creative and innovative solutions, including problems that have never been faced before by the organization, such as, for example, cyber risk:

> In the United States, the generalist director is still the rule. You don't see many HR, insurance or IT professionals on boards beside the finance, marketing and operations experts. But diversity is what can help solve even a problem that the company has never faced before. For example, in relation to cyber risk, even if he is not an expert on the topic, an IT director is able to provide guidance in terms of identifying potential risks and solutions. It is not compulsory to have a board member who has come from the IT are. What is crucial is that there is a wide and deep-level diversity among the directors. The time may come when it is more important to have someone from IT on the BoD, but for the time being, the crucial thing is to have diversity.

One of the most efficient ways to ensure increased diversity in the make-up of boards of directors is to renew the boards with shorter terms. **Fernando Carneiro,**[**] is of the opinion that, as well as bringing new perspectives into the boardroom, more frequent board turnover results in

---

[*] Herman E. Bulls is vice chairman of the board of Jones Lang LaSalle (JLL) Americas, is a member of the board of the American Red Cross, and serves on other boards in the United States. He has a degree in engineering from West Point and a master's degree in finance from Harvard. The author interviewed Herman E. Bulls in Washington, D.C., United States, on April 16, 2015.

[**] Fernando Carneiro leads CEO practices in Latin America and Brazil and was a member of Spencer Stuart Global Board. As a recognized expert in corporate governance, he conducted several board searches and board assessment projects for Brazilian and multinational companies. The author interviewed Fernando Carneiro in São Paulo, Brazil, on March 15, 2016.

a fresh look at the risks and opportunities and gives governance a new boost of energy: "The shorter terms of office facilitate the increasingly strong presence of minority shareholders, who want to be able to give a more forceful opinion on the fate of the company."

For another interviewee, shorter mandates even have the power to prevent detrimental behavior, such as the misuse of sensitive information for personal benefit:

> Another claim that is often made against younger board members is that, due to a lack of maturity, they may commit a breach of confidentiality in relation to the company's confidential strategic information. I look at it differently and think that it is a case of being a bit more daring in terms of the composition of boards. The figure of the "sly old fox" director comes to mind. Usually, he is a professional who has been with the board for a long time and who starts to use the position for his own benefit, in defense of opportunistic interests. So, my preference is for renewing the board more frequently and to have a young person there who unintentionally commits an indiscretion rather than a "experienced director" who knows only too well that he is only defending his own interests.

Independence

Much more than a mere formality and one of the best practices recommended by corporate governance manuals, the independence of the board members should be an integral part of the set of values exercised on a daily basis by boards of directors. One of the interviewees emphasized that, in addition to his own awareness of this, it is also vital that this independence of the board members is perceived by the group. According to his account, there are cases – fortunately, rarer – in which it is the imperative exercise of independence that ensures that the group of directors continues to "do the right thing":

> I have always believed in this set of attitudes and values; it has been inherent to my professional experience since I entered college at the age of 19. I think that board directors need to have at least two characteristics. The first is to find channels in which they manage not to be the only ones fighting. They have to be able to rely on good professional partnerships. For example, when I am going to take a firm stance against or in favor of a proposition, I try never to surprise anyone on the board. My peers are the first ones to be informed, even if it doesn't make them happy. And the second is independence above all. Professionals cannot depend on their positions as board members; if they have to quit, it cannot make

a difference in their lives. So, it may seem a little arrogant, but I think that's the way it should be: "If I have to quit before the end of my mandate, when asked why I left, I will be able to explain the reasons publicly." So, the price can be very high... and this gives the directors some leeway in terms of their behavior, I will not say to act fearlessly, but the fact is that the group is more motivated to keep doing the right thing.

Board Evaluation

When it comes to improving the workings of the BoD, the systematization of the assessment process has already proven to be an excellent tool. Even so, it continues to be underutilized. As recounted in Chapter 4, one of the results of the survey by **Guerra, Barros and Santos** was that 44% of the 340 directors operating in 40 countries state that their BoDs never carry out periodic evaluations or only do so at intervals of more than three years. The systematic evaluation of the Board is, however, the technique that best detects the group's as well as the individual's shortcomings, both in relation to cognitive biases and in connection with the group's own interactions. This is undoubtedly the reason why governance experts throughout the world regard board evaluation as one of the panaceas for all ills; at least as the initial and principal step in an improvement process. A vigorous assessment of the BoD provides a healthier environment in which there is respect for differences and relationships of trust. Only in this way can the conditions be created for information to be exchanged openly, allowing contradictory opinions to be used in a mature and constructive way in order to guarantee quality decision processes. This is a view shared by most governance gurus, as articulated by **Ira Millstein**[*] in an interview:

> Boards should be encouraged to self-assess to see if they are comprised of people whose values are in line with those of the organization. Therefore, one aspect of this assessment should be whether the director clearly expresses his/her position when something seems wrong. Does he/she take part effectively in the board meetings? I don't want board members who are giving their CVs a bit more sparkle, I don't want people who are just there for decorative purposes, I want people who really care about the company.

[*] Ira Millstein, corporate lawyer and a senior partner at Weil, Gotshal & Manges, is one of the most highly regarded corporate governance experts in the United States and headed up the committee that drafted the OECD's – Organization for Economic Cooperation and Development's – Corporate Governance Principles. The author interviewed Ira Millstein in New York, United States, on March 31, 2014.

In a similar vein, if **Sir Adrian Cadbury**[*] had to choose a single recommendation to make in governance, it would be to make room on boards for the assessment process, occasionally with the support of an external consultant:

> It's difficult to pick one piece of advice (...) but if I had to choose just one, I would say that boards must give time to thinking about how they are working collectively. A way to do that is to ask board members to reflect on board decisions they've made and give their opinion with hindsight, "Did we take the right decision? How did we make the decision? Are there ways we could do this better? And if so, how?" My advice is that there is a need for evaluation and, as a past chairman, I would want, at least on some occasions, to have an outsider assisting in the process of evaluation.

Chairs who head up the board assessment process can consider the priorities identified by the 102 directors who took part in the **Guerra and Santos'** survey (Graph 7.6 – see following page).[51]

BoD's Performance: Critical Initiatives

Governance Gurus Recommend

I. Before you become a director

Taking the initiative of opening up a dialogue before even accepting a position as a director of a company is a valuable preventive measure for the professional who is invited to join a BoD, especially if it is the first time that they will be serving in this position. Therefore, talking to the board's chair, other directors, the CEO and the auditor can be very revealing and guide the decision as to whether or not to accept that position. At this point, talking in advance with the board's chair is perhaps the most enlightening conversation, as they are the ones who will indicate how they define their own role and what type of performance is expected from the board – **protagonist** or **supporting**.[*] The adoption or not of a

---

[*] The concepts of protagonist BoD and supporting BoD were covered in Chapter 4.

---

[*] Sir Adrian Cadbury (1929–2015) was the author of the Cadbury Report, which, in 1992, established corporate governance standards for the United Kingdom. He was also the chairman of the board of Cadbury Schweppes. The author interviewed Sir Adrian Cadbury's in Dorridge, England, on December 4, 2013.

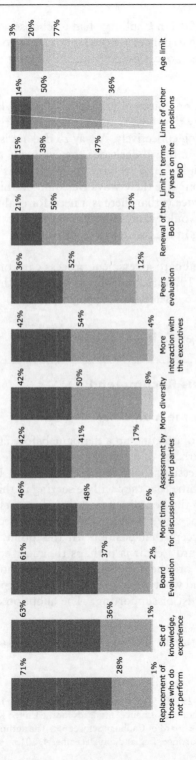

Graph 7.6 The importance of the initiatives to improve the board's performance.
Source: Guerra and Santos (2017).

systematic assessment process is also indicative of the BoD's willingness to continually face up to its shortcomings and limitations and, of course, how difficult it will be to become a director in that company. In fact, more than pre-acceptance discussions, **Mervyn King**[*] recommends that the future director carry out a two-way due diligence:

> If you invite me to be a board member, before I accept, I need to have an intellectually honest foundation. So, I need to do a due diligence on your company. What if you have a director on the BoD who has a bad reputation? The board is a collective body, and my reputation could also be affected. In the same way, the board should carry out a due diligence on me, not just whether I have skills, a good reputation, experience or already serve on many other boards. It is a two-way due diligence. If you are going to be an independent director, do you not have any links to a major shareholder, a large supplier or a major consulting firm? These preliminary tests should be done, since they are very useful.

In turn, **Robert Monks**[**] suggests that the future director should have talks beforehand until he/she and the company reach a very clear and well-defined agreement in relation to the scope of work, authority and responsibilities. According to **Monks**, in order for the director to always be able to act independently and in accordance with his/her values, first of all, they need to feel stable in the position:

> It is my opinion that the professional should have a legal agreement that clearly sets out their duties as a director so that they can serve in a proper way. It is not possible to be part of the decision-making process dealing with a situation of doubts or insufficient explanations. The director needs to achieve this stable position before they sit down at the board table; because after this it will be too late. The director has to know what he is going to do, how much time he will have to devote to the activity and his degree of authority and responsibilities. Based on this agreement, he can serve as a good board member.

---

[*] The author interviewed Mervyn King in New York, United States, on April 1, 2014.

[**] Robert Monks is a co-founder of Institutional Shareholders Services and the author of books such as Corpocracy and Watching The Watchers. The author interviewed Robert Monks in Pelican Hill, Newport Coast, California, United States, on September 13, 2013.

But, on top of this prior assessment of aspects of the business and of the company's governance, **Ira Millstein**[*] recommends that the professional who is a candidate to be a director should ask himself/herself what their most genuine interests are:

> When someone asks me whether or not they should be on a board, I ask if the person really likes the business. Even in my philanthropies, I try to search for directors who really like what they do. For example, if you are going to be on the board of a medical school or hospital, you have to be interested in healthcare; if you are going to join the board of a park or a reserve, you should be interested in environmental preservation. You do not want directors who sit there in silence and do everything that is suggested by the executives. You want them to ask smart questions, find out how to better understand the business, the community and the mission of the organization.

2. Already serving as a director

In addition to always being open to dialogue, upon sitting at the board table, the most valuable resource is continuous assessment – both individual as well as of the BoD as a group. The board's and the director's best performance depends on them being on guard to identify any factor that may be causing the decision-making process to deviate "from doing the right thing". Therefore, it is essential that the director dedicates himself/herself to constant self-criticism and analysis exercises, particularly during the board's assessment period. However, even if a systematic assessment is not a tool that is applied by the organization to its board, the director should not avoid the opportunity to carry out a self-assessment. Some exercises can – and should – be performed not only in relation to the technical skills for the business but also in terms of the behavioral profile. For example, with regard to the individual style of decision making, the researchers **Thuraisingham and Lehmacher** recommend the following individual questioning:

> "Over time we all develop a decision-making style – a set of habits that govern how we make decisions. We rarely stand back and reflect on this style. The best way to do this is to

---

[*] The author interviewed Ira Millstein in New York, United States, on March 31, 2014.

periodically review your performance on decisions you have been called upon to make. Look for patterns in the way you make decisions, the logic you use, the experience you rely on, the consultation you engage in, the scrutiny from others you encourage and so on. What does your behaviour tell you about your style? Use the following as a checklist:

- How often do you engage in second-order[*] thinking?
- Are your solutions imaginative enough?
- Do you spend too much time on the less important issues?
- Do you tend to gravitate towards choices that, after the fact, seem too conservative?
- Do you tend to miscalculate risk?
- Do you tend to sacrifice thoroughness for speed?
- Do you feel in control of your decision-making?
- Are there certain types of people that I engage with or whose opinion I rely on?"[52]

---

[*] Thuraisingham and Lehmacher refer to second order thinking (prior to making a decision) as 'thinking about your thinking' as opposed to first order thinking that relies on what is presented to you. Engaging in second-order thinking recognizes that the decision process is imprecise and departs from the assumption that examining one's thinking is important. Thuraisingham and Lehmacher assert that adopting second-order thinking reflects a conscious choice to question one's thinking more deeply, improving the quality of decision-making.

To a large extent, the quality of the board's performance results from its composition, its defined model of functioning (protagonist or supporting) and the performance profile of the board's chair. For this reason, it is necessary to make room for the directors to periodically assess their own performance, identifying points for improvement and planning initiatives that can be adopted. Nonetheless, it is still very common for some directors to argue that board evaluation may not be the best investment of precious board meeting time. The researchers **Pick and Merchant** assert that "the potential payoffs of doing so – or dangers of not doing so – are great"[53] and suggest alternatives so that, individually, the director can deal with even those boards that are the most resistant to his or her ideas:

- In addition to voluntarily playing the role of **devil's advocate**, it is recommended that directors, where appropriate, express their thoughts in such a way as to never put the board's chair in a difficult spot. **Pick and Merchant** even recommend that the questions should appear naive and show a "desire to learn," because the answers will be very informative. For example: "I wanted you to help me understand why Company X is our best target."

- If the board is very resistant to innovative ideas or to contradictory opinions, the two experts suggest prior conversations – outside the board meeting – with the board's chair or with the CEO explaining the assumptions behind a specific proposition.

- Another option is for the director to ask open-ended questions such as: "Has anyone among us worked with a client of this type before?" Or: "For me, this situation is an unusual one, what about for you?" According to the two experts, this "safe" divergence is a critical tool for the individual performance of the directors.

- Last but not least, another recommendation is to resist the temptation to isolate yourself in the BoD, particularly when alliances or coalitions already exist. "Creating and nurturing overlap with each board member is a way both of creating necessary social cohesion and fighting too much inappropriate social cohesion."

Culture or Character

Since the set of values, attitudes and behaviors expressed in operations and in the relationship with all its stakeholders, the organizational culture – which **Mervyn King**[*] prefers to call the corporate character – is what gives the company's performance context. Among the directors' roles is that of fostering the most appropriate organizational culture for the development of the adopted strategy, but always in line with the values and principles that guide the company. As **King** argued at the start of this chapter, it is critical that the BoD comes to a consensus regarding the company's character. He makes it clear that this is because that the board takes collective decisions, which will have to be adjusted to this character. And he gives a warning: if this is not done, the business will deteriorate or its character will have to be changed.

For those who view the word compliance as the panacea for deviations of all kinds – whether ethical or due to excessive risk or even inefficient practices – another warning: The most effective compliance processes and the most capable executives put in charge of this function – which is increasingly common – have a very limited role when the corporate culture or character does not provide them with

---

[*]   The author interviewed Mervyn King in New York, United States, on April 1, 2014.

the necessary support. There is no doubt that compliance mechanisms, headed up by an area or body created at the company for this purpose, can serve as a galvanizing element in the effort to adhere to practices aligned with upright behavior, as well as, for example, preventing excessive risks. But don't expect this to be enough. The *'tone at the top'* is what makes all the difference, as it builds the desired culture, shaping behavior without the need for excessive supervision. It is from the leaders that the behaviors and attitudes that will be replicated by everyone emanate. After all, what compliance department can really inhibit fraudulent behavior when the leaders use bribes as part of their business model?

On top of being the cornerstone for the daily management of corporate challenges, a healthy organizational culture's importance increases when the company is faced with critical challenges, as **Sir Winfried Bischoff**, chair of the United Kingdom's Financial Reporting Council, warns in a report dedicated entirely to the role of boards in relation to corporate culture:

> "A healthy culture both protects and generates value. It is therefore important to have a continuous focus on culture, rather than wait for a crisis. Poor behaviour can be exacerbated when companies come under pressure. A strong culture will endure in times of stress and mitigate the impact. This is essential in dealing effectively with risk and maintaining resilient performance."[54]

In this same document from the **Financial Reporting Council**[55] the essential recommendations are as follows:

- **Recognition of the value of culture** – a healthy corporate culture is a valuable asset.
- **Modeling by the leadership** – in all aspects and at all levels of the business, the leaders should incorporate the desired culture.
- **Openness and responsibility** – good governance entails respecting the interests of all stakeholders.
- **Integration and incorporation into practices** – the company's values should be practiced by all employees and suppliers.
- **Assessment, measurement and engagement** – the board should dedicate resources to assess the organizational culture and the items for improvement.
- **Value-aligned incentives** – the rewards system should support and encourage behavior that is consistent with the values.
- **Engagement of investors** – both majority as well as minority shareholders should question the behavior they encourage in business.

Boards and Directors: Looking to the Future

By discussing the current management context of organizations and presenting the behavioral approach as an efficient solution for reducing the potential dysfunctionalities and pathologies of boards, this book aims to help BoDs be better equipped for the new challenges they will have to face in the future. And everything indicates that, after the 'unforeseen' COVID-19 pandemic, the future challenges will not be insignificant. Having a healthy organizational culture is one of the most effective ways for companies to tackle – and get through – the resulting uncertainties. **Betania Tanure,**[*] who argues in favor of a culture based on openness, trust and discipline, claims that organizational culture and leadership are two sides of the same coin and that another responsibility of BoDs is to guide and continuously promote the practice of the company's set of principles and values:

> Leaders have a responsibility to direct the organization's natural flow and this holds true for board members. The BoD should promote and cultivate the company's health and vitality and culture plays an absolutely essential role in relation to this. If the flow is correct, the board's function is to accelerate; if the flow is not appropriate, its responsibility is to change, to transform. However, it is the BoD's job to guide the culture, rather than to operate it. It is up to the board to mobilize the CEO and C-level executives, when they do not respond to this need. It is the executive body that should manage a transformation process whenever necessary, but ensuring that it is carried out in alignment with the board of directors. In times of uncertainty, culture is also an important reducer of anxiety. But in order for that to happen, the leadership has to create an environment of trust, discipline and openness. Culture is the company's greatest sustainable competitive (dis)advantage, since it cannot be copied.

> **What is essential for the leader to give this direction to the organizational culture?**

> If the director identifies that he or she does not have certain necessary requirements, they should bear in mind that it is always time to learn, it is always time to add skills. One of the premises I use in my work is "no one is perfect, but a team can be." I recommend that the leader invest more and more in self-knowledge. Everybody

---

[*] Betania Tanure, who was director of the Fundação Dom Cabral for 15 years, is a psychologist, has a PhD in business administration and is a specialist in organizational culture. As well as currently working as a consultant, she also has experience as a board member. The author interviewed Betania Tanure, in a virtual internet room, on August 14, 2020.

should recognize their "sun" and "shadow" points and seek to develop them. Self-knowledge is what will enable professionals to better deal with business and management challenges in a world full of uncertainties, whether they are directors, executives or occupy any other position in the organization.

As an indication that perhaps self-knowledge is really one of the broadest paths for organizational improvement, **José Ernesto Beni Bologna** took a further step forward. As already mentioned in this chapter, as well as highlighting the power of desires – sometimes deviating from the best business decisions – he listed the three main contributions that psychology can offer leaders for improving risk management in business. According to **Bologna**, in addition to being aware of the gap between human reason and desire, leaders need to have the moral sensitivity and political courage to denounce deviations:

> "There are three contributions from psychology to risk management in governance. The first is: note that there is a difference between what people say and what they do. We create a rational speech, a rhetoric that justifies our desires. The second is to denounce the perception of this difference and its inferences. It is the leader's role to bring up what is hidden on the table. And the third contribution refers to how to make this complaint. Although the issue is a brutal one, the leader has to bring it out from underneath the rug in a delicate way, in a 'political' way in the best sense of the word, so as not to generate reactions of defense and protection against the brutality of the words."[56]

It is leaders such as this, who are ready for straightforward, mature dialogue, as well as being sensitive to the value of disseminating this culture in organizations, who will be able to create the environment of trust that is vital for addressing the huge challenges that face boards of directors. Especially in these post-COVID-19 pandemic times, the future is always just round the corner and requires immediate preparation, because a large number of these new issues are already recognizable on the horizon, including among others:

Business in a New World

Identifying the changes brought about by a new world, which may even be impossible to understand at first, is about more than being open to innovation, it is about leading it. Up until now the knowledge and experiences accumulated by the board members have played a fundamental role – allowing them to exercise the difficult task of deciding in an environment of constant uncertainty. But, because this knowledge is based on past assumptions, how long will it continue to be valid for viewing this new world, where what was unthinkable not long ago is today the norm? More than ever before, finding the means to enable companies to have a diverse collective decision-making body, which is open to contradictory opinions and mature in the sense of operating as a team, seems to be a much more conducive model for dealing with this challenging scenario. However, this path will also require a new attitude from the directors of the future: it is essential that they be open enough to recognize that the most brilliant solutions and insights may come from those of whom it would never have been expected.

Products and Services for a New Human Being

The gap between the generations is widening to an alarming degree and transformations, which formerly took decades, are now occurring in the space of a couple of years. Already nowadays, directors make decisions about products and services for customers, who could be called "mutants," so quick is their cycle of changing consumption habits. On top of this, these same products and services are developed by employees with professional aspirations and motivations that bear little resemblance to those of the directors when they were in the same age group. The political and social transformations have been so large and so fast that they leave everyone stunned, and seem to indicate that the means available for understanding human desires no longer detect them. Understanding these new human beings in order to satisfy their ever-changing needs will be one of the growing challenges that face directors.

The New Society of Stakeholders and the Emphasis on ESG

As part of this new world made up of new human beings, in addition to dedicating themselves to developing an organizational culture based on trust, directors and executives can no longer focus exclusively on the partners and shareholders, as this will no longer be enough to produce value – not even for these financial stakeholders. From this point on, it will be necessary to seek openness to understand the expectations of all those close to the company and obtain, in fact, and in law, the social license to operate: all stakeholders are a component part of the very fabric of which organizations are formed and none of them should be ignored. To build the future, either one embraces society's and all the stakeholders' expectations, or not even the other best governance practices will be able to become an effective instrument for improving the quality of management, the company's longevity and the common good.

The **ESG** agenda is here to stay. Despite the controversy narrated in Chapter 3 regarding the real commitment of the authors of business organizations' manifestos, it seems unlikely that there will be any retreat from such a forceful statement. The message that the model focused exclusively on the interests of shareholders is no longer appropriate for the reality of the 21st century and that each of the stakeholders is essential was clear, as was the commitment to deliver value to all of them. The experiences lived in the post-COVID world only highlight the urgent need for attention to be paid to **ESG** factors. Thus, it is most appropriate for business sustainability to get a head start and establish a broad dialogue with these stakeholders before their demands appear in the board rooms as yet another crisis that needs to be managed. The BoD needs to pursue a direct view of the concerns and expectations of stakeholders and, to this end must get out of the boardroom to visit the operations, customers and communities in which the company operates. It should do this carefully in order not to interfere in management, but in search of a direct line to the stakeholders. As BP's Senior Independent Director (SID) **Paula Rosput Reynolds**[*] states, "ESG is very real and investors want boards to do a better job [on it]." For the development of this **ESG** agenda, she mentions the importance of the quality of the conversation between the board and management and between the board and investors, an activity that as SID she carries out with investors on a regular basis, several times a year.

Based on her triple experience, as a director of listed and private companies, as an institutional investor for decades and as the former chair of GRI's (Global Reporting Initiative) board, **Christianna Wood**[**] reports that boards are increasingly investing time to discuss non-financial issues, such as cyber risk, compliance, risk management, codes of ethics and safety at work, among others. It is in this context that GRI's global standards are a facilitating mechanism for the performance of directors, who extend their scope of vision beyond the financial results.

By using standards such as GRI, SASB (Sustainability Accounting Standards Board) and TCFD (Task Force on Climate-related Financial Disclosures), as part of the reporting of their impacts on the

---

[*] Paula Rosput Reynolds is an Independent Director at BP and non-executive director of BAE Systems plcand General Electric Company. She was the former chairperson, president and chief executive officer of Safeco Corporation, a Fortune 500 company. The author interviewed Paula Rosput Reynolds, in a virtual internet room, on August 11, 2020.

[**] Christianna Wood was also the board chair of ICGN – International Corporate Governance Network, an international organization headed up by institutional investors, who account for US$ 54 trillion of assets. She has more than 25 years experience in the investment management industry.

environmental and social fronts and offering a structured view of all the business' other aspects, organizations give greater transparency to their initiatives. This is how they are able to anticipate and manage risks in all the dimensions that are gradually becoming of more interest to their various stakeholders and, in this way, create value. The problem is that boards do not always have the repertoire to understand and discuss in depth the impacts of the company's activities on society and the surrounding environment, particularly in relation to **climate change**. With this in mind, the **World Economic Forum** (**WEF**) has released a set of eight Principles designed to guide boards in steering their companies through an effective climate transition strategy. The **Climate Governance Initiative Principles**[57] set out a comprehensive and ambitious standard for directors to address the top risks facing society. The objective of the Principles is to assist directors in deepening their awareness of the implications of climate change for the businesses on whose boards they serve and to equip them with the necessary skills to navigate their way through this complex challenge.

The Era of Radical Transparency and New Technologies

The task of maintaining this dialogue with stakeholders has been greatly facilitated by the revolution in information technology and communications that have taken place over the past few decades. This same facility has added a new dimension to one of the fundamental principles of good governance: transparency. As **Christianna Wood,**[*] board director and former chair of GRI's board of directors, states, nowadays transparency is radical.

> "We live in a world of radical transparency. With social media, organizations have no choice but to be transparent. It is just a question of when and who will bring up bad practices."[58]

This new degree of media exposure imposes a great challenge on board members since companies are and under public scrutiny 24 hours a day in real-time. All of this, amplified by the "likes" of social media browsers, has the power to transform a minor slip-up into a viral posting on the internet, as those facts that gain huge notoriety, generating thousands – or even millions – of views, are called. Faced with this type of phenomenon, popular judgment is usually moved and devoid of any technical

---

[*]   Christianna Wood was also the board chair of ICGN – International Corporate Governance Network, an international organization headed up by institutional investors, who account for US$ 54 trillion of assets. She has more than 25 years experience in the investment management industry.

parameter or even any consideration regarding the relevance of the fact in that particular context. This new reality requires boards of directors to become freshly aware of their accountability in relation to a number of factors that did not previously receive much attention from them.

Integrated Thinking and Continued Value Creation

It is based on this context of transparency and the stakeholders' society that the **International Integrated Reporting Council's (IIRC)**[59] proposal emerged as an evolution of traditional corporate reports. Its own structure enables the company to communicate its strategy, governance, performance and prospects for creating short-, medium- and long-term values in a more efficient, interconnected, concise and intelligible way, to all of its stakeholders. Among those organizations that have adopted **Integrated Reporting (IR)**, the benefits go well beyond objective and transparent communication with society, as the execution process alone allows for a better understanding of the factors that materially affect the ability to generate value over time. This is what promotes performance gains as a whole and even behavioral changes. In his interview, **Sir Adrian Cadbury**[*] stressed that IR has been an incentive for companies to regain their sense of purpose:

> What needs to be done – and this is where governments and boards come in – is to help companies regain a sense of purpose, where they fit in in society and what is expected of them. I think that the work you are doing with Integrated Reporting[**] is very useful in that sense, because it takes human relations into account in a fundamental way for BoDs – not for everyone, because some do a great job – but, anyway, all boards need to have a broader focus, and this is what is proposed by IR with its integrated vision of how the business operates, but also with regard to its impacts on people, the community and the environment.

The IIRC's chairman emeritus, **Mervyn King**,[***] recalls that since the Great Depression of the 1930s, corporate reports traditionally remained exclusively focused on accounting and finance, only including other

---

[*] The author interviewed Sir Adrian Cadbury in Dorridge, England, on December 4, 2013.

[**] At the time of this interview, the author was a member of the IIRC's Council and was in the United Kingdom specifically for the meeting that approved the Conceptual Framework for Integrated Reporting.

[***] The author interviewed Mervyn King in New York, United States, on April 1, 2014.

dimensions of the business when there are regulatory obligations that have to be complied with. According to him, the execution of these documents is tiresome and bureaucratic, often generating a great deal of incomprehensible and, possibly, even useless information. In addition, as organizations have become multinationals, the degree of complexity has multiplied, given that each country or economic bloc has its own standards and requirements – some very specific. **King** points out that one of the benefits of IR is to inform and report to ordinary people as well, since the world's main stock markets are no longer made up of billionaire families, but rather of institutional investors, whose assets originate from savings or pension plans. As far as he is concerned, this means that "ultimately, the money invested in shares belongs to people who walk the streets of São Paulo, New York, Tokyo and London." In order to explain the benefits of the IR generated for companies themselves, the IIRC's chairman comes back here to his view of the Board as a collective mind:

> The Integrated Report tells the company's history in an understandable and interconnected way, enabling the directors to extract concrete information from it. Using the IR, the BoD identifies the resources used, capital, management's implementations and the relationship maintained with the different stakeholders, understanding their needs, interests and most legitimate expectations. Better informed and more in alignment with management, logically their contribution to the development of the short- and long-term strategy improves, generating continued and sustainable value. The Integrated Report allows the directors to reinforce their collective mind and maintain a relationship agenda with all of the company's stakeholders.

For **Paul Druckman**,* the IIRC's first CEO, who headed up the development of the Integrated Reporting framework, launched in 2013, it is precisely this integrated thinking that makes it possible to identify the interconnection between the business' various operational and functional units, the use of capital from different sources, as well as all the other factors that affect the ability to generate value over time. It is this broad, structured view that has the potential to steer the decision-making process toward a longer-term horizon – rather than maintaining the business strategy's focus on the short-term financial results. According to him, a growing number of organizations worldwide are adopting a more inclusive and integrated governance model, prioritizing communication

---

*   Paul Druckman was the IIRC – International Integrated Reporting Council's – CEO from its foundation up until October 2016.

with stakeholders. The objective is to attract more diversified and long-term investors, improve risk management and cut costs. **Druckman** regards Integrated Reporting as fundamental to the governance of organizations and the economy in the 21st century and explains why:

> How our capital markets system creates and distributes wealth and resources is a critical question that must be addressed with urgency. Our contribution to this debate has been the International IR Framework and the philosophical underpinning encapsulated by the six capitals: financial, productive, human, social, intellectual and natural. If economies, businesses and investors broaden their capital base, investment in their people, ideas and the protection of society and the environment will be prioritized alongside, and be consistent with, sustained financial performance. (...) In short, it contributes towards financial stability and sustainable development. This agenda is encapsulated by the work of global organizations such as the Coalition for Inclusive Capitalism and Focusing Capital on the Long Term, as well as national regulators such as the UK's Financial Reporting Council, which has done so much to bring attention to the importance of board culture in embedding long-term business success.[60]

The Imperative of Creating Long-Term Value in a Sustainable Way

This brave new world, which is already revealing itself as we move forward, will require an entirely new repertory from directors. Yesterday's way of doing things is no longer applicable to the present or to the future, as the vision of what is success for companies in this new world is undergoing a profound transformation. Gradually, but at an ever more rapid pace, governance "**in appearance**" with those boards that seek to embellish themselves with "the good and the great," those old directors who are full of airs and graces, excessively confident in their knowledge and experience, focused on their own ideas and with little interest in listening to others, will cease to have any relevance or impact. They will not last long.

The new profile of directors is that of someone who is part of the team, as they know that they are not playing alone. They are able to build a vast repertoire of skills and competences centered on relationships, with the aim of creating value as a group. Their deep knowledge and experience only make sense as part of this set of "**behavioral assets**," helping to mold an environment of trust and cooperation. These assets will enable the board members to be accessible to new knowledge and attentive to the disruption that will become the new normal.

Navigating skillfully in the behavioral dimension will thus become an essential competence, not just for this new board member, but also for all of those who interact with boards of directors – whether they be managers, consultants or even relevant stakeholders. All of the players in the corporate decision-making process need to incorporate this new knowledge and renew the skills that they have accumulated.

The expectation is that this book has been the first step, presenting the routes, maps and equipment for you to undertake the journey through this brave new world. And that, with these new resources, your performance – inside or outside of boards – will lead to a real difference in good governance. If desires are what truly govern the world, as already stated in this final chapter, my desire is that, with this behavioral compass, you will discover this new world and usher in a new phase in which value creation is for all people and is the destiny of all of us.

Notes

1 Thuraisingham, Meena; Lehmacher, Wolfgang. *The secret life of decisions: How unconscious bias subverts your judgement.* Aldershot: Gower Publishing, 2013.

2 Cadbury, Adrian. *Corporate governance and chairmanship – a personal view.* New York: Oxford University Press, 2002, p. 34.

3 Soll, Jack B.; Milkman, Katherine L.; Payne, John W. A user's guide to debiasing. *The Wiley Blackwell Handbook of Judgment and Decision Making,* v. 2, p. 924–951, 2015, p. 926.

4 Thaler, Richard H.; Sunstein, Cass R. Nudge: *Improving decisions about health, wealth, and happiness.* New York: Penguin, 2009.

5 Ibid. Location 173 of 5708.

6 Lovallo, Dan; Sibony, Olivier. The case for behavioral strategy. *McKinsey Quarterly,* v. 2, n. 1, p. 30–43, 2010.

7 Instituto Brasileiro de Governança Corporativa (IBGC). 17° Congresso do IBGC. São Paulo, October 2016.

8 Thuraisingham, Meena; Lehmacher, Wolfgang. *The secret life of decisions: How unconscious bias subverts your judgement.* Aldershot: Gower Publishing, 2013. Location 3009 of 3405.

9 Guerra, Sandra; Santos, Rafael Liza. *Headaches, concerns and regrets: What does the experience of 102 Brazilian directors tell us? Private sector opinion.* Washington, DC: IFC, 2017. Available at https://www.ifc.org/wps/wcm/connect/topics_ext_content/ifc_external_corporate_site/ifc+cg/resources/private+sector+opinion/headaches%2C+concerns%2C+and+regrets+-+what+does+the+experience+of+102+brazilian+directors+tell+us. Accessed on May 21, 2020.

10 Levitt, Theodore. Marketing Myopia. *Harvard Business Review,* BEST OF HBR, p. 1–14, 1960, p. 2 Available at https://www.google.com/url?sa=t&rct=j&q=&esrc=s&source=web&cd=&ved=2ahUKEwjz_LOTmLDrAhVW-JLkGHU1dAZUQFjARegQIARAB&url=https%3A%2F%2Fcanvas.harvard.edu%2Fcourses%2F8491%2Ffiles%2F1478568%2Fdownload%3Fverifier%3DU9bk8g6mgUQX6lDUcA7SChz40bDMdrRXKVMo-FubU%26wrap%3D1&usg=AOvVaw0BpFZwX2UJd9UICLvvdSW8 Accessed on August 22, 2020.

11 Frisch, Bob. When teams can't decide. Harvard Business School Publishing Corporation, November 2008. Available at https://hbr.org/2008/11/when-teams-cant-decide. Accessed on August 14, 2020.

12 Lovallo, Dan; Sibony, Olivier. The case for behavioral strategy. *McKinsey Quarterly*, v. 2, n. 1, p. 30–43, 2010.

13 Guerra, Sandra; Santos, Rafael Liza. *Headaches, concerns and regrets: What does the experience of 102 Brazilian directors tell us? Private sector opinion.* Washington, DC: IFC, 2017. Reference to Graph 7.1. Available at https://www. ifc.org/wps/wcm/connect/topics_ext_content/ifc_external_corporate_ site/ifc+cg/resources/private+sector+opinion/headaches%2C+ concerns%2C+and+regrets+-+what+does+the+experience+of+102+brazilian+ directors+tell+us. Accessed on May 21, 2020.

14 Thaler, Richard H.; Sunstein, Cass R. *Nudge: Improving decisions about health, wealth, and happiness.* New York: Penguin, 2009. Location 958 of 5708.

15 Reference to Graph 7.1. Available at https://www.ifc.org/wps/wcm/ connect/topics_ext_content/ifc_external_corporate_site/ifc+cg/ resources/private+sector+opinion/headaches%2C+concerns%2C+and+ regrets+-+what+does+the+experience+of+102+brazilian+directors+tell+us. Accessed on May 21, 2020.

16 Lovallo, Dan; Sibony, Olivier. The case for behavioral strategy. *McKinsey Quarterly*, v. 2, n. 1, p. 30–43, 2010.

17 Guerra, Sandra; Barros, Lucas A.; Santos, Rafael L. Decision-making in boards of directors: The roles of meeting dynamics and choice architecture. *Research Project*, 2020.

18 Janis, Irving Lester. *Groupthinking: Psychological studies of policy decisions and fiascoes.* 2nd ed. Boston: Houghton Mifflin, 1982.

19 Guerra, Sandra; Santos, Rafael Liza. *Headaches, concerns and regrets: What does the experience of 102 Brazilian directors tell us? Private sector opinion.* Washington, DC: IFC, 2017. Available at https://www.ifc.org/ wps/wcm/connect/topics_ext_content/ifc_external_corporate_site/ifc+cg/ resources/private+sector+opinion/headaches%2C+concerns%2C+and+ regrets+-+what+does+the+experience+of+102+brazilian+directors+tell+us. Accessed on May 21, 2020.

20 Guerra, Sandra; Barros, Lucas A.; Santos, Rafael L. Decision-making in boards of directors: The roles of meeting dynamics and choice architecture. *Research Project*, 2020.

21 Reynolds, Alison; Lewis, David. Teams solve problems faster when they're more cognitively diverse. *Harvard Business Review*, v. 30, p. 1–8, 2017.

22 Torchia, Mariateresa; Calabrò, Andrea; Morner, Michèle. Board of directors' diversity, creativity, and cognitive conflict: The role of board members' interaction. *International Studies of Management & Organization*, v. 45, n. 1, p. 6–24, 2015.

23 Lovallo, Dan; Sibony, Olivier. The case for behavioral strategy. *McKinsey Quarterly*, v. 2, n. 1, p. 30–43, 2010.

24 Bond, Samuel D.; Carlson, Kurt A.; Keeney, Ralph L. Generating objectives: Can decision makers articulate what they want? *Management Science*, v. 54, n. 1, p. 56–70, 2008.

25 Sunstein, Cass R.; Hastie, Reid. *Wiser: Getting beyond groupthink to make groups smarter.* Boston: Harvard Business Press, 2015.

26 Frisch, Bob. When teams can't decide. 2008 In: *HBR's 10 must reads on teams.* Boston: Harvard Business School Publishing Corporation, p. 135–147, 2013.

27 Ibid. Location 2264 of 3273.
28 Guerra, Sandra; Santos, Rafael Liza. Headaches, concerns and regrets: *What does the experience of 102 Brazilian directors tell us? Private sector opinion*. Washington, DC: IFC, 2017. Available at https://www.ifc.org/wps/wcm/connect/topics_ext_content/ifc_external_corporate_site/ifc+cg/resources/private+sector+opinion/headaches%2C+concerns%2C+and+regrets+-+what+does+the+experience+of+102+brazilian+directors+tell+us. Accessed on May 21, 2020.
29 Ibid.
30 Ibid.
31 Kahneman, Daniel. *Thinking, fast and slow*. New York: Farrar, Straus and Giroux, 2011. Location 4450 and 4457 of 9418.
32 Mckinsey. Flaws in strategic decision making. Global survey results, January 2009. Available at http://www.mckinsey.com/business-functions/strategy-and-corporate-finance/our-insights/flaws-in-strategic-decision-making-mckinsey-global-survey-results. Accessed on August 17, 2020.
33 Guerra, Sandra; Barros, Lucas A.; Santos, Rafael L. Decision-making in boards of directors: The roles of meeting dynamics and choice architecture. *Research Project*, 2020.
34 Pick, Katharina; Merchant, Kenneth A. Recognizing negative boardroom group dynamics. In: Lorsch, Jay William (editor). *The future of boards: Meeting the governance challenges of the twenty-first century*. Boston: Harvard Business Press, p. 113–132, 2012.
35 CEDR – Effective Dispute Resolution and IFC – International Finance Corporation. Managing conflicts and difficult conversations on the board. Interactive Training. Background Reading Material, 2015. Available at https://www.ifc.org/wps/wcm/connect/4d816348-7c63-48ba-95a2-849574020d0a/Boardroom_Disputes_Practical_Guide_for_Directors.pdf?MOD=AJPERES&CVID=kHGE9QV Accessed on August 14, 2020.
36 Pick, Katharina; Merchant, Kenneth A. *Blind spots, biases and other pathologies in the boardroom*. New York: Business Expert Press, 2010.
37 Masters, Jon J.; Rudnick, Alan A. *Improving board effectiveness: Bringing the best of ADR into the boardroom*. Washington, DC: ABA Section of Dispute Resolution, 2005.
38 Huse, Morten. *Boards, governance and value creation: The human side of corporate governance*. Cambridge: Cambridge University Press, 2007.
39 Kahneman, Daniel. *Thinking, fast and slow*. New York: Farrar, Straus and Giroux, 2011.
40 Thuraisingham, Meena; Lehmacher, Wolfgang. *The secret life of decisions: How unconscious bias subverts your judgement*. Aldershot: Gower Publishing, 2013.
41 IFC – International Finance Corporation and CEDR – Centre for Effective Dispute Resolution. Conflicts in the Boardroom Survey. Results and Analysis, 2015. Available at https://www.ifc.org/wps/wcm/connect/4d816348-7c63-48ba-95a2-849574020d0a/Boardroom_Disputes_Practical_Guide_for_Directors.pdf?MOD=AJPERES&CVID=kHGE9QV Accessed on August 14, 2020.
42 Pick, Katharina; Merchant, Kenneth A. *Blind spots, biases and other pathologies in the boardroom*. New York: Business Expert Press, 2010.
43 Kravitz, David A.; Martin, Barbara. Ringelmann rediscovered: The original article. *Journal of Personality and Social Psychology*, v. 50, n. 5, p. 936–941, 1986.

44 Latané, Bibb; Williams, Kipling; Harkins, Stephen. Many hands make light the work: The causes and consequences of social loafing. *Journal of Personality and Social Psychology*, v. 37, n. 6, p. 822, 1979.

45 Pick, Katharina; Merchant, Kenneth A. *Blind spots, biases and other pathologies in the boardroom*. New York: Business Expert Press, 2010.

46 Kahneman, Daniel. *Thinking, fast and slow*. New York: Farrar, Straus and Giroux, 2011. Location 1388 of 9418.

47 Torchia, Mariateresa; Calabrò, Andrea; Morner, Michèle. Board of directors' diversity, creativity, and cognitive conflict: the role of board members' interaction. *International Studies of Management & Organization*, v. 45, n. 1, p. 6–24, 2015.

48 Harrison, David A.; Price, Kenneth H.; Bell, Myrtle P. Beyond relational demography: Time and the effects of surface-and deep – level diversity on work group cohesion. *Academy of Management Journal*, v. 41, n. 1, p. 96–107, 1998.

49 Torchia, Mariateresa; Calabrò, Andrea; Morner, Michèle. Board of directors' diversity, creativity, and cognitive conflict: the role of board members' interaction. *International Studies of Management & Organization*, v. 45, n. 1, p. 6–24, 2015.

50 Guerra, Sandra; Santos, Rafael Liza. *Headaches, concerns and regrets: What does the experience of 102 Brazilian directors tell us? Private sector opinion*. Washington, DC: IFC, 2017. Available at https://www.ifc.org/wps/wcm/connect/topics_ext_content/ifc_external_corporate_site/ifc+cg/resources/private+sector+opinion/headaches%2C+concerns%2C+and+regrets+-+what+does+the+experience+of+102+brazilian+directors+tell+us. Accessed on May 21, 2020.

51 Thuraisingham, Meena; Lehmacher, Wolfgang. *The secret life of decisions: How unconscious bias subverts your judgement*. Aldershot: Gower Publishing, 2013. Location 3097 of 3405.

52 Pick, Katharina; Merchant, Kenneth A. Recognizing negative boardroom group dynamics. In: Lorsch, Jay William (editor). *The future of boards: Meeting the governance challenges of the twenty-first century*. Boston: Harvard Business Press, p. 113–132, 2012. Location 2054 of 2780.

53 Financial Reporting Council – Corporate culture and the role of boards report of observations from the financial reporting council July 2016. Available at https://www.frc.org.uk/Our-Work/Publications/Corporate-Governance/Corporate-Culture-and-the-Role-of-Boards-Report-o.pdf. Accessed on August 14, 2020.

54 Ibid.

55 Instituto Brasileiro de Governança Corporativa (IBGC). 17° Congresso do IBGC. São Paulo, October 2016.

56 World Economic Forum (WEF). Climate governance initiative principles. Available at: https://www.weforum.org/projects/climate-governance-initiative. Accessed on August 25, 2020.

57 Ibid.

58 More information about Integrated Reporting and its structure are available at https://integratedreporting.org/resource/international-ir-framework/ Accessed on August 14, 2020.

59 Druckman, Paul. We have made history together – thank you! Available at https://integratedreporting.org/news/we-have-made-history-together-thank-you/. Accessed on May 21, 2020.

60 Ibid.

Bibliography

Arnott, David. A taxonomy of decision biases. Monash University, School of Information Management and Systems, Caulfield, 1998. Available at: https://www.semanticscholar.org/paper/A-Taxonomy-of-Decision-Biases-Arnott/c58cca5c8e8774eb5b17ac3159914d1f1357a014. Accessed on May 21, 2020.

Arnott, David. Cognitive biases and decision support systems development: A design science approach. *Information Systems Journal*, v. 16, n. 1, p. 55–78, 2006. Available at https://www.researchgate.net/publication/220356732_Cognitive_biases_and_decision_support_systems_development_A_design_science_approach. Accessed on October 18, 2016.

Arnott, David; Pervan, Graham. A critical analysis of decision support systems research revisited: The rise of design science. 4th ed. *Journal of Information Technology*, v. 29, p. 269–293, 2014. London: Palgrave Macmillan.

Balestrin, Alsones. Uma análise da contribuição de Herbert Simon para as teorias organizacionais. *Revista Eletrônica de Administração (REAd)*, Escola de Administração: Universidade Federal do Rio Grande do Sul, UFRGS, v. 8, 2002. Available at: http://seer.ufrgs.br/index.php/read/article/view/44111. Accessed on June 14, 2020.

Barros, Lucas A. Vieses Gerenciais e o Conselho de Administração. *4º Curso Avançado de Conselheiro de Administração*. IBGC, June 2010.

Barros, Lucas A.; Da Silveira, Alexandre Di Miceli. Excesso de Confiança, Otimismo Gerencial e os Determinantes da Estrutura de Capital. *Revista Brasileira de Finanças*, v. 6, n. 3, 2008.

Baysinger, Barry; Hoskisson, Robert E. The composition of boards of directors and strategic control: Effects on corporate strategy. *Academy of Management Review*, v. 15, n. 1, p. 72–87, 1990.

Bebchuk, Lucian A.; Tallarita, Roberto. The illusory promise of stakeholder governance. *Cornell Law Review*, v. 106, p. 91–178, 2020. Available at https://ssrn.com/abstract=3544978. Accessed on April 24, 2021.

Becht, Marco; Bolton, Patrick; Röell, Ailsa. Corporate governance and control. *ECGI – Finance Working Paper n. 2*, 2002. Available at http://papers.ssrn.com/sol3/papers.cfm?abstract_id=343461. Accessed on December 2, 2015.

Better Governance. Conselheiros: dedicação de tempo dentro e fora das salas de conselho. *Pesquisa sobre conselhos de administração e consultivos*. June, 2020. Available at: https://bettergovernance.com.br/2020-06-01-Conselheiros_Pesquisa_Dedicacao_de_Tempo.pdf. Accessed on August 28, 2020.

Black, Bernard S.; De Carvalho, Antônio Gledson; Khanna, Vikramaditya; Kim, Woochan; Yurtoglu, Burcin B. Which aspects of corporate governance do and do not matter in emerging markets. *Northwestern Law & Economics Research Paper n. 14–22*, 2019; *ECGI – Finance Working Paper* n. 566/2018, *University of Michigan Law & Econ Research Paper*, p. 1–50. May, 2015. Available at http://ssrn.com/abstract=2601107. Accessed on January 1, 2016.

Bond, Samuel D.; Carlson, Kurt A.; Keeney, Ralph L. Generating objectives: Can decision makers articulate what they want? *Management Science*, v. 54, n. 1, p. 56–70, 2008.

Brancato, Carolyn K. *Institutional investors and corporate governance: Best practices for increasing corporate value*. Chicago: Irwin Professional Pub, p. xi–xxii, 1996.

Brull, Thomas. The Caspian Sea housing company: The role of board member in a two family business. 1st ed. In: Brisset, Leslie; Sher, Mannie; Smith, Tanzi Lorraine (editors). *Dynamics at boardroom level*. London: Routledge, 2020, p. 171–176, 2020.

Business Roundtable. Statement on the purpose of c Corporation. Published on August 2019. Available at https://opportunity.businessroundtable.org/ourcommitment/. Accessed on June 8, 2020.

Cadbury, Adrian. *Corporate governance and chairmanship: A personal view*. 1st ed. Oxford: Oxford University Press, 2002.

Cadbury, Adrian; Millstein, Ira. The new agenda for ICGN. *International Corporate Governance Network Discussion Paper*, n.1 for the ICGN 10th Anniversary Conference. London, July 2005. Available at http://www.icgn.org/conferences/2005/documents/cad bury_millstein.pdf. Accessed on October 10, 2006.

Capital Aberto. *Anuário de Governança Corporativa das Companhias Abertas 2019–2020*: As práticas adotadas pelas empresas com ações mais negociadas na B3. Capital Aberto, 11th ed. São Paulo: Editora Capital Aberto, 2020. Available at https://capitalaberto.com.br/edicoes/especial/anuario-2019-2020/. Accessed on June 3, 2020.

Catalyst. Why diversity and inclusion matter: Quick take. Published on August 1, 2018. Available at https://www.catalyst.org/research/why-diversity-and-inclusion-matter/. Accessed on June 13, 2020.

Catalyst. Women on corporate boards: Quick take. Published on March 13, 2020. Available at https://www.catalyst.org/research/women-on-corporate-boards/. Accessed on June 13, 2020.

Centre for Effective Dispute Resolution (CEDR); International Finance Corporation (IFC). Managing conflicts and difficult conversations on the board. Interactive training. Background reading material, 2015. Available at https://www.ifc.org/wps/wcm/connect/4d816348-7c63-48ba-95a2-849574020d0a/Boardroom_Disputes_Practical_Guide_for_Directors.pdf?MOD=AJPERES&CVID=kHGE9QV Accessed on August 14, 2020.

Chabris, Christopher; Simons, Daniel. *The invisible gorilla: And other ways our intuitions deceive us*. 1st ed. New York: Broadway Books, 2011. Video available at: http://www.theinvisiblegorilla.com/videos.html. Accessed on May 23, 2020.

Charan, Ram. Introduction: Advancing the practice of corporate governance. In: *Boards that deliver: Advancing corporate governance from compliance to competitive advantage.* 1st ed. São Francisco: Jossey-Bass, A John Willey & Sons Imprint, p. ix–xiii, 2005.

Charan, Ram. *Owning up: The 14 questions every board member needs to ask.* John Wiley & Sons, Digital Edition. Locations: 2507, 2514, 2522 of 3040, 2009. Available at https://www.wiley.com/en-us/Owning+Up%3A+The+14+Questions+Every+Board+Member+Needs+to+Ask-p-9780470397671. Accessed on June 08, 2020.

Clarke, Thomas. *International corporate governance: A corporative approach.* 2nd ed. New York: Routledge, 2017.

Collamer, Nancy; Avenue, Next. How to get on a board of directors. *Forbes,* September 11, 2017. Available at https://www.forbes.com/sites/nextavenue/2017/09/11/how-to-get-on-a-board-of-directors/#31bd99a51d56. Accessed on June 13, 2020.

Coutu, Diane. Why teams don't work. An interview with J Richard Hackman. In: *HBR's 10 must reads on teams.* Boston: Harvard Business School Publishing Corporation, p. 21–34, 2013.

Da Silveira, Alexandre Di Miceli. Corporate scandals of the 21st century: Limitations of mainstream corporate governance literature and the need for a new behavioral approach. *Science Research Network,* November 2015. Available at https://papers.ssrn.com/sol3/papers.cfm?abstract_id=2181705. Accessed on August 11, 2020.

Dabrowski, Wojtek. How companies can keep CEO behavior in check. *Harvard Business Review,* March 11, 2020. Available at https://hbr.org/2020/03/how-companies-can-keep-ceo-behavior-in-check Accessed on June 9, 2020.

Darley, John M.; Batson, C. Daniel. From Jerusalem to Jericho: A study of situational and dispositional variables in helping behavior. *Journal of Personality and Social Psychology,* v. 27, n. 1, 1973. Available at https://www.researchgate.net/publication/232591736_From_Jerusalem_to_Jericho_A_study_of_situational_and_dispositional_variables_in_helping_behavior. Accessed on October 16, 2016.

Dehaas, Deb; Akutagawa, Linda; Spriggs, Skip. Missing pieces report: The 2018 board diversity census of women and minorities on fortune 500 boards. *Harvard Law School Forum for Corporate Governance.* Published on February 5, 2019. Available at https://corpgov.law.harvard.edu/2019/02/05/missing-pieces-report-the-2018-board-diversity-census-of-women-and-minorities-on-fortune-500-boards/#:~:text=In%20the%202018%20census%2C%20representation, held%20by%20women%20and%20minorities. Accessed on June 12, 2020.

Deloitte. COVID-19 and the board: A chair's point of view. Available at https://www2.deloitte.com/global/en/pages/about-deloitte/articles/covid-19/covid-19-and-the-board-a-chairs-point-of-view.html. Accessed on July 17, 2020.

Deloitte. Data-driven change. Women in the boardroom. A global perspective. 6th ed. 2019. Available at https://www2.deloitte.com/global/en/pages/risk/articles/women-in-the-boardroom-global-perspective.html. Accessed on June 14, 2020.

Deloitte. EMEA 360 boardroom survey: Agenda priorities across the region – study carried out with 271 directors from 20 countries in Europe, the Middle East and Africa, June 2016. Available at https://www2.deloitte.com/content/dam/Deloitte/ch/Documents/audit/ch-en-emea-360-boardroom-survey-agenda-intercative.pdf. Accessed on August 30, 2020.

Deloitte. In the throes of a dual-front crisis. Establishing the road to a global consumer recovery. April 29, 2020. Available at https://www2.deloitte.com/us/en/insights/industry/retail-distribution/consumer-behavior-trends-state-of-the-consumer-tracker/covid-19-recovery/04-29-2020.html. Accessed on July 17, 2020.

Deloitte. The state of the deal: M&A trends 2020. Figures available at https://www2.deloitte.com/us/en/pages/mergers-and-acquisitions/articles/m-a-trends-report.html. Accessed on July 13, 2020.

Druckman, Paul. We have made history together – thank you! *Integrated Reporting.* October 27, 2016. Available at https://integratedreporting.org/news/we-have-made-history-together-thank-you/. Accessed on May 21, 2020.

Financial Reporting Council (FRC). Corporate culture and the role of boards report of observations, July 2016. Available at https://www.frc.org.uk/Our-Work/Publications/Corporate-Governance/Corporate-Culture-and-the-Role-of-Boards-Report-o.pdf. Accessed on August 14, 2020.

Fink, Larry. A fundamental reshaping of finance. *BlackRock.* Available at https://www.blackrock.com/corporate/investor-relations/larry-fink-ceo-letter. Accessed on June 8, 2020.

Forbes, Daniel P.; Milliken, Frances J. Cognition and corporate governance: Understanding boards of directors as strategic decision-making groups. *Academy of Management Review*, v. 24, n. 3, p. 489–505. 1999.

Frentrop, Paul. *A history of corporate governance, 1602–2002.* Amsterdam: Deminor, 2003, p. 480.

Frisch, Bob. When teams can't decide. *Harvard Business School Publishing Corporation*, November 2008. Available at https://hbr.org/2008/11/when-teams-cant-decide. Accessed on August 14, 2020.

Fuller, Joseph B.; Michael, C. Jensen. What's a director to do? In: Brown, Tom; Heller, Robert (editors). *Best practice: Ideas and insights from the world's foremost business thinkers*, p. 243–250. New York: Basic Books, 2003.

Gersick, Connie J.G.; Hackman, J. Richard. Habitual routines in task-performing groups. *Organizational Behavior and Human Decision Processes*, v. 47, n. 1, p. 65–97, 1990.

Governance Principles. Commonsense corporate governance principles. *Open Letter: Commonsense Principles 2.0.* July 2016. Available at http://www.governanceprinciples.org. Accessed on June 7, 2020.

Guerra, Sandra. Governança Corporativa e Criação de Valor. *Revista Criação de Valor.* Associação Brasileira de Companhias Abertas (ABRASCA), October, 2013.

Guerra, Sandra. Melhor não descuidar. As conquistas alcançadas em governança não eliminam os riscos de retrocesso. *Capital Aberto*, November, 2007.

Guerra, Sandra; Barros, Lucas A.; Santos, Rafael L. Decision-making in boards of directors: The roles of meeting dynamics and choice architecture. *Research Project.* 2020.

Guerra, Sandra; Santos, Rafael Liza. Headaches, concerns and regrets: What does the experience of 102 Brazilian directors tell us? *Private Sector Opinion 39*. Washington, DC: IFC, 2017. Available at https://www.ifc.org/wps/wcm/connect/topics_ext_content/ifc_external_corporate_site/ifc+cg/resources/private+sector+opinion/headaches%2C+concerns%2C+and+regrets+-+what+does+the+experience+of+102+brazilian+directors+tell+us. Accessed on May 21, 2020.

Harper, John. *Chairing the board: A practical guide to activities and responsibilities by institute of directors*. London: Kogan Page, 2010.

Harrison, David A.; Price, Kenneth H.; Bell, Myrtle P. Beyond relational demography: Time and the effects of surface-and deep-level diversity on work group cohesion. *Academy of Management Journal*, v. 41, n. 1, p. 96–107, 1998.

Henley Business School; Alvarez & Marsal. Boards in challenging times: Extraordinary disruptions leading through complex and discontinuous challenges. *Joint Research Programme on Board Leadership*. Available at: https://www.alvarezandmarsal.com/sites/default/files/am_boards_in_challenging_times_research_0.pdf. Accessed on July 14, 2016.

Huse, Morten. *Boards, governance and value creation: The human side of corporate governance*. Cambridge: Cambridge University Press, 2007.

Instituto Brasileiro De Geografia E Estatística (IBGE). Síntese de indicadores sociais: Uma análise das condições de vida da população brasileira. *Estudos & Pesquisas. Informação demográfica e socioeconômica n. 37*. Rio de Janeiro: IBGE, 2017. Available at https://biblioteca.ibge.gov.br/visualizacao/livros/liv101459.pdf. Accessed on June 6, 2020.

Instituto Brasileiro De Governança Corporativa (IBGC). *17° Congresso do IBGC*. São Paulo, October 2016.

Instituto Brasileiro De Governança Corporativa (IBGC). *Boas Práticas para Secretaria de Governança*. São Paulo: IBGC, 2015. Available at https://conhecimento.ibgc.org.br/Paginas/Publicacao.aspx?PubId=20996 Accessed on May 21, 2020.

Instituto Brasileiro De Governança Corporativa (IBGC). *Fundamentos para Discussão Sobre Cotas para Mulheres nos Conselhos no Brasil*. São Paulo: IBGC. 2013. Available at http://www.ibgc.org.br/download/manifestacao/IBGC_Pesquisa_CotasMulheres.pdf. Accessed on June 13, 2020.

Integrated Reporting. *International integrated reporting framework*. Available at https://integratedreporting.org/resource/international-ir-framework/. Accessed on August 14, 2020.

International Finance Corporation (IFC); Centre for Effective Dispute Resolution (CEDR). Conflicts in the boardroom survey – results and analysis. *World Bank*. Washington, DC: IFC and CEDR, 2014. Available at http://hdl.handle.net/10986/26116. Accessed on August 14, 2020.

International Finance Corporation (IFC); Centre for Effective Dispute Resolution (CEDR). Managing conflicts and difficult conversations on the board. Interactive training. Background reading material. 2016.

International Finance Corporation (IFC); Organisation for Economic Co-Operation and Development (OECD); Global Corporate Governance Forum. *Practical guide to corporate governance: Experiences from the Latin American companies circle*. Washington, DC: IFC, p. 1–276, 2009.

Janis, Irving L. *Groupthink:* Psychological studies of policy decisions and *fiascoes.* 2nd ed. Boston: Houghton Mifflin, 1982.

Johnson, Stefanie K.; Hekman, David R. e Chan Elsa T. If there's only one woman in your candidate pool, there's statistically no chance she'll be hired. *Harvard Business Review*, April 26, 2016. https://www.researchgate.net/profile/David_Hekman3/publication/303003812_If_There's_Only_One_Woman_in_Your_Candidate_Pool_There's_Statistically_No_Chance_She'll_Be_Hired/links/575eea9908ae9a9c955f8e2c/If-Theres-Only-One-Woman-in-Your-Candidate-Pool-Theres-Statistically-No-Chance-Shell-Be-Hired.pdf. Accessed on July 26, 2020.

Kahneman, Daniel. Thinking, fast and slow. New York: Farrar, Straus and Giroux, 2011. Digital Edition. Locations: 217, 331, 1388, 1422, 1607, 2001, 4450 and 4457 of 9418 and Location 462 of 10934.

Kahneman, Daniel; Tversky, Amos. Intuitive prediction: Biases and corrective procedures. *ResearchGate*. Cambridge University Press, 1977. Available at https://www.researchgate.net/publication/235103436_Intuitive_Prediction_Biases_and_Corrective_Procedures. Accessed on October, 1, 2016.

Kakabadse, Andrew; Kakabadse, Nada. *Leading the board: The six disciplines of world-class chairmen.* New York: Palgrave MacMillan, 2008.

Katzenbach, Jon; Smith, R.; Douglas, K. The discipline of teams. In: *HBR's 10 must reads on teams.* Boston: Harvard Business School Publishing Corporation, p. 35–53, 2013.

Klemash, Steve W; Rani, Doyle. Evolving board evaluations and disclosures. *Harvard Law School Forum for Corporate Governance*. Published on October 2, 2019. Available at https://corpgov.law.harvard.edu/2019/10/02/evolving-board-evaluations-and-disclosures/. Accessed on June 26, 2020.

KPMG. Impactos e respostas aos efeitos do COVID-19, June 2020. Available at https://assets.kpmg/content/dam/kpmg/br/pdf/2020/06/impactos-e-respostas-aos-efeitos-da-covid-19-saude.pdf. Accessed on July 16, 2020.

Kravitz, David A.; Martin, Barbara. Ringelmann rediscovered: The original article. *Journal of Personality and Social Psychology*, v. 50, n. 5, p. 936–941, 1986.

Larcker, David; Tayan, Brian. We studied 38 incidents of CEO bad behavior and measured their consequences. *Harvard Business Review*, June 9, 2016. Available at https://hbr.org/2016/06/we-studied-38-incidents-of-ceo-bad-behavior-and-measured-their-consequences. Accessed on June 7, 2020.

Latané, Bibb; Williams, Kipling; Harkins, Stephen. Many hands make light the work: The causes and consequences of social loafing. *Journal of Personality and Social Psychology*, v. 37, n. 6, p. 822, 1979.

Leblanc, Richard; Gillies, James. *Inside the boardroom: How boards really work and the coming revolution in corporate governance.* Mississauga: John Wiley & Sons, 2010.

Leblanc, Richard; Pick, Katharina. Separation of chair and CEO roles: Importance of Industry Knowledge, leadership skills, and attention to board process. *Director Notes*, August 2011. Available at http://www.yorku.ca/rleblanc/publish/Aug2011_Leblanc_TCB.pdf. Accessed on August 24, 2016.

Lechem, Brian. *Chairman of the Board:* A Practical Guide. Hoboken: John Wiley & Sons, 2002.

Leighton, David S. R; Thain, Donald H. How to pay directors. *Business Quarterly*, v. 58, n. 2, p. 30–44, 1993 apud Leblanc, Michel; Schwartz, Mark S. The black box of board process: Gaining access to a difficult subject. *The Authors*, v. 5, n. 5, p. 843–851, 2007.

Levitt, Theodore. Marketing Myopia. *Harvard Business Review*, Best of HBR 1960, p. 1–14, p. 2, 2004. Available at https://hbr.org/2004/07/marketing-myopia. Accessed on August 22, 2020.

Lorsch, Jay W. The future of boards: Meeting the governance challenges of the twenty-first century. *Harvard Business Review*. Digital Edition. Boston: Harvard Business Press, 2012. Locations: 382 and 405 of 2780. Available at https://store.hbr.org/product/the-future-of-boards-meeting-the-governance-challenges-of-the-twenty-first-century/10913. Accessed on June 7, 2020.

Lovallo, Dan; Sibony, Olivier. The case for behavioral strategy. *McKinsey Quarterly*, v. 2, n. 1, p. 30–43, 2010.

Malmendier, Ulrike; Tate, Geoffrey. Who makes acquisitions? CEO Overconfidence and the Market's Reaction. *Journal of Financial Economics*, v. 89, July 2008. Available at http://www.sciencedirect.com/science/article/pii/S0304405X08000251. Accessed on July 21, 2016.

Masters, Jon J.; Rudnick, Alan A. Improving board effectiveness: Bringing the best of ADR into the boardroom. *ABA Section of Dispute Resolution*, Washington, DC, 2005.

Mcgregor, Jena. These business titans are teaming up for better corporate governance. *The Washington Post*. Washington, DC. July 21, 2016. Available at https://www.washingtonpost.com/news/on-leadership/wp/2016/07/21/these-business-titans-are-teaming-up-for-better-corporate-governance/. Accessed on May 21, 2020.

Mckinsey & Company. Delivering through diversity, January 2018. Available at https://www.mckinsey.com/~/media/McKinsey/Business%20Functions/Organization/Our%20Insights/Delivering%20through%20diversity/Delivering-through-diversity_full-report.ashx. Accessed on June 12, 2020.

Mckinsey & Company. Flaws in strategic decision making. *Global Survey Results*, January 2009. Available at http://www.mckinsey.com/business-functions/strategy-and-corporate-finance/our-insights/flaws-in-strategic-decision-making-mckinsey-global-survey-results. Accessed on August 17, 2020.

Mckinsey & Company. *Investor opinion survey on corporate governance*, June 2000. Available at http //www.oecd.org/corporate/ca/corporategovernance principles/1922101.pdf. Accessed on October 4, 2016.

Merchant, Kenneth A.; Pick, Katharina. *Blind spots, biases and other pathologies in the boardroom*. New York: Business Expert Press, 2010.

Millstein, Ira M. A perspective on corporate governance: Rules, principles or both. In: *ICGN yearbook*. Washington, DC, 2006. Available at http://www.icgn.org/conferences/2006/documents/mill stein.pdf. Accessed on October 10, 2006.

Morgan, J. P. 2020 *Global M&A outlook: Navigating a period of uncertainty*. Published by J.P. Morgan's M&A team, January 2020. Available at https://www.jpmorgan.com/jpmpdf/1320748081210.pdf. Accessed on July 13, 2020.

Nadler, David A.; Behan, Beverly A.; Nadler, Mark B. *Building better boards: A blueprint for effective governance*. São Francisco: Jossey-Bass, 2006 apud

Guerra, Sandra. *Os papéis do CA em empresas listadas no Brasil*. Dissertation (Master's Degree in Administration) FEA/USP. 2009. Available at http://www.teses.usp.br/teses/disponiveis/12/12139/tde-11092009-141955/. Accessed on August 4, 2016.

National Association of Corporate Directors (NACD). *Governance challenges 2016: M&A oversight*. April 28, 2016. Available at https://www.nacdonline.org/Resources/Article.cfm?ItemNumber=27364. Accessed on July 21, 2016.

Noland, Marcus; Han, Soyoung. Women scaling the corporate ladder: Progress steady but slow globally. *Peterson Institute for International Economics*. May 2020. Available at https://www.piie.com/publications/policy-briefs/women-scaling-corporate-ladder-progress-steady-slow-globally. Accessed on June 7, 2020.

Organisation for Economic Co-Operation and Development (OECD). *G20/OECD principles of corporate governance*. Paris: OECD Publishing, p. 51, 2015. Available at https://www.oecd-ilibrary.org/governance/g20-oecd-principles-of-corporate-governance-2015_9789264236882-en. Accessed on June 10, 2020.

Organisation for Economic Co-Operation and Development (OECD). *OECD corporate governance factbook 2019*. June 11, 2019. Available at http://www.oecd.org/corporate/corporate-governance-factbook.htm. Accessed on June 9, 2020.

Phillips, Katherine W.; Liljenquist, Katie A.; Neale, Margaret A. Is the pain worth the gain? The advantages and liabilities of agreeing with socially distinct newcomers. *Personality and Social Psychology Bulletin* v. 35, n.3, p. 336–350, 2009.

Pick, Katharina. *Around the boardroom table-interactional aspects of governance*. PhD Thesis in Organizational Behavior, Harvard University, 2007.

Pick, Katharina; Merchant, Kenneth. Recognizing negative boardroom group dynamics. In: Lorsch, Jay William (editor). *The future of boards*: Meeting the governance challenges of the twenty-first century. Boston: Harvard Business Press, p. 113–132, 2012. Digital Edition. Location 2054 of 2780.

Pound, John. The promise of the governed corporation. *Harvard Business Review*, v. 73, n. 2, p. 89–98, 2000.

Pruitt, Dean G.; Rubin, Jeffrey Z. *Social conflict: Escalation, stalemate, settlement*. New York: Random House, p. 4, 1986.

PWC. Boards confront an evolving landscape. *PwC's 2013 Annual Corporate Directors Survey*, PwC, 2013. Available at https://corpgov.law.harvard.edu/2013/10/11/directors-survey-boards-confront-an-evolving-landscape/. Accessed on August 30, 2020.

PWC. Governing for the long term: Looking down the road with an eye on the rear-view mirror. *PwC's 2015 Annual Corporate Directors Survey*, PwC, 2015. Available at https://www.pwc.ie/publications/2015/annual-corporate-directors-survey.pdf. Accessed on July 15, 2020.

PWC. The collegiality conundrum: Finding balance in the boardroom. *PwC's 2019 Annual Corporate Directors Survey*, PwC, 2019. Available at https://www.pwc.com/us/en/services/governance-insights-center/assets/pwc-2019-annual-corporate-directors-survey-full-report-v2.pdf.pdf. Accessed on June 14, 2020.

PWC. The 'missing middle': Bridging the strategy gap in family firms. *Family Business Survey 2016*, PwC, 2016. Available at https://www.pwc.com/gx/en/family-business-services/global-family-business-survey-2016/pwc-global-family-business-survey-2016-the-missing-middle.pdf. Accessed on June 25, 2020.

Reynolds, Alison; Lewis, David. Teams solve problems faster when they're more cognitively diverse. *Harvard Business Review*, v. 30, p. 1–8, 2017.

Russel Reynolds and Associates; IESE Business School. *Survey of corporate governance practices in European family businesses*, Summer 2014. Available at http://www.russellreynolds.com/sites/default/files/europeanfamily businesspaper.pdf. Accessed on August 4, 2016.

Sherif, Muzafer. *The psychology of social norms*. New York: Harper, 1936. Also in Asch, Solomon E., *Effects of group pressure upon the modification and distortion of judgments*. In: H. Guetzkow (editor). Groups, leadership and men. Pittsburg: Carnegie Press, p. 177–190, 1951.

Simon, Herbert Alexander, *Administrative Behavior: A study of decision-making processes in administrative organization*. New York: Free Press, 1976.

Soll, Jack B.; Milkman, Katherine L.; Payne, John W. A user's guide to debiasing. *The Wiley Blackwell handbook of judgment and decision making*, v. 2, p. 924–951, p. 926, 2015.

Spencer Stuart. *2019 Brasil Spencer Stuart Board Index*. April, 2020. Available at https://www.spencerstuart.com/research-and-insight/brasil-board-index. Accessed on June 03, 2020.

Spencer Stuart. *Boards Around the World*. Available at: https://www.spencerstuart.com/research-and-insight/boards-around-the-world?category=all-board-composition&topic=independent-directors. Accessed on July 14, 2021.

Spencer Stuart. CEO transitions 2019. *Annual Review of CEO Transitions*. Available at https://www.spencerstuart.com/research-and-insight/ceo-transitions-2019. Accessed on July 15, 2020.

Sunstein, Cass R.; Hastie, Reid. *Wiser: Getting beyond groupthink to make groups smarter*. Boston: Harvard Business Press, 2015.

Surowiecki, James. BoardStiffs. *The Financial Page, The New Yorker*. March 8, 2004. Available at http://www.newyorker.com/magazine/2004/03/08/board-stiffs. Accessed on July 8, 2016.

Thaler, Richard H.; Sunstein, Cass R. Nudge: *Improving decisions about health, wealth, and happiness*, 1st. ed. New York: Penguin Books, 2009. Digital Edition. Locations: 171, 173 and 958 of 5708.

Thompson, Leigh. Desenvolvendo a criatividade dos grupos de trabalho organizacionais. GV executivo: Revista de Estratégia e Gestão. *Fundação Getúlio Vargas*, v. 2, n. 3, p. 63–81, 2003.

Thuraisingham, Meena; Lehmacher, Wolfgang. *The secret life of decisions: How unconscious bias subverts your judgement*. England: Gower Publishing, 2013. Digital Edition. Locations: 186, 3009 and 3097 of 3405.

Torchia, Mariateresa; Calabrò, Andrea; Morner, Michèle. Board of directors' diversity, creativity, and cognitive conflict: The role of board members' interaction. *International Studies of Management & Organization*, v. 45, n. 1, p. 6–24, 2015.

Tversky, Amos; Kahneman, Daniel. Judgment under uncertainty: Heuristics and biases. Oregon Research Institute. *ONR Technical Report*. 1973. Available at file:///C:/Users/user/Documents/arquivo%20indicado%20cap%206%20SG.pdf. Accessed on October 14, 2016.

Twain, M. Majority. Notebook, 1904. Available at: http://www.twainquotes.com/Majority.html. Accessed on July 28, 2020.

Valenti, Graziella. Acesso de Conselheiro a Dados Gera Debate. *Valor Econômico*, São Paulo, p. B2, July 20, 2016.

Wong, Simon. Boards: When best practice isn't enough. *McKinsey Quarterly*, June 2011. Available at http://www.mckinsey.com/global-themes/leadership/boards-when-best-practice-isnt-enough. Accessed on May 28, 2016.

World Economic Forum (WEF). Climate governance initiative principles. Available at: https://www.weforum.org/projects/climate-governance-initiative. Accessed on August 25, 2020.

World Economic Forum (WEF). COVID-19 risks outlook: A preliminary mapping and its implications. Available at https://www.weforum.org/reports/covid-19-risks-outlook-a-preliminary-mapping-and-its-implications. Accessed on July 17, 2020.

World Economic Forum's Global Risks Report 2015. Governing the global company. Oversight of complexity. Robyn Bew, from the National Association of Corporate Directors (NACD) and Lucy Nottingham, from the Marsh & McLennan Companies, 2015. Available at: https://www.mmc.com/content/dam/mmc-web/Global-Risk-Center/Files/governing-the-global-company.pdf. Accessed on July 20, 2020.

Zahra, Shaker; Pearce, John A. Boards of directors and corporate financial performance: A review and integrative model. *Journal of Management*, v. 15, n. 2, p. 291–334, June 1989.

Figures

Tables

Graphs

About the Author

One of the forerunners of corporate governance in Brazil, Sandra Guerra has served as a board member and chairperson of boards of directors since 1995. Her experience includes acting on the boards of listed, closed, family-controlled and state-controlled companies as well as of non-profit organizations both in Brazil and abroad. With 25 years' experience in corporate governance, she was one of the founding members of the Brazilian Institute of Corporate Governance (IBGC), where for four years, from 2012 to 2016, she was the chairperson of the board. On two occasions, she was also a member of the board of directors of the International Corporate Governance Network (ICGN). She was also board director of Global Reporting Initiative (GRI), from 2017 to 2019. Ever since she completed her Master's degree in Business Administration at FEA-USP (2009), her research has been focused on the board of directors. Certified as a Board Member by the IBGC and as a Mediator by the CEDR-Center for Effective Dispute Resolution (United Kingdom), Sandra continues to serve as a board director. In 2017 she published the book "A caixa-preta da governança. Conselhos de administração revelados por quem vive dentro deles" (The Black Box of Governance. Boards of directors revealed by those are part of them), published by Editora Best Business in Brazil and which is now in its 2nd edition.

Index